Feminist Intercultural Theology

STUDIES IN LATINO/A CATHOLICISM

A series sponsored by the Center for the Study of Latino/a Catholicism
University of San Diego

Previously published

Orlando O. Espín and Miguel H. Díaz, editors, *From the Heart of Our People: Latino/a Explorations in Catholic Systematic Theology*
Orlando O. Espín and Gary Macy, editiors, *Futuring Our Past: Explorations in the Theology of Tradition*
Raúl Gómez-Ruiz, S.D.S., *Mozarabs, Hispanics, and the Cross*

STUDIES IN LATINO/A CATHOLICISM

Feminist Intercultural Theology

Latina Explorations for a Just World

Edited by
María Pilar Aquino
and Maria José Rosado-Nunes

ORBIS BOOKS

Maryknoll, New York 10545

Founded in 1970, Orbis Books endeavors to publish works that enlighten the mind, nourish the spirit, and challenge the conscience. The publishing arm of the Maryknoll Fathers and Brothers, Orbis seeks to explore the global dimensions of the Christian faith and mission, to invite dialogue with diverse cultures and religious traditions, and to serve the cause of reconciliation and peace. The books published reflect the views of their authors and do not represent the official position of the Maryknoll Society. To learn more about Maryknoll and Orbis Books, please visit our website at www.maryknoll.org.

Published by Orbis Books, Maryknoll, New York 10545-0308.
Manufactured in the United States of America.
Manuscript editing and typesetting by Joan Weber Laflamme.

Library of Congress Cataloging-in-Publication Data

Feminist intercultural theology : Latina explorations for a just world / edited by María Pilar Aquino and Maria José Rosado-Nunes.
      p. cm. — (Studies in Latino/a Catholicism)
      ISBN 978-1-57075-741-9
   1. Feminist theology—Latin America—Congresses. 2. Christianity and culture—Latin America—Congresses. 3. Catholic Church—Latin America—Doctrines—Congresses. I. Aquino, María Pilar. II. Rosado-Nunes, Maria José.
      BT83.55.F446 2007
      230.082'098—dc22

                                                            2007006179

Contents

Foreword

Virginia Vargas Valente

Participating in the First Inter-American Symposium on Feminist Intercultural Theology—whose reflections gave birth to this book, *Feminist Intercultural Theology: Latina Explorations for a Just World*—was for me a political, epistemological, and feminist privilege. Invited as a feminist nonbeliever, I hesitated to accept. Except for my contacts with a few Latin American feminist currents with a faith commitment, such as Talita Cumi in Peru, which built up a collective movement, or Catholics for the Right to Decide, which expanded boldly and creatively to all Latin America, I knew little about the advances and reflections of feminist theologians. Those contacts became amazingly enriched and enhanced in the course of the discussions. The event was a crossroads of questions, reflections, uncertainties, all of which were very similar to those of other feminist currents that are seeking to respond to the paradigm changes of the new millennium, but which at the time were all very new for the place where they were now being expressed. From a common space of communication there emerged an earnest searching: a feminism that was trying to respond to these changes and contribute to them out of frameworks of justice and democracy. It was, as stated by Maricel Mena-López and María Pilar Aquino (in this same collection), a process of interchanging "contextual" wisdoms that are oriented toward achieving just alternatives on the basis of diverse sources and currents. It is a pilgrim theology that allows us to build, on the basis of diversity and plurality, as well as of inequalities and exclusions, forms of knowledge that are nourished out of the reality and the situation of each one of us.

The symposium made it evident not only that a Latina and Latin American theology exists, but also that it is a multiple critical theory that is nourished and fostered by the reflection and the rebellious transgression aroused by the marginalizing injustices strewn along the multiple paths of exclusion. The contributions to the symposium express theoretical analysis and reflection, not only about theology from a feminist perspective, but also about the feminist struggles for inclusion: in the democratization of discourse, in the sophistication of textual analysis, and in social, political, and religious practices. They are contributions to a critical political theory, a product of many years of readings, exchanges, complicities, new subjectivities, and new languages, which enrich the theological discourse of liberation. These contributions succeed in disturbing the bases of traditional theological discourse at the same time that they enrich and democratize feminist reflections, actions, and discourses.

An outstanding substantive aspect of these approaches is the fact that critical theories always have practices behind them, or to put it the other way around, every concrete practice has a concrete theory that emerges out of it. Recovering practices, says Boaventura De Souza Santos, means recovering theoretical frameworks, opening channels through which social transformation can flow.[1] And this is an epistemological wager in favor of discourse that emanates from concrete experience, on the basis of intellectual and social practices that nourish new paradigms sustained by new epistemological pathways.

In the course of the discussion the symposium signaled epistemological ruptures at many levels. Methodologically, there was the collective construction of knowledge on the basis of multiple positions, where differences are not taken to be social and cognitive inequalities, but rather "contextual wisdoms" (Mena-López and Aquino, in this collection) oriented toward the attainment of just alternatives. But also politically, there was a powerful recovery of "impertinent knowledge" for traditional imagery and discourse.[2] Such knowledge keeps emerging and keeps broadening the frames of reference through articulation and contextualization of the personal with the social, the political and the subjective, even while it promotes epistemological ruptures with a theology—and a theory—that proclaims eternal, absolute truths. Instead of these, the partial and incomplete character of our ways of knowing is assumed, so that our knowledge gains in complexity through its permanent dialogue with the diversity of other forms of knowledge. These are unfinished ways of knowing, which take on intricacy in their mutual recognition. It is precisely this process that progressively generates an alternative subjectivity, both in practice and in the theoretical and political imagery of the actors and of society. It is what nourishes an intercultural perspective in which gender will be subversive only insofar as it confronts the power structures and sexual domination at the level of their social, political, and religious norms and institutions, which continue to reinforce the subordination of women, and insofar as it provokes a challenge to the monocultural discourses that are framed within Western hegemony as an expression of the same system of domination, thus recovering the complex articulation of race, gender, class, ethnicity, age, and sexual orientation. It is impossible to imagine paradigmatic alternatives without this relational view in processes of democratic dialogue, from multiple autonomies.

As is well expressed in several articles in this collection, such processes succeed in recovering profoundly personal categories with high political content. The body is one of those impertinent ways of knowing that broaden the references of transformation; it recovers the diversity of ways that human beings exist in daily life; it recovers eroticism and pleasure, the sustenance of laughter and of desacralization. But memory is also critically recovered and articulated in the specific context in which the body is found: the memory of the suffering of the bodies, by reason of their different colors, odors, sexual expressions, ways of surviving, that is, by all the dynamics of exclusion, lack of redistribution and of recognition, for it is on the body that the forces of the "empire" leave their greatest impact: the neoliberal capitalist economy, the militarism, and the diverse fundamentalisms. For that very reason, the repoliticization of the body appears as theological discourse par excellence, since it is situated on an ethical, political, and sacred horizon within which relations of justice and democracy may be developed.

In this view, the body recovers the articulation between public and private; it confronts capital and the state; it confronts institutions that are national and global, religious and political; it confronts common traditional meanings and the growing fundamentalisms. It recovers what is most personal in people's lives, at the same time that it opens up a spectrum of possibilities of intercultural interaction on the basis of individualities charged with emancipatory political meanings. The body thus turns into a field endowed with citizenship.[3]

We are dealing also with a proposal that is global, first, because, while the content of the struggles emerges from a specific reality such as America's, it also has much in common with feminists of other regions, whose relation with religious experiences and discourses is also characterized by exclusion or subordination. But the proposal is global also because it takes part in a broader, worldwide movement, one which holds that *another world is possible*, precisely through challenging neoliberal globalization and creating new meanings and processes in favor of an alternative globalization, one that is in harmony with justice, the preservation of nature and the recognition of differences. Similarly, the proposal is global because it includes in these processes the exclusion and subordination of women as fundamental items on all democratic agendas; they are no longer just as women's business.

This dimension also includes other interactive and intercultural processes of a regional and global nature. Fed by the vital experiences of
exclusion and inclusion, a "frontier" type of thought is produced (among
Latino/a feminist theologians of the North, but with much wider theoretical and political reach); such thought crosses and connects the borders, and it nourishes a perspective of interculturality in creating a place
that is not completely either here or there. This is the place, according to
Maria José Rosado-Nunes (in this collection), that is proposed for the
construction of spaces where everybody will find room, without domi-
nances and with solidarity toward those who are marginalized. It is the
place of *Nepantla*—Middle Earth—where, from the fringes of the dominant cultures, Latino/a women make themselves visible, those whose
presence and influence have been rendered invisible by the existing
official history and by many others. Thus will they be victorious in
their historic battles for recognition and their efforts to recover the
biblical figures that reveal the processes of racialization, sexism, and
Eurocentrism.

Considering all this, the reflections we find here are of import not
only for feminist theology, but also for feminist theory more generally.
Their fundamental contribution is in offering a new source for undertaking a critical reading of our ways of being and our ways of interpreting the world from a feminist intercultural perspective. From this perspective, feminist theological activity is seen as an "alternative
ethico-political project" that nourishes that other feminist space, which
is not hegemonic or Western, but emerges from the fringes and from the
frontiers. In this process, feminist theological activity is conceived as the
expression of a project that allows us to "walk toward a new world of
justice," by engendering new forms of social coexistence (Rosado-Nunes,
in this collection). Such also is my cherished hope, and that of many
feminists on many other shores and other margins.

Finally, this book brings to feminism not only acknowledgment of the
struggles that feminist believers are waging, both inside and outside their
religious settings, but also it reveals their attitude of transgressive boldness with respect to the position they are in, a boldness that nourishes an
ethical, political, democratic perspective that can recover for all the different feminisms a space of emancipatory, diverse, multiple spirituality
as an inseparable part of all experiences of liberation.

Notes

[1] See Boaventura De Souza Santos, "Para Uma Sociologia das Ausências e Uma Sociologia das Emergências," *Revista Crítica de Ciencias Sociales* 63 (October 2002): 237–80.

[2] Diana Maffía, "Ciudadanía Sexual: Aspectos Legales y Políticos de los Derechos Reproductivos Como Derechos Humanos," *Feminiaria* 14, nos. 26/27 (July 2001): 28–31.

[3] See Betania Ávila, "Feminismo y Ciudadanía: La Producción de Nuevos Derechos" (AGENDA, Equidad de Género), *Mujeres al Timón: Cuadernos para la Incidencia Política Feminista* 2 (Lima: Flora Tristán, 2001), 1–16.

Symposium Abstract

Feminist Intercultural Theology

Religion, Culture, Feminism, and Power

Maricel Mena-López and María Pilar Aquino

This abstract presents a few of the multitude of perspectives that were shared during the first Inter-American Symposium on Feminist Intercultural Theology, which brought together Latina women who are prominent social scientists and feminist theologians in the United States and Latin America. The symposium was tremendously significant for us because, for the first time in the history of Christianity in the Americas, feminist theologians of the United States, Latin America, and the Caribbean were able to meet together to share our common concerns and visions about the present and the future of our theological work, on the basis of intercultural hermeneutical frameworks. Those of us who participated in this event brought with us a wealth of reflections that arises from our experience of life in thirteen different countries and that makes evident the ethnic pluralism of our region.

The general theme of this symposium was "Intercultural Feminist Theology: Religion, Culture, Feminism, and Power." This theme allowed us to enter into a space of respectful and critical deliberation about how feminist intercultural theology can contribute to the strengthening of present-day democratic movements, which seek to contribute constructively both to transforming the oppressive religious and cultural environments in which we live and to reorient the often ambiguous and controversial processes of contemporary globalization. Conducted entirely in Spanish, this symposium took place in Mexico City from July 5 to 11, 2004, as a collaborative project of the Center for the Study of Latino/a Catholicism of the University of San Diego (San Diego, California), the

Institute of Missiology Missio (Aachen, Germany), and the Iberoamericana University (Mexico City, Mexico).

The objectives proposed for this symposium were:

1. To analyze and to understand critically the relations among religion, culture, feminism, and power, with a view to developing a
   feminist intercultural theology;
2. To establish a space for dialogue concerning the conceptual frameworks and the key analytic categories that might ground a critical
   feminist theology of liberation in intercultural terms;
3. To seek the resources needed to facilitate the work of Latino/a feminist theologians in the United States, Latin America, and the Caribbean;
4. To contribute to the visibility of critical feminist theological perspectives in our region;
5. To gather the shared reflections into articles that would be published in a collective volume.

The present book is the concrete result of our week-long meeting. We
believe, however, that the attainment of these objectives cannot be judged
solely on the basis of the contents of this book. For us, these objectives
are still on the way to being achieved, for we still have many challenges
ahead in terms of promoting processes of feminist theological communication that is at once intercultural and inter-American.

THE PROCESS OF THE SYMPOSIUM

We approached the theme proposed for this symposium by using a
method of participation and deliberation that represented for us an *epistemological rupture,* insofar as all of us, rejecting a centralist and elitist
style of producing knowledge, participated in theoretical activity as students and teachers, as disciples and instructors, as apprentices and ex-
perts—in a word, as true companions and colleagues. This method was
designed jointly by the participants and the invited advisory team, which
was formed by feminist sociologists Maria José Rosado-Nunes (Brazil)
and Virginia Vargas Valente (Perú); feminist theologian María Pilar
Aquino (Mexico–United States); and philosopher Raúl Fornet-Betancourt
(Cuba-Germany). The decentralized, participative mode of creating
knowledge allowed us to share our varied wisdoms and to recognize
ourselves as a confederacy of feminist wisdom for change and liberation.

We learned that this is a key epistemological principle that feminist intercultural theology presents to us as a challenge.

As the meeting progressed, we stressed the importance of the dynamic of active memory for recovering our feminist theological development. We likewise placed importance on the dynamism of imagination as a means of forging new routes that might equip us better for designing theological responses to the concerns raised by the contemporary scenarios of a globalized world. As a starting point, we recognized that our theologies pass through our bodies and that they express experiences that are at once plural, common, and simultaneous. Such recognition means that we ourselves are "frontier bodies," because we move among different places: most of us do not work in our countries of origin, we drink of the wisdom that flows from other founts, and we assume that our identities are still in a process of construction. Our humanity as persons is constantly renewed on the basis of our joys, our cries, our shouts, our rhythms, our relations, our aspirations, and our spiritualities, all of which accompany us in the different contexts in which we live and work.

For that reason we proclaim and we celebrate the diversity of the faces of feminism: African American, Amerindian, Latina, Latin American—and every other frontier feminism that is open to the intermingling of wisdoms in the metaphorical space of *Nepantla*.[1] Among the many realities we experience, we also recognize the multiple, simultaneous forms of violence perpetrated again women because of their sexual condition, their social situation, their race, and their sexual orientation. Such realities lead us to affirm that our daily experiences are permeated with an ethical-political vision, since our theologies seek to overcome all forms of violence. Consequently, we also recognize that we have common objectives and that our bodies are historical subjects of change that proclaim that another world is indeed possible.

OPENING THE WAYS OF DIALOGUE

In the initial stage of our work, dialogue was opened up by a spontaneous exchange about the ideas, expectations, possibilities, and challenges that we found in the general theme and the proposed objectives of the symposium. We present below in summary form the four major themes that this dialogue brought to light. Since we do not accept historical linearity, these themes do not necessarily correspond to a preestablished chronological order, nor do they exhaust the contents of the dialogue; rather, they present the resonances of the whole group.

Gender, Race, and Identity

In view of the growing depoliticization of these concepts, we have taken as a common challenge the need to question their significance. For us, it is important to analyze how these concepts have functioned in academic and political rhetoric and what effects they have had in the practice of social change. The uncritical tendencies of those who would depoliticize these concepts challenge us to re-engineer our patterns of thought in order to propose new conceptual frameworks that support the visions of social and religious transformation in the complex contexts that we experience. We realize that it is necessary to approach these concepts in a way that allows us to overcome their reductionism, their provincialism, and their increasingly harmful effects in reproducing divided societies. We also see as important, however, the need to continue working on the deconstruction of the racial and sexual privileges that attribute superiority to the white race and to males, and the need to do so on the basis of the struggles for justice and cultural democratization undertaken by women and men.

Contextual Theologies

We affirm that all theology is contextual, the theologies of the North Atlantic and Western Europe as well as the feminist theologies of the northern hemisphere. These theologies have the duty to recognize and proclaim their own contextuality, just as does any other theology done in the context of the Two-thirds World. We believe that the different contextual situations will contribute to creating a community of theological subjects of equal intellectual dignity and to encouraging mutual communication and feedback among them. The consequence of this affirmation for us women is that we deem it necessary to continue fomenting a capacity for listening, learning, and interacting among the different types of feminism, whether Latina, Latin American, or Caribbean. By developing the capacity for mutual listening and learning, we place ourselves in the best position for intercultural communication.

Paradigm Changes and Theological World Views

The result of our theological activity expresses a systematization of our aspirations, experiences, and achievements. As discursive activity, theology expresses the values, visions, commitments and loyalties of those who practice it. In consequence, we agree to another epistemological rupture, one that leads us to criticize and reject the notion of theology as a mechanism for establishing eternal truths, and we consciously assert the historical partiality of our knowledge. We understand partiality as a way of thinking rooted in our diverse situations and realities, in what we experience through our historically situated bodies. We distance ourselves from the dominant monocultural centrism and objectivity of thought, and we draw close to the social and intellectual peripheries, that is, to other centers of thought and wisdom that find no place in the hegemonic centers. Affirming the partiality of knowledge assumes a recognition of the diversity of knowledge, and this recognition implies the need to affirm egalitarian interaction in the processes of generating theological knowledge. Our major challenge as women is how to interact with the women of our communities and how to share our wisdom with theirs.

Power, Economics, and Knowledge in the Academy

A broader and more critical discussion of these categories will help us to *empower women* in their struggles for self-determination and liberation. We consider it fundamental to continue affirming the political character of feminism within the academy, but we also recognize the need to continue creating new ways of transmitting our discourse. The connections among feminist academic work, civil society, and the pastoral world continue to be a challenge that requires new responses. Although we understand that the academy is a key arena for the transformation of systems of thought, we also consider it important to promote the theological community's participation in other spheres of social life in order to bring about a change in oppressive ideologies. Given our contexts, we consider it vitally important for women to participate in the design of theology programs, because only thus will we succeed in getting critical feminist analyses and hermeneutics consistently included in the programs.

EXPLORING VALID PATHWAYS

In the second stage of our work, we proposed a dialogue about the perspectives and dimensions (conceptual, analytic, rhetorical, methodological, political, and so forth) that we discovered in the reading we did by way of preparing for the symposium.[2] We found that many of the doubts and worries that presented themselves in the earlier stage were clarified by the perspectives offered in the readings. At the same time, though, we sought to turn the dialogue away from mere reaction to the readings and toward the framing of new questions, arising from both the earlier discussions and the readings.

The new questions that we shared had to do with the revision and subversion of our own concepts. We asked question such as the following: Why do the classical concepts of theology and of gender seem to us inadequate? What consequences does the recognition of cultural diversity have for our work? How should we approach theologically the themes of citizenship, politics, and the state? What hermeneutical and political implications flow from recognizing ourselves as feminists, or as simply women? With regard to the theme of interculturality we also had many questions. For example, when we adopt interculturality, are we reasserting the same notions of universality that we have been combating? Can it be that the perspectives of intercultural dialogue are more demanding than the cultural deconstruction proposed by critical feminism? Is there a danger that we will so focus on dialogue among cultures that we will abandon the critique of religion and its many manifestations of intolerance? How might we understand the critique and the transformation of racism and sexism within the context of the intercultural paradigm?

Our bodies in movement took still another step forward, raising questions about our situation in the academic realm. What challenges do we as feminists face in the teaching of theology? What is our experience in the institutions where we work? What feminist proposals are we making in terms of pedagogy? What are we doing so that feminist theology becomes an articulating axis of our study programs? What resources do we have for publishing our writings? How can we create intercontinental feminist networks in which our materials can circulate? How are our theologies affected by the fact that there is no place for us in our own countries? All such questions reveal the complexity of our contexts and the anxieties that we share. Without pretending to offer comprehensive answers, we managed to deal with some of these questions in two broad areas: gender theories and epistemological frameworks.

Gender Theories

Gender theories were incorporated into Latin American feminist theology only in the decade of the 1990s, and they helped us to delve into the problematic lived by women in the context of our patriarchal societies, cultures, and churches. The category of gender comes from feminist movements that saw a need to broaden their theoretical frameworks in ways that would help them achieve greater clarity and political commitment. We recognize, however, that those theories have their limitations and inadequacies for analyzing in depth the interstructural, multiplicative, and simultaneous nature of the present-day systems of domination. The greatest challenges for us today do not come from "gender," since our particular contexts do not produce "gender" movements as such. Rather, our challenges come from the social, cultural, and religious structures and institutions that keep women in positions of subordination.

We realize that the category of gender was initially well received in certain academic spheres, above all where feminist theoretical and political practices had been rejected. We understand that in such spheres the category continues to be a strategic instrument for introducing the conceptual frameworks of feminist liberation theology.

Some women's and feminists' movements have found in the category of gender a utopian horizon for inclusion. A few male theologians have belatedly adopted this category, and it has helped to gain some allies for the feminist struggles. Some theologians, nonetheless, especially Roman Catholic priests, but also certain groups of women theologians, have used and continue to use this category for the purpose of invalidating and denying legitimacy to critical feminist positions. In certain theological and ecclesiastical spheres, this category has also served to promote a revision of an understanding of "masculinity." Such conceptual approaches to masculinity are limited, however, not only because they perpetuate dualistic mentalities about differences between "feminine" and "masculine," but also because they fail to contextualize these approaches in feminist analytical frameworks that reveal quite clearly the sexual relations of power.

We view with concern the fact that in some countries programs have been developed for studying and reflecting on masculinity. Such programs seem to assume that it is historically necessary to maintain models of thought about "femininity," whose dualistic complement would be "masculinity." In such cases, the category of gender proves to be counterproductive as a way of attaining new modes of thought that are free of essentialist dualism. We are likewise concerned about the depoliticization of other categories, such as race and ethnicity. We therefore recognize the importance of questioning ourselves about the significance of these categories and about the ways we are using them in our own theological activity. What type of mentality do they help to promote, one that is liberating or one that is patriarchal? What type of activity do they help to develop, one of transformation or one of cooptation for what already exists? What kind of social project do they promote, a new world of justice or simply an entry into the system of power quotas? In examining these questions, we consider it fundamental to keep as a point of reference the historical contexts of poverty and dehumanization in which we live. Concentrating on the concrete reality that surrounds us helps us to focus our thought so as to discover what we wish to achieve in using these categories in our theological languages.

At the present time we see certain dangers in using the category of gender. A first danger is that the category can domesticate feminist discourse, insofar as it is used in some theological and ecclesiastical spheres as a strategy for minimizing critical feminist discourse. A second danger involves the depoliticization of feminism and the cooptation of the category of gender for the purpose of reducing feminism's political impact. We therefore believe it is necessary to rethink the epistemic and social function of the category of gender on the basis of the conceptual frameworks of critical feminism. A third danger is the risk of neutralizing the transformative effects of feminist thought, since the category of gender functions within kyriarchal thought patterns. This can result in a diminished understanding of how the feminist struggles contribute to a new world of justice and human rights for women.

Epistemological Frameworks

We start off from the premise that not every form of knowledge is valid or good for all women. There are forms of knowledge that, even if they are well intended and appear innocent, continue to maintain an intellectual hierarchy and a cognitive inequality. In many cases the modes of knowing practiced by peripheral cultures are considered inferior. Furthermore, we recognize the importance of words; there are words that engender life and words that engender death. Not every word spoken by a woman is liberating. We therefore seek to evaluate our own rhetorical practice and to face up to the epistemological challenge of continually developing a theological discourse of liberation. Our desire is to be able to find, by means of open communication and critical discussion, reliable orientations for the future.

For our epistemological discernment we propose to reflect on the relation that exists between thought and concept. Thought does not always produce liberating epistemological frameworks. In fact, hegemonic discourse justified the notions of nationality and pure theory and gave primacy to speculative, non-historical thought. From our viewpoint, it is precisely this monocultural, nationalistic discourse that has sought to invalidate all forms of thought that are not Western European. Our own epistemological proposal must break with Western European academic courtesy and name things by their name. The desire for theological dialogue certainly does not mean avoiding contradictions or hushing up disagreements.

We realize that in some countries of Western Europe and North America women theologians and social scientists speak of *post-feminism* and advocate the adoption of post-feminist positions. The use of this term possibly allows them to indicate that they find themselves in a different conceptual situation, one that is beyond the limitations of patriarchal thought. Thus, the use of the prefix *post* would seem to indicate that feminism is no longer necessary because the patriarchal environment has been wholly superseded. We believe that these post-feminist scholars are right to take such a position, since the domination of the patriarchal mind set has indeed been overcome within their own thought. This overcoming, though, has taken place only there, in their own thought, and not in the crude, naked reality that is experienced by the great majority of women around the world. We women scholars of the southern hemisphere, who do not benefit from a welfare state, cannot afford to indulge in any such "post-feminist" speculation. The harsh reality of the world in which we live imposes upon us the imperative of waging with ever greater determination the feminist struggles for transformation and emancipation. As long as the kyriarchal systems of domination last, critical feminism is for us an ethical, political and religious imperative. Many of the post-feminist scholars could well benefit from using an epistemology that historicizes concepts and avoids the superfluous use of words that have no backing in historical processes.

With a view to intercultural communication that goes beyond a dialogue made up of mere "discourses," we propose instead a dialogue among and with our bodies, our emotions, our flavors and aromas and colors. We must understand our bodies, though, within the context of struggle for a world of rights for women and of dignity and justice for all of humankind. We claim our right to think, to think incorrectly, to think subversively, to deconstruct and reconstruct concepts within theoretical frameworks that open up to us better roads for the present and the future. We believe that we can reinvent thought without fear of erring. In many circumstances the only option we have is to begin all over again. We propose a critical feminist epistemology because its grounding in social-change movements strengthens our hope that another world, one of rights and justice, is possible in this world. Such an epistemology infuses our visions of emancipation and human fulfillment with religious and political categories of hope.

We have also made an *epistemological break* with the kyriarchal epistemologies because these, besides being essentialist and monocultural,
also prevent us from naming the sexual violence committed against wom-
en. We hold that a critical feminist epistemology of liberation is different
from an epistemology of gender, since critical feminism proposes a type
of knowledge that emanates from the historicity of the experience of
struggle for a just world, not from the history of ideas or the definition
of concepts. Such knowledge is sensitive to the human aspirations of
emancipation and is therefore open to intercultural transformation.
The perspective of intercultural feminism is not in need of someone
else to legitimize it, for it is the very life of women, our bodies, our
struggles, our sufferings, and our hopes that legitimize our theological
practices.

We have also emphasized the horizon of justice and emancipation
that orients our work and that leads us to recognize the ethical, political,
and sacred dimensions of our religious discourse. Within this horizon
we wish to lay claim to the legacy of wisdom of our foremothers. The
women's voices that have been silenced and the women's presences that
have been denied in the African American and Amerindian traditions
challenge us to offer liberating alternatives for thinking. We wish to rescue and reconstruct all that the intercultural ethical proposals offer us in
the way of feminist thought and practice.

In our own contexts, where sexual violence is extensive and the human rights of women are ignored, there is a need to rescue the history of
women's suffering. In doing theology, we cannot leave out our own sufferings, or our joys and our hopes. Often we must ask ourselves: what is this
body that is creating such a literary body of works? Along with other
interpretative strategies, the hermeneutics of lament continues to be a liberating key to our bodies. If we cannot make public our laments, then
who will know of our existence? With whom will we be in solidarity?
Who will join us in our protest? For the good of all women who aspire
after basic well-being, we need to make public our irritation and our cry
for change. As an epistemological locus, our suffering is important and
should be viewed in relation to our longings for peace and happiness.

REIMAGINING THE PATHWAYS
OF FEMINIST THEOLOGICAL ACTIVITY

In a third stage of our work together we decided to compose a mosaic
based on words. Spoken works, unspoken words, words at times blessed,
and words often accursed. What were we to do with so many words?

We consider that reimagining the pathways of feminist experience and thought is the task we have before us. To that end we proposed creating a word mosaic that would reveal to us those pathways, oriented around four methodological axes: words, hermeneutical instruments, new paradigms, and theoretical knots that await future developments.

Words

Words that jump, that skip and that play
Words with body, everyday words
Words that sparkle with experiences, biographies,
    realities
Contextualities, movements, rhythms
Women, life, wisdom

Words that lament and that shout
Words weighty with suffering and complaint
Word: protest
Empire, poverty, Babylon
Women, life, wisdom

Words that flow, that evoke and that name
Indian, black, white, *mestiza*
Foremothers. . . .
Words that cross borders
De-northing: *Nepantla, Chacana*
Women, life, wisdom

Words that disrupt and disturb
Ambiguity, deconstruction, obscurity, clarity
Word: feminism
Women, life, wisdom
Words that embrace, that convoke, that defy
Word: silence
Liberty, empowerment, community
Women, life, wisdom

Words that jump, that skip and that play
Creativity, poetry, imagination
Dream, demand
Celebration, feast
Women, life, wisdom

Hermeneutical Instruments

The daily life of women; their negated, silenced, gagged bodies; their struggles, resistance, survival, and unfulfilled hopes oblige us to speak of the broader context that is empire. For the empire, those bodies have value only insofar as they are reserves for the laws of the market. Women's lives are inserted in the context of imperial capitalist globalization and impel us to view the exclusionary nature of its space, its place, and its geography. On all sides we find evidence of the growing feminization of poverty, and its countenance is notably black and indigenous. Considering the ambivalence and conflictual nature of the globalizing process and feeling its tentacles of centralization and poverty, we denounce the use of resources that benefit only privileged social groups. In our geographic contexts, exclusion and poverty are the most evident aspects of reality.

Before such a scenario, we are called to envision alternatives to empire. The present dominating globalization endangers women's lives, their millennial cultures, and their religious universes, because it does not offer spaces for them to organize their lives according to their community interests. The hyper-technology of globalization is of benefit only to a minute part of the world's population. More than two-thirds of the world's people receive no benefit at all. Geography has for us both a social and a political value. In our work we strive to connect the geographic context of earth with the geographic context of our bodies. For that reason we must think not only about where we are, but also about how we are.

We affirm that women's bodies are privileged spaces for our theological labor. They are sacred bodies, where divine Wisdom becomes manifest through their stories, their music, their liturgy, their religions, their celebrations. We are also challenged by the ambivalence of those bodies: they are bodies that become sick with myoma, with cancer, with HIV/AIDS, with depression, with cataracts, with exhaustion, with psychosomatic symptoms of so many problems that have no solutions. We ask ourselves: how is medicine treating the bodies of women, especially those who are black and indigenous? We are challenged also by those aesthetically beautiful bodies, with their liposuction and plastic surgery, that correspond to the patterns of beauty imposed by the dominant North Atlantic culture. We find on all sides the bodies of girls and young women, often malnourished, sexually abused, and prematurely pregnant. We find many bodies that are consumed by drugs, and many that are maltreated and aged beyond their years. We see that the repressed bodies of homosexual women have begun to come out into the open, and for that they are doubly punished. We find also the bodies of a migrating humanity, bodies persecuted and criminalized for the simple fact of seeking work "in the North." Many of these bodies have remained in silence, in anonymous graves. All these bodies deserve the attention of our theologies. In some ways, our epistemology is also itinerant, because it allows us to see the diversity, the plurality, and the inequalities of our reality. For that reason our epistemology requires us to undertake systematic analyses, which expose the interactions of racism, classism, religion, sexual orientation, and intergenerational relations. But it also requires us to recover disputed words, in order to affirm the conceptual force of our perspectives.

The hermeneutical instruments that support our labor are diverse, but we have recourse to feminist theological, political, and ethical categories in order to interpret our experience within the ambivalence and complexity of our contexts. The diversity of our interpretative instruments and categories has allowed us to make manifest in critical fashion the polyphony of voices and the wealth of meanings that we find in our reality. Nevertheless, we also find that we need to develop much more the theme of hermeneutical instruments, in order to clarify the nature of our own contribution to them.

New Paradigms and Pending Theoretical Knots

Intercultural perspectives require a dialectical intellectual praxis that allows social and cultural subjects to speak as equals and to forge alliances, on the basis of their real conditions and their diverse contextualities, for the purpose of achieving a common future of justice. An intercultural epistemology requires that we move beyond mere recognition of differences toward designing common spaces for affirming the common emancipative interests of the voices that the dominant culture wishes to suppress. Intercultural thought arises as a theoretical political proposal aimed at strengthening the search for new forms of living together (convivencia), where differences do not produce social and cognitive inequalities, but rather serve to unite together the diverse contextual wisdoms in order to achieve just alternatives for humankind and the world. Feminist intercultural theology seeks to participate in these perspectives and so adopts this same proposal. For us, the inclusion of the intercultural paradigm means renouncing the dogmatic absolutism affirmed by the present kyriarchal religions and denouncing the evils produced by the kyriarchal monotheisms and monocultures when they identify the divine presence with men. The tasks we see for the future are the following:

- The concept of cultural Mestizaje should be revised, since it is generally understood as a synthesis that represents a unitary and global cultural context. Such an understanding is inadequate because it suppresses the cultural diversity intrinsic to the cultures and religions of the indigenous and African American peoples. Furthermore, it also encourages the idea that these religions contain elements of witchcraft and idolatry and therefore should be censured and avoided.

- The feminist critique of kyriarchal reason continues to be an important connective theme in the development of our theologies. This critique should assist in the undoing of the universal organization of the existing dominant knowledge. We believe that this can be one of the most valuable contributions that intercultural thought can make to a critical feminist epistemology.

- In order to think interculturally, we need to "relearn" our thought by critically interpreting our own ways of life and thought within our concrete contexts. This relearning means entering into a process of suspecting our own suspicions and of allowing our hermeneutics to be reorganized in relation to other hermeneutics. It is not enough to affirm hermeneutical diversity; we must also recognize the partial and relative character of our own interpretations.

- In the process of producing theological knowledge, we find it necessary to repoliticize our bodies, since they are situated within an ethical, political, and sacred horizon. We hold that conditions of equality between women and men are a theological, ethical, and political imperative in our religions and our churches.

- In order for intercultural dialogue to come to be a reality, we consider it important to take account of the mobility and the transitory character of the knowing subjects. Nobody possesses absolute truth, but a common future of well-being and justice is something that should be shared by all humankind. A commitment to interculturality means that our theologies will build roads that join together to make the future possible.

- The invitation to establish intercultural dialogue does not mean covering up or ignoring the realities of racism and sexism that are present in our social and cultural environments. Rather, it means joining forces to bring about a radical transformation of those environments. The notion of dialogue among cultures requires of us greater consciousness of the visions and elements of emancipation that the different cultural traditions can contribute to the new realities that are already coming into existence.

Finally, among the various theoretical knots that have been insufficiently treated in our theologies and that still remain as challenges, we have tried to highlight the following: (a) the reinterpretation, from within our contexts, of concepts that communicate values such as truth, beauty, and personal security; (b) our activity and progress in academic institutions, and their relation with knowledge and authority; (c) an explicit theological approach to "dangerous" and controversial topics, such as the sexual and reproductive rights of women, abortion, homosexuality, and ordination of women to the Roman Catholic priesthood; and (d) the relation of our theologies with the organizations of civil society that work for human rights.

CONCLUSION

The dialogue proposed by this symposium has not ended, nor has it exhausted the wide field of our concerns and aspirations, but it has begun a process of dialogue that gives us joy and hope. In this process of production and exchange of wisdoms, we recognize that we drink from different founts a variety of liquids, with the flavors of diverse fruits and the pleasures our work arouses. We drink with pleasure the juice of our labor, which is the product of our medicinal plants for restoring health. We savor the fruit of our healing plants among ourselves, and we offer it to other women, to those who joined us in our memories, to those who did not arrive but with whom we communed by the art of imagination, and to those whom we do not know but who still inspire us to transform our reality. Their frontier presences, their movements, rhythms, songs, and prayers have come to give life to our feminist spiritualities. We offer that fruit also to our male theological colleagues and to other men who likewise seek healing for their kyriarchal infirmities. With gratitude we celebrate the support that we receive from many other persons, and we give thanks for the transforming action of the divine Wisdom in our lives, who is present as *aché*, as fount of energy, as liberating goodness.

Notes

[1] For the significance of these terms, see the Introduction by Maria José Rosado-Nunes and the chapters in this collection by Daisy L. Machado and Nancy Elizabeth Bedford.

[2] By way of preparatory reading for the symposium discussion, the whole group received the following works: Elisabeth Schüssler Fiorenza, *Jesus: Miriam's*

Child, Sophia's Prophet: Critical Issues in Feminist Christology (New York: Continuum 1994); Raúl Fornet-Betancourt, *Transformación Intercultural de la Filosofía* (Bilbao: Desclée de Brouwer, 2001); and *Antología de Teoría y Análisis Feminista*, selected by the organizers of the symposium, which included articles written by Virginia Vargas, Sonia E. Alvarez, and Maria José Rosado-Nunes.

Feminist Intercultural Theology

Introduction

New Paradigms in Feminist Theological Thought

The Longing for a Just World

Maria José Rosado-Nunes

The present book puts forward a proposal for new epistemological paradigms for feminist theological thought from the perspective of the Latina women of the Americas—Latin America, the Caribbean, and the United States. Presenting a radical critique of patriarchal reasoning in the field of theology, the book is the fruit of a rich collective experience that is described by Maricel Mena-López and María Pilar Aquino in the symposium abstract in this collection. The many authors of the essays in this book are Latina theologians who recognize that the theology elaborated by men and officially adopted by religions does not provide the categories that are necessary for incorporating and explaining the religious practices, experiences, and sentiments of women. The authors therefore propose a religious discourse constructed on the basis of a critical feminist epistemology that takes as a prime source for theological work the reality of women's lives.

Assuming the basic premises of interculturality, the varied approaches and subjects treated in the book highlight the powerful presence of the women in our hemisphere who are marginalized: poor women, black women, indigenous women. These pages give expression to the profound longing for a just world, where there is room for everybody and where the drums keep resounding and blending, along with the church bells, so that Jesus and Mary may dance in the great circle with all the *orishas*.

The theology that emerges from the fifteen chapters that make up the book is lively and dynamic, and it is deeply indebted to the context from

1

which it was born. In this way it demonstrates that theology is like all human discourse, whether religious, academic, or any other kind; that is, it is the result of the social, historical, and cultural conditions of its production. There is no "truth" or dogma proclaimed in this book. What it offers is a word that is open to confrontation, to dialogue, to the possibility of change. The essays also propose a new biblical hermeneutic by presenting strong arguments that question, deconstruct, and reconstruct many conventional interpretations of the sacred texts. This new way of reading scripture is not applied only to the textual content of the written word. The oral accounts, the myths, the lived histories, as well as the rituals, symbols, and gestures all become objects of theological reflection and instruments for its transmission. Women, their lives, their experiences, and their words are at the center of this theological endeavor, which seeks to be challenging and original.

It is well known from experience, and it is confirmed by statistical data, that women are more committed to religion than men. Women make up the clear majority of the faithful; they are the majority in the area of religious practice, in the rituals, in the transmission of the faith; and they are likewise the majority of those who act as guardians of the memory of any religious group. In the name of God, women take on many roles, such as religious workers, pastors, bishops, rabbis, and mothers of saints. Whether in the shadows or upon the stages and altars, most women believers work to connect others to the church—their husbands, their children, their family, the social or professional circles where they move. Why are there so many women in search of God? What do the religions give women, and what do they give the religions? If it is not a "natural" endowment, how do we explain the strong attraction that the religious realm has for women? In what way does their presence transform any religious project in which they become involved? From the viewpoint of feminist struggles, how ought we to understand the powerful presence of women in the religious field and in the churches? What are women looking for, and what do they find in the different religions?

Much research has been done on these questions, especially in the social sciences. Nonetheless, that massive presence of women in the temples and churches can lead to mistaken conclusions that need to be clarified. One such conclusion, widely disseminated, is that we women, by virtue or by grace of a "feminine nature," are "more religious" than men. Such a vision is based on the supposition that biology determines what is feminine, and it fosters the idea that what is proper to men is the realm of reasoning and cultural creation. This dualistic conception of masculine and feminine derives in large part from religious ideologies. The vast majority of religions are patriarchal; their theological roots and their historical and institutional practices are explicitly or implicitly influenced by a dualistic anthropological vision that establishes and enforces different roles for men and women, to the disadvantage of the latter.

The basis for this vision is found in a nonhuman, non-historical order that is therefore immutable and indisputable, since it takes the form of dogma and irrefutable truths. Thus, human nature is seen as the product of a decisive divine determination at the biological level that establishes rigidly defined gender roles.

Another popular error concerning women's relationship to religion is brought to light by the present fundamentalist forms of religion that are found both in the West and in the East. Indeed, religions are everywhere men's principal domain of empowerment. Historically men have dominated the production of what is to be considered sacred in different societies, and religious discourse and practice still bear the marks of that domination. In practically all the known religions the norms, the rules and the doctrines have been defined by men. Women continue to be absent in the spaces that shape the beliefs, the pastoral policies, and the organizational practices of religious institutions.

Nonetheless, in the same way that research has been done into the scientific transformations achieved by the work of feminist scientists, we can also ask about the significant changes brought about in the field of religions by the practice and the thought of women who have assumed a feminist perspective, whether as faithful, as theologians, or as students of the field.

In the last few decades, feminist ideas and political practice have had a significant impact both on religions themselves and on the fields of study that seek to understand and explain religions. Feminist thought has also had a strong influence on the development of a theological discourse that is produced by women and so is quite different from the discourse that men have produced. Religious feminists have undertaken a constant process of revising theories and proposing new interpretations of the sacred texts. The main targets of women theologians' critiques have been in the area of doctrine and institutional organization. In recent years, women believers have made a variety of bold claims, from access to the priesthood and pastoral ministry in Christianity to the rabbinate in Judaism; from the use of the veil to the rejection of its use among Muslim women. The types of worship undertaken by groups of women have also been spaces for imaginative response and recreation.

Evidence shows that there is no aspect of the established religions that has not passed through the critical filter of feminist examination. And this book is one more proof of that.

The first chapter, by María Pilar Aquino, demonstrates how the new frameworks of intercultural feminism produce changes, both in the dominant theological discourse and in various types of feminist discourse. Using analytic and experiential arguments, the author develops an understanding of feminist theological activity as an alternative ethical-political project that is directed toward achieving a new world of justice. Such an understanding is a historical necessity for our times and also helps us to rethink the social function of the other human sciences. Besides explaining the notion of interculturality, the author emphasizes that theological knowledge fulfills its function when it foments new forms of social living together *(convivencia)* that make "another world" of justice truly possible in this world.

In the following chapter Geraldina Céspedes analyzes the construction of knowledge, in which women have been refused participation. Many factors contribute to this exclusion of women, especially women who are poor, black, or indigenous. Among those factors should be mentioned especially the anthropological and philosophical conceptions that call into doubt and even deny women's reasoning ability; other factors include the link between knowledge and power and the unequal and unjust distribution of wealth. The author also questions those sources and processes of theological work that reinforce the dualism between theory and practice and fail to take into account oral traditions, women's experience, and personal biography. Women's attempts to construct an alternative *wisdom* require a search for alternative theological frameworks: the weaving together of inclusive wisdoms. The search for wisdom from a feminist intercultural perspective in the present-day context of globalization ought to be a prophetic task by which we make it possible to know and to think in a different manner. As feminist intercultural theologians, we are challenged to make of our search for wisdom an inclusive practice and a path toward justice and compassion with the poor and the excluded.

"Border thinking," as a basic epistemological tool of Hispanic and Latin American feminist theologies, is described in the texts of Nancy Elizabeth Bedford and Jeanette Rodríguez. "Borderlands" is the name of the geographical, emotional, and/or psychological space that is occupied by *mestiza* women, and it serves as a metaphor for the condition of living "in between" spaces, cultures, and languages. Neither belonging totally to the place where they live nor being recognized in the place from which they come, Latina and Chicana women in the United States experience an intermediate space that is especially challenging. From this space bursts a theology that proposes the construction of new spaces where there is room for everybody, without the need of some dominating others; and spaces for establishing bridges of solidarity to those communities whose members are tortured and marginalized and whose children run grave risks because they live where those who struggle for justice and peace are killed.

The experience of Latina women in the United States takes on a historical perspective in the essay by Daisy L. Machado. Recalling the relation between the construction of historical accounts and the use of power, the author inquires: how has American religious historiography managed to ignore the five centuries during which the Latino/a population has been part of North American Christianity? How can church historians pretend to be writing the religious history of the nation while they continue to ignore the participation of a whole people that has been present since the nation's founding? The author invokes the voices that come from *Nepantla*, Middle Earth, in order to remove Latino/a people from their invisibility in the official historical accounts. That people, that eternal "other," is unrecognized in its language, its culture, and its religious manifestations, and it still remains a foreigner in the United States, even though it has long lived there and has contributed much to the country's history. The history of those Latina women who celebrated, practiced, and maintained their faith for centuries must be narrated from the fringes of the dominant culture, from *Nepantla*.

In her contribution Clara Luz Ajo Lázaro, a Cuban theologian, invokes two of the central figures of Christianity, Jesus and his mother, Mary, in order to propose the possibility of dialogue between two religious universes that are very distant from one another and yet very close: the Christian world and the world of the *orishas*. The border between these two universes is not easy to establish because of the way in which their rituals and sacred figures intermingle. The author therefore presents an imaginary situation in which Mary, on leaving Mass, invites her son to accompany her to dance with the *orishas*. Drums blend with organs and bells, the Our Father and lively Yoruba chants mix together, all of them announcing a simple form of interreligious dialogue, so different from the official ecumenism of the churches.

We see more of the religious reality of Cuba in the essay of Michelle A. González, who treats the interesting relationship between Latin American and Latina theology through the study of two key figures in Afro-Cuban history: the intellectual Lydia Cabrera, and Our Lady of Charity of Cobre (La Cachita, as she is known). The author's interpretative intention is to break through the categories of identity that operate in those theologies. The crucial question raised in this article is how to write a Latina theology that is historically informed by Latin America without negating our distinctive characteristics as Latinas. Her comparative study yields a methodological proposal that involves consideration of the contexts and the ambiguous situation of Latina women who live between two or more cultures—*Nepantla*. She especially examines Afro-Latino religion as a source for theological study.

Maricel Mena-López immerses herself in the biblical world to recover the figure of the Ethiopian woman and to reflect on the complex relations that exist among race, gender, and religion. This mysterious figure, never mentioned in the sermons heard in Christian churches, is Zipporah, the wife of Moses—we know of him, of course, the great patriarch! Kenite (Egyptian) in some sources and Cushite in others, Zipporah is the prime example of Ethiopia's contribution to the biblical religions. Introducing her as a source for biblical hermeneutics means studying the process of racialization and of sexism that is present in the traditional exegesis of Eurocentric stamp. The author's aim is to support the development of new epistemological paradigms in biblical studies. In this way, black feminist biblical interpretation challenges the erudition of traditional biblical theology to view history from another place, from a center that is not necessarily Western and Semitic.

The bold demand for a future that is black and beautiful, achieved through recovery of traditions that affirm the dignity of people of African descent, is enunciated in the chapter by Silvia Regina de Lima Silva. The author presents the challenge of rediscovering the forgotten black legacy. The memory of the bodies of so many black women, as a new theological locus, is what will set the foundation for the creation of a new black feminist Christology. That memory, in dialogue with the biblical text, recovers the many stories of Jesus and breaks free of the logic of Western European identity.

Black women are present once again in the essay of María Cristina Ventura Campusano. Once again we find intermingled the stories and memories of real women and those of biblical characters. United to the midwives drawn out of the biblical narrative are fictional women who help give birth to children. With respect to this activity the Bible is read as an ambivalent text: on the one hand, the Bible proceeds from a colonial project that is destructive of cultures and associated with a patriarchal, androcentric system; on the other hand, it allows us to dialogue with the ancient memories of women and different cultures. From this dialogue emerges the possibility of bringing about *interculturality as a political act that affirms the valuing of difference* as a way of living in liberty.

The chapter by Christa P. Godínez Munguía takes up this same theme of intercultural dialogue. Her treatment of the wisdom and the spirituality of indigenous women shows us that we can be enriched by listening to them with open heart.

Celebration, joy, and suffering merge together in the lives of the Brazilian women who are infected with HIV/AIDS. In writing about them, Yury Puello Orozco reveals that what is most surprising in these women's stories is not so much their ability to bear the pain without denying it, but their capacity for finding and generating life far beyond the pain. The harsh reality of discovering themselves to be infected by the virus allows them the unexpected experience of recognizing themselves as subjects. Confidence and gratitude are the constant feelings of these women, and solidarity is their daily practice. Despite everything, they are still alive, and hope is their horizon.

Violeta Rocha Areas's article revisits the book of the Apocalypse from the perspective of critical feminist hermeneutics. It is quite a challenge to interpret this mysterious biblical text, with all its signs and symbols, its images and enigmatic works, but critical feminism can help us to recover the liberating pedagogy contained in the text and to discern its call for a new order of justice and peace, in which the community dimension is fundamental.

María del Carmen Servitje Montull undertakes, from a critical feminist perspective, a theological reflection on the Virgin of Guadalupe, that takes into account the Latin American context in which that devotion was born and was nourished. The essay recognizes the *mestiza* character of Our Lady of Guadalupe and explores the diverse ways of viewing her—an example of women's submission or an expression of women's refusal to submit. The author concludes by invoking the Virgin as an ally in our constant struggle against the machismo that still prevails at all levels of our cultures.

To round off the collection, Olga Consuelo Vélez Caro adopts the theoretical perspective developed by Raúl Fornet-Betancourt to explain the epistemological premises for the construction of a feminist intercultural theological paradigm. The author starts off by explaining the concept of interculturality, the contemporary notion of culture, and the development of feminist theological thought in Latin America. With this conceptual base, she then proposes three constitutive elements for feminist theological work from an intercultural Latin American perspective: (1) that all the voices of women and men speak out, even the most diverse; (2) that the existential dimension be incorporated into a knowledge that goes beyond elaboration of concepts; and (3) that the transformation of mind sets make possible a world that does not exclude people because of sexual orientation.

I hope this brief presentation of the various texts that make up this book constitutes an enticement to readers to study them and to commit themselves also to this process of creating other possible ways of living in this world. May Sor Juana Inés de la Cruz bless us and guide our steps toward the future!

1

Feminist Intercultural Theology

Toward a Shared Future of Justice

María Pilar Aquino

This chapter represents a modest effort of reflection on my under-standing of feminist intercultural theology as an alternative ethical-po-litical project for advancing toward a new world of justice. The central concern guiding my reflection has reference to the need to clarify the social function of a critical feminist theology of liberation that is ex-pressed in intercultural terms. From my point of view, the recent devel-opment of critical intercultural theories offers us new theoretical tools and new conceptual resources for enriching and expanding the emancipatory vision of feminist theologies.

The themes I present in this chapter are inconclusive, because a femi-nist intercultural theology, with its distinctive frameworks of intercul-tural praxis, has hardly begun to be developed in many parts of the world. Therefore, my contribution to this book is simply an initial ex-ploration of how a feminist intercultural theology might contribute to the search for answers to the problems and concerns presented to us by today's realities. I have divided my reflection into three parts. First I put forward some arguments for the need to strengthen interactive commu-nication between the feminist theological frameworks and the emergent intercultural frameworks. In the second part I present some key under-standings of the concept of *interculturality*, and I also consider some approaches to the basic conditions for intervening in the intercultural deliberations that aim at a continued development of a *critical ethical-political* paradigm of theological interpretation.[1] In the third and final part, I focus my reflection on the contribution that a feminist intercul-tural theology makes to the development of new ways of knowledge

9

that bolster our conviction that another world of justice is truly possible
in this world.

ARGUMENTS FOR INTERCULTURAL FRAMEWORKS

Intercultural philosophical approaches are proving to be a valuable
resource for clarifying the social function of religious discourses and
have already begun to bring about changes in the theological sciences,
especially in the understanding of their ethical horizon. Among the many
possible explanations for this, I consider relevant only three arguments
that are important for the purposes of my reflection. The first argument
states that the multidimensional, simultaneous processes being impelled
by the present social model of imperial capitalist globalization are raising questions and concerns that the Western European Christian tradition is unable to deal with in any significant fashion.[2] Due to its
kyriarchal[3]-monocultural and Eurocentric character, this tradition appears to be obsolete and incapable of offering visions that are convergent with the values and aspirations of the social, intellectual, and religious movements that seek answers to the growing problems of social
injustice. While more than two-thirds of the world's population experiences on a daily basis the heavy burdens of the profound social inequalities produced by that social model, only a privileged minority of the
world enjoys its benefits. The most immediate experience of people
around the world is shaped by the suffering and the anxieties that come
from poverty, social violence, fatal infirmities, and increasing human
insecurity. The present epoch is characterized by a worldwide crisis of
human rights. It is precisely in terms of such experience that people are
interpreting their human and their religious existence. From my own
experiential position in the Americas, I can see clearly that this kyriarchal
Christian tradition not only has not contributed to forging systems that
engender social justice, but that it also is still failing in its mission to
provide people reasons to assert their hope that another world is possible.

The second argument recognizes that in the context of Latin America,
even though the political panorama has changed significantly in the last
few years, the cultural and religious ambience not only continues to be
adverse to women's dignity and human rights but has actually gotten
worse. Recent studies point out that, although there is some evident
reform of political and social institutions, there has been no advance in
terms of developing and consolidating a democratic culture.[4] M. Lagos,
director of the prominent firm Latinobarómetro, states: "Unfortunately,

after ten years, almost nothing in the region has happened as regards democracy. . . . Everything changes so that everything stays the same."[5] Among other causes, these studies point out that the attitudes and the values in favor of an antidemocratic political culture remain constant. The inadequate development of a culture of respect for human rights finds expression in poverty and the deepening of social inequalities, which affect principally the lives of women. From my viewpoint, another main cause, ignored by these studies, is the antidemocratic presence and activity in the region of Roman Catholicism and the fundamentalist Christian churches. By virtue of their hierarchical, authoritarian, and sexist character, these churches act as real obstacles to the development of democratic cultures. In many countries conservative Roman Catholicism, with its absolutist dogmatism, has intervened in the public realm in order to prevent the juridical recognition or the approval of changes in legislation to protect the human rights of women.[6]

Latin America and the Caribbean are not the exception, however, for in recent years the attacks against the human rights of women have increased similarly in other countries as well. Amnesty International points out that "this attack, especially regarding women's sexual rights and reproductive rights, was led by conservative U.S.-backed Christian groups and supported by the Holy See and some member states of the Organization of the Islamic Conference."[7] For the Latin American and Caribbean region it would be naive and absurd to ignore the negative function that kyriarchal Roman Catholicism exercises as regards the achievement of human rights for women. Going back to its origins in the Eurocentric colonial project, kyriarchal Roman Catholicism has historically had, and continues to have, a major influence in the cultural frameworks that ground the values, visions, and forms of life in this region. The kyriarchal theology of Roman Catholicism continues to give backing to cultural environments that accept the subordination of women and that give permission for men, as a social body, to function as a privileged human grouping that is allowed to degrade, humiliate and violate women. In most countries the Catholic Church has failed to offer alternative cultural models for transforming the apparent inertia of the cultural and social privileges enjoyed by men, and it has been negligent in abandoning the mentality of privileges that the present cultures reproduce.

In order to illustrate this assertion, I will describe a situation that I recently experienced, a sordid scene that still seems to me to be strewn with absurd images.[8] As associate director of the Center for the Study of Latino/a Catholicism, I happened to be visiting a Latin American country to explore the possibilities of holding a symposium on feminist intercultural theology, similar to the symposium that produced this book. In the midst of many meetings that I had, one afternoon I was to be present in a session that was attended by several colleagues and friends, all men. Upon entering the meeting, I did not think it unusual that my presence was unacknowledged, because I understood that my first duty was to familiarize myself with the topic that the group was discussing. However, after forty minutes of feeling not only that my presence there was being ignored, but that I was being rendered invisible, I was gripped by a distinct sense of being excluded for the simple fact of being a woman. I was not wrong in feeling that way. A few minutes later I tried to intervene in the conversation, which was on a topic of much interest for me, related to the processes of the commissions of truth and reconciliation in Latin America. At the moment of seeking to utter my first words, however, one of the participants said to me in a strong, serious, authoritarian voice: "Ma'am, shut your mouth. Did you ask your boss for permission to speak?" At that I became frozen, as if I were petrified by the horror of the situation. Suddenly, the scene was blanketed in a solid silence, which nobody dared to break. I seemed to be living in a mean, unreal world, but that situation was quite real and those of us who were there were real people. What was absurd about the situation is that I was there precisely to seek out spaces for organizing an event on feminist intercultural theology, and that in such a circumstance my person suffered aggression for no reason at all.

Experience revealed to me that that participant who so despotically silenced me thought that he had permission to degrade me as a person. But he revealed also that another participant in the meeting believed he had permission to convey the idea that I was his subordinate and that somehow I owed obedience to a person who gave the erroneous impression of being my "boss." In that dynamic of power and control, in order for that person to be recognized as "the boss," it was necessary for me to be degraded. In the midst of my amazement, I was able to realize that the consummate arrogance and overinflated egos of those colleagues and friends had been nourished by cultures and religions that were profoundly sexist. In my view, those dynamics of kyriarchal power continue to function because the dominant antidemocratic cultures have not changed at all, and the mentalities of dominion and control continue the same as always. With the exception of one other participant, I have not received any apologies from those perpetrators of women's degradation for that aberrant and unnecessary disgrace that they made me undergo. This personal experience only confirmed for me the need we have of intervening theologically for the radical transformation of the kyriarchal cultures, and religions that dominate the world. In my opinion, there will be no changes in our societies without radical changes in the cultural frameworks. There will be no respect for women without radical changes in the kyriarchal societies, cultures and religions. The conceptual frameworks of the intercultural critique seek to contribute to the development and the consolidation of democratizing environments, so that present-day world realities cease being forever the same. For that reason, interculturality is not so much a new theme for theology as it is a new rationality that expands the ethical-political horizon of theology.

The third argument asserts that the function of theological knowledge can be clarified by answering these questions: What happens to the world's reality when God's presence and activity takes place there? And what happens to God's reality when it takes place in the world? According to Ignacio Ellacuría, the central concern of theology is making clear "which historical acts bring salvation and which bring condemnation, which acts make God more present, and how that presence is actualized and made effective in them."[9] This concern leads me to recognize that for present-day world realities, so characterized by the universality of social injustice and women's subordination, theological activity can and should understand that its function is in direct relation to those currents of thoughts and emancipatory social movements that seek to fortify processes favoring a social justice paradigm. In my view, the processes of struggling to make a new social paradigm possible in the world are precisely those where God's presence and activity become real in the world. Feminist liberation theologies, by keeping step with the processes aimed at promoting transformative visions and practices in favor of a new world of justice, are becoming increasingly integrated into the frameworks of critical intercultural thought.

Nonetheless, in light of these three arguments, we should recognize that the intercultural theological frameworks are not products already assembled, much less finished goods. What is more, these frameworks can come into existence only when there are people like you and me, interested in contributing to the creation of intercultural feminist processes and spaces. Intercultural perspectives do not happen outside of what we are and what we do; rather, they develop in those metaphorical and physical border spaces where we relearn the thinking process on the basis of new situations of interaction and contextuality and a new consciousness of cultural diversity. The processes of communication among the diverse contextualities are producing a new notion of universality, one based on our shared struggles to make concrete the conviction that another world is possible. The development of a feminist intercultural theology in different contexts around the world is a sign of hope, because it shows that alternative modes of critical thought are already coming into existence.

FEMINIST INTERCULTURAL APPROACHES:
UNDERSTANDINGS AND CONDITIONS

First, I wish to state that it is difficult for me to offer a univocal under-standing of the meaning of the concept of interculturality. In fact, the mere attempt to offer such a univocal understanding would be contrary to the very nature of intercultural frameworks, insofar as they are con-tinually being elaborated and expanded in every process of cultural in-teraction.[10] Cultures are not fixed products, but processes that change through human intervention and that are continually affecting the whole social context in its different local, regional, and global levels. In gen-eral, the common tendency of the kyriarchal mode of knowledge is to-ward seeking and establishing definitions that explain things in a clear and distinct fashion. The monocultural and Eurocentric character of kyriarchal knowledge functions as a key that locks off the possibilities for modifying such definitions by other modes of knowledge, since the definitions are already unilaterally established. However, the meaning of the concept of interculturality cannot be encapsulated in locked-up definitions, since people themselves are the actors and the subjects of the intercultural process. People, therefore, enter into the dynamics of trans-formation as interacting participants of diverse cultures and as bearers of agendas for change.

Along the same line, there is another difficulty in defining this con-cept. On the one hand, the meaning of interculturality is linked to the historical context of each people and each culture, so the meaning de-pends on the realities, the resources, and the challenges of that context. For example, due to the particular configuration, significance, and im-plications of the intercultural processes, they will necessarily be differ-ent in contexts as diverse as Rwanda, Guatemala, Nepal, or the United States. Naturally, the priorities, the strategies, and the resources involved in intercultural processes will show variations, depending on the par-ticular contexts of each people. On the other hand, in present-day global contexts, the processes generated by imperial capitalist globalization produce the simultaneous interaction—usually on unequal terms—of peoples and cultures all around the planet. In such contexts, according to the Korean feminist philosopher Choe Hyondok, intercultural praxis requires that we take into account the different constellations of power in order to analyze the implications and the consequences of intercul-tural processes.[11] We must therefore ask questions about what interests are represented worldwide, what type of values underlie the cultural interaction promoted by the present globalization, and who is obtaining the benefits of such interaction. Even so, taking into account the difficulties mentioned here and being conscious of the dimensions and the complexity of intercultural processes, I continue to emphasize the importance of fomenting spaces of critical deliberation for the purpose of developing understandings of interculturality that express shared commitments. Through communication and shared dialogue, intercultural approaches offer alternatives for deliberating about our common commitment to forging, out of our diverse cultural contexts, a world free of violence and injustice. To this end I here present briefly some of the understandings of interculturality that have helped orient my own reflection.

- In its most existential dimension, interculturality is understood as taking a position before life or as a "conscious way of life in which an ethical position in favor of living together *(convivencia)* with differences takes form."[12] In this sense, interculturality is an experience that emerges from daily life because that is where human interaction occurs and that is what people use to explain their existence.[13] Such an experience goes beyond mere tolerance or simple recognition of cultural diversity, for it understands that diversity as an opportunity for improved human development, cultivated by dialogue. Interculturality, in the words of Raúl Fornet-Betancourt, is a form of "consciously knowing the finality for which we work . . . in order to know what we should take care of today and how we should do it."[14]
- As a social force for change,[15] interculturality is an international social movement composed of practitioners who are present at different levels of existing social institutions and who work in diverse fields of human activity, including churches and universities. For S. Wesley Ariarajah, "intercultural hermeneutics has been used to denote a number of movements within the theological scene that relates to interpretation and explication that involves two or more cultures."[16] This social movement seeks to strengthen the relations among different cultures so that they can develop jointly, as equal subjects, "a model for living together"[17] in solidarity and peace. By affirming an ethical horizon of emancipation, interculturality can also be understood as a current of thought and action that is committed to the "emergent and insurgent moral forces of our epoch,"[18] those that have as their project the construction of a just world.
- In its development as a framework for thought and action, interculturality is understood fundamentally as an *alternative political-cultural project* that seeks, according to Fornet-Betancourt,

"the reorganization of current international relations . . . [and] the correction of the asymmetry of power that exists today in the world of international politics."[19] As such, interculturality aims at transforming the relations of domination and subordination that are rooted in today's cultures and societies. The objective of this transformation is the creation of just conditions that affirm the rights and the human dignity of marginalized social groups.[20] In order for theologies and religions to participate in this objective, it is imperative to strive for their intercultural transformation in such a way that "they become what they should be: ways of participating in God's truth."[21]

- As a new scientific paradigm or disciplinary model, interculturality is understood as a "methodology that allow us to study, describe and analyze the dynamics of interaction among different cultures and that views interculturality as a new discipline."[22] In this understanding, interculturality "is the theory and method of interpreting and understanding across cultural boundaries."[23] This is not, however, a narrow methodology, but rather "an interaction of diverse methods"[24] that intersect and enrich one another so as to participate more effectively in the project of constructing a new world based on justice.

By joining together these understandings of interculturality, I can discern their distinct orientation toward the transformation of existent realities, with the aim of modeling a world where there is a place for all peoples and where human dignity and human rights become possible. In this new world, the subordination of women will no longer exists because the kyriarchal cultures and religions will have ceased to exist. In order for such a world to be possible, however, it is necessary to participate actively in the design and the expansion of the spaces of intercultural dialogue. The conditions for participating in this dialogue include the following.

According to Fornet-Betancourt, the intercultural frameworks of thought present, above all, a hermeneutic challenge that involves the "need to reconsider the presuppositions of our own theory of understanding."[25] In order to intervene in theological dialogue in intercultural terms, at least four basic conditions are necessary.[26] First, we must historicize the hermeneutical question. Such historicization refuses to continue fomenting the creation of theories based on purely abstracting thought; that is, theories disconnected from the social contexts in which marginalized cultures have developed plural forms of knowledge for the purpose of supporting visions and practices of social change. The intercultural proposal undertakes the task of analyzing and evaluating the models of human knowledge that have dominated the world from antiquity up to the present. From an intercultural feminist perspective, the dominant models of knowledge known to us have been and continue to be kyriarchal-monocultural and Eurocentric. Since these models continue to declare themselves to be universal, it is not surprising that they ignore or subordinate the emergent models of rationality, like critical feminist theory, that develop theories that are rooted in processes of social change and propose emancipation and justice as the primary objectives of knowledge. For intercultural frameworks of thought, it is important to pay heed to the words of caution offered by Uma Narayan, who recommends that we avoid replicating the limitations of the previous theories of knowledge, including even the emancipatory theories, since they "constructed their emancipatory projects and subjects as Universals, even as they excluded many groups of people from their political vision. We need to remember that many political projects that sought to redefine and empower marginalized groups constructed their own forms of exclusion and marginalization."[27] For that reason, hermeneutical historicization requires that we transcend any theories that promote the fragmentation and dispersion of the social groups that develop emancipatory kinds of knowledge, and it also requires the transformation of the material conditions where the diverse cultural voices enter into contact on unequal terms.

A second condition is relativizing our own ways of thinking. In order to enter into the spaces of intercultural dialogue, each participant in the dialogue must relativize his or her own ways of understanding humanity and the world. This relativization means that the different parts in the dialogue renounce the prescribed certainties that kyriarchal-monocultural and Eurocentric knowledge has bestowed on them. Historically, such certainties have prevented cultures and peoples from knowing and understanding other peoples and other cultures in terms of their equal originality, dignity, and value. However, since the dominant forms of knowledge express the values and interests only of those social groups that are situated in structural positions of power and privilege, this relativization of one's own ways of thinking also involves a turning toward the emancipatory modes of knowledge developed by the subordinate cultures. Possibly the major challenge here is how to accede to those emancipatory modes, not from the customary kyriarchal horizons of understanding, but from a new situation of egalitarian encounter and exchange. In order to reach a common future of well-being and justice that benefits the whole of humankind, it is essential to have discursive exchange on the basis of equality.

The third basic condition for intercultural dialogue is renouncing dogmatic attitudes and unilateral positions. Such renunciation means that the parts interested in the dialogue recognize that the world can and should be different, and that they understand that there are other models of thought that can help bring about this different world. In this sense, intercultural dialogue does not promote recuperation or reconstruction of the kyriarchal-monocultural frameworks of thought, but rather supports the radical transformation of the current models of thought. From an intercultural feminist perspective, the renunciation of conceptual absolutisms and doctrinal dogmatisms is essential for making egalitarian communication and open deliberation possible. To attain this perspective, the plural voices in theology are invited to become involved in processes of interchange and critical deliberation with the aim not only of overcoming fragmentation, but also of working together for a new organization of religions and of the world. In this way, the feminist practice of interculturality seeks to transform the supposedly universal character of kyriarchal-monocultural knowledge and to offer emancipatory models of knowledge so that justice comes to be truly universal from within each culture and society. Thus, the intercultural theological approaches seek to make universal a proposal for discourse that affirms the dignity and human rights of every person and promotes the integrity of creation in all parts of the world. For this reason, not only do intercultural theological frameworks accept and value cultural diversity, but they also recognize and affirm that it is precisely in the ethical-political space of justice where cultures and religions should join together.

The fourth basic condition for intercultural theological dialogue is having a keen awareness, as a starting point, that the cultures known by humankind up to the present time have produced values and ways of life that perpetuate a *politics of inequalities*, especially in the relations between men and women. In general, the existing cultures have found in religions the ethical-political arguments needed to establish patterns of thought and behavior that place women in positions of subordination. Intercultural approaches to religion and theology, therefore, deliberately avoid any romanticization or uncritical understanding of one's own cultural tradition. However, such approaches also recognize that cultures, in their diversity, offer emancipatory visions of the world and of human relations that are helpful in searching for new ways of living that banish the subordination of women. In this regard, Fornet-Betancourt states that each culture, as a vision of the world, "has something to say to

everybody," so that all cultures come to be valuable resources "for seeking a common life strategy for all."[28] An intercultural understanding of
religions and theological activity, then, involves a commitment to elimi-
nating that politics of inequalities because, theologically, it is contrary to
God's purpose for humankind and the world. Fornet-Betancourt points
out that cooperation or interaction among cultures can be deceitful if
there is no clear affirmation of a *politics of transformation* "that combats effectively and unequivocally the asymmetry of power that charac-
terizes the current world 'order' and that becomes more acute as globalization progresses. Only by creating conditions of equality and social
justice at a global level will it be possible to guarantee a free interaction
in which all cultures can . . . promote, from within, mutual transformations in their ways of life."[29] Consequently, feminist intercultural theology affirms as an ethical-political religious imperative the transformation of those cultures and religions that have bred values and ways of
life that are hostile to the dignity and human rights of women.

These four conditions for intervening in theological conversations on
intercultural terms support the continued development of a feminist intercultural theology that (1) contributes to the search for answers perti-
nent to the aspirations and struggles of social groups committed to the
transformation of kyriarchal cultures, religions, and societies, and that
(2) provides support for the religious visions and spiritualities needed to
maintain such commitment. In the present contexts of imperial capitalist globalization, there is multiple and simultaneous incidence of cultural fragmentation, neoliberal homogenization of cultures, and social
inequalities. Since the harmful effects of this situation mainly affect wom-
en, a feminist intercultural theology is the one most able to respond to
questions about the function of religions in bringing about social and
cultural conversions from a global politics of *subordination* to a global
politics of *emancipation*. What is equally important, this type of theology helps us to achieve better the radical turn away from the divisive
politics inherent in the logic of identities toward the integrative politics
inherent in the logic of emancipatory democracy.[30] With the aim of facing the challenges that the present contexts present for theological activity, feminist intercultural theology seeks to strengthen the development
of a *critical ethical-political paradigm of biblical and theological interpretation*. Since the dominant interpretative paradigms continue to be
kyriarchal-monocultural and Eurocentric, their transformation must be
a common task shared by the theological community in its diverse cultural spheres. In the words of Elisabeth Schüssler Fiorenza, an emancipatory feminist paradigm of interpretation understands that

the task of interpretation is not just to understand biblical texts and traditions but to analyze their power of persuasion in order to change and transform western malestream epistemological frameworks, individualistic apolitical practices, and sociopolitical relations of cultural colonization. . . . Biblical [and theological] interpretation, like all scholarly inquiry, is a communicative practice that involves interests, values, and visions. Only in such a rhetorical-emancipatory paradigm of biblical [and theological] studies will liberation theologies of all colors have the possibility of engaging the discourses of biblical [and theological] studies on their own terms and on equal terms with Eurocentric malestream scholarship. By beginning with the religious experiences and articulations of the marginalized and colonized—of those wo/men traditionally excluded from interpreting the Bible, articulating theology, and shaping communal Christian self-understanding—they can change the starting point of traditional biblical [and theological] interpretation.[31]

FEMINIST INTERCULTURAL THEOLOGY:
FOR A NEW WORLD OF JUSTICE

"Another World Is Possible" is the declaration or slogan that each year brings together hundreds of social movements, human rights organizations, religious leaders, government representatives, public-policy leaders, researchers, intellectuals, and activists from all parts of the world. Organized by the World Social Forum,[32] this encounter joins together all these organizations and individuals who "are committed to building a planetary society directed toward fruitful relationships among Humankind and between it and the Earth."[33] Those of us who hold that another world is indeed possible are guided by a new vision, one that supports the struggles to overcome the destructive processes of the present-day kyriarchal globalization[34] and that illuminates the search for alternatives that open the way to a world free of divisions and violence. This vision speaks of a new kind of globalization in solidarity, one which "will prevail as a new stage in world history. This will respect universal human rights, and those of all citizens—men and women—of all nations and the environment and will rest on democratic international systems and institutions at the service of social justice, equality and the sovereignty of peoples."[35] The feminist theories and theologies of liberation that have emerged around the world share this vision and are actively working to make it a reality in the world. Moreover, they are just as insistent that the systemic subordination and dehumanization of women and the sexual violence against them should be a central part of every agenda of transformation, so that these realities are eliminated from all cultures, societies, and religions.

From the viewpoint of Christian tradition, feminist theologies of liberation imagine and visualize a new world, and they use their interpretative resources to create religious languages that sustain every effort to establish the social conditions most compatible with that world of justice and liberation desired by God. The redeeming and creative presence of God in the world is truly expressed only by the historical realities of justice, solidarity, peaceful living together *(convivencia)*, and human fulfillment. The very content of these realities, therefore, is understood to be the expression of God's glory on earth. According to Elizabeth Johnson, "In biblical terms, yearning for salvation, for victory in the struggle with evil, for deliverance of the poor from want and of the war-torn from violence is consistently expressed in the hope that God's glory will dwell in the land or will fill the earth or will shine throughout heaven and earth."[36] The central role that this vision has for every struggle for social change means that, in the present context of kyriarchal globalization, feminist theologies have committed themselves to developing and promoting the kinds of knowledge and practice that transform those conditions that are contrary to God's purpose. Their function is to foment and sustain, in religious-political terms, visions of justice that give impulse to every effort to change the present situation. For the Christian community, the duty of working for justice emanates from the biblical affirmation that all of humankind—men and women alike—has been created in the image of God and that the equality and dignity of each person, as a child of God, is affirmed in Christ Jesus (Gal 3:26–28). For that reason, no person has reason or is permitted to subordinate another person or to destroy God's creation. According to this biblical affirmation, everything that harms the world or degrades humanity is contrary to God's liberating purpose and so formally constitutes a sinful reality that must be eradicated. For feminist liberation theologies, the struggles for justice and for the elimination of violent cultures is a historical, theological, and ethical-political necessity, given the present situation of the world and of the kyriarchal-monocultural religions.

If I could name one aspiration that people of all cultures value and share in common, it would be the aspiration to experience the well-being and happiness of their everyday life. Experiencing a peaceful existence and the satisfaction of one's basic emotional and material needs is something that all persons treasure for themselves and for those around them. I believe that this aspiration is universal and that it exists in all the world's cultures. In the current model of society, however, its fulfillment is literally impossible for more than two-thirds of the world's population. What is more, the present kyriarchal cultures and religions not only have been useless in preventing this situation, but they have also contributed to exacerbating the politics of inequalities, with its exclusionary institutions and its monocultural and sexist discourses. Nevertheless, as Tapio Kanninen points out, "in the light of the unfortunate but increasing prominence of religion as a divisive force in our world, the time has come for religion also to play its role in uniting people and creating conditions for peace."[37] The proposal to develop a feminist intercultural theology is concerned with making explicit the relation that exists between the real conditions in which people live, the function of cultures in inculcating values and aspirations, and the role of religious discourses in maintaining or changing the values and aspirations that originate in the conditions in which the people live.

The intercultural conceptual frameworks, according to Hyondok, have "the intention to transform reality, and not simply describe and explain the reality."[38] It is for that reason, in my opinion, that feminist intercultural theology broadens its array of instruments: in order to make more evident the roads that lead to the strengthening of visions of a world transformed on the basis of the contexts of each culture and the new scenarios of communication and interaction among the cultures. In view of the widespread aspirations for a new world of well-being and justice, contemporary processes of social change must amplify and intensify the spaces of communication and dialogue that exist among the emancipatory traditions present in the different cultural worlds. For feminist intercultural theology, a new world of justice is the only world that we can call our home. In this regard, Mercy Amba Oduyoye states that "our future as women is in living our true humanity in a world that we have helped to shape, and in which even now we have begun to live and enjoy, conscious of our situation and seeking consciously to change structures and attitudes. Even the prospect of being a part of this calls for celebrating."[39] For me, participation in this change of structures and attitudes already aims toward the creation of new cultural environments that respond to people's profound aspirations. What is more, people's active involvement in the present processes of change makes it evident that, in the crossing of cultural frontiers, we are already living in that different future of which we dream. For many of us women, the reason for our hope lies in the fact that, by our feminist theological practices in diverse cultural environments, we are intervening together in opening up and exploring what María Cristina Ventura calls "the new possibilities to exist with human dignity."[40]

From the viewpoint of the frameworks of intercultural thought, these possibilities of living in a human and dignified manner are broadened at the world level because, from within each culture and from the global interaction of cultures, an *alternative politico-cultural project* is already under way, and a *critical ethical-political paradigm of biblical and theological interpretation* is burgeoning. Feminist intercultural theolgoy seeks to express these developments in a form that is systematic and coherent in its methods and contents. For feminist theological activity, intercultural thought is an aid for clarifying the function of theology in present-day contexts, and it contributes to visualizing conceptual strategies for advancing toward new cultural environments that support just and humanizing social relations. According to Fornet-Betancourt, cultures "are not roads already made, ready to be traveled on with a pre-arranged itinerary,"[41] but are concrete processes "by which a given human community organizes its materiality on the basis of the ends and values that it wishes to attain."[42] Because cultures are not static historical formations, reality itself generates plural discursive practices that often are divergent and favor interests that are contrary to the people's aspirations. In this context, it is important for me to affirm that feminist intercultural theological activity deliberately accepts its ethical-political dimension, especially as regards its commitment to the struggles for human dignity, the human and reproductive rights of women, and a new world of justice.

The proposal for a feminist intercultural theology is not a prescription or a finished product. I propose that it can be understood as a process of critical deliberation, which, in interaction with other liberating theological languages, seeks to contribute to the construction of different realities. With its religious language and resources, this theology seeks to participate in processes of change in order to replace:

> the paradigm of domination with the paradigm of justice,
> the paradigm of subordination with the paradigm of emancipation,
> the paradigm of capital with the paradigm of human dignity,
> the paradigm of a predatory market with the paradigm of an inclusive community,
> the paradigm of domesticating religion with the paradigm of transformative religion,
> the paradigm of absolutist Christianity with the paradigm of dialogical Christianity,

the kyriarchal-monocultural paradigm of
    interpretation with the critical ethical-political
    paradigm of interpretation, as proposed by
    feminist intercultural theology.

Taking these hoped-for changes into account, I have no hesitation in
recognizing that this theology affirms an option for hope. Fornet-
Betancourt holds that intercultural thought affirms such an option because it enters into the scenario of present-day reality "as an alternative
for articulating the concrete hopes of every person who dares today to
imagine and to rehearse still other possible worlds."[43] In our present
historical reality, the option for hope and the affirmation that another
world is possible are ethical and religious imperatives for the theological
community in every part of the world.

To conclude my reflection, I would like to note also that, by adopting
the inputs of other theologies of liberation, feminist intercultural theology affirms that theological knowledge should function as a principle of
liberation in the church and society.[44] Theology is therefore obliged to
abandon its historical function as a mechanism for producing dehuman-
izing discourses and for validating systems of domination. Consequently,
feminist intercultural theology, both in its aims and in its contents, is
articulated according to the simple criterion of what harms or what helps
"the very fact of living"[45] of the people. In the same way, for its epistemological coherence and consistency, this theology assumes the *feminist
option for the poor and the oppressed* as its fundamental principle of
biblical and theological interpretation.[46] This option has a twofold consequence for feminist intercultural theology: its contents are developed
in response to the aspirations and struggles of women for an existence
free of human degradation, and primacy is given to those insurgent traditions for a just world that are born in our own cultural environments.

Finally, I would suggest that this type of theological discourse needs
to be undertaken as a collective task and as a reflection rooted in the
concrete, lived contexts of our communities. As I mentioned at the beginning of this essay, the most common experiences of people in these
contexts have to do with poverty and the lack of basic human rights.
The immediate consequence for our theological work is our need to continue raising questions about how religious languages operate in social
life, what ethical-political consequences they have, what type of relation
they establish with social and religious movements involved in social
transformation, what impact they have in the local struggles to promote
justice, what types of answers they offer to the struggles for the human
and reproductive rights of women, what religious resources they provide

for affirming the human rights of the homosexual community, what incidence they have in "the very fact of living" of the people, and what type of common future we can visualize on the basis of the cultural and religious frameworks of interpretation advocated by intercultural thought. Even though further explorations are needed, I believe that a feminist intercultural theology has abundant religious resources that can offer visions and interpretative strategies that affirm the right of every person to live free of misery, fear, violence, and social insecurity Still another part of our task, as Narayan points out, is to continue opening up spaces within the institutions of society, so that there is a place for every person, especially for "those who are socially marginalized and powerless, so that they may become active participants in articulating their interests, commitments, and visions of justice."[47] This is so precisely because intercultural frameworks are aimed at fomenting interaction among cultures for the sake of achieving justice at the global level. Our own work is dedicated to the continued strengthening of the imagination of the theological community so that we may contribute better to the design of viable routes toward a common future for the whole of humankind. With our religious languages and resources, our work is called upon to show that another world of justice is possible in this world.

Notes

[1] On this paradigm, see Elisabeth Schüssler Fiorenza, *Rhetoric and Ethic: The Politics of Biblical Studies* (Minneapolis: Fortress Press, 1999), 32–33.

[2] On this, see S. Wesley Ariarajah, "Intercultural Hermeneutics: A Promise for the Future?" *Voices from the Third World* 29, no. 1 (2006): 91.

[3] The term *kyriarchy* is a feminist analytical category. This is "a neologism coined by Elisabeth Schüssler Fiorenza and derived from the Greek words for 'lord' or 'master' (*kyrios*) and 'to rule or dominate' (*archein*) which seeks to redefine the analytic category of patriarchy in terms of multiplicative intersecting structures of domination. Kyriarchy is a socio-political system of domination in which elite educated propertied men hold power over wo/men and other men. Kyriarchy is best theorized as a complex pyramidal system of intersecting multiplicative social structures of superordination and subordination, of ruling and oppression" (Elisabeth Schüssler Fiorenza, *Wisdom Ways: Introducing Feminist Biblical Interpretation* [Maryknoll, NY: Orbis Books, 2001], 211). Also, as explained by Schüssler Fiorenza, "the neologism *kyriarchy-kyriocentrism* (from Greek *kyrios* meaning lord, master, father, husband) seeks to express this interstructuring of domination and to replace the commonly used term "patriarchy," which is often understood in terms of binary gender dualism. I have introduced this neologism as an analytic category in order to be able to articulate a more comprehensive systemic analysis, to underscore the complex

interstructuring of domination, and to locate sexism and misogyny in the political matrix or, better, patrix of a broader range of oppressions" (Schüssler Fiorenza, *Rhetoric and Ethic*, 5).

[4] Daniel Zovatto, "Cultura Democrática: Poco Cambia Pese a los Cambios," Latinobarómetro, Observatorio Electoral Latinoamericano, Noviembre de 2005, available from http://www.observatorioelectoral.org/informes/tendencias/; Internet (accessed December 11, 2006).

[5] Cited by Zovatto, "Cultura Democrática."

[6] See, for example, a typical case from Nicaragua in Roland Membreño Segura, "Deshumanización y Fundamentalismo Cristiano: A Propósito del Aborto Terapéutico," *El Nuevo Diario* (Managua, Nicaragua), edición 9425, Miércoles 8 de Noviembre de 2006, available from http://www.elnuevodiario.com.ni/2006/11/08/opinion/33345; Internet (accessed December 13, 2006); Violeta Otero Rosales, "La Iglesia Católica y el Aborto: Por Abortos Clandestinos Mueren Mujeres," *El Nuevo Diario* (Managua, Nicaragua), edición 9392, Viernes 6 de Octubre de 2006, available from http://www.elnuevodiario.com.ni/2006/10/06/opinion/30665; Internet (accessed December 13, 2006); Tania Sirias and Edgard Barberena, "Más Voces Internacionales en Defensa del Aborto Terapéutico," *El Nuevo Diario* (Managua, Nicaragua), edición 9435, Sábado 18 de Noviembre de 2006, available from http://www.elnuevodiario.com.ni/2006/11/18/nacionales/34263; Internet (accessed December 13, 2006).

[7] Amnesty International, "Key Issues: Stop Violence against Women: Women's Right to Freedom from Violence," in *Amnesty International Report 2006: The State of the World's Human Rights*, available from http://www.amnesty.org/ailib/aireport/index.html; Internet (accessed December 12, 2006).

[8] I have slightly changed some elements of this scene in order not to reveal the names of the place or of the actors, but I have not forgotten any of them.

[9] Ignacio Ellacuría, "The Historicity of Christian Salvation," in *Mysterium Liberationis. Fundamental Concepts of Liberation Theology*, ed. Ignacio Ellacuría, S.J., and Jon Sobrino, S.J. (Maryknoll, NY: Orbis Books, 1993), 251.

[10] Concerning this, see Raúl Fornet-Betancourt, *Filosofar Para Nuestro Tiempo en Clave Intercultural* (Aachen, Germany: Verlag Mainz, 2004), 12–14.

[11] Choe Hyondok, "Introduction to Intercultural Philosophy: Its Concept and History," in *In Quest of Intercultural Philosophy: Communication and Solidarity in the Era of Globalization*, ed. Department of Philosophy (Gwangju, Korea: Department of Philosophy, Chonnam National University, 2006), 8.

[12] Unless I indicate otherwise, this paragraph has as its primary source Fornet-Betancourt, *Filosofar Para Nuestro Tiempo*, 12–13.

[13] Raúl Fornet-Betancourt, *Interculturalidad y Globalización: Ejercicios de Crítica Filosófica Intercultural en el Contexto de la Globalización Neoliberal* (Frankfurt/IKO; San José, Costa Rica: Departamento Ecuménico de Investigaciones, 2000), 68.

[14] Raúl Fornet-Betancourt, *La Interculturalidad a Prueba* (Aachen, Germany: Verlagsgruppe Mainz in Aachen, 2006), 22.

[15] On the understanding of the social forces that orient history, see Ignacio Ellacuría, *Filosofía de la Realidad Histórica* (Madrid: Trotta, 1991), 449–57.

[16] Ariarajah, "Intercultural Hermeneutics," 93.

[17] Hyondok, "Introduction to Intercultural Philosophy," 7.

[18] Fornet-Betancourt, *La Interculturalidad a Prueba*, 18.

[19] Fornet-Betancourt, *Filosofar Para Nuestro Tiempo*, 13.

[20] Fornet-Betancourt, *Interculturalidad y Globalización*, 85.

[21] Fornet-Betancourt, *La Interculturalidad a Prueba*, 113.

[22] Fornet-Betancourt, *Filosofar Para Nuestro Tiempo*, 13.

[23] Ariarajah, "Intercultural Hermeneutics," 92.

[24] Fornet-Betancourt, *La Interculturalidad a Prueba*, 116.

[25] Raúl Fornet-Betancourt, *Trasformación Intercultural de la Filosofía: Ejercicios Teóricos y Prácticos de la Filosofía Intercultural Desde Latinoamérica en el Contexto de la Globalización* (Bilbao: Desclée de Brouwer, 2001), 39.

[26] See Fornet-Betancourt, *Transformación Intercultural*, 39–43. Concerning this, see also Raúl Fornet-Betancourt, *Hacia una Filosofía Intercultural Latinoamericana* (San José, Costa Rica: Departamento Ecuménico de Investigaciones, 1994), 19–26.

[27] Uma Narayan, *Dislocating Cultures: Identities, Traditions, and Third World Feminism* (New York: Routledge, 1997), 37.

[28] Fornet-Betancourt, *Transformación Intercultural*, 195.

[29] Raúl Fornet-Betancourt, "Interacción y Asimetría entre las Culturas en el Contexto de la Globalización: Una Introducción," in *Culturas y Poder: Interacción y Asimetría Entre las Culturas en el Contexto de la Globalización*, ed. Raúl Fornet-Betancourt (Bilbao: Desclée de Brouwer, 2003), 25.

[30] Elisabeth Schüssler Fiorenza, *But She Said: Feminist Practices of Biblical Interpretation* (Boston: Beacon Press, 1992), 150–56; see also 176–80.

[31] Schüssler Fiorenza, *Rhetoric and Ethic*, 46–47. Bracketed material is mine.

[32] World Social Forum, "Another World Is Possible," English version available from http://www.forumsocialmundial.org.br/; Internet (accessed November 14, 2006).

[33] World Social Forum, "Charter of Principles," English version available from http://www.forumsocialmundial.org.br/; Internet (accessed November 14, 2006).

[34] On my understanding of the term kyriarchal globalization, see "The Dynamics of Globalization and the University. Toward a Radical Democratic-Emancipatory Transformation," in *Toward a New Heaven and a New Earth: Essays in Honor of Elisabeth Schüssler Fiorenza*, ed. Fernando F. Segovia (Maryknoll, NY: Orbis Books, 2003), 385–406.

[35] World Social Forum, "Charter of Principles."

[36] Elizabeth A. Johnson, *Friends of God and Prophets: A Feminist Theological Reading of the Communion of Saints* (New York: Continuum, 1999), 53–54.

[37] Tapio Kanninen, "Prevention and Reconciliation in a World of Conflicts: The United Nations Perspective," in *Reconciliation in a World of Conflicts*, ed. Luiz Carlos Susin and María Pilar Aquino (London: SCM Press, 2003), 99.

[38] Hyondok, "Introduction to Intercultural Philosophy," 17.

[39] Mercy Amba Oduyoye, *Daughters of Anowa: African Women and Patriarchy* (Maryknoll, NY: Orbis Books, 1995), 207.

[40] María Cristina Ventura, "Prácticas e dasafíos de la teología Afro-dominicana en un mundo globalizado," in *Teología Afroamericana II: Avanços, Desafíos e Perspectivas: III Consulta Ecumênica de Teologia Afroamericana e Caribenha*, ed. Antônio Aparecido da Silva and Sônia Querino dos Santos (São Paulo: Centro Atabaque de Cultura Negra e Teologia, 2004), 139.

[41] Fornet-Betancourt, "Interacción y Asimetría," 24.

[42] Fornet-Betancourt, *Transformación Intercultural*, 181.

[43] Ibid., 209.

[44] Ignacio Ellacuría, *Conversión de la Iglesia al Reino de Dios: Para Anunciarlo y Realizarlo en la Historia* (Santander: Sal Terrae, 1984), 211.

[45] Ibid., 86.

[46] Concerning this, see María Pilar Aquino, "The Feminist Option for the Poor and Oppressed in the Context of Globalization," in *The Option for the Poor in Christian Theology*, ed. Daniel Groody (Notre Dame, IN: University of Notre Dame Press, 2007), 191–215.

[47] Narayan, *Dislocating Cultures*, 37.

2

Sources and Processes of the Production of Wisdom

An Approach from Intercultural Feminist Criticism

Geraldina Céspedes, O.P.

> For us women, the invitation to disturb the patriarchal waters at all levels of knowledge becomes more urgent today than ever; it is a requirement of justice for ourselves and for humankind.
>
> —IVONE GEBARA

> There are moments in life when the question of knowing if one can think differently from the way one thinks and if one can perceive differently from the way one perceives is indispensable for continuing to see and to reflect.
>
> —MICHEL FOUCAULT

Both of these quotations, one from philosopher-theologian Ivone Gebara and the other from philosopher Michel Foucault, leader of the "Spirit of May 1968" in France, present us with the challenge of questioning our habitual ways of perceiving and thinking of reality. Both authors insinuate that daring to seek out new avenues for knowing and thinking about reality is inherent to the struggle for justice and the whole endeavor of searching for and reflecting on what we as human beings do. The quotation from Foucault encourages us to believe that it is possible to think differently and to perceive differently from the way we usually think and perceive. Attempting to change the way we perceive and think is today indispensable in all areas of knowledge that seek to exercise critical thinking and not simply repeat what we have always been taught and what we have always learned. One crucial area for such a change of practice is the field of theology, done from the feminist perspective.

We should recognize that until now we feminist theologians have done very little investigation about how the actual process of acquiring and producing wisdom takes place in us. Rather, the great majority of us have limited ourselves simply to introducing new contents and new nuances into an already given theological arena. Meanwhile, the structures of knowledge, the sources used, and the procedures followed have until now remained, if not invariable, then at least relatively unexplored. We must deepen and systematize our understanding of how we in fact develop our process of production and transmission of wisdom. We believe that study of this process is one of the most important tasks in women's struggles; besides strengthening our practical and political resistance, we must also strengthen our intellectual resistance by daring to challenge the realms and the processes that produce our wisdom.

In this essay I take a critical approach to the models of producing and transmitting wisdom that have been characteristic of the dominant cultures, which pay little heed to other world views. Such processes have been carried out from a masculine, kyriarchal perspective that has left women out of consideration. When we speak of intercultural feminist criticism, we are not claiming only that a given subordinate culture should be considered to have a valid model for producing and reproducing wisdom, but we seek also to analyze how, even within that same marginalized culture, women have been officially left out of the process of production of wisdom. Nor do we claim that we should accept a production of wisdom, which may come from women or from a feminist perspective, but which fails to take into account the intercultural dimension or the class perspective. After presenting my criticism, I point the way toward proposals that are able to offer alternative models, ones that include intercultural feminist categories in the process of acquisition, production, and multiplication of wisdom.

BEGINNING THE SEARCH FOR WISDOM

We may begin by asking about the conceptual framework that we use in our teaching and in our communication of knowledge. To make the matter a bit more concrete, we ask some questions. What categories do we use, where do they come from, how do we use them? What are our epistemological and hermeneutical frameworks for creating theological concepts? Do they help women in their process of emancipation and resurgence?

We have learned much from the efforts of other researchers, both in the field of theology and in that of the social sciences. On the theological side we have been greatly helped by theologians such as Elisabeth Schüssler Fiorenza, who has taught us to include in our analyses and reconstructions certain concepts that are vital for being able to effect a reconstructive feminist analysis.

Among the critical concepts that Schüssler Fiorenza offers us are the following: "wo/men," oppression, gender, androcentrism, partriarchy, kyriarchy, and kyriocentrism. This author also suggests other concepts that provide a theoretical space for alternative interpretation, such as the categories of "androgyny, gynecentrism/gynaikocentrism, matriarchy, relationality, and the *ekklesia of "wo/men."*[1]

In this essay I concentrate especially on the work that feminist theologians have done in the critical recovery of the sapiential categories and especially the wisdom traditions. As Schüssler Fiorenza indicates, one of the characteristics of the feminist theology of the last two decades has been rediscovering and re-creating the buried traditions of wisdom.[2]

This essay argues for the need not only to treat wisdom as a category apart, but also to reflect on it within a framework in which wisdom, feminism, and interculturality are interconnected. I seek to weave together these three dimensions and in so doing provoke a dialogue that allows us to seek out the elements that feminism and interculturality can contribute to our very way of asking, knowing, formulating, and transmitting our thoughts and our dreams. This essay is also an invitation to question ourselves about how the feminist and the intercultural lenses affect and transform our theological concepts, our understanding of reality, and our production of wisdom.

If we examine the meaning of the concept of wisdom in everyday language, we find that in ordinary life having wisdom is generally understood as having knowledge that comes from experience, or perhaps as having a suitable, prudent attitude and conduct in a given situation or stage of life. Wisdom is also understood as profound knowledge in some science or art, or as a state of mind or spirit that is characterized by great lucidity.

Going a little deeper into the meaning of wisdom, we might understand it as a capacity for discernment, deep intelligence, or creativity; it is the ability to move and dance, to make association, to savor life, and to learn from experience.[3] All these characteristics offer us a broader, more reflective idea of what wisdom is. They are all facets that we find present in the wisdom that is possessed by many peoples and cultures. Such wisdom has for the most part been woven together, silently and stealthily, by women, even though, paradoxically, they are made invisible and marginal within this process.

In religious and biblical language, wisdom is understood both as representative of divinity and as characteristic of people's lives. While we recognize the value of reflections on wisdom as representative of divinity and, more recently, as an interpretative key for an emancipative feminist Christology, we prefer to turn our attention for the moment to considering wisdom as part of the lives of persons, peoples and cultures.

In the Bible, wisdom is not generally the object of philosophical speculation, as it was among the Greeks, nor is it the orderly study of the phenomena of the cosmos in order to dominate them technologically. Rather, biblical wisdom is oriented more to understanding the mysteries of life and the suffering of human beings.[4] Wisdom, therefore, draws on life experiences and attempts to extract from them practical norms of conduct for helping human beings to live in justice and harmony among themselves, as well as with the cosmos and with God.

Wisdom is a practical kind of knowledge that is obtained through reflection on people's daily lives and through study of the events of nature and history. Schüssler Fiorenza situates wisdom in the confluence between knowledge acquired by experience and that acquired by critical analysis. Thus she writes: "Wisdom is intelligence shaped by experience and sharpened by critical analysis. It is the ability to make sound choices and incisive decisions."[5]

In this essay I argue for a production of knowledge that is at once a type of wisdom and a critical and liberating analysis. I think it is important to take these criteria into account in doing theological work. Furthermore, in view of the key role that experience plays in the process of acquiring wisdom, feminist theology is called upon to place more value on experience as an indispensable source for molding and integrating our wisdom.

Directing our gaze to the sources and processes of the production of wisdom has important consequences also for our evaluation of biblical texts. An example of this is the way in which many feminists are recovering and reinterpreting the Wisdom traditions of the Bible, after the example of Elisabeth Schüssler Fiorenza and also of Elizabeth Johnson, and applying them to the field of systematic theology.[6] We should recall that in the centuries following the Enlightenment there was a tendency to ignore the sapiential writings in favor of the prophetic and historical books, since these express the essential characteristics of the Jewish faith in a God who reveals himself as acting in history. One of the important discoveries of modern scholarship is that the sapiential tradition is not a perspective that excludes history; rather, the tradition simply has a different way of perceiving God's revelations. Its focus is not so much on the sacred events in Israelite history, although it does recall them, but rather on the interpersonal, social relationships, the problems of everyday life, the enigma of suffering, the experience of the world. The Wisdom tradition thus makes it clear that God's salvation is not only found in historical events; rather, people also connect with the mystery of the sacred in that which surrounds them, in non-heroic moments, in the daily efforts on behalf of justice, in the difficulties and the afflictions, in the enjoyment of nature, and in the search for harmonious relationships.[7]

THE EXCLUSION OF WOMEN
FROM THE SPHERES OF PRODUCTION OF WISDOM

Speaking of wisdom is not the same as speaking of knowledge, although some current expressions of wisdom in everyday life include and/ or identify wisdom and knowledge. In a way, the two terms imply one another, but each has its own connotations. Wisdom is continually acquired in the course of life experience and through the patient exercise of making errors and starting over, of being attentive and listening in order to learn from others.

If wisdom is acquired through experience and through a process of reflection on life and events, then women should in no way be excluded from the processes of acquiring and producing wisdom. Rather, it is more than obvious nowadays that women should be positively included in the processes of production of knowledge. We should keep in mind that, according to most definitions of wisdom, knowledge is a fundamental dimension and an integrating part of wisdom, although it does not exhaust its meaning. From this starting point, then, we have the right to speak of the egalitarian inclusion of women in the process of production and reproduction of wisdom.

What is understood and accepted as wisdom at the level of officials and others who hold power, however, is something different. It is usually identified with a kind of knowledge in which women generally have not taken part, unless as consumers of that "wisdom" produced by the elite circles that hold not only sociopolitical power, but also the power of knowledge, science, and technology. Taking these elements into account, we become aware that women have been excluded from the process and the spheres of the production of knowledge all through history. All that has to do with knowledge and the production of knowledge has been linked to elite groups, dominant cultures, and males, who have proposed and developed it on the basis of their own experiences and their own interests. As Ivone Gebara points out, the result of this is that all true, scientific, philosophical, or theological knowledge is thought to be gained and transmitted only by men, while women, poor people, and oppressed cultures are thought to exist on the margins of this process and to have access only to the "inferior" knowledge that is based on the experiences of everyday life and is not readily recognized as "true."[8]

Rather than simply describe the fact of the exclusion of women from the spheres of knowledge, we consider it more important to examine some of the elements that have caused this exclusion of women from the processes of production of wisdom. What have been the grounds for the exclusion of women and the poor from the production and the multiplication of wisdom? The exclusion of women and poor people from the process of production of knowledge may be traced to the interaction of multiple factors.

First, there are the *philosophical theories and anthropologies* that in the course of history have sustained and spread ideas *that place in doubt or actually deny women's ability to reason.* Although this view of women lasted for centuries, it is today dismissed in studies and analyses about men and women. Nonetheless, while it is true that now nobody maintains this perspective theoretically, in practice and at the deepest levels of the subconscious, this idea still has a strong hold on many men and women. We find proof of this in the suspicion that is cast upon many books written by women; any works by feminist theologians that fall outside the kyriarchal framework are quickly disqualified. We find proof also in the doubts that assault many students as to whether a woman theologian will be able to give a course as good as the male professors' courses and in the general lack of seriousness with which theology done by women is studied.

Second, there is *the question of power.* At base, women's lack of access to the spaces of knowledge production is a problem of their lack of participation in the spaces of power and decision-making. We cannot forget the famous slogan that affirms that knowledge is power. Whoever controls knowledge and information can control power and can control all the personal and collective processes in society's organizations. Knowledge is today more than ever a power,[9] and it is a power we use either for oppression or for liberation. I believe that only wisdom is capable of giving us a liberating perspective and of transforming our way of knowing and our horizon of knowledge; only wisdom can help orient knowledge toward the search for a life that promotes relations of justice between men and women. This perspective of knowledge as power is even more relevant today, when the unequal distribution of power between men and women, as well as between dominant cultures and dominated ones, has become even more pronounced. We live in a neoliberal, globalized world that produces an ever greater gap between those who know and those who do not know. This divide is perhaps most obvious in the case of access to technologies, but we will not go into that topic here, for it is one thing to speak of technology and quite another to speak of knowledge or wisdom. What I propose to treat here is something more profound and more meaningful, namely, the seeking, the producing, and the transmitting of wisdom.

Many people in our society have attained a high degree of expertise in technology and have amassed large amounts of knowledge, but that does not mean that they have attained wisdom. That is to say, some people accumulate knowledge but have little idea of what a wise person is, especially the wise person described in the sacred scriptures and in the writings of other religions and cultures. Indeed, all that accumulated knowledge is often managed not wisely but foolishly. Being a wise person involves a way of positioning oneself in life and of dealing with the events that come with life; it is understanding reality and undertaking its transformation; it is assuming the pains and mysteries of life; it is knowing how to bear suffering in a liberating way. A wise person today, understood from a Christian perspective, is one who is expert in humanity, in the style of Jesus.[10]

Third are *relations of injustice and unequal economic distribution.* Those who have no economic power unfortunately also have no power of accessing the spaces of production of knowledge. That is the problem experienced by many impoverished people, in their majority women, who have to overcome many obstacles in order to be able to reach the higher levels of education and in some cases even to attain a basic education. In so saying, I am not claiming that the lack of access to spaces of knowledge identifies them as persons lacking in wisdom. Wisdom is not acquired only in books or in schools; rather, it settles into people and groups through their reflection on their life experiences. Without justice and economic equity, however, and without the economic emancipation of women, there cannot be real participation of women in the spaces of acquisition and production of power.

Finally, there are *the sociocultural patterns imposed* by those who hold power and *internalized by the marginalized sectors,* among whom are women. In many places, even when groups and families are convinced of women's intellectual capacity and the economic resources are available, the women of the family are often still denied the possibility

of acceding to higher levels of education. Such denial is the remnant of
an old taboo that has still not been rooted out of the collective consciousness of our cultures and that continues to keep women subjugated.
Religious institutions are by no means free of such exclusionary practice. Even today the number of women who have access to theological
studies is quite low, and many of the women who earn the highest academic degrees afterward have difficulties and suffer many tensions, since
the academic system generally contemplates only two possibilities with
regard to those who dare to think differently and to propose new avenues for theology: cooptation or exclusion.

SOURCES OF WISDOM THAT HAVE BEEN EXCLUDED

Exclusion is a practice that directly affects the subjects, in this case
women, but we must also speak of the exclusion that affects those sources
of wisdom that might contribute a critical, transformative vision of reality of our peoples and our cultures. Especially excluded are those sources
that are considered unofficial, that is, those that are not designed within
the realms of power and domination. Such sources have been, and continue to be, discredited or negated by the academic world, since they are
not thought to contain or to structure the wisdom that is traditionally
accepted.

One of the excluded sources comprise *the oral traditions*, which have
considerable force in the indigenous and African cultures of our continent and which have been kept alive thanks to the transmission work
carried out mainly by women. Among oppressed cultures and disregarded
peoples, oral culture has always had great importance. In a society in
which access to reading and writing was and still is in the hands of only
a few, oral culture constitutes a condemnation, because it makes manifest how some groups are excluded from the whole process of written
production, precisely by those few who control what we must learn and
what we must teach, what we must read and what we must write, just so
the established order need not be disturbed. The recovery of the oral
traditions is a tremendous challenge for us; we must try to analyze their
messages, which at times legitimize oppression, but which also often
provide us with great strength for resistance and sustain us in our struggles
for liberation. From an intercultural feminist perspective we must critically analyze how the oral traditions portray women, indigenous peoples,
blacks, and others, and thus move toward a recovery of the wealth and
wisdom that those traditions bear within them.

Besides oral culture as a source and a form of expression of the wisdom of our peoples and cultures, there is another sphere that has been excluded as a source of wisdom: *the body*. Our body is a privileged site of wisdom; it contains a great wisdom that is longing to be revealed. The recovery of the body as a source of wisdom is one of the great challenges that awaits us in our theological work. The body has its own wisdom; it reveals to us the truths of our lives and our history. It has recorded in it our stories of struggle, resistance, and liberation. In the production of intercultural feminist wisdom, the body cannot be reduced to a simple topic of study and reflection. Rather, the body must be a central theme inasmuch as it is a source, a mediator, and a channel of all our vital experiences and all our processes of knowledge.

Another source of wisdom that today nourishes the theological activity of feminists is *women's experience*. Such experience has no place in the hegemonic models of wisdom, but it is considered fundamental in the democratically conceived models, which are more intimately connected with the life and the experience of women and the poor. In the case of feminist theology, the experience of women constitutes one of the fundamental themes that define the task at hand. The very category of women's experience has become widely studied by many feminist theologians, including Elisabeth Schüssler Fiorenza, María Pilar Aquino, Rosemary Radford Ruether, and Elizabeth Johnson.[11]

Biblical studies on the theme of wisdom highlight the fundamental role of experience in the configuration of wisdom. Given the feminist intercultural perspective that we are using as a background and that we wish to strengthen, we should make clear that we are not dealing with just any experience or any interpretation. Fundamentally, we are considering those experiences that in the course of history have not been considered sources of wisdom because they came from subordinate groups, especially from silenced cultures in socially marginalized regions. In such settings women experience with double or triple intensity the afflictions of exclusion, silence, and marginalization. We do not claim either that all experience is valuable just because it comes from a woman, whether black, indigenous, or *mestiza*. Wisdom may be extracted from such experience only when the experience is analyzed critically, interpreted with new lenses, confronted with wisdoms that emerge from other contexts, cultures, and religions—such a process will yield a praxis that is truly transformative. However, if we do not start from this perspective of learning from our experiences and the events of our personal and collective lives, then we will never be able to give expression to all the wisdom that our experiences contain.

Personal narrative biography is also a source of knowledge, for wisdom is present in the telling of our life story. The theology being done, therefore, must be related to the biographies of the theologians, through reflections on topics, questions, and problems that involve us directly; we should feel personally part of the process and try to go deeper into what we have lived through and what we are experiencing now. We must analyze how we are affected and touched by the problems, the dreams, and the hopes that we see in other women. The perspective of personal biography has to do with the interpreted experience of women. That is, we should not simply view our lives naively but should mold them into a biography that is interpreted now with different lenses. For this task we need intercultural, feminist tools that are capable of throwing new light not only on the global reality and world history, but also on our own personal history, our own daily lives as women theologians. Often the academy, in the name of a supposed objectivity, teaches us to give concrete, written form to our wisdom in a quite aseptic way; it does not permit us to involve ourselves personally in our production. Our main task sometimes seems to be simply to write about what happens to other women, and we do not touch on what is happening to us personally or on how we are personally being affected by our conversion toward a new way of thinking and living.[12]

EXCLUSION BORN OF DUALISTIC POSTURES

In the light of biblical wisdom we must also question our dualistic interpretations and practices. In the sapiential tradition the world, reality, and life are all part of God's creation and so cannot be divided into sacred and profane times and places.[13]

We have to overcome every type of dualism. In dealing with the present topic, a dualism exists between the academic world and the world of praxis, and praxis is the primary place from which true wisdom emerges. The overcoming of dualism allows us to remove the walls that separate the public and the private, academic praxis and everyday praxis. Moreover, overcoming such dualism involves the need "to break down the barrier between expert and everyday language," in the words of Schüssler Fiorenza.[14]

The task of intercultural feminist wisdom is not limited, however, to overcoming the dualism between academia and praxis; it must also lead us to question our own role in academia and help us to convert academia into a place of struggle. In this arena also we must overcome many barriers and learn to open up spaces for other forms of thought, other ways of doing theology, other ways of presenting problems. We must exert our influence and make our contribution not only in the classrooms, but well before entering them, for example, in the design of academic programs; the selection of contents, method, and sources; and the perspective employed to frame a given question. Our aim should be to have our whole life, inside and outside of academia, impregnated with what we consider vital for the construction of a new way of thinking and of living. To this end we must learn to demythologize the structures of the dominant way of thinking and open up spaces on the basis of our own experiences and convictions. As Schüssler Fiorenza points out, "Wo/men and other theologically muted persons must learn to demystify the dominant structures of knowledge in order to find our own intellectual voices, exercise personal choice, and achieve satisfaction in our intellectual work."[15] To this end we must challenge the traditional academic scene in its pretensions to monopolize and commandeer wisdom; we must validate other forms of production of knowledge.

As regards the sources and the processes of our knowledge, many dichotomies must be overcome. Often in our acquisition of knowledge contradictions and exclusions become evident in the final formulations and theories, but they remain hidden in the inner parts of our being. In order to free ourselves of these dualisms, we need to produce knowledge that has as its framework and its setting a radically democratizing feminist practice. Only such radically democratic perspectives will make it possible for us to question the standard models of reasoning and of intellectual production that are dominant in scientific theology. Such models are characterized by a mainly masculine way of thinking and generally derive from the upper socioeconomic and cultural strata of society. Such knowledge tends to dissociate reason from feelings and emotions for the sake of reaching objective and impartial knowledge.[16]

In our labor of producing wisdom and designing new frameworks of understanding and analysis, we are also tempted by the patriarchal system's inducements to establish absolute, arrogant formulations that have an air of universality and immutability. Feminist intercultural theology must avoid any form of dogmatic declarations and must steer clear of absolute statements that tend to identify reality with our interpretations of same. As Ivone Gebara well reminds us, we must keep in mind that "our knowledge, which is partial, localized, dated and therefore marked by our subjectivity, cannot set itself up as universal objectivity and as the criterion for all forms of knowledge. The tension between our perceptions and our theories should always be maintained, towards the end of dethroning all absolutisms and destabilizing all definitive theories. Only thus will we be able to conform better to the creative flow of life that makes the flowers bloom, the cocoons open up, the storms rage and old structures decay, far beyond all our scientific predictions."[17]

WEAVING THE INTERCULTURAL FEMINIST ROAD OF WISDOM

One of the most notorious exclusions that most of us women have suffered in the course of history has been our exclusion from the realms of production of knowledge. Today we are witnessing a new awakening as women discover themselves to be producers of meanings, of knowledge, and of wisdom.

We women define ourselves as eternal apprentices. The great majority of men have problems in accepting this concept of learning as a process that places humans in a humble, dialoguing position. In this regard, Sor Juana Inés de la Cruz had clear ideas about what it meant to acquire knowledge. Her words reflect her conviction that learning is not aimed at knowing more or at dominating others but is rather the humble road to being less ignorant: "I have desired to study only to be less ignorant."[18]

The intercultural feminist road of wisdom must be paved with confidence in our own ability to engender wise discourse and praxis. As women theologians we need this attitude of confidence in ourselves and in other women, because we are surrounded by distrust and disdain of women's knowledge. Making an intercultural feminist critique of the way in which we cultivate, acquire, and transmit wisdom leads us to ask: Do we women really accept ourselves, and are we accepted by others as producers of wisdom on a level of full equality? Do we recognize value in the wisdom that is produced by the muted cultures and by the resistance movements that have risen in the midst of peoples who have been disregarded by the world? The patriarchal system has taught us that there is a division between the producers and the consumers of knowledge, and in that division women and subordinate groups have been relegated to the role of mere consumers and reproducers of the wisdom produced by the elites of the dominant groups.

In our intercultural feminist analyses we cannot forget the close linkage that exists between the themes of wisdom and of power. We must recognize that connection if we wish to understand some of the exclusions to which women and oppressed peoples are subject. In the course of history, we women have been excluded both from the realms of production and acquisition of knowledge and from the realms of power. Our aim, though, is not simply to move into those realms, but rather to redesign the very ways of understanding power and wisdom. Today many women are doing just that, inspired by Jesus as the power and wisdom of God. We are developing the praxis of an alternative power and an alternative wisdom: a power not for dominating others but for promoting justice, and a wisdom that works for the expansion of life.

From this perspective, wisdom ceases to be something private and enclosed in academic limits and instead begins to integrate a variety of visions and to manifest itself in a series of new spaces. Academia is just one of these spaces, though it certainly is quite important, since it is where systems of thought are engendered and where the programs of what is to be transmitted and how it is to be transmitted are designed. In this respect, our access to that space turns out to be crucial, but we cannot enclose ourselves only in an academic institution, for wisdom is found especially in the streets. Wisdom is rather vagrant; it reveals itself in open spaces, in the midst of public transactions, wherever there is a call and a cry for life. Wisdom goes far beyond the different boundaries that we are accustomed to establish. It continually teaches us to nourish ourselves discerningly, both from the private realm and from the public. Moreover, our wisdom is called upon to infuse every dimension of our personal and social lives with its transforming action and influence. In this way, the dualistic schema that would establish arbitrary boundaries between spaces is demolished by women's perspective and by wisdom's vision, as we delve into weaving together our everyday reality with our political reality, our domestic sphere with our public sphere.

THE COLLECTIVE SEARCH FOR WISDOM

The search for wisdom is, above all, a collective endeavor. One cannot be wise if one is not searching with others, learning together with others, entering into the circle in which many other people are dancing. All this means making the words of other people and other cultures constitutive elements in our own thinking process.[19]

Wisdom of the patriarchal type generally produces categories and concepts that are meant to be consumed by a collectivity. As women, we seek to reverse these processes through the exercise of collective criticism. We need to produce wisdom together, with a communitarian meaning. Through this new vision, which is based on the practical experiences we have had as Latin American and Latina Hispanic women, we hope not so much to shine as brilliant theologians as to pave a new collective avenue for acquiring and producing wisdom. We do not idolize the "stars" or the "luminaries," but rather those women who are able to enter into a dynamic of collective empowerment.

Only a collective search for wisdom will facilitate the task of giving visibility to women's wisdom and to the wisdom hidden in oppressed peoples and cultures. Our aim must be to make it possible for all of us women to sit down and dine at the banquet of wisdom, since, as we have already stated, knowledge is a sphere in which injustice, inequality, and exclusion are today most clearly manifest.

The shared elaboration of wisdom increases our force and our spirit, and, even as it enriches us, it reaffirms in us a practice that is critical, participative, and democratic. Furthermore, out of the spaces of collective production we will gain confidence and authority among ourselves. In the face of the constant questioning to which many women theologians are subjected, concerning the authority by which we say what we say and do what we do, we need to appeal to our own authority, which comes to us from our experience, our intuitions, our sufferings, and our struggles. Such authority comes to us, above all, from the Spirit of Jesus, and not from some established laws and norms that supposedly have the power to determine what is wisdom and what is not. Rather than seek external approval, which often does no more than imprison us within the patriarchal mental mold, we ought to appeal to the authority of the experience and wisdom that we ourselves have woven together over the course of time.

WISDOM SEEKS OUT
ALTERNATIVE THEORETICAL FRAMEWORKS

The search for alternative forms of producing wisdom leads us necessarily to pose the problem of the theoretical frameworks that will serve as a foundation for our constructions. We cannot use just any framework, if we truly wish to transform our thought and our reality. Rather, we need to propose a fresh type of wisdom, one based on our own creative capacity and the requirements of the avenue that we wish to create. Often wisdom, when it explores outside the conventional frameworks, creates shock and rejection, but such reaction is only to be expected in the face of alternative thought that is dissident and seeks to transgress the established order.

The intercultural feminist critique of the processes of production of wisdom leads us to touch on a key aspect of the frameworks in which we feminists are moving and in which we must continue to move. One of the tasks required for developing knowledge from a women's perspective is critiquing the traditional epistemological frameworks, which are incapable of accommodating other cultural and sexual variables and are therefore exclusionary.

At the same time that it is performing this critique, feminist theological work has the serious responsibility of creating alternative theoretical frameworks that are able to include a variety of experiences and wisdoms and that make possible the development of other ways of understanding and other theological analyses and explanations. Today the interpretative and epistemological frameworks that have formed us no longer suffice. Even some frameworks that speak of liberation are basically still trapped in ethnocentric, monocultural, patriarchal meshes that interpret reality from a perspective that excludes indigenous peoples, blacks, women, and the poor generally from the production of knowledge. Such a perspective, therefore, is far removed from what we are seeking today with our proposal for a feminist intercultural theology in Latin America.

Often, in our process of acquiring and transmitting knowledge, whether through our pastoral work, our teaching, or our own practice and lifestyle, we women have unconsciously employed theoretical frameworks that end up reinforcing our submission and domination. All of us have adopted certain theoretical frameworks that are like a loamy soil in which distorted forms of apprehending reality burst forth, take root, grow, and fructify. Since the framework is such a decisive issue, we women theologians are obliged to undertake the laborious, difficult, but not impossible task of reconfiguring and reconceiving the epistemological frameworks that we have been using in our theological work. We need to discern the nature of the forms of knowledge that will lead us to a radical transformation and adopt them in our work. In so doing we will perforce learn to think in new ways and to reinterpret critically our own discourse and the epistemological paradigms we are using.

As women with multiple presences, in the sense that we move in various spheres, from those of everyday life to those of sociopolitical action and academia, we are all in some way producers and transmitters of wisdom. Not only should our self-criticism be directed at the substance of what we are transmitting in each of those spheres, but it should also reflect and evaluate the ways in which we are carrying out that process. We should especially examine the nature of the frameworks that we are starting out from and that we are inculcating in those who are the recipients of our education. If the traditional frameworks in which we have always moved are not demolished, we cannot hope to achieve a creative, distinct theology, done from an intercultural, feminist perspective. Trying to create this fresh theology, from the perspective of new subjects, and leaving it in the old theoretical frameworks would be equivalent to what Jesus called pouring new wine into old wineskins or putting a new patch on an old garment (Mt 9:16–17).

Critically revising our processes of knowledge is of great importance if we really want to do theology in a different way. In order to do feminist theology in an intercultural key, we must start out from an attitude of epistemological suspicion that makes us pose questions rather than affirm truths or take for granted certain axioms. Often true wisdom reveals itself more by letting questions "loose" than by "tying up" answers and conclusions.

THE ENCOUNTER OR THE CRISSCROSSING OF WISDOMS

In these times of globalization we are greatly challenged to weave together relations and build bridges among different wisdoms; only thus will we be able to open up a wide field of mutual enrichment. A feminist intercultural theology makes possible, as well as quite constructive and challenging, the coexistence and simultaneity of different paradigms that aim at a transforming dynamic. The bridges that are today being built among the different wisdoms on our continent keep enhancing the feminist theological labors in Latin America. We see this clearly in the case of the interactive theologies, such as the feminist, the African American, and the indigenous theologies.

In this interweaving of wisdoms it is important to keep in view the horizon that emancipates women. All the wisdoms found on our continent are confronted by questions that have the same ground and come out of the same cry: Is our way of knowing one that frees us or is it one that keeps us submitted, dependent, stuck in the traditional paradigms? Is our knowledge a knowledge that is capable of unleashing a liberating praxis? Does our knowledge remain confined among us, in our own circles, or do we search for creative and effective ways to pass it on to other women? With regard to our intuitions and our findings, we are called and challenged to be like the personified biblical Wisdom that becomes a street preacher, a prophetess that goes forth into the public plaza. The sacred scriptures show us how Wisdom goes out into the public arena in order to illuminate and teach the people, guiding them along the way of peace.[20]

Wisdom is all encompassing: it includes all of us, even as it draws together all the threads of the different types of wisdom. In these times we are invited to acquire that wisdom which makes us multidimensional subjects, so that we may learn how to live, learn, relate, and work on an interdisciplinary basis. Dialogue with and acceptance of the different wisdoms involve, to be sure, a variety of disciplines, but they also encompass the different ways in which we women express our understanding of ourselves and of our processes of liberation. For example, the diverse manifestations of the feminist movement are not really evidence of fragmentation, even though the patriarchal system, in order to weaken our struggle, tends to interpret them so. Rather, we should understand such diversity as proof of our ability to create multiple formulations, which help us invent varied readings of the same reality as our answer to a specific time and place. In this way, in the face of the ecological crisis and the exclusion of women, ecofeminism is presented as "a wisdom that attempts to recover the ecosystem and women."[21] Feminist intercultural theology comes to be seen as theological activity that aims at weaving together and clarifying the intersections among religion, cultures, feminism, and power within the context of neoliberal globalization.[22]

The wisdom produced by us women should seek a greater integration of those poles that the patriarchy has taught us to separate in an antagonistic, dualistic manner. What was said earlier about the need to weave together public and private spaces holds also for the treatment of the spheres of reflection and action, theory and praxis, the very way in which we know and create wisdom. As Ivone Gebara points out, "We need to overcome the dualistic, hierarchical divisions of our forms of knowledge and stress the connections and interdependences among them. We also need to escape from the Euro-centrism of knowledge and from the different imperialist controls over truth that are maintained by the western world."[23]

Our knowledge should help to transform both the practices and the concepts that shut us up in narrow visions of reality and of ourselves. In order to acquire this deeper, broader vision, we need to be connected with our own lives and our struggle for transformative action, and at the same time with the academic world, always helping both spaces to nourish and critique one another. This is fundamental, for as Schüssler Fiorenza points out, "Intellectuals will be able to articulate knowledges and visions that engender and empower socio-political action and change in relation to domination only if and when we as participants in a socio-political movement for justice attempt to 'hear into speech' the theoretical problems and challenges of a group of people involved in grassroots democratic struggles."[24]

Wisdom is capable of integrating the variety of voices and experiences in a dynamic that is respectful of each and every one, at the same time that it is critical and radically democratic. Our knowledge and our vision of life, of things, of creation, of the relation between men and women, and of our image of God become enriched when the different wisdoms intersect and interact in ways that promote a decent, just existence for people who have been discounted and dismissed by society.

This interweaving of the different wisdoms keeps revealing itself as a festive and hopeful encounter in which we celebrate and enjoy the fruits that give us life and nourish us one and all. Instead of hoarding knowledge or holding tight to the keys of wisdom, our encountering and engaging others on the basis of plurality lead us to a practice of sharing wisdoms as a form of solidarity and communion among human beings.

The inclusive character of wisdom is demonstrated in the experience of the people of Israel, who in developing their sapiential discourse knew how to receive and savor the wisdom of the peoples that surrounded them. The Bible shows that wisdom was not exclusive to Israel but was closely related to the sapiential knowledge of Egypt and of other advanced cultures of the ancient Near East, and often borrowed from them.[25]

Taking this fact into account, but also situating ourselves in the present-day context of globalization, we are necessarily led to assume not just an intercultural and transcultural perspective, but also an interreligious one. Both dimensions are fundamental and flow from the very character of wisdom, for wisdom is not the particular possession of any one group, religion or culture. As Schüssler Fiorenza points out, wisdom is found to be present in the symbolism and the writings of all the known religions. It is characterized by its transcultural, international, and interreligious nature.[26] Wisdom is not the private property of anybody. It has an all-inclusive, democratic character that we are today called upon to recover in our practices, both ordinary and political. This democratization of wisdom is today one of the great challenges not only for theology, but for all spheres of knowledge. The processes of acquiring, producing, and multiplying knowledge cannot be democratized, however, if this same democratic current does not flow through all human relations and all levels of our sociopolitical and economic life.

The search for wisdom from an intercultural feminist perspective in the modern context of globalization will be a prophetic task in which we will make possible another way of knowing and thinking. As feminist intercultural theologians, we are challenged to make our search for wisdom an inclusive praxis and a way of justice and compassion for all the poor and excluded.

Notes

[1] See Elisabeth Schüssler Fiorenza, *Wisdom Ways: Introducing Feminist Biblical Interpretation* (Maryknoll, NY: Orbis Books, 2001), 107.

² See ibid., 21.

³ Ibid., 23.

⁴ See Xavier Pikaza, *Dios judío, Dios cristiano* (Estella: Verbo Divino, 1996), 167.

⁵ Schüssler Fiorenza, *Wisdom Ways*, 23.

⁶ See Elisabeth Schüssler Fiorenza, *Jesus: Miriam's Child, Sophia's Prophet: Critical Issues in Feminist Christology* (New York: Continuum, 1994); Elisabeth Schüssler Fiorenza, *Jesus and the Politics of Interpretation* (New York: Continuum, 2000); Schüssler Fiorenza, *Wisdom Ways*; María Pilar Aquino and Elisabeth Schüssler Fiorenza, eds., *In the Power of Wisdom: Feminist Spiritualities of Struggle* (London: SCM Press, 2000); Elizabeth A. Johnson, *Consider Jesus: Waves of Renewal in Christology* (New York: Crossroad, 1992); Elizabeth A. Johnson, *She Who Is: The Mystery of God in Feminist Theological Discourse* (New York: Crossroad, 1992); Elizabeth A. Johnson, *Friends of God and Prophets: A Feminist Theological Reading of the Communion of Saints* (New York: Continuum, 1999).

⁷ Elizabeth A. Johnson, "Wisdom Was Made Flesh and Pitches Her Tent among Us," in *Reconstructing the Christ Symbol: Essays in Feminist Christology*, ed. Maryanne Stevens (New York: Paulist Press, 1993), 97.

⁸ Ivone Gebara, *Intuiciones ecofeministas: ensayo para repensar el conocimiento y la religión* (Madrid: Trotta, 2000), 45.

⁹ It is interesting to note that feminism understands power differently from the way it is understood by the masculine-kyriarchal perspective, which conceives power as dominion and control over others. Power in the feminist mode is conceived rather as energy that fills our lives and moves us forward. See Schüssler Fiorenza, *Wisdom Ways*, 8.

¹⁰ I borrow here the words of Xavier Pikaza, who speaks of Jesus as a wise man in the world but insists that this must be understood as saying that Jesus, as an expert in humanity, unmasks organized violence and overcomes the pervasive patriarchal mentality. See Xavier Pikaza, *Este es el hombre* (Salamanca: Secretariado Trinitario, 1997), 35. Jesus is presented as a wise man also with regard to the style of his discourses. We see this above all in the Synoptic Gospels (Mt 12:38–42; Mk 1:11; Lk 21:15), where Jesus frequently appears teaching in the manner of the masters of wisdom of the Old Testament and adopting in his preaching the sapiential genre. In this regard, see Martin Hengel, "Jesus as Messianic Teacher of Wisdom and the Beginning of Christology," in *Studies in Early Christology* (Edinburgh: T & T Clark, 1995).

¹¹ Women's experience, considered to be both part of the content and a criterion of truth in feminist theology, has often been misinterpreted as being opposed to theology's two objective sources, holy scripture and tradition; we should not forget that these two sources are also codifications of collective human experiences. See Rosemary Radford Reuther, *Sexism and God-Talk: Toward a Feminist Theology* (Boston: Beacon Press, 1993), 12.

¹² The relation of one's own biography to the research one does is a question being posed today by feminists of various disciplines. In the field of sociology,

for example, Gayle Letherby puts it thus: "In producing feminist work it is important that we recognize the importance of our 'intellectual biography' by providing 'accountable knowledge' in which the reader has access to details of the contextually located reasoning process which gives rise to the 'findings', the 'outcomes'" (Gayle Letherby, *Feminist Research in Theory and Practice* [Philadelphia: Open University Press, 2003], 9).

[13] See Elizabeth A. Johnson, "Wisdom Was Made Flesh," 97.

[14] Schüssler Fiorenza, *Wisdom Ways*, 8.

[15] Ibid., 34.

[16] See ibid., 16.

[17] Gebara, *Intuiciones ecofeministas*, 26–27.

[18] See the complete phrase in Sor Juana Inés de la Cruz, *Respuesta a Sor Filotea de la Cruz, Obras Completas* (Mexico City: Porrúa, 2002), 844.

[19] See Raúl Fornet-Betancourt, *Trasformación intercultural de la filosofía: Ejercicios teóricos y prácticos de la filosofía intercultural desde Latinoamérica en el contexto de la globalización* (Balboa: Desclée de Brouwer, 2001), 53–55.

[20] See especially the three public apparitions of Wisdom in Prv 1:20–33; 8:22–31; and 9:1–6.

[21] Gebara, *Intuiciones ecofeministas*, 18.

[22] See Maricel Mena-López and María Pilar Aquino in the symposium abstract in this collection. The background information on this symposium is available in English and Spanish on the website of the Center for the Study of Latino Catholicism, http://www.sandiego.edu/theo/Latino-Cath/teofemint.php and http://www.sandiego.edu/theo/Latino-Cath/feminttheo.php; Internet (accessed October 20, 2006).

[23] Gebara, *Intuiciones ecofeministas*, 42.

[24] Schüssler Fiorenza, *Wisdom Ways*, 82.

[25] Pikaza points out that it is clear that the Wisdom of Israel shared common roots in Near Eastern history with Egyptians, Canaanites, Syrians, and Babylonians and also had close contact with Hellenism, above all from the time of the conquest by Alexander the Great (Pikaza, *Dios judío, Dios cristiano*, 167).

[26] Schüssler Fiorenza, *Wisdom Ways*, 23.

3

Making Spaces

Latin American and Latina Feminist Theologies on the Cusp of Interculturality

Nancy Elizabeth Bedford

It was a soft, sunny, July day in the streets of the historical core of Mexico City. We congregated near the door of what had been the convent of San Jerónimo, where Sor Juana Inés de la Cruz spent many years of her life and where she died in 1695. The site has changed its identity many times since she lived there; after the convent was closed in the nineteenth century due to the nationalization of ecclesiastical properties, it became a marketplace, a cabaret, a factory and most recently, a university. Still, we hoped to find some traces of the lives of the nuns who once lived and worked there, and so we walked through the excavated cells and stared at the walls. We admired the ancient bathtubs and drains, and the thick stone walls. We pondered the life of the woman sometimes called the Tenth Muse, and we recalled some of the wonderful poems and essays she was able to write in the relative isolation of the cloister, surrounded by her four-thousand-book library and her musical and scientific instruments. The physical walls of the convent and the layout of its remaining foundations reminded us sharply that Sor Juana's life of learning was made possible in part by other women, who took on necessary and menial tasks of service without receiving the honor given to the nuns of high social standing.[1]

Our own group was made up of women of different shapes, sizes, ages; the tint of our skins, the shape of our lips, the texture of our hair, the timbre of our voices varied greatly, and yet, for all our differences, we had a certain air in common—the curious glances and insistent questions of scholars, the buoyancy of women who love the gift of life, of song, of conversation. Though the chapel where Sor Juana worshiped and probably was buried was closed for renovations, we found ourselves inside its dusty walls; the university officials did not have the heart to turn away such an unusual group of pilgrims. The construction workers faded quietly away, as if on cue. Several women pulled off their shawls and scarves to make a soft, pliable altar; someone else provided votives. We stood, then sat, in a circle and improvised a fluid liturgy, remembering the life of Sor Juana and honoring the high price she paid for her love of learning and for her theological expression. We prayed for women around the world. We felt thankful to be together. When we left the chapel, the votives were still burning; the room smelled of sawdust and of melted wax. We set off for the *Zócalo* with a sense of wholeness; we had made time and found a place for remembering the past, enjoying the moment, and dreaming of the future. It seemed to me we had somehow stumbled into what coming together for our first symposium of Latina[2] and Latin American feminist theologians was really all about: making spaces.

OF MELTING, SHIFTING AND SPACES IN BETWEEN

Our votives in Sor Juana's chapel seemed solid enough but soon melted away, consumed by their own heat. Their melting away, it would seem, mimics what many of us experience in our lives: the evanescence of what once seemed quite solid. I notice as I write this essay how even the solidity of books dissolves in the face of my use of Internet-based resources. As often as I can, I use such sources in the hopes that they will be accessible to friends in the southern hemisphere who can more easily find their way to a cybercafé than to a well-stocked library; yet I am aware that such resources are ephemeral and furthermore fall far short of the solid, comforting presence of a book. "All that is solid melts into air." Marx's phrase—accessed on the Internet—has indeed become a description of the ephemeral nature of so many aspects of late modern culture,[3] even as that same culture paradoxically produces mountains of solid waste that are quite tangible and not at all ephemeral. It is worth looking at the entire sentence in its context within the *Manifesto*:

> All that is solid melts into air, all that is holy is profaned, and man is at last compelled to face with sober senses his real condition of life and his relations with his kind. The need of a constantly expanding market for its products chases the bourgeoisie over the

entire surface of the globe. It must nestle everywhere, settle everywhere, establish connections everywhere.[4]

The "melting" and the "profanation" that were part and parcel of nine-
teenth-century capitalist globalization are also, in Marx's prescient though
androcentric words, precursors of our own experience. The fragment of
the *Manifesto* is of particular interest because it ties together themes that
continue to be *theologically* relevant in our own time: the liquidation of
space in conjunction with the continual expansion of the capitalist market, and the profanation of "all that is holy" within that shifting framework. It seems to me that theology in general—and feminist theology
most particularly—is called to pay attention to place and its relationship
to the "holy." It desires to seek out, for instance, in what spaces women
and those they love are able to flourish, for indeed such flourishing, at
least according to some strands of the Christian tradition, is an indicator
of God's pleasure and serves to glorify God.[5]

Raúl Fornet-Betancourt puts a similar idea to that of Marx in contemporary terms, when he describes neo-capitalist globalization as the
systematic expansion of a political and economic project that takes hold
of the material base of cultures. As he puts it, cultures are left literally
"in the air" because the market occupies their times and places in a way
that no longer allows those cultures to configure their space according
to their own desires.[6] This rather violent process, which at times takes
on the misleadingly irenic guise of "multiculturalism," is no placid interchange of cultural goods among equal partners but rather is traversed
by many asymmetries of power. Precisely an awareness of these asymmetries is one of the principal markers of the sort of *interculturality* that
serves as one of the transversal themes of this collection.[7] I would like to
focus for a moment on this tension of asymmetry and interculturality by
bringing to mind two events of 1848, the same year in which Marx
spoke of the solid melting into the air. That moment in history, besides
serving in a very real sense as a backdrop for the relational dynamic
between Latinas and Latin American feminist theologians, showcases
two strands that I hope can be intertwined in the context of interculturality
to the benefit of a critically minded theology: the *border* as a significant
space for an epistemology and *feminism* as a critical discourse of modernity.

The two significant events of the year 1848 in the North American
subcontinent to which I refer are, in shorthand, Guadalupe-Hidalgo and
Seneca Falls. In February of that year Mexico signed the Treaty of
Guadalupe-Hidalgo, by which it ceded more than half of its territory to

the United States.[8] The treaty, in itself a concession almost unbearable to the Mexicans ("a peace that seemed almost worse than war"),[9] was never respected in its entirety, particularly as regards the property rights of the Mexican inhabitants of the territory. Abraham Lincoln, who at that time was a U.S. Representative from Illinois, was highly critical of that war and of the rationale used to launch it by the Executive Branch of the United States. In his "Spot Resolutions" of December 22, 1847, he challenged the administration to show proof of the exact "spot" where U.S. blood had supposedly been shed by Mexicans on U.S. soil. As in the case of the nonexistent weapons of mass destruction in Iraq, which were used by the U.S. Executive Branch as a pretext to invade that country in 2003, the "spot" alleged by then U.S. president James Polk was never shown to have existed in reality.[10]

Though the "spot" had no true or verifiable place, its virtual reality became a wedge by which the apparent solidity of an established international border soon melted into the air. As a consequence, a new border—and with it new borderlands—emerged, along with new ways of negotiating the asymmetries of power among the groups who came into contact; it can even be argued that a new people emerged as a result of the shift, even as new configurations had emerged in the sixteenth century as a result of the initial European invasion of what came to be known as the American continent. Though the movement toward the Pacific of U.S. Americans had begun some decades previously, bringing with it a series of cultural and political changes, many Chicanos and Chicanas commemorate February 2, 1848, as the birthdate of the Chicano Mexicano Nation, not because they consider the U.S. invasion or its aftermath an event to celebrate, but rather as an acknowledgment that the retracing of that border led to cultural and linguistic shifts: "Our point here is not that we see the Tratado as our salvation, but rather a fact of history, a part of our history that has formed who we are as Chicano Mexicanos. . . . Even though *Raza* from here and *Raza* from across the border have the same cultural background, our social and political experiences are different."[11]

In the group of women who came together for the symposium of Latina and Latin American feminist theologians in Mexico City, the border drawn in the Treaty of Guadalupe-Hidalgo was continually present, both implicitly and explicitly. The feeling in Latin America, perhaps especially among critical intellectuals, tends to be that of suspicion toward the United States and those who inhabit it. As Jeanette Rodríguez expresses in her essay in this collection, one of the first questions that is asked of Latinas and Latinos by Latin Americans is "¿Dónde naciste?" (Where were you born?) The subtext is, "From what side of the border are you, really?" When I heard her speak of this, I immediately thought of how I have always enjoyed answering that question precisely because I was born in the Argentine province of Chubut, a place so far to the South that it subverts every North American preconception of Latin America as a tropical or subtropical paradise; it is a harsh, wind-swept landscape by the cold South Atlantic, where the Southern Cross shines intensely among innumerable bright stars.[12] However, the same question, heard from the perspective of those with Latin American roots but not born in Latin America, can be a cruel one. It functions in a subtle way as a burden of proof almost impossible to resolve, because it requires a person to prove a negative: Latinas born North of the Río Grande must show that they are "not" somehow alien to Latin America and Latin American interests. The place of their birth or of their upbringing becomes a barrier rather than a gift to be shared.

At the same time, they are expected to be fluent and articulate in a language that may indeed be close to their hearts, but in which (if they received schooling in the United States) they most likely received little formal education, nor in which (if they were trained and work in the U.S. academy) are they accustomed to lecture or write academic papers. Spanish may be precious but very private to them, a language of intimacy but not their preferred medium for public discourse. This point was brought home to me at the airport, the moment that I encountered two of the Latina theologians headed toward our symposium. When they spoke to me in English, I immediately answered in Spanish, assuming somewhat defensively that they thought that my English last name or light skin marked me as a non–Latin American. The conversation went on from there in Spanish, in a desultory fashion; a little later I noticed that among themselves, they shifted to English, peppered liberally and rather charmingly with Spanish expressions. Spanish was the condiment, not the main fare of their manner of communicating. It was the first of many illuminating moments in those days together.

The border, which had melted away in 1848 and reemerged further to the south, functions in palpable and exclusionary ways in both directions; it is not only a barrier for those who wish to migrate northward for economic reasons but also serves as an invisible fence southward toward those, such as the Latinas in our group, who might desire to extend their hands to the South, but too often feel that their hands are slapped rather than clasped. I began to see that they had been rather brave even to travel to Mexico City and expose themselves to the scrutiny and skepticism of their sister theologians from Latin America. When—after some initial hesitation—the Latin Americans in our group did extend our hands, palms up, we received from the Latinas among us the gift of a greater awareness and understanding of a space: the border-lands or *Nepantla*.

The Náhuatl word *Nepantla* means "in the middle," or as Gloria Anzaldúa liked to translate it, "torn between ways."[13] The borderlands are symbolized by the U.S.-Mexican border but are not limited to that area; they extend to wherever the forty million Latinos, Latinas, and Latin Americans in the United States congregate, and beyond them to other groups "torn between ways." Significantly, Anzaldúa also answers the implicit question about where she was and *was not* born: "I was not born at Tenochitlan in the ancient past, nor in an Aztec village in modern times. I was born and live in that in-between space, Nepantla, the borderlands." In her work, she gradually widened the concept of *Nepantla* to include not only the place of the "Mexican immigrant at the moment of crossing the barbed-wired fence into the hostile 'paradise' of el Norte, the United States," but also "that uncertain terrain one crosses when moving from one place to another, when changing from one class, race or gender position to another, when traveling from the present identity into a new identity." Thus, she could imagine *Nepantla* in terms of Borges's Aleph as "the one spot on earth which contains all other places within it."[14]

Perhaps, in her enthusiasm, Anzaldúa goes further than the metaphor warrants, but I do think that she points to a rich space for living out and thinking about interculturality. It is one that, as Latina theologians insist, is too important to be ignored by theology, for among its other virtues, it allows one to visualize interculturality in a complex fashion, fruitfully. I have made reference to interculturality several times already, and yet I have not yet defined what I mean by it. By not doing so too hastily I am heeding Fornet-Betancourt's warnings about the danger entailed by too narrow and perhaps too Eurocentric a definition of interculturality. He reminds us that speaking of interculturality in a monocultural manner would be counterproductive; what is necessary—he argues—is on the one hand to recognize our need to learn new ways to look at the world from within the diversity of alphabets provided by different cultures, and on the other to recognize the contextual nature of our definitions. Interculturality can of course be contrasted to monoculturalism, but it also goes beyond the tolerance of a shallow "diversity," inasmuch as it desires to find cultural and political ways for mutual transformation and the flourishing of all.[15] Fornet-Betancourt proposes the metaphor of mutual translation *(traducción recíproca)*, by which we attempt to put in our own words the experiences and realities of others and, by so doing, modify our own vision and language and realize just how contextual and contingent our concepts really are.[16] The metaphor of translation is, of course, a tricky one because if the process is not reciprocal, as well as somewhat symmetrical in terms of power dynamics, it easily becomes a simple instrument of domination.[17]

Another way of thinking of interculturality is simply to get to know the people of the borderlands along the Río Grande (or Río Bravo, as it is usually called in Latin America), as the Latinas in our symposium repeatedly invited us to do. Gloria Anzaldúa, who writes of herself in her characteristic mixture of English and Spanish, is a case in point:

> *Hay muchas razas* running in my veins, *mezcladas dentro de mí, otras culturas* that my body lives in and out of. *Mi cuerpo vive dentro y fuera de otras culturas* and a white man who constantly whispers inside my skull. For me, being *Chicana* is not enough. It is only one of my multiple identities. Along with other border *gente*, it is at this site and time, *en este tiempo y lugar* where and when, I create my identity *con mi arte*.[18]

In Anzaldúa one sees an awareness of interculturality within her own body and biography ("many races running in my veins") and in her interactions with others ("along with other border people"). Her body is within and without other cultures: interculturality. Furthermore, as Walter Mignolo puts it, interculturality it is not a matter only of "being together" in the sense of the Spanish verb *estar* (that would be a simple multiculturalism), but rather accepting also the diversity of being in the sense of *ser*; there are many ways of needing, thinking, desiring and knowing.[19]

Not to acknowledge or—better—to come to know *Nepantla* is a disservice to reality, the reality we as theologians are committed to probe honestly. Few situations illuminate both the glories and the limitations of a critical discourse within a hegemonic cosmology that is oblivious to what *Nepantla* symbolizes as clearly as an event that also took place in North America in 1848, only a few months after the signing of Guadalupe-Hidalgo. In July of that year, a group of around three hundred women and men, most of them Quakers and many of them abolitionists,[20] gathered at Seneca Falls, New York, where they debated and then signed a "Declaration of Sentiments" based on a text by Elizabeth Cady Stanton and modeled on the U.S. Declaration of Independence. In it, they demanded for U.S. women "immediate admission to all the rights and privileges which belong to them as citizens of the United States." It also called for the "zealous and untiring efforts of both men and women for the overthrow of the monopoly of the pulpit."[21] First-wave feminist theology subtly resonates throughout the text, and the historic meeting was a turning point for early U.S. feminism in general, wielding great influence on the movement in the United States and elsewhere. Nothing was recorded there, however, of an awareness of the ramifications of the Treaty of Guadalupe-Hidalgo. It seems sad—even tragic—that no analogy was perceived by the Seneca Falls signers, whose declaration spoke of the "entire disfranchisement of one-half the people of this country, their social and religious degradation," between the disenfranchisement of "white" women and that of one-half of the sovereign country of Mexico; their feminist sensibilities and convictions lacked a sufficient measure of intercultural awareness, and one might argue that for that reason its critical edge was necessarily blunted as well. Furthermore, women of African ancestry, despite their extraordinary importance in facilitating both the birth of U.S. American first wave feminism and the abolitionist movement, were entirely absent at Seneca Falls, physically and theoretically.[22] If one applies the lens of "border thinking" to the event, it is clear that the people involved were hampered by their blind spots, though they did exercise a fair amount of critical thinking from within their paradigm; at least in this case it is clear that a feminism hatched within the confines of modernity is not in itself enough to provide a wider lens to view the disenfranchisement of the subaltern.[23]

BORDER THINKING

By speaking of *Nepantla* and of subalternity almost in the same breath I am, of course, making use of a theoretical instrument lately most developed by postcolonial thinkers. In Edward W. Said's seminal work *Orientalism*,[24] he sketches out the basis of what is now known as postcolonial theory by arguing that the "Orient" was basically an ideological and discursive creation of North-Atlantic cultures in order to control the shape and dissemination of knowledge. This is indeed a useful insight. From a Latin American point of view, however, it is also very clear that our subcontinent and its history are often left out of the Oriental-Occidental equation (despite the fact that after the European invasion it was initially constructed as the East Indies, a significant hybrid of East and West). If to that omission we add the suspicion often found in Latin American academic circles that cultural and postcolonial studies are an ideological export of the North American intelligentsia—even if it is an intelligentsia partly composed of third-world expatriates—we can begin to see why postcolonial theory has generally not shown itself to be the most fruitful of critical instruments in the Latin American context, though that is perhaps slowly beginning to change.[25]

Upon first hearing of postcolonialism, Latin Americans often ask, right-fully: How can we speak of *post*-colonialism if we continue to be colonized by the forces of capitalist globalization and renewed U.S. imperialism, regardless of the formal independence of our countries?[26] In the face of such questions, Walter Mignolo maps out a necessary distinction between the *colonial period* (that is, the period of Spanish and Portuguese colonization) and *coloniality of power* (the continuing colonial structures that discipline and punish Latin America in the interests of capitalist globalization).[27] Latin America is no longer in the colonial period (and in that sense, the postcolonial period began with the formal independence of most of our countries in the nineteenth century); however, Latin America continues to be subject to the coloniality of power. Mignolo also points out, usefully, that whereas for Latin Americans it may seem obvious that modernity and coloniality are two sides of the same coin because historically they encountered both of them simultaneously, from the perspective of other third-world/southern nations (for example in the Mahgreb), coloniality comes *after* modernity.[28] That is why some of the postcolonial analysis born of South Indian or North African contexts cannot be directly translated to the Latin American situation. What all countries and peoples suffering under the coloniality of power do have in common, however, is the need for *decolonizing* thought and praxis.

Franz Fanon's concept of decolonization[29] is appealing to me from a Latin American feminist perspective; it implies action and historical process, conversion and a praxis of liberation. It addresses needs of both the "colonized" and the "colonizer"—a distinction that in itself is, of course, not always cut and dried. As Chandra Talpade Mohanty points out, such decolonization involves

> profound transformation of self, community and governance structures. It can only be engaged through active withdrawal of consent and resistance to structures of psychic and social domination. It is a historical and collective process, and as such can only be understood within these contexts. The end result of decolonization is not only the creation of new kinds of self-governance, but also the "creation of new men" (and women).[30]

As Talpade Mohanty rightly underlines, this transformative dimension is central to third-world feminist theorizing—and, I would add, to feminist theology as well. If we tease out the logical consequences of this perspective we will note that modernity and coloniality are closely linked (appearing either simultaneously or concurrently) and that without the normative horizon of "decolonization," coloniality of power, in its present form of capitalist globalization, will continue unchecked to effect its ends in ways deadly particularly to the subaltern. At the same time, many of the theoretical options we use to understand and counter this coloniality of power—such as Gramsci's idea of the subaltern—themselves come from the critical edges of "modernity." So, too, does much of feminism. Celia Amorós, for instance, celebrates feminism as an "undesired" child of the Enlightenment, whose insistent questions expose the latter's inconsistencies, but whose parentage is not in doubt.[31] Does this need for a normative horizon and for tools of analysis born of modernity mean that liberation theologies and feminist theologies are too embedded in the logic of modernity for their own good? In fact, one of the critiques that tend to be aimed at liberation and feminist theologies alike is that they are too dependent on emancipatory discourses that emerged at the rise of modernity but in the end are totalizing, dangerous, and unfaithful to the Christian message.[32]

It seems to me that an awareness of border thinking along the lines proposed by Walter Mignolo is useful in showing how and why this kind of criticism, while warranted in some measure (and thus worth considering), falls short of an accurate understanding. Awareness of *Nepantla* or thinking of the border allows us literally to develop what Mignolo terms *border thinking* or *border gnosis*, a way of knowing that disrupts dichotomies from *within* a dichotomous situation: "thinking from dichotomous concepts rather than ordering the world in dichotomies." It is worth recalling that the very word *Nepantla* was only coined in the sixteenth century and was only "possible in the mouth of an Amerindian, not of a Spaniard." Yet thinking in *Nepantla* or "border thinking" is "more than a hybrid enunciation. It is a fractured enunciation in dialogic situations."[33] As such, it is located "at all the borders (interiors or exteriors) of the modern/colonial world system."[34] For Mignolo, what people such as Gloria Anzaldúa with her "mestiza consciousness" or W. E. B. Du Bois with his "double consciousness" provide, is precisely an epistemology that avoids being entrapped within the logic of the dominant world view while still able to make use of critical instruments forged within that world view. As Mignolo sees it, such an epistemology can establish alliances with the critique of modernity from within modernity itself (and thus with Kierkegaard, Marx or Derrida, among so many others), but at the same time it marks the "irreducible difference of border thinking" by its capacity to critique the modern world system also from its "exterior." [35]

What allows for this latter capacity is the *colonial difference*. This difference is not usefully thought about in a metaphysical fashion. It does not mean, for instance, that Latin American human beings are some-how essentially different from North American ones; it refers, rather, to a difference constructed historically that has real epistemological conse-quences. Mignolo argues that "Latin America" is a product of a geo-politics of knowledge, a way of understanding the world fabricated and imposed by European modernity. This way of knowing presents itself as objective and discards the validity of other ways of understanding the world. In reality, however, it is not objective but a way of thinking born in a given part of the world (around the Mediterranean basin and then moving northward), no more and no less. The epistemology of moder-nity is therefore not a disembodied knowledge to which all regions of the planet should aspire to ascend. Seen from this perspective, the thought of Christendom, Liberalism, and Marxism are more similar than differ-ent; they have all served in varying degrees to justify the "coloniality of power" that disregards epistemologies with other cultural roots and tra-jectories.[36]

As Mignolo points out, if we try, for instance, to understand the Zapatistas merely on the basis of Bourdieu or sociological methods born of modernity, we will simply reproduce the colonization of knowledge, denying the possibility that perhaps the thought generated by the Zapatistas is more relevant for understanding Latin America than that of Jürgen Habermas, for instance, as valuable as that may be.[37] Simi-larly, for Latin Americans, Gramsci's model of the organic intellectual is insufficient, because its context in European modernity orients it en-tirely toward the written word. A Latin American interculturality re-quires the engagement of oral traditions and of the knowledge of the "unlettered," who by the mere standard of the Enlightenment would be seen as having no "lights."[38] It is thus not a matter of rejecting the tools offered by the critical tradition of modernity, but rather of seeing their limitations. They only are capable of answering the questions that they ask, but they may not ask the questions that we need to pose.

Border thinking seems to me to constitute a fundamental epistemo-logical tool for Latina and Latin American feminist theologies. At one point during our discussions in the symposium in Mexico City, María Pilar Aquino asked a fundamental question: "¿Con qué epistemología quiero comprometer mi vida?" The force of her question is in one sense untranslatable, but I take it to mean roughly, "To what epistemology can I commit my life?"[39] That question seems to me to constitute one of the central questions for theology today. It should be noted that in Latin America, *epistemology* usually does not mean simply a "theory of mean-ing"; it is also often used in reference to how knowledge is produced, structured, and validated. In other words, epistemology is not only seen as a subset of human philosophical discourse but rather is embedded materially in the world.[40] Epistemology is a matter of life and death. As Tirsa Molina put it in one of our group discussions, as feminist Latina and Latin American theologians we are producing these epistemologies from our *entrañas*—from our very entrails.

This capacity for using the critical tools born of modernity in a creative way is one way of interpreting Audre Lorde's dictum, "The master's tools will never dismantle the master's house." She asks, "What does it mean when the tools of a racist patriarchy are used to examine the fruits of that same patriarchy? It means that only the most narrow perimeters of change are possible and allowable." She posits that using such tools in the ways prescribed by the "masters" does not allow for genuine change; at the same time she uses the tools of argumentation and academic discourse to propose ways of dismantling that "house." In my opinion, she is not saying that the "tools" should be discarded, but rather that they should be used in ways for which they were not necessarily designed: swords into plowshares. Thus, she deconstructs the theory behind a racist feminism that tries to homogenize all women by paying close attention to material reality and asymmetries of power:

> Poor and third world women know there is a difference between the daily manifestations and dehumanizations of marital slavery and prostitution, because it is our daughters who line 42nd Street. . . . If white American feminist theory need not deal with the differences between us and the resulting difference in aspects of our oppressions, then what do you do with the fact that the women who clean your houses and tend your children while you attend conferences on feminist theory are, for the most part, poor and third world women? What is the theory behind racist feminism?[41]

Lorde is speaking from the awareness of the coloniality of power, and this allows her to see differently, pose different questions, and use the "master's tools" in unexpected ways; it is an example of border thinking.

In the face of the limitations and blind spots of critical discourses within hegemonic cosmologies, border thinking thus opens up new critical horizons. But border thinking is neither seen nor understood by persons who have not reflected sufficiently on the colonial difference or—better yet—experienced it themselves. Nelson Maldonado-Torres makes the important point that what seems to remain hidden to John Milbank and other "radically orthodox" critics of Latin American theology is precisely the "colonial difference." As Maldonado-Torres lucidly puts forward, Latin American theologies cannot be accounted for simply with reference to European theologies, for they assert "theological difference from the space of enunciation of the colonial difference."[42] Radical Orthodoxy presents itself as a "participatory" theology, understanding participation "as developed by Plato and reworked by Christianity." If that were as far as it went, such a statement might function as a salutary recognition of the contextual nature of that theology; the mistake is to then add that "any alternative configuration perforce reserves a territory independent of God," which in turn "can only lead to nihilism."[43] The supposition that "any alternative configuration" to its own Eurocentrically configured theological proposal *necessarily* leads to "nonsense" amounts to participation, consciously or unconsciously, in the dynamics of the coloniality of power.

What is very exciting to me about the potential of Latina and Latin American feminist theologies is that because they are cognizant of the "colonial difference," they are quite capable of making use of critical instruments indebted to modernity while at the same time bringing a critique to the table that is not simply in the "custody" of hegemonic forms of knowledge.[44] It also allows for the possibility of reappropriating emphases in the Christian theological tradition that have had little "space" in the logic of Christendom. Feminist theology has indeed been characterized by the latter search, which has been a keystone of its method.[45] As a feminist Latin American theologian indebted to the practices and convictions of the Anabaptist tradition—and as a follower of Jesus in the rhythms of that sensibility—I am heartened by the possibilities I envision in applying border thinking and awareness of the "colonial difference" to retrievals from the Anabaptist tradition that may contribute to *making space* in peace and justice.

I am aware of Peter Phan's dictum to the effect that all theology is autobiographical, yet not all autobiography is theological,[46] and so I do not want to tell too many stories. Yet, as I write, the memory of another space comes to mind and insists on asserting itself. I think of the serene waters of the Neckar River in Germany, on the banks of which lies the university town of Tübingen, where I lived as a doctoral student. A few kilometers away, also nestled on the Neckar's banks, lies Rottenburg. I first visited Rottenburg to enjoy its *Fasnet*, wondering if it would be like or unlike the *carnavales* I knew in Argentina. The pre-Lenten celebration was indeed amusing and joyful, yet I soon realized that this beautiful little city was also the place I knew from history as a Golgotha for Anabaptists. A rock engraved with simple letters reminds visitors that in 1527 Margaretha and Michael Sattler were executed on this site.

Margaretha had been a Beguine. She married Michael Sattler, the former prior of a Benedictine monastery in the Breisgau who became a leader of the early Anabaptist movement. Their adherence to the Anabaptist way came in the context of the sixteenth-century peasant unrest.[47] In May 1527, Margaretha was tried for heresy in Rottenburg and "after being subjected to many entreaties, admonitions, and threats, under which she remained steadfast, was drowned."[48] Some days previously Michael Sattler had been tortured and likewise killed. Detailed testimonies of his trial and execution are preserved; they have a hagiographic flavor but contain worthwhile insights nevertheless. It is clear that he and the thirteen men and women accused along with him, including Margaretha, were particularly worrisome to the authorities because of their position concerning nonresistance in the hypothetical case of an invasion by the Turks. Sattler, having conferred with his "brethren and sisters" and speaking for the group, pointed out that for confessing Christians, Jesus' command in Matthew 5:21 ruled out warfare and killing. From the perspective of "border thinking" it is of particular interest to note his reasoning:

> We must not defend ourselves against the Turks and others of our persecutors, but are to beseech God with earnest prayer to repel and resist them. But I said that, if warring *were* right, I would rather take the field against so-called Christians who persecute, capture, and kill pious Christians than against the Turks for the following reason. The Turk is a true Turk, knows nothing of the Christian faith, and is a Turk after the flesh. But you who would be Christians and who make your boast of Christ persecute the pious witnesses of Christ, are Turks after the spirit![49]

Certainly, Sattler's language with regard to the "Turks" is not the language of present-day intercultural sensibilities, and yet his argument is important. Whereas it makes no sense to expect a "Turk" (presumably a Muslim) to act according to Christian convictions, those who call themselves Christians and use violent means to propagate their beliefs are in truth much more objectionable than the "Turks." A Christian who resorts to the sword is distorting the message of Jesus from within. Sattler argued that "neither I nor my brethren and sisters have offended in word or in deed against any authority"; actually, their position was deeply offensive to those in power because it showed up the inconsistencies of a Christendom model in which Christianity becomes an ideological justification for state terrorism. This is the same sort of stance that earned present-day Dominican nuns Jacqueline Hudson, Ardeth Platte, and Carol

Gilbert prison sentences for protesting nonviolently against the U.S. nuclear arsenal in Colorado.[50]

It is also worth noting how Sattler is willing to use whatever critical tools he has at his disposal, asking his accusers to "send for the most learned men and for the sacred books of the Bible in whatever language" in the hope that the authorities might "be converted and receive instruction." We can detect in his argument both the recourse to the humanist critical tools of an incipient modernity and a perspective from the "exteriority" of the message of Jesus as spoken outside the logic of Christendom.

The same year that Margaretha and Michael Sattler were executed, Sebastián Caboto founded the Sancti Spiritus fort at the confluence of the Carcarañá and Paraná rivers. That fortification serves as a symbolic beginning of the invasion and colonization of what is now Argentina by the strength of the sword in the name of the Holy Spirit. Though Sattler was undoubtedly unaware of this occurrence, his non-Christendom stance, and that of his companions, is extremely relevant in illuminating why Caboto's incursion was a tragic symbol for the Christian faith. The biblical admonition is for Christians to let the Spirit be their defense, not to use the sword in the name of the Spirit; it follows that a fortified place of intrusion such as Caboto's "fort of the Holy Spirit" is a travesty of pneumatic "space." Ivone Gebara proposes the metaphor of *breathing* to speak of God and imagines that it is within this "breath" that is God that we "organize our life, interact, struggle for justice, look for love and even produce very different discourses about this same breathing."[51] Her metaphor is very much in tune with the idea of "making spaces" in which to breathe, live and flourish, and is fundamentally a pneumatological image (Jn 3:8). What we need, rather than the "fort of the Holy Spirit," is the Spirit's strength to find places to breathe and flourish in peace and justice: Sor Juana, Margaretha Sattler, and many others knew this, yet space was denied them. So did Jesus. When he says that "the Son of the Human Being has no place to lay his head" (Mt 8:20), he does not mean that he lacked the hospitality of friends and family, but rather that there was little "space" for the life he wanted to bring. Yet, though his life was cut short, that was not the end of the story, for by the Spirit we are still able to find and make spaces for the flourishing of life.

The Zapatistas speak of the need for a world with space enough for all *(un mundo donde todos quepamos sin necesidad de dominar a los otros);*[52] their proposal has been echoed by many in Latin America and beyond, in the face of the liquidation of cultures and spaces presently taking place in the world. Yet how might we contribute as feminists to configuring such a space? As Daiva K. Stasiulis cogently puts it:

The dilemmas faced by women's movements in dealing with simultaneous nationalist and ethnic minority claims within the same geopolitical space suggest the need to develop a conceptual apparatus
that can analytically deal with not merely the *plurality* but also and
more importantly the *positionality* of different nationalisms, racisms, ethno-cultural movements and feminisms *in relation to one
another*.[53]

An awareness not only of plurality (as in the discourse of diversity or
multiculturalism) but also of positionality (that is, of relations of power)
forces us to exercise discernment and judgment. It is a kind of thinking
that requires a contextualized, three-dimensional theoretical model able
to take into account many factors at once; it has, in short, to be both
analytic and synthetic in nature. It seems to me that theologians, particularly those cognizant of the "colonial difference," are trained to think
in such ways. Furthermore, Latina and Latin American feminist theologians are well-seasoned practitioners of the nonviolent art of "making
spaces" for themselves and for others. The tender, fearless manner in
which our group of women in Mexico City worked together to make
spaces leads me to wonder whether perhaps we—along with many others—have been called and trained for just a moment such as this, at the
cusp of interculturality. As in the beautiful Psalm 31, beloved by the
gospel writers, we can say thankfully to God: "You have set my feet in a
spacious place" even as we add: "Be gracious to me, Lord, because I am
in distress" (Ps 31:8–9, Homan Christian Standard Bible). For we know
that, in the matter of finding and making spaces, God's Spirit is nearer to
us than the air we breathe.[54]

Notes

[1] When she entered the convent in 1669 her mother gave her a slave, Juana de
San José, whom she sold to her sister fifteen years later. See Luis M. Villar,
Chronology, at the Sor Juana Inés de la Cruz Project of Dartmouth College,
available from http://www.dartmouth.edu/~sorjuana/Chronology.html; Internet
(accessed May 15, 2005).

[2] I understand *Latina* as denoting a woman who either was born in the United
States of Latin American ancestry or is a Latin American who has spent a significant portion her life in the United States, adopting it as her primary place of
residence and struggle; furthermore, she is a woman who uses this word to
describe herself, as do the authors in María Pilar Aquino, Daisy L. Machado,
and Jeanette Rodríguez, eds., *A Reader in Latina Feminist Theology: Religion
and Justice* (Austin: University of Texas Press, 2002). On Latinas in the United

States and their history from a religious point of view, see particularly Daisy Machado's essay herein.

[3] Marshall Berman, *All That Is Solid Melts into Air: The Experience of Modernity* (New York: Penguin Books, 1982).

[4] Karl Marx and Friedrich Engels, *Manifesto of the Communist Party* (1848), available from http://www.meehawl.com/Asset/Manifesto%20of%20the%20Communist%20Party.html; Internet (accessed May 16, 2005).

[5] On this, see Nancy Elizabeth Bedford, "Mirar más allá de Babilonia: La teología como teoría crítica para la gloria de Dios," *Cuadernos de Teología* 23 (2004): 203–19.

[6] Raúl Fornet-Betancourt, *Transformación Intercultural de la Filosofía* (Bilbao: Desclée de Brouwer, 2001), 280–81.

[7] In the sense of a variety of "traditions" recognized superficially by the hegemonic culture and incorporated in a token fashion in some of its institutions; it is worth remembering that multiculturalism can also be understood critically in a sense similar to the interculturality presupposed in this book and discussed particularly in the essay by Olga Consuelo Vélez Caro. It might be useful to distinguish between a critical multiculturality as a dimension of interculturality and multiculturalism. On this, see also María Xosé Agra, "Multiculturalismo, justicia y género," in *Feminismo y filosofía*, ed. Celia Amorós (Madrid: Síntesis, 2000), 135–64, who points out that multiculturalism is a word that necessarily needs an adjective because it is so multivalent. One must always ask, what *kind* of multiculturalism do you mean?

[8] A transcription of text of the treaty is available from http://www.cervantesvirtual .com/servlet/SirveObras/chic/46826397115794495222202/index.htm; Internet (accessed May 16, 2005).

[9] Tulio Halperin Dongui, *Historia contemporánea de América Latina* (Buenos Aires: Alianza Editorial, 1992), 186.

[10] For Lincoln's speech in the House of Representatives, see Roy P. Basler, ed., *The Collected Works of Abraham Lincoln*, vol. 1 (New Brunswick: Rutgers University Press 1953), 420–22; also available from http://www .animatedatlas.com/mexwar/lincoln1.html; Internet (accessed May 16, 2005).

[11] Statement of the Partido Nacional de la Raza Unida, San Fernando, California, February 1997, available from http://larazaunida.tripod.com/docs/feb2.htm; Internet (accessed May 16, 2005).

[12] In the first visit to the United States of which I have a clear memory, I remember the surprise I felt as a six year old at a recurring question from other children when they heard I was from Argentina: "Do you eat monkeys?" The youngsters had already picked up the idea that Latin America was the exotic "other" where such food would presumably be expected fare. Another common question, arising from the fact that in the southern hemisphere December constitutes the beginning of summer, was if it was possible for us to "have Christmas."

[13] Gloria Anzaldúa, "La Conciencia de la Mestiza: Towards a New Consciousness," in *Feminist Theory Reader: Local and Global Perspectives*, ed. Carole R.

McCann and Seung-Kyung Kim (New York: Routledge, 2003), 179–87. On the matter of the *nepantleras* and on migration, see my essays "Escuchar las voces de las nepantleras: Consideraciones teológicas desde las vivencias de latinoamericanas y 'latinas' en Estados Unidos," *Proyecto* 15 (2004): 204–24, and "To Speak of God from More than One Place: Theological Reflections from the Experience of Migration," in *Latin American Liberation Theologians: The Next Generation*, ed. Iván Petrella (Maryknoll, NY: Orbis Books, 2005), 95–118.

[14] Gloria Anzaldúa, "Chicana Artists: Exploring *Nepantla*, el Lugar de la Frontera," *North American Congress on Latin America NACLA: Report on the Americas* 27 (1993): 37–43. Borges's phrase is "uno de los puntos del espacio que contienen todos los puntos . . . el lugar donde están, sin confundirse, todos los lugares del orbe, vistos desde todos los ángulos."

[15] As is the case with *multiculturalism,* the codeword *diversity* tends to mask asymmetries and in fact in business and educational institutions is often described as something to be "managed." For a short and vivid description of this problem in academic circles, see Marisela B. Gómez, "Council Meeting," in *This Bridge We Call Home: Radical Visions for Transformation*, ed. Gloria Anzaldúa and Analouise Keating (New York: Routledge, 2002), 293–94.

[16] Raúl Fornet-Betancourt, *Filosofar para nuestro tiempo en clave intercultural* (Aachen, Germany: Wissenschaftsverlag Mainz, 2004), 9–14.

[17] On this, see Claudia de Lima Costa, "Repensando el género: Tráfico de teorías en las Américas," in *Perfiles del feminismo iberoamericano*, ed. María Luisa Femeninas (Buenos Aires: Catálogos, 2002), 189–214.

[18] Anzaldúa, "Chicana Artists," 43.

[19] Walter Mignolo, in Catherine Walsh, "Las geopolíticas del conocimiento y colonialidad del poder: Entrevista a Walter Mignolo," interview by Catherine Walsh, available from http://www.campus-oei.org/salactsi/walsh.htm; Internet (accessed May 27, 2005).

[20] Frederick Douglass was present and—according to the report in the *North Star* (his newspaper)—"in an excellent and appropriate speech, ably supported the cause of woman"; his report is available from the American History website, at http://www.nps.gov/wori/report1.htm; Internet (accessed May 16, 2005).

[21] The text of the declaration is available from the American History website, at http://www.nps.gov/wori/declaration.htm; Internet (accessed May 16, 2005).

[22] A fundamental transversal strand of discussion in our symposium was the matter of race, particularly as regards white privilege and the experiences of Afro-Latin American women; this is reflected particularly in this collection in the essays by Michelle González and Maricel Mena, but indirectly in many of the others as well.

[23] *Subaltern* in a Gramscian sense refers to those excluded from any meaningful role in the prevailing "common sense" (see Antonio Gramsci, *Prison Notebooks* [New York: Columbia University Press, 1992] and *The Modern Prince and Other Writings* [New York: International Publishers, 1967]). His term was reappropriated and is used in a widened fashion by the postcolonial theorists of

the subaltern studies group, perhaps most famously by Gayatri Chakravorty Spivak.

[24] Edward W. Said, *Orientalism* (New York: Vintage Books, 1978).

[25] A good (because nuanced) example of this reticence is Eduardo Grüner, *El fin de las pequeñas historias: De los estudios culturales al retorno (imposible) de lo trágico* (Buenos Aires: Paidós, 2002). For a lucid example of the complexity of borrowing postcolonial theoretical tools, written from a Latina feminist perspective, see Michelle A. González's use of Bhabha's notion of hybridity in her essay "Who Is Americana/o? Theological Anthropology, Postcoloniality, and the Spanish-Speaking Americas," in *Postcolonial Theologies: Divinity and Empire*, ed. Catherine Keller, Michael Nausner, and Mayra Rivera (St. Louis: Chalice, 2004), 58–78.

[26] Contemporary U.S. imperialism can be described simply as a further stage in the development of capitalism. As Atilio Borón puts it, globalization consolidates imperialist domination and deepens the submission of peripheral capitalisms, which are increasingly incapable of exercising control over their domestic economic processes. This leads to ever greater structural asymmetries. See Atilio Borón, *Imperio e Imperialismo: Una lectura crítica de Michael Hardt y Antonio Negri* (Buenos Aires: CLACSO Consejo Latinoamricano de Ciencias Sociales, 2002), 11.

[27] Walter Mignolo, *Local Histories/Global Designs: Coloniality, Subaltern Knowledges and Border Thinking* (Princeton, NJ: Princeton University Press, 2000), esp. xiv.

[28] Ibid., 50.

[29] Franz Fanon, *The Wretched of the Earth* (Harmondsworth: Penguin Books, 1963).

[30] Chandra Talpade Mohanty, *Feminism without Borders: Decolonizing Theory, Practicing Solidarity* (Durham, NC: Duke University Press, 2003), 7–8.

[31] Celia Amorós, "Presentación (que intenta ser un esbozo del *status questionis*)," in Amorós, *Feminismo y Filosofía*, 9–112 (and throughout her work).

[32] See, for instance, John Milbank, *Theology and Social Theory: Beyond Secular Reason* (Cambridge: Blackwell, 1991), 207ff.; Daniel Bell, Jr., "Sacrifice and Suffering: Beyond Justice, Human Rights and Capitalism," *Modern Theology* 18 (2002): 333–59, and *Liberation Theology after the End of History: The Refusal to Cease Suffering* (New York: Routledge, 2001), 63–65, 100ff.

[33] Mignolo, *Local Histories/Global Designs*, x.

[34] Ibid., 85.

[35] Ibid.

[36] See Walsh, "Las geopolíticas del conocimiento y colonialidad del poder."

[37] A collection of essays and communiqués of the EZLN is available from the website of the Ejército Zapatista de Liberación Nacional, at http://www.ezln.org/documentos/; Internet (accessed May 27, 2005).

[38] Walsh, "Las geopolíticas del conocimiento y colonialidad del poder"; Mignolo, *Local Histories/Global Designs*, 91ff.

[39] "Vaciado de deliberaciones," Primer Simposio Interamericano de Teólogas Feministas Latinas, Latinoamericanas y del Caribe, 6–11 de julio de 2004 (unpublished minutes of the conference), 8.

[40] See Gregorio Klimovsky, "Epistemología," in *Diccionario de Ciencias Sociales y Políticas*, ed. Torcuato S. Di Tella et al. (Buenos Aires: Emecé, 2001), 222–26.

[41] Audre Lorde, "The Master's Tools Will Never Dismantle the Master's House," in *This Bridge Called My Back: Writings by Radical Women of Color*, ed. Cherríe Moraga and Gloria Anzaldúa (New York: Kitchen Table Press, 1983), 94–101.

[42] Nelson Maldonado-Torres, "Liberation Theology and the Search for the Lost Paradigm: From Radical Orthodoxy to Radical Diversality," in *Latin American Liberation Theology. The Next Generation*, ed. Iván Petrella (Maryknoll, NY: Orbis Books, 2005), 39–61.

[43] John Milbank, Catherine Pickstock, and Graham Ward, eds., *Radical Orthodoxy* (New York: Routledge, 1999), 3.

[44] Most of the essays in this book reflect just such a move: Clara Luz Ajo by describing the dancing of Jesus and Mary with the *orichas*, Christa Godínez when she speaks of Xochitlalpan and Amerindian wisdom, Michelle González when she reflects on La Caridad del Cobre and Lydia Cabrera. All incorporate varieties of "border knowledge" with particular clarity into their theological projects.

[45] The classic methodological statement in this vein is Rosemary Radford Ruether, *Sexism and God-Talk: Toward a Feminist Theology* (Boston: Beacon Press, 1993), 20–46.

[46] Peter C. Phan, "Preface," in *Journeys at the Margin: Toward an Autobiographical Theology in American-Asian Perspective*, ed. Peter C. Phan and Jung Young Lee (Collegeville, MN: Liturgical Press, 1999).

[47] Arnold C. Snyder, "Revolution and the Swiss Brethren: The Case of Michael Sattler," *Church History* 50 (1981): 276–87.

[48] "The Trial and Martyrdom of Michael Sattler: Rottenburg, 1527," in *Spiritual and Anabaptist Writers. Documents Illustrative of the Radical Reformation*, ed. George H. Williams and Angel M. Mergal (Philadelphia: Westminster Press, 1957), 144. The men in this group were put to death by the sword, whereas the women were drowned; the latter manner of death was often cruelly called the "third baptism" by the authorities. Some nine hundred persons were put to death in Rottenburg for "heresy" in a period of approximately ten years.

[49] "The Trial and Martyrdom of Michael Sattler," 141.

[50] Parts of their dialogue with the authorities read strangely similar to the accounts of Sattler's trial; a transcript of Sister Platte's opening statement is available from http://www.jonahhouse.org/platte_openstm.htm: Internet (accessed May 30, 2005).

[51] Ivone Gebara, "Nuevas vías para la transformación de la estructura de la teología: Una propuesta de la teología feminista latinoamericana," in *Resistencia*

y Solidaridad. Globalización Capitalista y Liberación, ed. Raúl Fornet-Betancourt (Madrid: Trotta, 2003), 319–33.

[52] "La jornada 4 de enero de 1996: Construyamos un mundo de respeto y tolerancia: EZLN," available from http://www.ezln.org/documentos/1996/19960103.es.htm; Internet (accessed May 30, 2005).

[53] Daiva K. Stasiulis, "Relational Positionalities of Nationalisms, Racisms, and Feminisms," in *Between Woman and Nation: Nationalisms, Transnational Feminisms, and the State*, ed. Caren Kaplan, Norma Alarcón, and Monoo Moallem (Durham, NC: Duke University Press, 1999), 183.

[54] Many thanks to the postcolonial reading group at Garrett-Evangelical in the northern hemisphere spring of 2005, for our discussions on these and similar topics: Matthew Charlton, Yoojin Choi, Ric Hudgens, Kathleen Kordesh, Lallene Rector, and particularly Donna Techau.

4

Tripuenteando

Journey toward Identity, the Academy, and Solidarity

Jeanette Rodríguez

In the summer of 2004, I attended the first symposium of Latin American feminist theologians, titled "Feminist Intercultural Theology: Religion, Culture, Feminism and Power," held in Mexico City. I was very excited to attend this conference knowing that I would be intellectually stretched and forced to identify my epistemological markings and hermeneutical instruments within a global context. The four days of intense intellectual interchange brought to the forefront various perspectives of conceptually based frameworks that can only further enhance the study of critical feminist theology.

I begin this article, however, with my very first contact with my Latin American sisters. It was at the Mexico City airport. Upon arrival, I met the delegation from Colombia and Brazil. In a pre-conference mailing packet, each participant had already received a list of the participants from the particular country that they represented. Next to my name, Jeanette Rodríguez, was "Ecuador/U.S.A." Immediately following the initial greetings of "How are you?" and "It's a pleasure to meet you," I was asked the first critical question, the litmus question, "Donde naciste tú? En Ecuador o en Los Estados Unidos?" (Where were you actually born? Was it in Ecuador or in the United States?) I could feel my body tense up immediately, feeling, "Oh no. Once again I'm being asked to state my position, perhaps state my loyalty, my primary identification." I responded that I was born in the United States, the firstborn daughter of Ecuadorian parents. I suppose that makes me a *gringa*. My response was an attempt to divert any criticism I might receive for claiming a Latina identity and being born in the United States.

The response of my Latin American sisters was, "Pues no te vamos a felicitar" (well, we are not going to congratulate you), at which point I took a deep breath and responded as quickly as possible with, "Claro que no, estoy acostumbrada de ser puente donde me pisan por los dos lados" (Of course not, I am already accustomed to being a bridge where they step on me from both sides). There was an uncomfortable laugh and an unspoken repositioning of how we were going to engage one another. We then proceeded to greet the rest of the participants in what would be a very exciting five-day intellectual exchange.

This story directs what I choose to write about in this anthology. It reaffirms the necessity of bridge building. Gloria Anzaldúa best articulates my understanding of bridges when she states, "Bridges are thresholds to other realities . . . passageways, conduits, and connectors, that connote transitioning, crossing borders and changing perspectives. Bridges span limitable spaces between worlds. . . . Transformations occur in this in-between space, an unstable, an unpredictable, precarious, always-in-transition space lacking clear boundaries."[1]

In this chapter I explore three particular areas that involve crossings, bridges, and exchanges: (1) the intrapsychic crossing, which is not limited to but includes identity and belonging, (2) the intersection of race, class, and gender in the academy, and finally, (3) the bridging necessary to live out our commitment to solidarity. The title of this chapter, *tripuenteando*, is a play on words. It includes *tri* (three), and *puente* (bridge), but its meaning is "tripping." The slang *tripear* for tripping in some parts of the Spanish-speaking world is colloquial. The word *toward* in the title is also significant because it involves a process and offers an alternative to a fixed and static notion within these three areas. In the intrapsychic section, I identify who are Latinos/as in the United States and what their context is. I give one specific contextual example—mine—of crossing more than one world, and how issues of race, class, and gender intersect in the formation of that identity. In the second section I use both narrative and insights from women of color who confirm this issue of race, class, and gender being played out in the academy. Included in this section are the significant contributions that we bring. In the third section I focus on solidarity and discuss briefly two venues to that solidarity. One is with theological method—hermeneutics; the second is the call on the part of the university to participate in the social transformation of the world.

IDENTITY AND BELONGING[2]

Who we understand ourselves to be will have consequences for
how we experience and understand the world. (Paula M. L. Moya)

I grew up in the Astoria projects by the Hudson River, an area in New
York City that was poor. It housed a factory, contained eighteen six-
floor buildings, where mostly African American, poor Irish, and first-
generation Latinos lived. I remember having to cross over a variety of
worlds even as a young child. The world within my family felt safe and
spoke Spanish. They were humble, relational, open, and affectionate.
When I stepped through the doors of our apartment I entered a world
that was hostile, dirty, and dangerous. In this world I created an ar-
mored persona in order to not be hurt and to mask my fear. The survival
was complicated by the fact that although I spoke Spanish I was fair
skinned. Initially I was accosted by the nonwhite kids for being what
they perceived as "white." My ability to speak the language was one of
the things that saved me. At the same time the white communities in the
area did not accept me because I had an Indian mother and I was a
Rodríguez "spic."[3]

It was difficult enough to have to cross between these worlds. However, matters were more complicated when I started to bring the values
and cultural mannerisms of one group into another. Let me try to explain this. Given my context, I grew more bilingual, assertive, and independent, while acting as a buffer between my family and the new social
context they found themselves in here in the United States. I became this
buffer or ambassador, or bridge, for three reasons. First, I was bilingual.
Second, I was the firstborn girl and learned early that it was my responsibility to take care of the family. Finally, I had blue eyes. "Ojos azules
abren las puertas," as my parents would say. Blue eyes open doors. In
the brown eyes of my parents, my fair skin and blue eyes would open the
world for me. In other words, the U.S. world would say yes more quickly
to me more often than they would say yes to them or my brothers, who
were dark skinned and brown eyed. *Ojos azules abren las puertas.*

At first hearing you might think this is a privileged position. In some
cases it is. You may also pick up the inherent and transformed racism in
this statement. What it meant for me was that I was constantly being put
in a position of negotiating, defending, and advocating for my family
and others. These skills were further enhanced by a working-class posture of persistence, reciprocal relationship building, and tenacity. These
skills developed for personal and communal survival may also, however,

be critiqued and rejected by one's own community. In my Latino community, and even from my own mother's lips, I would be told things like, "Mija, deberias de ser hombre" (My daughter, you should have been a man). Was that a compliment or an insult? Was my assertiveness within the dominant culture seen as aggression in the Latino community? Later my mother would tell me that she was just concerned that I would suffer in the world because the world did not like smart women.

While this is a personal story, it is also an urban story. A short vignette demonstrates how a Latina in Texas experienced discrimination as well as the internal conflict that one carries as a colonized Latina living in the underbelly of U.S. triumphalism.

> My grandmother was a very special person in my life. I grew up in Texas and we were poor. I was very aware of our status because every day at school I was ostracized by the predominantly white children who did not like my clothes, my hair, my skin, my name or my lunches. My little old grandmother would deliver my lunch to me every day. I always had a warm taco with beans and meat or rice and a small thermos of milk. Everyone else had white bread sandwiches with cold cuts. I always felt pained at lunch time because part of me didn't want to see my grandmother and the other part of me felt so guilty for feeling that way. She knew that children made fun of me and of her but she acted as if she was oblivious to it. She always brought certain differences to my attention, never explicitly saying what she really meant but laying a foundation of thought in my head. If a different colored plant grew out of place she could comment on how its difference made things more interesting. She would brush her long hair at night and comment on how some people didn't like it when gray hair began to grow into their natural color but she said that she liked it because it meant something different and it gave more strength to her dark hair. She said everything in nature should be appreciated because it was part of God's design.[4]

This story illustrates the inner conflict and wisdom of our grandmothers that coexist in our intrapsychic world. In the late 1980s, writer and poet Gloria Anzaldúa developed and articulated an understanding of *la conciencia de la mestiza.*[5] This *conciencia* is a consciousness of the mixed blood. As Anzaldúa states, *la conciencia de la mestiza*

> is a product of the transfer of the cultural and spiritual values of one group to another. Being tricultural, monolingual, bilingual, or

multilingual, speaking *a patois,* and in a state of perpetual transition, the *mestiza* faces the dilemma of the mixed breed. . . . She has discovered that she can't hold concepts or ideas in rigid boundaries. . . . *La mestiza* constantly has to shift out of habitual formations; from convergent thinking, analytical reasoning that tends to use rationality to move toward a single goal (a Western mode), to divergent thinking, characterized by movement away from set patterns and goals and toward a more whole perspective, one that includes rather than excludes.[6]

Chela Sandoval echoes Anzaldúa by proposing that *la mestiza* "develops a subjectivity capable of transformation and relocation, movement guided by the learned capacity to read, renovate and make signs on behalf of the dispossessed."[7] This particular ability and skill Anzaldúa calls *la facultad. La facultad* is the capacity to see in surface phenomena the meaning of deeper realities, to see the deep structure below the surface. It is an instant "sensing," a quick perception arrived at without conscious reasoning. It is an acute awareness mediated by the part of the psyche that does not speak, that communicates in images and symbols that are the faces of feelings, that is, behind which feelings reside/hide. The one possessing this sensitivity is excruciatingly alive to the world.[8]

Philosopher Maria Lugones concurs with Anzaldúa and claims that the theory and method of U.S. third-world feminism requires of its practitioners nomadic and determined "travel" across "world"-traveling.[9] Anzaldúa brings to this argument the formative process that constitutes the essential elements of Latino/a community: language, history, religious and cultural practices, etc. This constitutive piece develops the subjective person as of the community, for example, the individual's important place in the process of community. It is through the individual subjective dialogue with other that the trans-historical identity of "Latino/a" is developed and understood. It is, in brief, the living words of a community.

Who are we Latinos/as in the United States that contribute to these living words? According to the U.S. 2000 census, the total population is 35.3 million; this is not taking into account the undocumented workers in this country. Interestingly enough, 64 percent of this Latino population is nativeborn to the United States. Of the 35.3 million Latinos in the United States, the Mexican community is the largest group, representing 59 percent of this total Latino population. Among Central Americans, Salvadorians make up the largest group, 39 percent, followed by Guatemalans, 22 percent, and Hondurans, 13 percent. From the South American group, 35 percent were Columbian, 19 percent were Ecuadorian, and 17 percent were Peruvian. Overall, this population is young, with over one-third of its members under eighteen years in age.[10]

While these numbers reveal the growing demographic challenge of understanding and taking seriously this community, it really does not tell us who this community is. In order to truly understand this population we ask the following questions: Are the Latinos/as we are speaking of those who were born in the United States or who immigrated to the United States? If they immigrated to the United States, did they come thinking that this was the land of milk and honey providing opportunities for them and their children? Did they come to the United States as refugees or as political exiles, perhaps believing that someday they will return to their home country? If they were immigrants, did they come from the city? Or did they come from the rural area? What is their level of education? What is the socioeconomic status of these individuals and/ or families? What is their language of preference, their language of proficiency? What is their religious orientation? What is their sexual orientation? These questions put flesh on the numbers that many times lead to sterile understanding of these communities and/or stereotypical presuppositions.

The large majority of Latinos in the United States are Mexican/Mexican American. Therefore, I draw on their epistemological contributions as a way of understanding the process of Mestizaje that occurs in the United States. I use the terms *mestiza* or *U.S. Latina* interchangeably to indicate an individual who, on a daily basis, navigates between the U.S. dominant culture and a specific Latina ethnicity.

This particular Latino/a culture has evolved from a tradition that is often described as *flor y canto* (flower and song). According to this world view, the deepest recesses of being human can only be expressed in the poetry of metaphor and beauty. While it recognizes the significances of reason and logic, this particular world view takes seriously the affect, the intuitive, and the aesthetic. As a way of articulating the kinds of questions and the interior reflection of a *mestiza*, I offer a poem by Gabriella Gutiérrez y Muhs, a poetry and language professor:

Las Granadas (Pomegranates)

The chambers of my disposition
Divided by fleshly porous walls,
Blood filled portions of me.
Could I be a Buddhist Catholic?
Will the pope invest on my illegal condition of hope?
Have the Virgin of Guadalupe and Tonantzin

Merged with Ixtlacíhuatl inside my pomegranate?
Cartas a nadie
Does Santo Clos live with The Three Reyes?
Do I write to my 98 cousins I will never meet?
Is there peace in the salsa made with fire?
Can I sup at the table of the monks
That speak only Spanish?
Could the war of streets, barrios, and belongings
end with a granada or with a pomegranate?

Can an alcoholic swim herself back to the Tierra
    Santa?
Does la madre patria marry a passport
In her dreamy trench of identitad?

Is there soul food in the atrium of forgiveness?
Will the pomegranate evolve into a grapefruit?[11]

The pomegranate is a metaphor for *Latinidad,* holding in tension the feeling of isolation and the desire for unity. It is a beautiful metaphor for suffering, blood, alienation, and undiscovered potential. In Spanish, fruit is more personified than in English. Fruit has skin, bones, and heart. Food carries multilayered meanings. For example, Mexico's most popular national dish is *chiles en nogada.* The colors that make up this dish represent the blood of the heroes (red), integrity (white), and hope for the future (green). In the case of the pomegranate, this fruit has rooms, chambers, and cities. *La granada* in Spanish may either be a food delicacy or a weapon, a true antithesis. So many times Latinos are inside a granada suffering quietly, perhaps waiting for it to explode, reinventing their own systematic pains, not knowing that in other chambers of our *Latinidad* the same process has been repeated. We may isolate ourselves thinking that we are the only Chicano Muslims, or Texan Buddhists; the only ones that criticize the church for its hierarchical structure; the only ones that speak the language of our pre-Columbian ancestors. But really we all are part of the tree of *granadas* that feeds and softly kills part of us when we enter another chamber. Each of us is a *granada,* or a chamber, whatever we resolve to be. Will we ever evolve into a citrus, and see the rest of us, of our own self? Henceforth, the dialectical discussion of self-becoming allows for a dramatic expansion of subjectivity to occur through a variety of interdisciplinary lenses.

Gutiérrez y Muhs uses the term *subjectifying entities.* She uses the word *subject* as a verb, not "to subject," but "to subjectify" or "subjectifying."[12]

She contends that subjectivity is constantly being reconstituted and that this subjectivity is constructed through "representations circulated by society's major institutions of social reproduction, the family, school, church, advertising, culture, i.e., the ideological state apparatuses. These are systematically but independently organized to hail us as their subjects."[13]

U.S. Latinas' (*mestizas* in particular) self-concept is determined in relationship to others. These relationships manifest themselves in the links that are woven between them and their families, friends, co-workers, and relationships with the saints, the divine, and creation. Chicanas in particular have enjoyed a multiplicity of roles. Another Latina colleague who identifies herself as a *mestiza* describes it this way:

> Initially, for me, mestiza acknowledges my Spanish and indigenous blood. More profound is my experience as a Chicana living in the Northwest. It would be one thing to be a Chicana living in the Southwest or East Coast where there are significant Latino populations. It is a completely different experience to be a Chicana living in areas that have small populations of Latinos. The visual image that best describes my experience is the teeter-totter, where you are up in one end while the other is down. Experiencing success in one cultural group (Latino vs. mainstream) has historically meant that I have been down in the other cultural group. This experience has been physically, mentally, and emotionally draining. Balancing was an act that took me a long time to learn. I became motivated to balance my Mestizaje experience after being down on both ends of the teeter-totter for long periods of time. I concluded that there had to be a way to balance this experience. However it took me a long time to come to this conclusion because those before me had always accepted one reality over the other, never attempting to balance. Who knows, maybe they did try to balance but the experience became too emotionally draining. Throughout my experience, I have learned that it is okay to be up on one end of the teeter-totter and down on the opposite. I have also learned that is possible to balance both experiences but that doing so requires a lot of thought and emotional energy.[14]

The primary metaphor utilized in the writings of women of color for women's consciousness is that of multiplicity. Many women of color, and in particular Chicana writers, speak about developing this multiple identity at an early age, juggling a variety of social groups, serving as bridges between their traditional monolingual family context and the dominant culture. Many Latinas joke that while they see this ability as an asset, it has come at the price of being walked on by both sides. This constant crossing becomes the most ordinary thing in *mestizas'* lives. Although they cross back and forth between these multiple identities, they sometimes feel terribly unaccepted—orphaned. Some do not identify with the Anglo-American cultural values, and some do not identify with, for example, the Mexican American cultural values. Mexican Americans are a key example of the synthesis of these two cultures, with varying degrees of acculturation. The synthesis brings conflict. Latinas describe their experience with a litany of words such as *conquest, resistance, borderlands, integrity, anger, pain, economically and politically marginalized,* and *multiple identities.* The nexus of rationality in this potentially fragmented *realidad* is found in the very spirituality that explains and reinforces the cosmology of *Latinidad.*

The term *borderlands* refers to the geographical, emotional, and/or psychological space occupied by *mestizas,* and it serves as a metaphor for the condition of living between spaces, cultures, and languages. A Chicana feminist epistemology acknowledges that Chicanas and other marginalized peoples often have a strength that comes from their borderland experiences. So another part of a *mestiza* consciousness is balancing between and within the different communities.[15]

Gloria Anzaldúa captures a compelling description of what it is like to cross between cultures and epistemological perspectives: "Like corn, the *mestiza* is a product of crossbreeding, designed for preservation under a variety of conditions. Like an ear of corn–a female seed-bearing organ– the *mestiza* is tenacious, tightly wrapped in the husks of her culture. Like kernels she clings to the cob; with thick stalks and strong brace roots, she holds tight to the earth—she will survive the crossroads."[16]

INTERSECTION OF RACE, CLASS, AND GENDER

There is difference and there is power. Who holds power decides the meaning of difference. (June Jordan)

Questions revolving around belonging and acceptance, crossing and tenacity, are not the sole fragments of our intrapsychic journey and workings. These dynamics also play a significant role in the issues that women of color face in the academy. A review of the limited amount of research in this area, plus some qualitative analysis that I have conducted in discussions with women of color in a variety of different higher education institutions, report the experience of feeling isolated or out of place in their departments, colleges, and/or universities. When people ask me about my graduate-school experience, I often tell them I would rather go through another military coup than go through that experience again. What was so awful about that experience? You would think that I would be happy and that people would be proud that a Latina finally made it through to a graduate program in theology. There were so few of us in the 1980s. Instead, I walked into my graduate program feeling that perhaps I didn't belong. There was no one like me, so what was I doing here? This personal narrative by Laura I. Rendon reflects the experience of many Latinas entering higher education.

> Many of us enter higher education consumed with self doubt. We doubt our intellectual capacity; we question whether we really belong in the academy; we doubt whether our research interests are valid. This doubt is reinforced by the subtle yet powerful messages that higher education institutions communicate. Only white men can do science and math, that only the best and the brightest deserve to be educated, that white students are inherently smarter than non-whites, and that allowing people of color to enter a college diminishes its academic quality.[17]

My insecurity or lack of confidence slowly transformed into anger about several issues: my perspective and my experience were not taken seriously, Western constructs were seen as the norm for humanities thinking and reflection, and thinkers who were not part of the U.S. North American–European system were not respected. Perhaps most upsetting was the realization that they tried to make me in their image and expected gratitude for the opportunities and doors soon to open to me. My field made it more difficult because I took seriously the insights and method of liberation theology before it gained credibility. My first major work was on our Lady of Guadalupe, which at that time was seen as "soft theology" because it lived in the realm of popular religion. As Rendon puts it, "'Pure' academics who subscribe to Euro-centered rationalism and objectivity do not wish to read personal, emotional, or intuitive essays like mine. To them, these recollections are, at best, primitive and self-serving and, at worst, romanticized nonsense."[18] I am grateful for Orlando Espín, Virgilio Elizondo, María Pilar Aquino and the whole of ACHTUS (the Academy for Catholic Hispanic Theologians of the United States), whose scholarship in U.S. Hispanic theology contributes to the larger theological enterprise.

Upon graduating, a number of universities expressed interest in hiring me. The interviewing process made me realize that while I would have made a good token, fulfilling some quota for Latina representation at the university level, I really needed to find a place where my work would be taken seriously. The institution did not have to demonstrate knowledge of my work, but it needed to indicate an authentic interest in the experience of Latinos/as. It also had to be open to the contribution U.S. Hispanic theologians would make to the theological enterprise. I found this at Seattle University.

The good news was that I found a place that I believed was authentic, that was open to the "other," willing to enter into dialogue and exchange with a person and an area with which they were not familiar, and to recognize their significance. The bad news was that I was the only Latina in the College of Arts and Sciences. As one of three women of color in the entire university (this was in the early 1990s), I learned quickly the importance of forming alliances, and developing not only interdisciplinary but intercultural dialogue, specifically with women of color on the faculty.

My experience demonstrates the reality of other U.S. Latinas. We are often the only ones in our neighborhood, our school, our profession. The struggle to maintain our identity, let alone our language, is significant. For this reason the following section reflects on race, class, and gender in the academy drawing from the experiences of a variety of women of color, not specifically Latinas.

This essay began with a narrative that exposed the identity litmus test. In my discussions with women of color in the academy, this test surfaces as a concern for authenticity. For one woman of color, authenticity has become quite a discussion in her field (South Asian Studies):

> The criticism is if you write in English you're not authentic, you can't write about India, especially because you don't live in India, especially because authenticity is so strongly connected to location. When people make that assumption, I have trouble with it because there is something called authenticity and I don't know what authenticity is, because traditions change. What is authentic to me is different from another part of India. The way we experience life, my religion, my class, ethnicity, my language are very subjective in India. I cannot translate that as this sort of norm for everybody else. But in this discussion of authenticity, what is being highlighted is the idea that I don't think there is something essential about authenticity.[19]

Similarly, in a questionnaire given to women of color in the discipline of geography, the study reported that women of color faculty members experienced a challenge to their legitimacy as professional scholars. This challenge was initiated by other faculty members: "Several tenured interviewees explained that people assume they were only appointed or awarded tenure because of their minority status, or through affirmative action policies, rather than for the quality of their scholarship or their teaching abilities. The perception among interviewees is that they are then expected to take on extra committee work to make up for these supposed 'deficiencies.'"[20]

Women continue to enter one the most guarded institutions in the nation—higher education. As tenured professors, women of color faculty members rank the lowest in numbers: only 38 percent of Latinas are tenured, 41 percent of Asians, 41 percent of Native Americans, 46 percent of African Americans. These numbers compare to 47 percent for Anglo-European females and 68 percent for Anglo-European males.[21] Scholars Anna M. Agathangelou and L. H. M. Ling analyzed tenure as a narrative of institutional power, "This narrative integrates and rationalizes racism, sexism, and classism in order to screen out persons who do not fit the academy's designation of who and what the faculty of color should be."[22] These authors identify and articulate the tremendous challenge of the tenure process. In addition to this challenge, the authors further report that there are additional scripts or roles assigned to women faculty of color:

> For example, African-American women risk being seen as the ghetto "hussy"; Latinas, the uncontrollable, barrio "spitfire"; Asians, the red-taloned, red-light district "dragon lady." Ironically, these stereotypes heighten their sexualization since women of color are not allowed, like Anglo-European women, to "pass" for men. Neither can women of color rely on a strategy of feminization: e.g., African-American women become the "slave" or "mammy"; Latinas, the "slut"; Asian, the "lotus blossom baby."[23]

The tenure process further aggravates women's marginalization through the pre-scripted roles and racist presumptions inherent in the tenure process. At most universities a non-tenured faculty person is evaluated in three categories: research, teaching, and service. The number of one's publications in refereed journals, or full manuscripts, defines research. Co-authorship and therefore collaborative and interdisciplinary work, is frowned upon as a sign of intellectual inefficiency. There is a hierarchy of preference in terms of publications with university press and scholarly books being at the top and book chapters, poems, and reports at the bottom. Teaching is assessed primarily through student and peer evaluations, and service covers everything else in which the candidate is involved in terms of the academy: student advising, mentoring, committee work, service learning, and community involvement. These three categories—research, teaching, and service—are evaluated by institutional decision-makers on at least three levels—the department, the college, and the university. Tenure processes ignore the subtle episodes of gender discrimination. Recent studies include such categories as "'inequitable distribution of resources' (rank and wage disparities, hiring and firing inequities), 'work-family burdens' (child care, maternity/paternity leave), 'hostile work environment' or 'chilly climate' (sexual harassment, heterosexism, preferences for male students or 'masculine' traits). . . . Recent studies on gender equity in international relations affirm the importance and salience of these issues for this subfield."[24]

Anna M. Agathangelou and L. M. H. Ling move us to deeper insight and a more profound source of gender discrimination, which is the intersection of race and class. "Nowhere in MIT's (1999) supposedly path-breaking study of discrimination, for example, does it consider the issue of race—not to mention the triple impact of race, gender and class on a woman's faculty career."[25]

My own informal discussions with faculty members from other institutions support the findings above. Women of color faculty members experience the academy as marginalizing them into a domestic, underclass, outsider status. When a woman of color refuses to play the role of domestic outsider, the academy's gatekeepers are outraged. This fuels the indignation of women of color, whose perception is that they work twice as hard to be seen as equals to their Euro-American counterparts. How can women of color succeed in such an environment? In conventional, social-science language, this discussion raises a hypothesis that is difficult to test. Though anecdotes abound, few are documentable, given the rule of confidentiality that binds tenure cases. Risk of litigation prohibits any party from divulging the materials/rationales involved, and injured parties rarely litigate for lack of funds and/or fear of institutional retribution. Accordingly, the academy escapes accountability because discrimination is so easily hidden. It places under arbitrary closure the very terms and processes that the academy claims to be "rational" and "fair." It is not enough to allow women of color access to institutions of higher education. Institutions themselves must change. What women of color bring to this much-needed transformation is an interdisciplinary perspective, an ability to struggle in the intersections of race, class, and gender, and they bring an openness with facilitation skills for dialogue.

TOWARD SOLIDARITY

To cross the boundaries of one's culture without realizing that the other may have a radically different approach to reality is today no longer admissible. If still consciously done, it would be philosophically naïve, politically outrageous and religiously sinful. (Raimon Panikkar)

The challenge to understand reality and God's activity in that reality is necessarily an intercultural activity. Theological hermeneutics offers a key. Hermeneutics, historically the science of interpretating sacred texts, may apply to interpreting persons and cultures. Hermeneutics asks, What do I know, when I know another reality outside myself? According to religious scholar Raimon Panikkar, Western hermeneutical philosophy has leaned toward a monocultural understanding when some degree of pre-understanding can be presumed. However, he argues, in interreligious or intercultural contexts, such pre-understanding may give rise to the hermeneutical circle that may not exist. Panikkar asks, "How can we understand something that does not belong to our circle," and in response to this question offers us the tool of diatopical hermeneutics. Diatopical hermeneutics is "literally, the art of coming to understand (across places) our traditions which do not share common patterns of understanding and intelligibility. . . . Diatopical hermeneutics arises in response to the challenge of interpreting across cultural and religious boundaries where the hermeneutical circle has yet to be created."[26]

This postmodern hermeneutics refuses to colonize the "other." The narratives I offered in the first section of this chapter and the intersection of race, class, and gender that emerged in the example of the academy prepare us for this challenging and indispensable tool for our theological scholarship. Panikkar introduces what he calls the imperative method. This is "learning from the other and the attitude of allowing our own convictions to be fecundated by the insights of the other. As distinct from the comparative method, which privileges dialectics and argumentative discourse, the imperative method of diatopical hermeneutics focuses on the praxis of dialogue in the existential encounter." Panikkar is explicit on this point: "It is only in doing, the praxis, that diatopical hermeneutics function."[27]

Panikkar further introduces dialogical dialogue, which begins with the assumption that the "other," whoever the other might be, can be a source of human understanding and that "at some level persons who enter the dialogue have a capacity to communicate their unique experiences to reach others."[28] These tools of diatopical hermeneutics and dialogical dialogue are necessary so that the participants might establish common ground or a circle of meaning; the ground of understanding needs to be created in the space between the traditions or the cultures through praxis of dialogue.[29] This hermeneutical instrument is vital for our future work. "Dialogue seeks truth by trusting the other, just as dialectics pursues truth by trusting the order of things, the values of reason and weighty arguments."[30] Foundational for this dialogical dialogue is honesty, openness and a willingness to forego prejudice in the search for truth while maintaining profound loyalty towards one's own tradition."[31] An example of this method and tool in practice would be the work done by U.S. Latina theologians, as well as activists committed to social justice and social transformation.

In the process of interdisciplinary and collaborative endeavors we find that there are points of intersection and common cause/interest. In 1982, Gloria Anzaldúa edited a book titled *This Bridge Called My Back,* which captured the challenges facing women of color. It articulated the experiences of women of color utilizing the bridge metaphor. Julia Sudbury explains the development of the metaphor:

> The bridge metaphor captured the challenges facing women of color as they negotiated the radical social movements of the 1970s and 1980s in the United States. Expected to act in feminist spaces (as if gender were the primary oppression structuring their lives) in radical movements of color (as if the struggle against white supremacy were the only meaningful engagement) and in leftist organization (as if gender and race were distractions to the fight against capital), women of color struggled to generate a politics that could honor the complex intersections of race, class, and gender in their lives. Working with white women to challenge violence against women, and with men of color to defend their communities against police brutality and institutional racism, women of color frequently found themselves acting as the bridge between a multiplicity of social movements. Yet this role, while critically important as a basis for coalition-building, was also draining.[32]

Twenty years later Anzaldúa, in conjunction with Analouise Keating, continues to expand on this bridging concept in another anthology titled *This Bridge We Call Home: Radical Visions for Transformation.* In this work the writers raise the questions of institutional authority and continuing race, sex, and class inequality as well as the "politics and effects of globalization in its relation to histories of colonization and de-colonization."[33]

We know that the Latino/a community, and communities of color in general, are the most vulnerable in the United States. Every indicator of poverty, crime, unemployment, education, and health issues confirms this. The powers-that-be want us to accept this and to believe that the world is impoverished, never to be changed.[34]

We need to understand who we are, what kind of community we want, what kind of world we want, and what we need to build it. What are our resources? Our resources are the strength of our communities. The wisdom and courage of the lived experience provide us with perspectives that enable us to discern the underlying meaning of choices we make and need to make. As theologians, we promote choices for life that bring forward communities that have been marginalized, voiceless, and not allowed at the table. I do not pretend to speak as an expert in political matters, but, as a theologian, I believe that our actions can be guided by the Spirit, who wants us to live in light more than in darkness.

I began this essay by calling upon my experience with Latin American feminist theologians in Mexico City. It was obvious to me that all of us yearn for peace and justice in the world. Many of us have seen, with our own eyes, the cost of human greed and social conflict. These experiences have led us to work for the basic right of every person to a life of dignity. Building bridges has been made difficult by the cultural baggage we carry and the manner in which the dominant culture has structured our roles.

This bridge work is necessary because countless communities of our brothers and sisters across the globe are being assaulted. Our role is to remember our own journeys as well as build bridges of solidarity to those communities whose members are tortured, marginalized, and whose sons and daughters are at grave risk. Our collective wisdom will build bridges to those communities in which mutilated cadavers appear in cemeteries, where those who struggle for justice and peace are assassinated.

The mothers and fathers of these missing sons and daughters transformed these monstrosities as they formed groups to pray for peace, advocate for reconciliations, witness to the power of solidarity, and plead to the world for peace and justice. Intercultural dialogue and interreligious activity are essential to move this process forward. Intercultural dialogue and interreligious activity provide opportunities to create places where people can flourish and live in peace with one another. Intercultural dialogue and activity create communities of reciprocal care and shared responsibilities. A hallmark of Latino communities then becomes a rich pattern of life in the world we now inhabit, where every person matters and each person's welfare and dignity is respected and supported.

The prophets and the teachings of Jesus constantly remind us of a new vision and hope for humanity. Grounded in a covenant relationship with God, these texts remind us that we are one people, God's people. The covenant they reveal asks us to make a preferential option for the poor, to do justice, and to choose life. This is the prophetic vision of our faith.

The prophets were called from the people, yet stood apart from the people in that they challenged those sinful structures in which human life and dignity were not fully embraced. They were men and women whose lives were intimately intertwined with God, and who wholeheartedly embraced, believed, and were faithful to this covenant. The work of the Latino community is to make visible the power of the community within the world in the twenty-first century. The prophets were persons of prayer, faith, courage, and patience. We look at our ancestors, at members in our own academy, at activists, and learn that they have been people of prayer. Sustained by prayer, they came to know the immensity of God's love and the depths of God's mercy. It is this faith tradition, of which we are a part, in which blood has been spilled, in which children have been killed, that calls to task the structures of authority that condemn the poorest of the poor.

As outlined in all three sections of this chapter, it is clear we have the tools. We need moral courage. In the words of Archbishop Oscar Romero, "We believe in Jesus, who came to bring the fullness of life, and we believe in a living God who gives life to humans and wants them truly to live."[35] The church thus faces the fundamental option of faith: to be in favor of life or of death. "With great clarity we see that in this no neutrality is possible. Either we serve the life of Salvadorans or we are accomplices in their death. It is the expression in history of what is most fundamental in the faith: either we believe in a God of life, or we serve the idols of death."[36] This conviction ultimately challenges people of faith to choose life, even to give of one's life. Our faith, culture, intellectual, and activist communities have prepared us for this challenge. Creating cultures of conversations may provide the means to cross these bridges over chasms of separatism and instead foster understanding and solidarity for the common good.

Notes

[1] Gloria Anzaldúa and Analouise Keating, eds., *This Bridge We Call Home: Radical Visions for Transformation* (New York: Routledge, 2002), 1.

[2] Parts of the first section were initially included in the article "Mestiza Spirituality: Community, Ritual and Justice," *Theological Studies* 65 (2004): 317–39.

[3] *Spic* is a derogatory term that was used during that time period to refer to Latinos.

[4] Jeanette Rodríguez, *Stories We Live Cuentos Que Vivimos: Hispanic Women's Spirituality* (New York: Paulist Press, 1996), 29–30.

[5] Gloria Anzaldúa, *Borderlands: The New Mestiza* (San Francisco: Aunt Lute, 1987), 79–91.

[6] Anzaldúa, *Borderlands*, 78–79.

[7] Chela Sandoval, "Mestizaje as Method: Feminists of Color Challenge the Canon," in *Living Chicana Theory*, ed. Carla Trujillo (Berkeley, CA: Third Women's Press, 1998), 359.

[8] Anzaldúa, *Borderlands*, 38.

[9] Maria Lugones, "Playfulness, 'World'-Traveling, and Loving Perception," *Hypatia* 2, no. 2 (Summer 1987): 3–19.

[10] U.S. Department of Commerce, *We the People: Hispanics in the U.S.*, U.S. Census Bureau, Census 2000 Special Reports, U.S. Department of Commerce, 3.

[11] Gabriella Gutiérrez y Muhs, unpublished (2002).

[12] Gabriella Gutiérrez y Muhs, *Subjectifying Entities/Emerging Subjectivities in Chicana Literature* (Ph.D. dissertation, Stanford University, 2000).

[13] Gutiérrez y Muhs, quoting Griselda Pollack, *Vision and Difference: Femininity, Feminism and the Histories of Art* (New York: Routledge, 2000).

[14] Interview with "Marina," November 2000.

[15] Dolores Delgado Bernal, "Learning and Living Pedagogies of the Home: The Mestiza Consciousness of Chicana Students," *Qualitative Studies in Education* 14, no. 5 (2001): 632.

[16] Anzaldúa, *Borderlands*, 78–81.

[17] Laura I. Rendon, "From the Barrio to the Academy: Revelations of a Mexican American 'Scholarship Girl,'" *New Directions for Community Colleges* 80 (Winter 1992): 61.

[18] Ibid., 59.

[19] Personal interview with Dr. Nalini Iyer, director of the Center for the Study of Justice in Society and Wismer Professor of Diversity, Citizenship and Social Justice, Seattle University, Fall 2004.

[20] Mineelle Mahtani, "Mapping Race and Gender in the Academy: The Experiences of Women of Colour Faculty and Graduate Students in Britain, the U.S. and Canada," *Journal of Geography in Higher Education* 28, no. 1 (March 2004): 91–99.

[21] Alison Schneider, "Proportion of Minority Professors Up to about 10%," *The Chronicle of Higher Education* (June 20, 1997): A12.

[22] Anna M. Agathangelou and L. H. M. Ling, "An Unten(ur)able Positon: The Politics of Teaching for Women of Color." Paper presented at the Wismer Center Lecture Series, March 2003, Seattle University, Washington, 2.

[23] Ibid., 8.

[24] Ibid., 4.

[25] Ibid., 4–5.

[26] Raimon Panikkar, quoted in Gerald Hall, *Intercultural and Interreligious Hermeneutics: Raimon Panikkar*, 2, available from http://dlibrary.acu.edu.au/research/theology/ghall_panikkar.htm; Internet (accessed March 10, 2007).

[27] Ibid., 3.

[28] Ibid., 6.

[29] Ibid.

[30] Raimon Panikkar, *Myth, Faith, and Hermenutics* (New York: Paulist Press, 1979), 243.

[31] Raimon Panikkar, *The Unknown Christ of Hinduism*, 2nd. rev. ed. (Maryknoll, NY: Orbis Books, 1981), 35.

[32] Julia Sudbury, "Toward a Holistic Anti-Violence Agenda: Women of Color as Radical Bridge-Builders," *Social Justice* 30, no. 3 (2003): 134

[33] For a review of *This Bridge We Call Home*, see Heather Love, "The Second Time Around," *Women's Review of Books* 20, no. 4 (January 2003): 2.

[34] See United States Census Bureau Facts for Hispanic Heritage Month, 2, available from http://www.census.gov/Press-Release//fs97-10.html; Internet (accessed January 23, 2005).

[35] Archbishop Oscar Romero, *Voice of the Voiceless: The Four Pastoral Letters and Other Statements*, trans. Michael J. Walsh (Maryknoll, NY: Orbis Books, 1985), 184–85.

[36] Ibid., 185.

5

Voices from *Nepantla*

Latinas in U.S. Religious History

Daisy L. Machado

In the September 1993 issue of the journal *Church History*, published by the American Society of Church History, Martin E. Marty wrote an article entitled "American Religious History in the Eighties: A Decade of Achievement."[1] It was an extensive article, or rather a detailed bibliography, in which Marty looked at works written by historians of American (meaning U.S.) religion that were published from 1980 to 1989. Working with a variety of journals up to 1992, Marty presented in his article a survey of what books became what he called "part of the public record" in the area of the history of Euro-American religion. Marty's survey was divided into twelve general topic areas, the fifth of which was called "Minorities." In this topic area the last paragraph was on Hispanic Americans and in a short seven sentences we were told: "Sadly deficient was the attention paid to the largest non-English speaking group in America, Hispanics. . . . Anyone looking for a dissertation-book area, or who would like to make contributions to a neglected force in the American mix, should explore Hispanic topics."[2] While the invitation Marty made to church historians well over a decade ago seemed one of great promise, the fact that the religious academy in general and the church historians in particular had for so long overlooked the story of Latinos in U.S. religious life seems more than a sad deficit. We must ask: How can the five centuries that Latinos have been a part of Christianity in North America still be considered so unimportant? However, in order to pose a more accurate set of questions one needs to look at the religious academy and at the field of church history in the United States itself. This then leads one to ask: How can church historians pretend to write the religious history of a nation if they continue to ignore the participation of an entire group that has been present in the nation since its founding? What does this say about how history is used to tell a "national" story that is really about exclusion and not inclusion?

Few would deny that history is a powerful tool used to scrutinize and interpret. In the telling of history both events and people are critically examined in their particular space and time. Yet history can also serve to provide the type of historical "evidence" that serves to undergird the political, economic, racial, social, and religious agendas of institutions. If an entire population group has no historical voice, and if that group seems to have occupied no significant historical space, then it is very easy to relegate that group to the margins of a national and religious epic. It is this very marginalization that can then facilitate the claim to hegemony and the appeal to the ideals of inclusivity, diversity, equality, and justice of that nation. Because there is no written mainstream record to threaten the national epic, whether religious or political, there is also no dissenting historical memory to say it was and is not so. In this manner the non-writing of a people's history finally becomes an act that ultimately promotes invisibility.

Almost fifteen years have passed since the publication of Marty's survey article, and we can say that the historical production about and by Latinos/as has increased, albeit in small numbers and with the caveat that the majority of publications have focused on general or secular histories. Some of the welcomed additions to the "public record" Marty talks about include three important books: Emma Pérez's *The Decolonial Imaginary: Writing Chicanas into History* (1999), Vicki L. Ruíz's *From out of the Shadows: Mexican Women in Twentieth-century America* (1998), and *Las Tejanas: 300 Years of History* (2003) by Teresa Palomo Acosta and Ruthie Winegarten.[3] Notice that all three books were published only in the last few years, and none is about the religious history of Latinas; so while these books represent gains in the historiography of Latinas, the undeniable reality is that there is much more work to be done. And this is especially true for the religious historiography of Latinas.

In the Latino/a community in the United States women have played a major role in the transmission of the faith. Through the decades, whether Roman Catholic or Protestant, women have been the faithful transmitters of religious belief and practice; they have kept alive the traditions of their faith. Whether it was maintaining home altars or actively participating in the *sociedades guadalupanas,* Roman Catholic Latinas have contributed to the spiritual life of their families and communities. For Latina Protestants it was their work as non-ordained *misioneras* in the early to mid-1900s that made it possible for Protestantism to be carried into the Spanish-speaking Caribbean. Some of these Latina evangelists, following the migratory patterns of their communities, came to the large urban centers of the United States and became revival preachers in places like New York.

However, the existing historical writings give little evidence of the many roles Latinas have conscientiously played in the spiritual life of their communities and churches. There are, I believe, many issues that have contributed to this void in the historical writings about Latina religious life. First, there is the very basic problem of lack of primary source materials, which cannot be discounted. Many denominations and parishes have not kept records about their work among Latinos, and so materials are not available. In many cases source materials about Latino churches and church leaders, especially women, have been gathered in a variety of places and not been catalogued, so historians are not even aware of what is available to them. However, I believe that even more influential in creating this historical silence are the attitudes toward and interpretations made about Latinos/as since the early 1800s when the first encounters between Euro-American settlers and Mexicans took place in the southwest territory known today as Texas. These attitudes and interpretations make up what can be identified as a *historical imagination* that has influenced and continues to influence what is written and not written about the Latino communities in the United States. That is why, in answer to the Euro-Americans who have told me that what we need is more Latino/a historians to tell "our stories," I say that a community must first be acknowledged or become visible before its story can be told.

U.S. RELIGIOUS HISTORY AND *NEPANTLA*

The widely known novelist Carlos Fuentes is reputed to have said, "The United States has no history; it only has the movies." To this Arturo Madrid, a professor of humanities at Trinity University, has replied, "My statement would be that the United States has no history, rather it has images and stories that have dissembled a history. These images and their accompanying stories predate the movies. Notwithstanding the continuing struggle to eliminate them from U.S. culture, they continue to be present in the consciousness of the citizenry of the United States, and to manifest themselves in their outrageous forms and in more subtle but no less nefarious ways."[4]

As a historian of Christianity, I know very well what both Fuentes and Madrid are trying to say. Their focus is not that there is really no

history, but that history in the United States, the national historical epic
that is at the heart of U.S. self identity, is not so much about fact but
about what is being called a historical imaginary (historical imagination). And this imaginary, for Fuentes, can be found on the screen of
movie theaters; for Madrid, it can be found in the many images and
stories that are embedded in the national consciousness. Stories about
those Madrid calls "aliens, misfits and interlopers." It seems as if we,
the Latinos/as in the United States, embody a series of contradictions
that evoke from those in the mainstream of this culture surprise, anger,
acceptance, rejection, celebration, disapproval.

I want to use the words of Otto Santa Ana from his book *Brown Tide
Rising: Metaphors of Latinos in Contemporary American Public Discourse* to paint one picture that shows how Latinos/as have been historically imagined in the United States.

> The Mexican Sleeping Giant never woke up. It died in its sleep in
> the summer of 1993 [with California's Proposition 187]. At this
> time, the image of the Mexican and other Latinos maintained by
> the public in California and the rest of the United States changed,
> seemingly almost overnight. For fifty years, the Sleeping Giant im-
> age sustained the general view that Mexican posed no threat to the
> Anglo-American hegemony in the United States. . . . For the U.S.
> public, no matter how large the Mexican Sleeping Giant was, it
> simply could not menace the Anglo-American way of life any more
> than could the Jolly Green Giant. Anglo-America has a history of
> dismissing the Population as inconsequential. Although by the late
> 1990s Latinos would be the largest minority group in the United
> States, the U.S. public still tended to see Latinos as the silent ser-
> vants who made its beds or bussed its tables, the humble gardeners
> who pruned overgrown shrubs in the backyard, and those uniformed
> parking attendants who rushed to open the car door. These brown
> people were expected to perform their menial roles quietly, effi-
> ciently, and without dissent. While white Americans came into con-
> tact with lowly Latino service workers, or quite anglicized Mexi-
> can Americans, the preponderance of the Latino population was
> invisible. In California and elsewhere in rural areas they worked in
> the fields out of sight. In urban areas, they had been redlined into
> residential isolation. The greater part of their children attended
> segregated public schools. And their brown faces never appeared
> in national news or entertainment media, except in safely circum-
> scribed ways.[5]

What Santa Ana is focusing on when he talks about the uses of metaphors for Latinos/as in U.S. public discourse is directly related to what I, as a historian, call the historical imagination. By historical imagination I am talking about how those in the dominant group of a nation who have the power to tell its history perceive the "other." This is done not only through metaphor, as Santa Ana clearly shows in his book, but also through national myths, through a national memory that creates a blameless and noble history of that nation. Creating dichotomies that describe people and their relations of power such as winner/loser, civilized/savage, insider/outsider, religious/superstitious, hardworking/siesta lover, educated/backward, clean/greaser, and so forth also does it. Chicana historian Emma Pérez says this about the critical/reflective/interpretative process of historiography: "If history is the way in which people understand themselves through a collective, common past where events are chronicled and heroes are constructed, then historical consciousness is the system of thought that leads to a normative understanding of past events. Historical knowledge is the production of normative history through discursive practices."[6]

This is very important to remember when we think about the Latino community. I say this because there is ample evidence that in this country this national historical imagination has been at work since 1823, when the first Anglo-American colonizers crossed into Mexican territory; it was at work during the war that led to the creation of the Republic of Texas in 1836; it was manifested in the political maneuvering that led to the Mexican American War in 1848; it was alive and well during the Great Depression, when thousands of Mexican Americans who were U.S. citizens were unjustly deported to Mexico; it was evident in the mid-1950s when the Immigration and Naturalization Service conducted the shameful Operation Wetback that lasted into the 1960s, deporting about 600,000 Mexicans, the majority born in the United States; and continued into the 1990s, when agribusiness obstructed the farmworkers' peaceful struggle for a just wage and humane working conditions. It is also present with ballot initiatives like Propositions 187 and 209 that opened the doors for public expressions of anti-Latino sentiments.

What is ironic about all this is the unrelenting fact that a demographic "browning" of this country is taking place. The numbers don't lie. Statistics tell us that the Latino population will grow from its present figure of more than thirty million (legally documented) to what demographers estimate will be approximately thirty-six million in 2010 and to forty-six million in 2025 or almost 25 percent of the total U.S. population.[7] And despite what the media may want to portray about what this browning of the United States means, I can clearly state that there is more depth and complexity to this process than "yo quiero Taco Bell" and Cinco de Mayo. Yet, despite this browning that is taking place, Arturo Madrid, writing about race and the Latino community, says that we are still in a particular place in the national consciousness:

> The U.S. communities labeled Latino are a diverse set of populations whose roots grow deep in the soil of the United States. Their members, however, have not, either as individuals or as a collectivity, ever been considered part of the "imagined community" of this nation. We have been consistently defined out. . . . That is the subtext of the question all Latinos are asked: And where are you from? We are not perceived as being "from here." Rather, we have been considered to be a "foreign other," regardless of our individual or collective histories. Moreover, our imagined "otherness" is shaped by deep-rooted images and stories concerning our ancestors and ancestry. . . . We have been imagined and we have been found wanting.[8]

Fernando F. Segovia, New Testament scholar at Vanderbilt University, has described the reality of Latino life in the United States as being "the eternal Other." The Latino community in North America is both citizen and foreigner; it has been conquered and colonized. The Latino community in the United States is an imagined community, and by this I mean a community that has been created or imagined by those outside our community. Let me give you another example. The term *Hispanic* as a racial category was developed in the 1970s for purposes of the census. It is a political creation, a way to describe difference in race and culture. Prior to the invention of the term *Hispanic*, all persons living in the United States who came from a Spanish-language culture were categorized as Caucasian. But now all this has changed, and as a result of the creation of this new category by the federal government the only place in the world where Hispanics exist is in the United States. This is how Richard Rodríguez describes the creation of the term *Hispanic*:

> "Hispanic" is not a racial or a cultural or a geographic or a linguistic or an economic description. "Hispanic" is a bureaucratic integer—a complete political fiction. How much does the Central American refugee have in common with the Mexican from Tijuana? What does the black Puerto Rican in New York have in common with the white Cuban in Miami? . . . Think of earlier immigrants to this country. Think of the Jewish immigrants or the Italians. . . . Ger-

man Jews distinguished themselves from Russian Jews. The Venetian was adamant about not being taken for a Neapolitan. But to America, what did such claims matter? . . . A Jew was a Jew. And now America shrugs again. Palm trees or cactus, it's all the same. Hispanics are all the same.[9]

The Latino history is in many ways similar to the story of all immigrants, but it is also different in very particular ways. In reality, Latinos/as never stopped being "foreign" to the Euro-American citizens of this nation. That is why to talk about race in this nation must mean to talk about more than just the black-and-white racial dichotomy. For Latinos/as to talk about race is to talk about nationhood, to talk about being imagined by the dominant culture as foreigner/stranger, and to discover that we have been left on the margins as "other." This is how sociologist Suzanne Oboler explains it:

> The struggle for Mexican-Americans and Puerto Ricans for civil rights and equality before the law has necessarily taken a different form from that of the African-Americans, precisely because, at least since the Civil War period, the exclusion of blacks has not been couched in distortion stemming from xenophobic portrayals of them as foreign born. Indeed, the experiences of Mexican-Americans and Puerto Ricans in the United States (legally fellow citizens since 1848 and 1917 respectively) exemplify the ways xenophobic nationalism and domestic racism have been conflated since the early nineteenth century.[10]

As a result, the Latino/a has been historically imagined as "other," foreigner, non-native, which have ultimately been ways of excluding. To help you better understand the power of being imagined as non-native, even if that Latino/a was born in the continental United States, let me share with you a court case that dates back to 1896. Rodríguez, despite the guarantees of the Treaty of Guadalupe-Hidalgo, was denied his final naturalization papers. Rodríguez went to court. "In making their case against Rodríguez 'the authorities argued in court that Rodríguez was not white nor African' and 'therefore not capable of becoming an American citizen.' Noting that they wanted to keep 'Aztecs or aboriginal Mexicans' from naturalization."[11] Here we have a clear example of how the national imagination played out in the court system supported the exclusion of Mexicans who not only lived on U.S. soil before the war with Mexico, but also were guaranteed the right to citizenship by the Treaty of Guadalupe-Hidalgo. Here we see how domestic exclusion was based on the racial understandings of the black/white dichotomy, which is still seen as *the* legitimate racial categories for the nation. This national understanding of race has continued to reinforce the idea of nationhood and nationality that has rendered "Mexican-Americans invisible both as citizens and as native-born members of the nation."[12]

And so we are outsiders, the "eternal Other," the native-born foreigner. This is what I call life in *Nepantla*. In the indigenous Mexican Nahuatl, *Nepantla* means "land in the middle." What does it mean to feel as though you never belong? What does it mean that you are always seen as the interloper who has come to take advantage of the wealth and the largesse of those who hold power? What does it mean to have as your first language a language that is deemed inferior, so that your bilingualism is not valued? However, what is ironic in the debate over Spanish is the fact that in this country "Spanish has been spoken for more years than any other European language . . . and counts more native speakers than ever before. Yet with insistent reinforcement, the conventional script designates Spanish as a foreign language and its native speakers as aliens."[13]

Therefore, as we consider the historical task before us, the principal goal of the Latina (or any racial-ethnic) historian is to make Latinas (and racial-ethnic people) more than historical objects. It is not enough to include women or Latinos or Asians or African Americans in the history being written. The more difficult but significant task for the Latina historian is what J. Derrida has called "deconstruction," which "makes it possible to study systematically (though never definitively or totally) the conflictual processes that produce meanings."[14] Chicana historians Emma Pérez and A. Castañeda take Derrida's process of deconstruction even further. Pérez, Castañeda, and other Chicana historians are developing their own voice and methodologies. They are not only concerned with the production of historical knowledge and the issue of gender, but they are also interested in the issues of race and class as these are constructed or omitted in the historical narrative. Like Euro-American feminist historians, Chicana historians also believe that the creation of knowledge is a political process that centers on the issue of power, and they use Foucault's idea of a "third space."

Foucault's idea that history can have gaps is very important to the work of Latina and other racial-ethnic historians. These gaps are of importance because they represent the places where the "unspoken and unseen" unfold.[15] Foucault's gaps or third space between power and knowledge is understood by Latina historians as important because it is filled with movement, alive, a place where life is negotiated by those who live on the margins. It should not be dismissed or ignored. For

Pérez, it is in this third space that one can uncover the "hidden voices of Chicanas that have been relegated to silences, to passivity."[16] It is also where one can uncover the process of colonization of the entire Chicano community. What Latina historians share with all racial-ethnic historians is the desire to rethink the dominant history in a way that will give them historical agency, which is ultimately transformative.

Pérez advocates for a critical self-reflection (or archeology of knowledge) that will challenge "from within but against the grain"[17] and that will help to undo the nature of present-day Chicano historiography, which, she believes, has failed to challenge the accepted systems of thought that are replete with colonial relations. Pérez also believes that the transformative history of Chicanas can be found especially in that border space between colonialism and postcolonialism. This is the space she calls the "decolonial imaginary." Like all border regions, Pérez also finds that this in-between place, this third space, is one of "fragmented identities, fragmented realities . . . [that are] partially seen yet unspoken, vibrant and in motion."[18] One senses that for Pérez this third space is a place of possibilities where the uncovered can be discovered, where the suppressed can be claimed, and where the devalued can be celebrated. I understand that the historical narrative can be a powerful and subversive tool because it can be used as the means to give voice to those whose biographies have been traditionally ignored and left out of the bigger national or political or denominational narrative because of race, ethnicity, class, or gender.

Given the realities of our communities, we Latinos/as are daily border crossers who must learn early to interpret life on both sides—life in the dominant culture and life in the Latino community. This is how we learn to survive and how we are able to be who we really are. We have historically lived in this nation's third space, in the paradox of belonging yet not really belonging, this space where the history of Latinos begins to be understood, not just nationally but also within the denominational histories of Protestants and Roman Catholics. This is also where we need to begin our analysis of what this paradox implies for the writing of religious history in the twenty-first-century United States. To write history from the reality of Latinos/as is first to acknowledge the vibrancy of life in the margins of the dominant culture where Latinos/as have been placed in the national historical narrative, that place I call *Nepantla*. The next step is to create a historical space within the accepted, normative religious national history for the many voices from *Nepantla*. To write the religious history of Latinas is to tell the story of those many remarkable women who have celebrated their faith, who have practiced their faith, who have been sustained by their faith from that social location known as *Nepantla*. It is to tell their story not as objects but as the subjects of the historical realities that surrounded and shaped their lives—despite the obstacles placed before them by denominations and the religious hierarchy. This history is about those women who have found in their faith the hope and strength to struggle for justice, for dignity, and for the right to participate in the creation of a better future for themselves and their communities. To tell the religious history of these Latinas is talk about women of faith who found in God the acceptance and empowerment that both society and denominations often denied them. To tell their stories is to enter into that third space and to examine carefully their stories against the backdrop of a historical imagination that defined these women as outsiders, foreigners, never full participants because of their nationality, race, gender, and language.

VOICES FROM *NEPANTLA:* TELLING THE STORIES OF LATINAS

I want to use this section to tell briefly the faith stories of a handful of Latinas. I also examine those expressions of faith within the context of race, gender, and language as understood and defined by the dominant historical imagination. I look into that third space where Latinas have lived and continue to live as invisible and marginal members of denominational bodies. Because of the wealth of practices and expressions of faith found in the religious life of Latinas in the United States, this section can be only a brief overview. However, it represents an effort that despite its brevity is an attempt to begin to tell the stories of the faith of Latinas and in doing so creates a space for the many voices from *Nepantla*.

The Roman Catholic Experience

The majority of Mexican Americans are Roman Catholic, with a vibrant devotion to Nuestra Señora de Guadalupe. This is a brief retelling of what happened on the hill of Tepeyac outside of Mexico City.

The foundation legend tells of a Nahua commoner named Juan Diego, recently converted to Christianity, to whom the Virgin Mary appeared on four occasions in December, 1531. [When the bishop, the Franciscan Juan de Zumárraga] dismissed [Juan Diego's] story, the Virgin told Juan Diego to pick the flowers that bloomed on the hillside and take them to the bishop. He gathered them into his cloak, and when he shook it out before the bishop, the Virgin's image was miraculously imprinted on the rough fabric. . . . [Many] native people embraced Christianity in the wake of these apparitions . . . [and popular tradition asserts that] Our Lady of Guadalupe is some sort of amalgam of Aztec mother goddess and Christian saint. To many, *la virgen morena* "the dark Virgin" is more indigenous than European.[19]

Through the centuries the Mexican people's popular devotion has continued to shape Our Lady of Guadalupe so that she has become the symbol of the mother of all Mexicans, the protector of her children-nation, the figure around which an entire people have learned to gather no matter what their geographical location. It was the figure of Nuestra Señora de Guadalupe that was raised in a flag by Father Miguel Hidalgo when he launched his movement for independence from Spain's colonial rule known as the Grito de Dolores in 1810. By using the image of *la virgen morena* as a rallying cry for independence from Spain, the Virgin was moved to a new position as political icon. Nuestra Señora de Guadalupe was now the representative not only of political freedom and self-determination of Mexicans, but also of the religious soul of the Mexican people that was their strength.

The popular religiosity of the Mexican people has continued to give shape to Our Lady of Guadalupe so that in the borderlands of Texas she has become a symbol of the Latino/a Roman Catholicism that has often stood in contrast to the Roman Catholicism brought to this nation by European immigrants.

She has been and continues to be especially important to Mexican American Latinas. Nuestra Señora de Guadalupe is especially important to Mexican American women who must contend with racial prejudice, poverty, and sexism. For them, she represents a sympathetic mother who hears their requests for assistance in daily life. She is thus the mediator of their entreaties to God for help in overcoming difficult circumstances. . . . By 1750 public expressions of devotion to her were common in San Antonio. Women assembled jewelry and other ornaments for adorning the church and the image of Guadalupe. . . . During the community processions that were part of the festivities, women were the immediate attendants of the image of Nuestra Señora. Their prominent place in this annual display of *guadalupanismo* (a strong devotion to Guadalupe) reflected Tejanas' leadership in the community's spiritual practices. . . . *Sociedades guadalupanas* carry out their devotion to Nuestra Señora de Guadalupe in a variety of ways. They pray together and receive

Holy Communion as a group. Members practice other acts of devotion, such as carrying Guadalupe's image in a public pilgrimage through a neighborhood to extend the protection of the Virgin to the area. . . . The Guadalupanas also perform charitable acts and involve themselves in the community to represent the "all encompassing" love of Nuestra Señora de Guadalupe.[20]

The charitable acts performed by these Mexican American women were carried out through *sociedades guadalupanas* (Guadalupe societies). By identifying with the love of Nuestra Señora for the community, Mexican American women had a role model that helped them to move beyond their roles within the family and become social activists. It was also through the *sociedades guadalupanas* that Mexican American women were given opportunities to develop leadership skills for both the church and society. Using their membership in the *sociedades*, the women were also able to create a bridge between the realm of religious ritual that expressed their faith in Nuestra Señora and the realities of the daily lives of their communities. Many of the *sociedades guadalupanas* made it possible for poor and working-class Mexican American women to work with battered women, illiteracy programs, ministries to Latino/a inmates, campaigns to promote good health. The dual benefits of membership in the *sociedades*—religious leadership and community activism—cannot be dismissed. In establishing a base for Mexican American women in the church, the women also learned and applied new leadership and organizational skills; many participated in the grassroots group Communities Organized for Public Service.[21]

The Missionary Catechists of Divine Providence congregation[22] was created specifically for Mexican American women to serve the needs of Mexican Americans and Mexican immigrants in Houston. The congregation was founded by Sister Mary Benitia Vermeersch, who in 1915 was assigned to Our Lady of Guadalupe School in Houston. When she began to visit the families in the community she found many had fled Mexico when President Plutarco Elías Calles began persecuting Catholics. The majority of these families lived in great poverty and suffered from poor housing, poor medical care, and malnutrition as well as religious neglect. Seeking the help of citizens and businessmen in the community, Sister Mary Benitia sought to change the lives of these families. In 1930 she gathered a group of young Mexican American women to help the children in the community and teach them the basics of the Catholic faith. A house was built for these women in 1935 so they could live under religious rule. Sister Mary Benitia continued her work in San Antonio, starting a second congregation in 1938 that would also serve the poor Latino residents of the city. In 1946 the Missionary Catechists of Divine Providence were granted approval as a filial branch of the Congregation of the Sisters of Divine Providence. To this day the Missionary Catechists continues to be made up entirely of Mexican American women who have not only faithfully and diligently ministered to the poor Latinos/as in Texas but have also expanded their ministry to include New Mexico and California. What is unique about this religious group is how its members have made their culture, ethnicity, and language the primary assets for their ministry. In stark contradiction to the mainstream Euro-American push for assimilation, the Missionary Catechists makes a proud claim to who its members are. This is clearly stated in its Constitution, which says: "As a religious community of Mexican American women, the Missionary Catechists bring their language, culture, and rich faith to build the church, working as God's instruments of warmth, compassion, truth and love" (1.2).

The third and final Roman Catholic group I want to examine is Las Hermanas.[23] Las Hermanas is a national organization for lay and religious Catholic women that was founded in 1970 by Gloria Gallardo, S.H.G., and Gregoria Ortega, O.L.V.M. The first meeting took place in Houston in April 1971, when fifty Mexican American women representing a variety of religious communities came together to discuss and determine the organization's national agenda for the next two decades. What these women wanted was to create a clearinghouse of information to increase awareness of the needs of the community; work for social change; provide leadership training for organization and community members; and, the most challenging, exert pressure on the Catholic hierarchy so that these national goals would be achieved. After having established a national office in Houston, the first national meeting was held in November 1971, in Santa Fe. Bringing in religious and lay women from twenty-one states and working with a national vision that favored the *comunidades de base* (base communities) model, Las Hermanas sought to make a difference in its church and in its communities.

One of the early projects supported by Las Hermanas, Proyecto México, was designed to get religious women who had come from Mexico out of the kitchens of the U.S. seminaries where most had been assigned and into community work in the parishes. In this one project we see how Las Hermanas refused to accept the passive and stereotypical role the dominant culture had traditionally assigned the Latina—that of cook. Here we have Catholic Latina women, religious and lay, working on a national level to change this historical imagination that was limiting the ministry and aspirations of those women from Mexico who had entered religious life not to be cooks in a U.S. seminary but because they had a sense of ministry, of vocation, a call to service. In the 1990s Las Hermanas located to a permanent site in San Antonio on the campus of Our Lady of the Lake University at its Center for Women in Church and Society. Las Hermanas continues its work today through a number of groups in Texas and across the nation. National meetings are held every two years at different locations.

The Protestant Experience

The first encounters Latinos/as had with Protestantism in the United States began in the late 1800s when denominations, following the movement of Euro-American settlers, came to the southwest. Protestant denominations began to make their presence known in colonial Texas in the 1820s, when it was still the Mexican province of Coahuila y Texas. This occurred despite the fact that the official Mexican Constitution clearly stated that Roman Catholicism was the one and only religion of the new Mexican republic. It is believed that Freeman Smawley (or Smalley), from Ohio, preached the first Baptist sermon in Texas, at the home of William Newman, in the year 1822.[24] Joseph L. Bays, from Missouri, held the first Methodist worship services in Stephen Austin's colony at San Felipe de Austin in 1823, which resulted in his arrest by Mexican authorities.[25] The first Sunday School in Texas was established by the Baptists in 1829, but when the suspicions of the Mexican authorities were aroused, Austin closed the Sunday school.[26] Collin McKinney and his family, who came from Kentucky and who identified themselves with the newly emerging Stone-Campbell movement, were the first Disciples to cross into Texas in 1831.[27]

As Protestantism continued to grow, the reality of the Mexican presence came into greater focus, yet it was not a concern that immediately dominated the energies or the resources of any one of the Protestant denominations. This may have much to do with the continuous arrival in Texas of North American settlers in the 1840s and 1850s. This growing number of Euro-American settlers became the main focus of ministry for denominations in Texas. However, historians have been able to trace an aggressive marginalization of the Mexican Texan through the decades right after the Revolution of 1846.[28] This occurred despite the public and political statements of concern made for nonwhite people by the expansionists of the nineteenth century. In reality the expansionist agenda of North America was based on calculations about how to best control the borderlands of Texas and the people who inhabited that land.

When the Mexican-US border was put into place after 1848, as a result of the Mexican American War, the issues of immigration and illegal border crossings also became of utmost concern for the northern nation. By the late 1800s and into the mid-1900s secular historical writings, as well as the religious reports of Protestant denominations in Texas, concerned themselves with the "Mexican Problem." Writers of this era, which included social scientists as well as missionaries, were troubled by the large and continuous immigration of Mexicans into the United States. Why? "The overall sentiments held by secular authors were that Mexicans lacked leadership, discipline, and organization; that they segregated themselves; that they were lacking in thrift and enterprise . . . that they did not measure up to the intellectual caliber of Anglo-American[s]."[29]

Like the missionary efforts to Native Americans, the "Mexican Problem" was interpreted as a window of opportunity for evangelism. The Great Commission was now the rallying call that brought Protestants to the Texas missions fields to bring to fruition the two important and related activities of Christianizing and Americanizing. This was how authentic kingdom building was understood. Consider the wording of an article written by Disciples missionaries in the 1920s: "The 'Mexican Problem' is ever present with us. It is inescapable. The border line between Mexico and the United States is 1,833 miles long. It is a political rather than a natural barrier and is therefore artificial and easily crossed. . . . The Christianization and Americanization of this large body of alien people is a task for the whole church."[30]

The words used in such denominational reports support the idea that the primary task for missionaries was the uplifting of a people truly perceived as "other." Notice how the idea of a "duty" to be performed by faithful Protestants is emphasized. What is being communicated is a forceful theological assumption about evangelism and mission work. In this assumption there is a direct association between Christianization and Americanization. And it was in this great effort that Mexican Americans were incorporated into the many denominations that became a permanent part of the religious landscape of the southwest in the early 1900s.

As Latinos/as in the southwest became Protestants, they began to give shape to their religious experience. Even though their Protestant faith was initially received from North American missionaries, as leadership indigenous to the Latino communities began to emerge Latino Protestantism began to take on a flavor of its own. These efforts at self-definition and self-determination within their faith can be seen in the organization of the Texas-Mexican Presbytery in 1908, of the Baptist-Mexican Convention in 1910, and the Texas-Mexican Mission organized by the Methodists in 1914.[31] Women were also important contributors to the shaping of a Latino Protestantism in the southwest. One such Latina contributor was Élida García de Falcón (1879–1968).[32] Born in Tamaulipas, Mexico, after both her parents died Falcón moved to Texas to live with her sister, who was married to one of the early Mexican American Methodist ministers. She attended the Laredo Seminary, operated by the Methodist Women's Missionary Council for Texas Mexican Women, on a scholarship. Graduating from that school in 1900, she continued training as a teacher, completing her studies at age seventeen. She immediately began teaching in the towns of the Río Grande Valley in south Texas. Falcón's main contribution to Latino Methodism in Texas was her work as translator. For more than twenty years Falcón worked as translator in the women's division of the Methodist Church and in 1955 she helped translate the official Methodist hymnal into Spanish, the *Himnario Metodista*. She also helped to translate another very important document of the Methodist Church, the *Book of Rituals (Ritual Metodista)*. By making these two printed tools available to Latinos/as in Spanish, Falcón helped to make the Methodist church more accessible to the Latino community.

A second important Latina Protestant in the southwest was Jovita Idar (1885–1946).[33] Like Falcón, Idar was a teacher, but she was also a journalist who contributed with her brothers to her father's newspaper and she was an activist who used her voice to call attention to the educational, economic, and social discrimination faced by Mexican Americans in the southwest. Born in Laredo, Texas, she attended the Methodist Holding Institute, where she obtained her teaching degree in 1903. She began to teach but was soon frustrated by the inadequate conditions she found in the schools for Mexican Americans. It was this frustration that led her to begin her work as a journalist for her father's newspaper, *La Crónica*. During the years 1910 and 1911 Idar wrote weekly articles that featured the poverty of Mexican Americans, the educational discrimination, and the lynching of Mexican Americans by the Texas Rangers. "She wrote about the lynching and hanging of a Mexican child in Thorndale, Texas, by the Texas Ranchers [*sic*] and the brutal burning at the stake of 20 year old Antonio Rodríguez in Rocksprings, Texas."[34] In September 1911 she joined the First Mexican Congress held in Laredo, which met to discuss the issues of concern to Mexican Americans: education, labor, and the economy. One of the key results of this gathering was the formation in October 1911 of the Liga Femenil Mexicanista (League of Mexican Women), which was the first feminist social movement among Mexican American women, and Idar became its first president. Idar helped the league focus on the education of poor children as its principal effort, though it also provided free food and clothing.

In 1913 Idar joined the staff of the newspaper *El Progreso*, where one of her articles was very critical of the use of U.S. troops dispatched by

President Wilson to the border. When the Texas Rangers arrived to close down the newspaper, Idar stood in the doorway to keep them from entering. Despite her willingness to stand up for her rights and her desire to give voice to the problems in her community, Idar was no match for the Texas Rangers, who closed down the newspaper despite her protests. The next year, 1914, Idar took over her father's newspaper after his death. In 1917 Idar married Bartolo Juárez, and the couple moved to San Antonio. There Idar continued her activism, joining the Democratic Party, establishing a free bilingual kindergarten, and working as a Spanish-language interpreter for patients in the county hospital. It was in San Antonio where Idar also became the editor of *El Heraldo*, which was a publication of the Río Grande Conference of the Methodist Church.

The third and final Protestant woman I want to discuss comes from the Pentecostal religious experience that is found in Latino communities across the United States. Leoncia Rosado Rousseau (b. 1911), affectionately called Mama Leo, is a widely known Latina Pentecostal preacher in the northeastern United States. The Rev. Rosado came to New York City in 1935 with her husband-pastor, and together they founded the Concilio de Iglesias Cristianas de Damasco (Council of Damascus Christian Churches). After her husband was drafted in World War II, the church called on her to be its minister, making her perhaps the first Latina Pentecostal pastor in New York City.[35]

With her role as pastor giving her new authority, Rosado began to carry out a ministry that was in many ways tailored for the Puerto Rican community—she focused her energies on the Puerto Rican drug addict and gang member. Working in the most dangerous neighborhoods in the city, Rosado became a familiar street preacher and slowly began filling the larger Pentecostal church buildings and then local arenas. Even though her preaching was imbued with fiery enthusiasm, basic biblical teachings, and a claim to power and liberation by the Holy Spirit, Rosado did not allow her message to be a merely spiritualized one. She also focused her energies on the human need of the people she preached to, establishing a rehabilitation center for drug addicts and alcoholics in the church's building. Through the years Rosado saw her ministry expand to the point that it now includes "eight congregations on the East Coast, thirty-nine churches and missions in Ecuador, fourteen in Mexico, and nineteen in the Caribbean and elsewhere. The denomination also operates a school and an orphanage."[36]

What is significant about Rosado's ministry is that she was able to combine the Pentecostal theological discourse about the Holy Spirit with the commitment to social justice. She espoused a message that called for the holistic care of the person. This meant not only a religious rebirth or conversion but also giving attention to the physical and material needs of the new convert. Needless to say, when Rosado first started preaching her message, many other Pentecostal leaders thought her ministry to be "too worldly" because of its emphasis on the social realities of those being preached to. They also felt that the population group she focused on in her work—drug addicts, alcoholics, and gang members—was too dangerous. However, Rosado refused to bow to pressure and continued her work with a strong belief that her community "needed both spiritual hope and physical renewal."[37] To her credit Rosado not only broke out of her prescribed cultural role as a woman and Latina, which is quite remarkable given the fact she began her ministry in the 1940s, but did the same as a pastor. In her role as leader Rosado also broke out of the prescribed role of the Latino Pentecostal pastor by making *both* the soul and the body important to her preaching and teaching.

CONCLUSION

As we can see the religious history of Latinas in the United States is a rich field that needs continued attention. There are so many women whose stories are just being discovered, and others who continue to wait in silence. As the historians of the religious history of this nation, we face the challenge not to allow our research and writing to continue to be defined and imagined for us as it has been in the past. We are called to reimagine the past and in so doing to liberate the future writing of religious history so that it can truly become more inclusive and representative. And in the twenty-first century this inclusivity must mean more than just the normative Protestant/Catholic/Jewish realities so that the great mosaic of religion in the United States can begin to take shape as other religions also become part of the meta-discourse of religious history. But as we struggle toward this goal, we Latinas will continue to live out our faiths and contribute to our denominations and communities. And it is to be hoped that with each passing year we will become less invisible so that our stories will begin to fill in the gaps of a national religious history that will remain incomplete until *all* the stories have been acknowledged and included.

Notes

[1] Martin E. Marty, "American Religious History in the Eighties: A Decade of Achievement," *Church History* 62, no. 3 (September 1993): 335–77.
[2] Ibid., 353.

[3] Emma Pérez, *The Decolonial Imaginary: Writing Chicanas into History* (Bloomington: University of Indiana Press, 1999); Vicki L. Ruíz, *From out of the Shadows: Mexican Women in Twentieth-century America* (New York: Oxford University Press, 1998); Teresa Palomo Acosta and Ruthie Winegarten, *Las Tejanas: 300 Years of History* (Austin: University of Texas Press, 2003).

[4] Arturo Madrid, "Aliens, Misfits, and Interlopers: The Racialized Imagining of the U.S. Latino Communities at the End of the Twentieth Century," in *Race in Twenty-first Century America*, ed. Curtis Stokes, Theresa Meléndez, and Genice Rhodes-Reed (Lansing: Michigan State University Press, 2001), 100.

[5] Otto Santa Ana, *Brown Tide Rising: Metaphors of Latinos in Contemporary American Public Discourse* (Austin: University of Texas Press, 2002), 1, 2, 3.

[6] Pérez, *The Decolonial Imaginary*, 7.

[7] Strategy Research Corporation, *1998 U.S. Hispanic Market* (Miami: Strategy Research Corporation, 1998), 48.

[8] Madrid, "Aliens, Misfits, and Interlopers," 100.

[9] Richard Rodríguez, *Days of Obligation, An Argument with My Mexican Father* (New York: Penguin Books, 1992), 70.

[10] Suzanne Oboler, "So Far from God, So Close to the United States," in *Challenging Fronteras: Structuring Latina and Latino Lives in the U.S.*, ed. Mary Romero, Pierette Hondagneu-Sotello, and Vilma Ortiz (New York: Routledge, 1997), 41–42.

[11] Ibid., 42.

[12] Santa Ana, *Brown Tide Rising*, 313–14.

[13] Ibid.

[14] In Joan Wallach Scott, *Gender and the Politics of History* (New York: Columbia University Press, 1999), 2.

[15] Pérez, *The Decolonial Imaginary*, xvi.

[16] Ibid.

[17] Ibid., 7.

[18] Ibid., 6, 7.

[19] Louise M. Burkhart, *Before Guadalupe: The Virgin Mary in Early Colonial Nahuatl Literature* (Albany, NY: Institute for Mesoamerican Studies, University at Albany, 2001), 1.

[20] Palomo Acosta and Winegarten, *Las Tejanas*, 202.

[21] "Sociedades Guadalupanas," *The Handbook of Texas Online*, http://www.tsha.utexas.edu/handbook/online/articles/view/SS/ics10.html; Internet (accessed October 6, 2006).

[22] "Missionary Catechists of Divine Providence," *The Handbook of Texas Online*, http://www.tsha.utexas.edu/handbook/online/articles/MM/ixm3.html; Internet (accessed October 6, 2006).

[23] "Las Hermanas," *The Handbook of Texas Online*, http://www.tsha.utexas.edu/handbook/online/articles/LL/ixl3.html; Internet (accessed October 6, 2006).

[24] William Stuart Red, *The Texas Colonists and Religion, 1821–1836* (Austin, TX: E. L. Shuttles, 1924), 75.

[25] Ibid., 74.

[26] W. R. Estep, "Religion in the Lone Star State: An Historical Perspective," *International Review of Mission* 78 (April 1989): 181.

[27] Colby D. Hall, *Texas Disciples* (Fort Worth: Texas Christian University Press, 1953), 38.

[28] See Richard Griswold del Castillo, *The Treaty of Guadalupe-Hidalgo: A Legacy of Conflict* (Norman: University of Oklahoma Press, 1990); Arnoldo De León, *Mexican Americans in Texas* (Arlington Heights, IL: Harlan Davidson, 1993).

[29] Arnoldo De León and Kenneth L. Stewart, *Tejanos and the Numbers Game: A Socio-Historical Interpretation from the Federal Censuses, 1850–1900* (Albuquerque: University of New Mexico Press, 1989), 4.

[30] *Survey of Service*, The United Christian Missionary Society (St. Louis: Christian Board of Publication, 1928), 127.

[31] Palomo Acosta and Winegarten, *Las Tejanas*, 207.

[32] "García De Falcón, Élida," *The Handbook of Texas Online*, http://www.tsha.utexas.edu/handbook/online/articles/GG/fga90.html; Internet (accessed October 6, 2006).

[33] "Idar, Jovita," *The Handbook of Texas Online*, http://www.tsha.utexas.edu/handbook/online/articles/II/fid3.html; Internet (accessed October 6, 2006).

[34] "Por la raza y para la raza," *La Voz de Aztlán* 1, no. 5 (February 27, 2000); also http://www.aztlan.net/default5.htm; Internet (accessed October 6, 2006).

[35] María E. González y Pérez, "Latinas in the Barrio," in *New York Glory: Religions in the City*, ed. Tony Carnes and Anna Karpathakis (New York: New York University Press, 2001), 291.

[36] Ibid., 291–92.

[37] Ibid., 294.

6

Jesus and Mary Dance with the *Orishas*

Theological Elements in Interreligious Dialogue

Clara Luz Ajo Lázaro

He was standing in one of the last benches of the old church of Pueblo Nuevo. His white clothes stood out in the tenuous, welcoming shadows. As he approached me, I could see his kindly, smiling mulatto face and his green eyes that shone as he beheld his mother, who was coming toward him, trailing the golden cape of her virginal attire. The Mass was ending, and many people were in a hurry to leave, making the classic sign of the cross after hearing the final blessing. Mary, also in a hurry, was gesturing to her son, "Come on, son, it's getting late." He got up. Despite his handsome, attractive appearance and the brightness in his expressive eyes, people hardly looked at him. Making his way forward among the crowd, greeting here and there, Jesus reached his mother, and both went out onto the street.

In the distance the drums announcing the *Wemilere*[1] could already be heard. Holding hands, Jesus and Mary quickly moved in the direction of the house-shrine where the saint's feast being announced by the drums would be celebrated. The house was close, in the same neighborhood as the church they had just left after taking part in Sunday Mass.

The day was becoming liturgy, was becoming shared life, life in the realm of the sacred, and Jesus and Mary were totally involved in the celebrations, first in the church and afterward in the *Wemilere*. A Sunday of celebration, a meeting of the sacred and the human in a blend of all the gestures, sounds, aromas, colors, form and content, words and

109

images, through which ordinary people orient their daily lives within celebrative moments and in intimate relation with the sacred.

MARY AND JESUS LEFT FROM MASS
AND WENT TO DANCE WITH THE *ORISHAS*

This story, fruit of my imagination, is simply a fanciful way of expressing what can be experienced in a transcultured[2] religiosity, which in the Cuban context finds daily expression in constant exercises of enculturation. This experience is one of dialogue and interaction, not for the purpose of imposing forms, ideas, or concepts, but for sharing and being enriched in a mutual interchange of expressions that become blended and fused almost imperceptibly for ordinary people, who are the prime subjects of this experience. They have known how to draw on, and at the same time contribute to, a rich spirituality that has dialogued with itself since the epoch when our ancestors arrived from Africa, made into slaves—and it still continues that dialogue.

My interest is to study some of the theological elements that express the faith of a large part of our Cuban people, elements that are created and re-created by the people through their religious experiences and practices. To that end I take as points of reference two diverse Cuban religious universes, namely, the Rule of Ocha or Santería and Christian belief and practice. In both traditions Jesus and Mary constitute important figures in people's experience of the sacred. This experience has been transformed by a process of transculturation. Above all, through the faith of the slaves, it has produced an enriching encounter between the Catholic saints and the *orishas* of African origin.

The religious factor is a decisive component in the whole formation process of the Cuban ethnic character, and it displays a great wealth of theological elements that have been reshaped by the people's faith. In the course of almost four centuries these elements have been engaging in a constant process of interchange, assimilation, and fusion. Such experiences open up for us today new avenues of theological reflection.

FROM THE MASS TO THE *WEMILERE*
AND FROM THE *WEMILERE* TO THE MASS

For many people in today's Cuba, it is quite natural to participate both in the Mass and other church activities and also in rituals of Santería or other Afro-Cuban religious worship. When I speak of church, I am referring to the Catholic Church or the Episcopal Church, which are the Christian denominations that in some way allow their members to live this religious duality.

If we examine the origins of Santería, we find that this interrelation between Christianity and elements of the African traditions arose through a process of transculturation that structured and shaped Cuban society. This process began at the very start of colonization and took place primarily among the indigenous cultures of the peoples that originally populated our lands; it then took place between these cultures and the culture of the whites who came from Spain; later, large numbers of Africans of different ethnic groups, brought to Cuba as slaves, became integrated into this process; and eventually others also were included: Jews, French, English, Chinese, and people from all corners of the earth.[3]

The Africans, however, were a most important element for nurturing and molding Cuban culture. Of all the different ethnic groups that were introduced into Cuban territory,[4] the Yorubas, who came from former Dahomey, Togo, and especially southeastern Nigeria, were those who had the greatest cultural influence.[5] They came from urban civilizations that were culturally quite advanced; they had a developed agriculture, traded with other regions, and possessed artistic skills that made their cultural influence dominant in Cuba, especially in the more western parts of the country, such as Matanzas and La Habana. The Yorubas, called *lucumíes* in Cuba, also brought with them their religious beliefs, for their divinities *(orishas)* traveled along with them in the slave ships. Slowly but surely, many of the religious practices of the *lucumíes* were assimilated into the Christian tradition they found here.

Certain social and cultural factors contributed to this interchange and assimilation of religious elements between the two traditions. First of all, although the Catholic Church of Cuba sought to evangelize the slaves and rid them of their native religious beliefs (at least, this was one of the arguments given for participating wholeheartedly in the slavery business), a major part of the clergy were slave-owners, so that their material interests ended up prevailing over their supposedly missionary intentions. That is to say, the priests did not concern themselves much with catechizing the slaves, since that would mean taking slaves away from their work. At the same time, the colonialist masters applied cruel and violent methods, which made the slaves reject both their unethical behavior and their Christianity as unworthy of imitation. Besides these problems there were linguistic difficulties, for the custom of performing the Catholic rituals in Latin was quite foreign to African customs and

traditions. Moreover, the slave-owners sought to preserve ethnic, linguistic, and religious differences among the slaves in order to avoid up-
risings and riots in the barracks. On some feast days, though, there was
a certain tolerance of organization, which allowed the people to play
their drums and dance according to their traditions. Such moments were
taken advantage of by the slaves to celebrate their liturgical rites and
invoke their divinities.

In addition, there existed among the Africans associations called
cabildos or *cofradías*, which provided them a legal space for organizing
meetings. In the *cabildos* men and women of one ethnic group met together for the sake of helping one another and maintaining their culture.[6] The *cabildos* allowed the slaves to preserve their own customs and
traditions as if they were still in their places of origin, and they were also
able maintain their own religious hierarchies, which were recognized
and respected by all the members. The *cofradías* were somewhat similar,
but they were of Spanish origin, and they brought together Africans of
different ethnic groups to celebrate Christian feasts.

Although these organizations had functions that were ostensibly social, they were of fundamental importance for the religious life of the
African slaves and for freed persons as well. These spaces allowed them
to keep alive their traditions and religious customs, disguised behind
Christian norms and practices. The ceremonies with African rituals joined
together and fused with those of the Catholic tradition. In some cases
the organization was given the name of a saint, and processions were
made to the parish church so that the priest in charge could bless the
saint's image. Afterward the people celebrated the feast by playing their
drums and dancing according to their own traditions. The *cabildos* often took the name of an African deity; they were spaces in which the
language of origin was recalled and taught, and the traditional African
religious rituals found protection there.

In the course of time the *cabildos* and the *cofradías* extended to all
parts of the country, and the colonial government placed many limitations on them. They finally underwent a process of fusion, so that not
only people of African descent but also people of other ethnic groups
participated in them. At the end of the nineteenth century many of these
organizations were transformed into house-shrines, where a saint or a
deity was worshiped and where African rituals with Christian elements
were practiced.

The transcultural give-and-take gradually transformed many aspects
of ritual, customs, and traditions. Throughout this whole process, the
slave *lucumíes*, from the Yoruba tradition, put Christian names on their

gods and goddesses, taking cues from external similarities that they found between the deities and the saints; they also borrowed elements of the Catholic liturgy to celebrate their own religious rites. The result of this process was that the *orishas*, African divinities of the Yoruba tradition, were commonly "canonized." At the start, this was a strategic act aimed at hiding or disguising the African deities, but little by little these strategies became new pathways, new cultic elements, and new ritual expressions. As a genuinely Cuban creation, Santería transformed the original African elements, keeping some of them and adding new elements.

The saints of the Christian tradition came down from their altars to join with the African *orishas* and to share with them their characteristics, virtues and defects, ritual elements, spiritual gifts, and healing energies. The saints came out from the parish Mass to become part of the *Wemilere*. They entered into the people's humble houses, communing closely with the men and women, children and elders, and in the process became much more human. In this way, the *orishas* have themselves been transformed, taking on a Cuban identity and becoming Cuban gods and goddesses of African origin. For that reason we find a major portion of the Cuban population who, with no feeling of dogmatic sectarianism, proceed tranquilly from the Mass to the *Wemilere* or from the *Wemilere* to the Mass. The people themselves have established the interreligious dialogue; they have broken the barriers and the limits between the Mass and the *Wemilere*, between the parish church and the house-shrine.

ELEMENTS THAT DIALOGUE

The theological elements that enter into the dialogue between these two religious universes come from all levels of the religious expression of those who are the prime participants in the dialogue: from their world view, from their myths and symbols, from the characteristics of the divinities and the believers' relationship with them, from their rituals and other aspects of life. All this is reflected in ordinary human relations and in the way people face their day-to-day problems.

Of course, Jesus and Mary are sacred images that form a very important part of the religious symbolism of believers, but the people have practiced a certain deconstruction on the traditional images. Believers have developed a new relation with these two figures as a result of their proceeding back and forth between the *Wemilere* and the parish Mass, and that new relation challenges us to find new ways of formulating our theological reflection.

The Child Jesus and the Old Jesus

In Santería, the creation of the world and of people is not done by the supreme God.[7] Rather, God creates the *orishas*, and it is they who make the earth, the universe and people—and afterward they come to live with them. The supreme God breathes life into people, but afterward he draws apart and remains distant and indifferent to human problems. The *orishas* are the ones who govern the world and remain in contact with people. These divinities have attitudes that are completely anthropomorphic; they have all the imperfections and virtues of human beings. In Yoruba tradition, good and evil are two inseparable aspects of existence, and both are mixed together in the divinities; they behave like humans and live intimately related to them. Each one of them has been endowed with one of the powers of the supreme God.[8]

In Cuba these divinities are individual and personal, and each believer has his or her own. The relation between the *orisha* and the believer is described by Verger as "pure force, immaterial *aché*[9] that becomes perceptible only to those persons who incorporate themselves into one of them, . . . who become a vehicle that allows the *orisha* to return to earth in order to greet and to receive tokens of respect from the descendents who have evoked him."[10]

The figure of Jesus appears in relation to the manifestations, avatars, or "ways"[11] of two important *orishas*, Obatalá and Elegguá.

The child Jesus, through the transculturation[12] process, is related with Elegguá, the *orisha* who is owner of the ways, the one who opens and closes the ways of people's destiny. One has to count on him for any major life decision. He not only opens up the ways but also cares for houses, and for that reason his image is generally positioned behind the doors. What is interesting is that since the time of our African ancestors Elegguá has been conceived of as a mischievous child; he is unpredictable, as is destiny, which can be either very good or very bad. He is the messenger of Olófin, who told him, "Since you, the smallest one, are my messenger, you will be the greatest on earth and in heaven, and people will not be able to do anything without counting on you."[13]

Believers and practitioners of this Cuban religious tradition consider this relationship to be perfectly valid. Elegguá is a child, owner of the ways and the life destinies of people; he can open or close horizons; he can provide well-being and growth in the future life; he is the messenger of Olófin—after all, he is the child Jesus! This strategic relation was established by our African foreparents, but today it is fully accepted by all who practice Santería, even while they confess themselves to be Christians and attend church.

An ancient story, the Child of Atocha, tells of a boy who went to a prison carrying a basket full of bread and a bucket full of water. He gave food and drink to countless prisoners, but the basket of bread and the bucket of water always remained as full as when he started. According to the legend, this child was the same Jesus Christ who came as a child to attend to the material and spiritual needs of the prisoners.[14] This story was told by old African slave women to illustrate the relationship between Elegguá and the child Jesus. We see the miracle of feeding, of filling hungry stomachs, as a gesture that identifies Jesus. This story of the child recalls the words of the gospel: "But Jesus called for them [the children] and said, 'Let the little children come to me, and do not stop them; for it is to such as these that the kingdom of God belongs. Truly I tell you, whoever does not receive the kingdom of God as a little child will never enter it'" (Lk 18:16–17; cf. Mt 19:13–15; Mk 10:13–16).

It is significant that Elegguá is first in everything: the first to eat at the time of the ritual sacrifices, the first to be offered gifts, the first to be praised in the *Wemilere*, which begins with drumming and songs to Elegguá and also ends with hymns to this mischievous, playful little god. Elegguá is always present in the homes; he is the guardian and the caretaker of domestic space. He is also the first to be consulted when future plans and projects are being prepared or when people have problems or difficulties in their lives.

The symbol of the child is an important part of people's faith; it is synonymous with security, future growth, creativity, and foresight. Popular mysticism makes freshly present the messianic prophecy of First Isaiah (chapters 1—39). As Nancy Cardoso Pereira points out: "The child is just this: he is and will be. Through this ambiguity of present and future we can approach the child as a prophetic category. The child is event, expectation, incarnation."[15]

Of course, the wisdom of the people's mysticism allows for Elegguá to take on negative characteristics. Indeed, all the *orishas* can show a negative side: none of them represents extreme purity. All of them represent the contradictions of life, so that each may present certain negative aspects. Elegguá's negative side is called Echu, which is the incarnation of the bad things, the human problems, and the tragic misfortunes that come along in life. According to tradition, Echu lives in the streets and in the bush; if he manages to enter into a house, difficulties and tragedies will start for the family.

Natalia Bolívar Aróstegui states that

the Elegguá-Echu pair is the mythical expression of the inevitable relationship between the positive and the negative. For the Yorubas, the house signifies the refuge *par excellence*, the privileged place to escape the avatars of destiny. Elegguá dwells at the very door of the house, marking with his presence the boundary between two worlds: the internal world of security and the external world of danger. Security cannot exist, however, without danger, nor can calm exist without anxiety; for that reason, the Elegguá-Echu pair is indissoluble, despite their opposition.[16]

That is the reason, in my opinion, that the saints of the church became more human in the process of transculturation. Such human qualities as fragility, error, and evil are also found in these anthropomorphic manifestations of the divine; the gods and the saints are seen as persons who have their defects and their virtues. The experience of the sacred forms an integral part of the mystery that includes the ambiguous and paradoxical character of existence.

The old Jesus is a figure that appears in some of the manifestations of Obbatalá, who is one of the principal *orishas*. His statue is placed in the first division of the shelf called *canastillero*, where the devotees of the saints keep their images.[17] Obbatalá is considered to be the creator of human beings, the one who sculpted them from clay so that Olófin would then place the breath of life in them. He is the deity that represents purity; he is master of all that is white; and he is lord of the head, of thoughts, and of dreams. In various of his manifestations or ways, he is associated with Jesus of Nazareth,[18] but he is generally pictured as a stooped, trembling little old man. He is the *orisha* of peace and harmony, much respected by all, capable of calming the worst manifestations of wrath in the rest of the *orishas*. White is his color, and he is a symbol of intelligence, experience, and discretion.

Apart from being identified with Jesus of Nazareth, Obbatalá assumes another interesting form in the process of transculturation, namely, a feminine image that relates Obbatalá to the saints of the Christian tradition, and especially to the Virgin Mary as Our Lady of Ransom. On the altars of the house-shrines we will find images of Jesus and Our Lady of Ransom placed quite close together beside the container for the natural elements that represent Obbatalá, this *orisha* who is master of all that is white.

In keeping with Yoruba tradition, the Cuban gods and goddesses of African origin behave like humans and show human imperfections. One of the old stories of the Yoruba tradition tells that when Olódùmaré gave Obbatalá the task of creating the earth and human beings, Obbatalá did not make the things the way he should have. Rather, he got drunk on palm wine and his rival Odduwa had to take over the job of creating earth. Obbatalá was then given the task of creating human beings, and he was forbidden to drink palm wine. According to the story, however, he sometimes gave in to his vice, so that some of his human sculptures came out badly shaped—thus does the tradition explain birth defects.

Important elements of this interreligious dialogue are the way humans are formed from the dust of the earth and the way people's lives are inevitably interwoven with good and evil. The earth is seen as a great womb, a giant pumpkin, a fertile belly in which all life comes to birth. The first ancestors were born of the clay of the earth, which was their original matter. Death returns to the earth all that belongs to it, thus allowing rebirth; when biological life ceases, the earth receives the bodies back into itself, thus regaining its generative capacity. The origin of life and of bodies is closely related to nature's vital elements: light, air, water, and earth. In these elements are found the principles or forces *iwà, axé,* and *àbá,* which are divine energies regulating all existence.

Each *orisha* represents the archetype of a different personality, and we find in the Yoruba pantheon almost all the most general archetypes of human psychology. At the same time, each *orisha* is related to one of the forces of nature. In this way important relationships are established among divinities, personalities and natural forces.

Jesus and Mary also form part of these interrelationships. It is significant that in the process of transculturation Jesus assumes archetypal forms that have generally been avoided by Western civilization, such as the young and the elderly. Also, when Our Lady of Ransom is related to the *orisha* that is responsible for the creation of human beings, we become aware that many symbolic elements involved in the deconstruction of traditional images have ended up enriching the people's spirituality.

Two Faces of Mary:
Goddess Mother and Goddess of Love and Sensuality

The process of transculturation has given Mary many faces that become manifest through the feminine *orishas* and the relationships between them and the saints of the Catholic tradition. Mary has come down from her high altar, donned the clothes of the common women, and remained there with them—for that reason she is much loved and venerated. We would like to examine now two faces of Mary that are of great importance in the religiosity of the Cuban people: Mary the mother, related to Yemayá, the goddess of the seas; and Mary the goddess of love and sensuality, related to Ochún, the goddess of fresh water.

Mary and Yemayá are two divinities that in Cuba have become united in the transculturation process, whereby they have come to share many elements that transform and enhance both of them. The Virgin of the Regla is the name of the black Mary, who is patroness of fishers; her sanctuary is located in the town of Regla, in La Habana province, where she is venerated both by Christians and by devotees of Santería.

The Virgin of Regla and Yemayá represent the archetype of the mother who protects and gives life. In the Santería tradition, Yemayá is the queen of all waters, mistress of the fresh water that she gives to Ochún and also of the salty sea waters from which life emerged. She is considered the mother of all the *orishas*, the mother of all life. The name Yemayá means "mother whose children are fish." Originally she was the *orisha* of a Yoruba nation called Egbá, in a part of Africa where there still exists a river that bears her name, Yemoja.

In Cuba she is called the goddess of intelligence and is the symbol of the balanced person. She is considered to be a mother who is judicious, kind, protective, understanding of her children, and rather stern; when she becomes angry she can be quite terrible. She is like the sea, which can be quite beautiful when calm but quite fearful in times of tempest.

The fusion of Yemayá with the Virgin of Regla shows a face of Mary quite different from the traditional image of the humble and chaste Virgin, since Yemayá, though she is a good mother, is also a single mother. The stories tell of her love affairs with various *orishas* and also of her strong character, expressed in her tenacity and valor. Yemayá therefore is not a model of maternity that can be used for controlling the sexuality and the bodies of women. The fusion of the two images has been enriched with the common people's spirituality, which brings them close to the real lives of women. Thus these images become creative and transformative forces that destroy the traditional stereotypes of the Virgin Mary and project rather the image of a mother who affirms her body and her sexuality in a free and responsible manner.

Mary and Ochún, the goddess of love and sensuality, show us the other face of Mary, one that is a good mirror of the Cuban woman. Ochún is a goddess of the Yoruba pantheon that has passed through a process of transformation and adaptation and thus become one of the most important deities in Santería. In Cuba, Ochún ceases to be African and becomes mulatto, Creole, or Cuban; she is the muse of many poets and painters, who re-create her cinnamon-colored skin, her long tresses, and her warm sensuality. She is the symbol of coquetry, of grace, of beauty, and of feminine sensuality. She is the goddess of love and fecundity, the patroness of pregnancies, the protectress of women with child. The devotees of Santería say that she takes care of women's wombs and recently born children.

When we study the African roots of this *orisha*, we see that her origins go back to Nigeria, where she is the goddess of the river (Ijebu/Ijexá) that bears her name and that runs the length of Nigeria. Her great ancestral mothers are the Iyàmi-Ajé or the Iyàmi Osàròngà, which in the Yoruba tongue mean "my mother sorceress"; they are also called *iyá àgbá* (old, respectable mother) or *eleye* (mistress of the birds). As the stories go, Ochún maintains strong ties with these ancestral mothers, thanks to which she possesses the power of fertility.[19]

In the Yoruba region the Iyàmi traditionally represented the mystical powers of women, which were feared and respected. These ancestral mothers were considered sorceresses and might be called the matriarchs of Yoruba tradition. They appear in the ancient myths of the creation and so reveal an epoch when women were the ones who had charge of the most important matters of the community, including the cult to the ancestors. They had control of the powers of the tradition, which later passed into the hands of the men.

In this tradition the Iyàmi represent those feminine powers in their most dangerous and fearful aspect. They were the so-called Great Angry Mothers, without whose leave life could not continue; they were considered sorceresses *(àjé)*, but not in the popular meaning that that word has today. According to Pierre Verger:

> The matter of the sorceresses in relation to the so-called traditional religions was not always treated with due caution. That is to say, since sorcery was always from the start considered to be an extremely anti-social activity, people thought it could not form part of the religion of a human community. In the Yoruba religion, however, these women were considered sorceresses because their activities were directly related to the divinities, to the *orishas* and to the myths of the creation of the world.[20]

In Cuba, just as in Brazil, the powers of the Iyàmi appear in the more socialized form of the feminine *orishas*, such as Ochún, Yemayá, Oyá Yansá, Nanà Burukú, Obba, and Yewa.

In Cuba, as in Africa, Ochún is called Iyálóde, a title conferred on her to indicate that she is the person who occupies the most important place among all women. According to Verger, she is the one who controls women. In one story she is presented as the head of the sorceresses, and she distributes among them birds, the power source of the *àjé* (sorceresses). She sells in the marketplace, but she also represents women in the king's palace and in the council of the elders. She is also present in the local tribunal if a woman is involved in a trial. Outside the tribunal, she herself performs the function of arbiter of the problems that might arise among women. This is the most honorable title that a woman can receive; it places her automatically at the head of women and makes her the representative of the *àiyé* of the ancestral feminine power.

Water and earth are the conducting elements for the *axé*, the feminine generative force that is in the earth's waters: the water of rain, rivers, lakes and springs, and even the water of the sea. In the Santería tradition Ochún is closely linked to Yemayá, and in some of her manifestations or "ways," she dwells beside Yemayá in the mouth of the rivers, where river and sea join together. The Cuban tradition contains stories that tell how Yemayá cares for Ochún, protects her as a sister, and shares her riches with her, including the river as a place to dwell.

Ochún is transformed into the Cuban mulatto woman throughout all the process of transculturation. If we ask practitioners of Santería what Ochún is like, they will always describe a Cuban woman, sensual, flirtatious, happy, amusing, a lover of dancing and feasting. She loves to entice by adorning herself and dressing up in fine clothes. She is generally described as a honey-skinned mulatto with clear eyes, long curly hair, and a beautiful, sensual body. While possessing great powers, she is compassionate and miraculous; she is affectionate and as sweet as the honey she loves, but also willful and harsh when she gets angry.

She is considered mistress of the earth's fresh waters, without which life would be impossible, but she is also mistress of the sweet waters of the sexes, also essential for life. She represents the lively, free, daring woman who is mistress of herself. She possesses femininity, but not of the submissive, complacent type. Rather, her femininity is powerful, liberated, sensual, sure of itself, and in control of its sexuality; it is a femininity that is able to obtain anything through its charms. The African slaves called her the *panchákara*, which in the Lucumi language spoken in Cuba means "prostitute" or even "whore goddess." To be sure, this title is considered one of power and is used only by the more experienced practitioners of Santería, and always with the greatest respect and admiration, not in a pejorative sense. This is one of the most popular and best known ways or manifestations of Ochún, in which she is known by the name Yeyé Kari or Yeyé Moró.

Ochún is also associated with the Virgin of Charity of Copper (Cobre), the patroness of Cuba. What has made possible this relationship between the sensual Ochún and the pure and chaste Virgin?

Poets have called her the dark-skinned Virgin, and historians have called her the Mambisa Virgin, as have all the people who have felt her support during the long years of struggling for freedom. Much venerated by the Cuban people, she is a *mestiza* or mulatto Virgin who reflects in her face a broad blend of Hispanic, Indian, African and Creole origins. Precisely that blend of races of our Cuban ethnicity has made Cachita or Cari, as she is affectionately called by devotees, a most important part of popular religious expression in Cuba. In her there takes place an integration of many devotions that have been the heritage of centuries of Hispanic, Native American, African, and Creole traditions. In her, all of them become fused and transculturated, producing a popular Cuban religious expression that is today practiced by the great majority of our people. From the sixteenth century down to the present, such devotion has been capable of uniting the faith and the beliefs of all the different social groups that make up our nationality.

One day in 1613 a statue appeared floating in the waters of the Bay of Nipe, on the northeastern coast of the island; it was recovered by two Indian farmworkers and a ten-year-old African slave. Attached to the statue was a small tablet with an inscription that reads, "I am the Virgin of Charity."

A number of factors led the slaves to associate the Virgin of Charity with the goddess of African origin. First, the Indians had already associated the Virgin with their own goddess Atarex, adored as the engendering mother, and this association must in some way have influenced the later relations between the Indians and the Africans. Second, the Virgin was the patroness who presided over the religious celebrations in the copper mines of El Cobre, where women worked at removing the mineral from the river. Ochún's traditional mineral was copper, and her traditional color was yellow. In Africa, Ochún was the goddess related to the river waters, the goddess of fertility who gave women their children. The Virgin, wearing a yellow cape, held a child in her arms, and she had been found floating in the water. All the legends told of her disappearing and then reappearing again, soaking wet.

This fusion of Virgin and goddess took place in a process that was accompanied by struggles and rebellions, in the midst of a long history in which *mestizos*, mulattos, blacks and whites united and fought for their rights to land and independence. Meanwhile, the dark-skinned Virgin and the goddess of love became blended to the point of forming an integral part of people's daily life. The pure Virgin was humanized and transformed into a real woman of the people, a joyful, dancing, sensual Cuban *mulata*, thus breaking with the stereotypes that Western tradition had imposed on her by making her forbiddingly holy.

In our days Ochún and Cachita are joined together; they are one and the same divinity, although with very different historical origins. Santería has fused them, and they are found one beside the other on the altars, in

the rituals, and in the feasts dedicated to Ochún. September 8, the day
when people traditionally celebrate the appearance of the Virgin of Charity in the waters of the Bay of Nipe, is a feast day both for the Catholic
Church and for the devotees of Santería; the one has Masses, processions, and other activities for the dark-skinned Virgin of Charity, while
the others adorn her altars with flowers and hold a vigil in which candles
are lit before her image. The Virgin, dressed in her golden tunic, is always brightly shining beside the *asentamiento* of Ochún, which is a porcelain or clay recipient in which are kept the elements of the river that
contain the *axé* of the *orisha*. The candles are lit at midnight, and at that
moment everyone prays and asks the Virgin for peace, health, and pros-
perity. Christian prayers such as the Our Father and the Hail Mary are
said, and Christian hymns are sung, while a bell is sounded for Ochún
(called *agogo*); finally, some hymns are sung in Yoruba. It is a unique
blend of traditions that the people have achieved by breaking through
the barriers of religious sectarianism, in the same way that Ochún and
Cachita were able to break down and deconstruct the barriers of con-
ventionality and traditionalism that have kept women imprisoned in rig-
orous patterns of conduct.

Inexhaustible is the wealth of symbols, ritual elements, spiritual gifts,
and sacred energies that we find in the relationship that the Cuban faithful have established between these two expressions of traditional religion. By means of such simple, sincere interreligious dialogue, which
seeks not to impose criteria or concepts but rather to give and receive
with the believers' open, faith-filled hearts, we find ourselves challenged
to open up new avenues in Cuban feminist theological reflection. The
drums continue to sound, blending with the church bells. And Jesus and
Mary are still dancing in the great circle, with all the *orishas*.

Notes

[1] The religious expression called Rule of Ocha or Santería is one of the most
extended religious traditions of African origin in Cuba. It arose at the end of the
sixteenth century through a process in which elements of the African cultures
and religions, introduced into the island in the epoch of slavery, became mixed
and fused with elements of Christian tradition and with other social and cultural factors. Such blending gave rise to this popular religious expression, which
is today practiced by a large part of the Cuban population. The *Wemilere* is one
of the liturgical rituals of Santería.

[2] "All transculturation is a process in which something is always given in
exchange for what is received; it is a give-and-take [*toma y daca*], as the Spanish
say. It is a process in which both parts of the equation end up changed and in

which a new reality emerges, one that is not simply a mechanical agglomeration of features, or even a mosaic, but a new, original and independent phenomenon. . . . Transculturation as a term describes a process in which there is no one given culture to which another has to conform, but there is rather a transition between the two cultures. Both are active and contribute with their respective features, and both cooperate in the advent of a new reality to civilization" (Fernando Ortiz, *Contrapunteo cubano del tabaco y el azúcar* [Havana: Ciencias Sociales, 1983], xxxiii).

³ Ibid., 243.

⁴ Fernando Ortiz mentions ninety-nine different ethnic groups. See *Los negros esclavos*, 3rd ed. (Havana: Ciencias Sociales, 1975), 100. Other authors have furthered the studies made by Ortiz; among them, Rafael López Valdez states that the number of ethnic groups introduced into Cuba reached one thousand (see "Presencia étnica de los esclavos de Tiguaboa (Guantánamo) entre los años 1789 y 1844," *Revista José Martí* 77, no. 3 [1956]: 14–21).

⁵ All the peoples and tribes living in this region and speaking the Yoruba language were identified by this name. Yoruba is therefore "a basically linguistic denomination, although these tribes were linked by the same culture and their belief in a common origin" (Natalia Bolívar Aróstegui, *Los orishas en Cuba* [Havana: P. M. Ediciones, 1994], 3).

⁶ This organization arose at the beginning of the slave epoch, during the sixteenth and seventeenth centuries, when slavery in Cuba had not acquired the rigor and violence that it had in later centuries.

⁷ The name of this supreme god is Olòfin Olóòrun Olódùmarè. Each of these names represents functions and forces that are active in the world. Olòfin is the creative force that made the *orishas*, the world, the animals, and the people; it is the cause and the reason-for-being of all things. Olóòrun is the sun, heat, light, the basic vital energy for all that makes up life on earth. Olódùmaré represents universal law, the laws of nature and of all existence.

⁸ "Each *orisha* becomes an archetype of an activity, a profession or a function; they are complementary to one another and represent the whole complex of forces that govern the world" (Pierre Verger, *Orixás: Deuses iorùbás na Africa e no novo mundo* [São Paulo: Editora Corrupio, 1981], 21).

⁹ For the Yorubas there are three forces that make possible and regulate all that exists in the universe: *iwà*, *axé (aché)* and *àbá*. The *iwà* allows generic existence; the *axé (aché)* is the power of realization that energizes existence and allows it to arise; the *àbá* is the power that endows purpose, gives direction and accompanies the *axé (aché)*. Existence develops through these tissues of forces and principles, in a continual search for balance among the elements.

¹⁰ Verger, *Orixás*, 19.

¹¹ All these divinities have different ways of manifesting themselves, which in Cuba are called ways or avatars.

¹² I do not use the term *syncretism* because it is not the most appropriate for describing the fusion that comes about between the African divinities and the

saints of the Christian tradition. Besides, it is a term that has been quite manipulated. I prefer to use the term *transculturation*.

[13] Verger, *Orixás*, 27.

[14] This legend, inherited from Spanish Catholicism, is known as the story of the Child of Atocha. For more details see Aróstegui, *Los orishas en Cuba*, 35.

[15] Nancy Cardoso Pereira, "El Mesías siempre debe ser niño," *Revista Ribla* 24 (1996): 17–24.

[16] Aróstegui, *Los orishas en Cuba*, 28.

[17] The *canastillero* is a piece of furniture that has an important ritual function; all devotees of Santería have one. It is a sort of cupboard with various divisions and is kept in the room of the saints in the house-shrines. In the *canastillero* are placed the *asentamientos* of the *orishas* in accord with their hierarchy, as well as a series of objects and attributes that correspond to them according to the tradition. The *asentamientos* are containers of clay or porcelain that contain natural objects that are charged with the energies of the different *orishas*. To indicate its hierarchical importance, the *asentamiento* of Obbatalá is always in the first division of the *canastillero*. Generally, domestic cabinets and cupboards are modified to serve as *canastilleros*.

[18] In these ways or avatars he is known as Obbatalá Ocha Griñán, Obbatalá Obá Lufón, or Obbatalá Obá Moró. For more information on this, see Lydia Cabrera, *El Monte* (Miami: Ediciones Universal, 1992), 306–9; and Aróstegui, *Los orishas en Cuba*, 94–120.

[19] Pierre Verger, "Grandeza e decadência do culto de Iyàmi Òsòròngà (Minha Mãe Feiticeira) entre os Yorùbá," in *As senhoras so pássaro da noite: Escritos sobre a religião dos orixás V*, ed. Carlos Eugênio Marcondes de Moura (São Paulo: Universidade de São Paulo (Edusp), Axis Mundo, 1994), 16.

[20] Verger, "Grandeza e decadência," 16–17.

7

The *Virgen* and the Scholar

Afro-Cuban Contributions
to Latino/a and Latin American Theologies

Michelle A. González

For over thirty years Latino/a theologians have articulated a contextual, liberationist discourse that centers on the Latino/a community in the United States. Focusing on the everyday religiosity of these communities, Latino/a theologians bring forth the particular theological world view underlying Latino/a faith and religious practices. Similarly, since the late 1960s Latin American liberation theologians have articulated a theological perspective that emphasizes the particularity of Latin American religiosity in light of its complex historical and contemporary contours. Feminist voices form part of the canons of Latino/a and Latin American theologies, highlighting the function of sexism and the exclusion/silencing of women in their perspective communities and the broader Christian tradition. While Latino/a and Latin American theologies have emerged from distinct social locations, with their own theological voice and emphases, there is obvious historical and contemporary overlap between the two. Though I do not want to collapse the Latino/a and Latin American contexts, one cannot deny that the borders between the Americas are not quite as rigid as our rhetoric often implies.

One feature that marks Latino/a and Latin American theologies is a certain silence regarding Afro-Cuban culture and religiosity in particular and Cubans and Cuban Americans in general. This silence is found within a larger omission, that of Afro-Latino/a and Latin America. While the North American theological academy has been marked by the presence of Cuban American scholars, there has been little reflection on Cuban

American religious life in general and Afro-Cuban experience in particu-lar.[1] In a similar vein, the Cuban context is often overlooked in Latin American liberation theology. This is due to the various historical fac-tors that set apart the Catholic Church in twentieth century Cuba from its Latin American counterparts. John M. Kirk notes that, unlike in other Latin American countries, liberation theology did not spread in Cuba. Also, the violence that the church has experienced in other Latin Ameri-can countries did not occur in Cuba.[2] Kirk reminds us that Cuba and Puerto Rico remained colonies of Spain a good eighty years after main-land Latin America. "Had the Cuban revolution taken place after the Second Vatican Council or the CELAM meetings, perhaps the bitter in-vective of the early 1960s could have been avoided. For most of Cuba's Catholics, Vatican II arrived too late."[3] The revolutionary meetings of Vatican II and Medellín had little effect on the church in Castro's Cuba. Had the revolution occurred ten years later, or the radical changes that transformed the Latin American church ten years earlier, one might be discussing a very different church in Cuba.

My article is a modest attempt to break this silence and offer an Afro-Cuban contribution to Latino/a and Latin American theologies through a study of two key figures in Cuban and Cuban American history, religi-osity, and scholarship: La Caridad del Cobre and Lydia Cabrera. The national patroness of the island, La Caridad del Cobre is arguably a religious symbol that has come to represent what it means to be Cuban, both on the island and in the Cuban diaspora. Religious anthropologist, folklorist, and painter Lydia Cabrera is an often overlooked intellectual foremother in Latino/a and Latin American studies. Underlying my re-search on La Caridad and Cabrera is a desire to crack open the catego-ries of identity operating in Latino/a and Latin American theologies. In emphasizing an Afro-Cuban contribution, my intention is to evoke more explicit attention to black Latino/a and Latin American culture, history, and religiosity. My focus on Cuba is also a deliberate Caribbean contri-bution to these discourses. Lastly, as a Cuban American emphasizing historical Cuban sources, my hope is to broaden and challenge a static understanding of Latino/a and Latin American theologies.

LA CARIDAD DEL COBRE

La Caridad del Cobre, or Cachita, as Cubans affectionately call her, is a vital symbol of Cuban religious and national identity. She is, even for those without religious beliefs, a symbol of what it means to be Cuban. La Caridad began as a local devotion among a community of slaves in the seventeenth century and has grown over the years to become the national patroness of the island. Perhaps for this reason alone she represents not only Cuba, but also the Afro-Cuban roots of Cuban identity and religiosity, for in La Caridad we have an example of an Afro-Cuban practice that has grown to represent what it means to be Cuban regardless of one's race. She is revered both on the island and among Cubans in the diaspora. Shrines to her exist in Cuba and in Miami. Even in Castro's Cuba, among a community that has grown without a heavy emphasis on (and at some points a discouragement of) religious beliefs, thousands flock to her shrine on her feast day, bearing sunflowers as offerings to her.

Throughout Cuban history the image and story of La Caridad have been vastly transformed within Cuban mythology, so much so that the narrative and iconography surrounding her today differ sharply from historical accounts of her actual appearance. La Caridad that exists in the minds of present-day Cubans and Cuban Americans is not quite La Caridad of the seventeenth century. Much of this transformation occurred during Cuba's wars of independence from Spain, during which La Caridad rose in prominence as a national symbol. La Caridad, therefore, is not only a symbol of Cuban identity but represents the Cuban process of identity making, Cubans' self-construction as they articulated a distinctive identity from Spain.

If one looks at a prayer card or statue of La Caridad del Cobre in a Cuban American's home in this day and age, one is usually confronted with a representation of Mary looming large over three men in a rowboat. She is dressed most often in blue. Carrying the baby Jesus, she stands enormous over the three helpless men. Her skin is light brown. The sea is stormy, with waves crashing over the boat. The man in the middle, of African descent, is holding his hands in prayer. The two other men, one Caucasian (Spanish) and the other of ambiguous racial descent (biracial? Indigenous?) clasp their oars. In Cuban mythology these men are known as the "three Juans." If one were to interpret this image at first glance, it would seem as if Mary appeared *over* these three men during a great storm, and they are pleading for her aid. A powerful image, especially within a community where thousands have risked their lives in homemade rafts, facing turbulent waters as they attempt to flee Cuba, this depiction of La Caridad is close to the hearts of both Cubans and Cuban Americans, though far from the historical account of her apparition.

La Caridad did appear before three men in a rowboat on the Bay of Nipe, but she was a statue floating in the water, and it was not during a storm. The men were not all named Juan, and none of them was Caucasian. The actual date of this discovery is contested, though scholars

today agree that it occurred in the first fifteen years of the seventeenth
century.[4] The earliest account of La Caridad is a 1687 interview of Juan
Moreno, an African slave who claimed to be one of the three who discovered the statue.[5] This narrative was recorded in 1703 by Father Onofre
de Fonseca. Forgotten for centuries, this testimony was revived in the
1970s by Cuban scholar Leví Marrero and is now considered the au-
thoritative historical narrative of the apparition. Prior to its revival scholars assumed that the discovery of the statue occurred much later in the
seventeenth century.

Juan Moreno recounts that he and two Indigenous brothers, Rodrigo
de Hoyos and Juan de Hoyos, were searching for salt in the Bay of Nipe
early one morning. Moreno was a royal slave in the copper mines in El
Cobre. In the distance they saw an object that they first mistook for a
bird. Instead, they discovered a statue floating in the water with the
words "Yo soy la Virgen de la Caridad" (I am the Virgin of Charity)
attached to it. They gathered in the statue and quickly turned it over to
Spanish authorities.[6] Miraculously, they note, though she was floating
on the water her clothes were dry. An altar was dedicated to her in a
hospital chapel, and shortly after her apparition miracles began to occur
within the community that were attributed to her. After its discovery, for
example, the image was moved around to various places, though it kept
vanishing and resurfacing at the first altar dedicated to La Caridad. In
1613 the statue was brought to El Cobre, where she remains today. It
was not until 1640 that she was moved to the main altar of the sanctuary in Cobre.

Devotion to La Caridad spread, at first among slaves in the region of
El Cobre. At the time of her appearance, Cobre was primarily a copper-
mining community of slaves. The slaves, however, were royal slaves and
were the direct property of the Crown, meaning that the king of Spain
owned the mines and the slaves. Royal slaves were primarily involved in
the construction and operation of the Crown's projects. By the second-
half of the eighteenth century the town had become a community of
blacks, with a combination of slaves and freed people. The community
in Cobre was designated as a *pueblo*, which gave it special status. Privileges of a *pueblo* included a limited local government and a local militia
with its own officers.

The first altar dedicated to La Caridad was located near the copper
mines, where slaves toiled under Spanish rule. It is significant that
Cachita's first altar is located in the area of Barajagua, lands that a decade earlier had been threatened to be taken from the slaves. In other
words, her first altar was situated in lands that were vital to the slave
community. The altar was ordered by the head of the mines, Captain

Don Francisco Sánchez de Moya. The importance of her clothing reenters the narrative at this first altar. As mentioned in the previous section, when she was found in the ocean her clothes were dry. At this first site she continually disappeared at night and reappeared, now with wet clothes. She inverted the order of things, appearing wet on dry land and dry on the waters. This inversion is symbolic of her upsetting the social order of the era. It is also seen in her apparition to a slave and two Indigenous and her appearance in the waters, away from the colonial order. "While the Virgin appeared to him [Juan Moreno] and the Indians outside or beyond the colonial social order—in nature—they took her back into 'culture' or 'civilization' through the prescribed social political channels, which at the time she subverted."[7] The story of La Caridad is one of a Marian image that appears to and accompanies the slave community in Cobre. When Sánchez de Moya ordered that a new shrine be built to her on a quarry hill, away from the mines, La Caridad protested. She sent lights into the sky and eventually was returned to her desired space next to the mines. She thus moves from the marginalized (in her apparition) to the centers of power and back to the marginalized (the miners).

La Caridad eventually became the object of national devotion. During the latter half of the nineteenth century she became a central feature of Cuban national identity. "Although devotion to Our Lady of Charity did begin in the seventeenth century in Oriente, it was only during the nineteenth century that nationalist sentiment arose in Cuba—the last of Spain's colonies in the Americas to secure independence—so it was only then that the Virgin could become so closely identified with the nation."[8] During the second war for independence (1895–98) Cuban soldiers began to appeal to her to act in their behalf, and they began to wear images of her on their uniforms. By the time the Cuban Republic is established in 1902, she had become "the rebel Virgin, the patriot Virgin, the national Virgin."[9] In 1915 a group of veterans petitioned Pope Benedict XV that she be named the patroness of Cuba. On May 10, 1916, she was named patroness, and a new shrine was constructed for her. Prior to this pomp and circumstance, however, she was a local devotion, the patroness of a slave community in eastern Cuba. Throughout Cuban history her significance and her very appearance have shifted to meet the needs of the Cuban community, whose devotion to her grew from a local to a national level.

With La Caridad's growing prominence as the official patroness of Cuba, however, her narrative altered to accommodate the broader Cuban population. The origin of the different transformations of the three figures in the narrative remains unknown. What is clear, however, is that the story and the iconography surrounding Cachita are whitened as her prominence among all Cubans grows. An 1874 painting by Joaquín Pérez Ordaz shows the black Juan in the classic prayerful pose, Cachita in blue, and what could be interpreted as a white Juan. The sea is stormy and she appears as a large figure before them. This painting was placed on an altar to the Virgin in her shrine.[10] A mid-nineteenth-century painting by the Spaniard Víctor Patricio de Landuluze shows a similar image, though he also lightens the skin of Cachita and definitely makes one Juan white.[11] The whitening of Cachita's story not only affects her visual representation but also the very narrative of her apparition. In 1935 the chaplain of the sanctuary, Juan Antonio Veyrunes Dubois, reedited Fonseca's history of La Caridad. In this edition La Caridad is white, and from then on the three Juans are depicted as black, white, and mixed.[12]

La Caridad was transformed into the symbol of Cuban nationalism during the Cuban struggles against colonial rule. The nationalist fervor associated with La Caridad has not disappeared in the diaspora but has been transformed to mirror the political consciousness of the Cuban American community. Thomas Tweed argues that La Ermita, La Caridad's Miami shrine, is a site of diasporic nationalism. "Through symbols at the shrine, the diaspora imaginatively constructs its collective identity and transports itself to the Cuba of memory and desire."[13] Thus La Caridad comes to symbolize a preferential option for the exile community, one that has been wrongly forced to leave Cuba. As the pamphlet detailing the history of the shrine outlines, La Caridad entered into exile with the Cuban people who were escaping Cuba's totalitarian government. She stands in solidarity with this community. What is not explained, however, is the original image's continued presence in Cuba and how the two relate to each other. In a manner resonant with the transformation of her historical narrative and presence throughout the history of Cuba is yet another rewriting of her history by Cubans in the United States. With all these twists and turns, however, there remains the core devotion and figure.

LYDIA CABRERA

Afro-Cuban scholar and pioneer Lydia Cabrera was born in 1900 in Havana, Cuba. In the late 1920s she moved to Paris, where she lived until 1938. While living in Paris she visited Cuba various times until her permanent move back to the island. The 1940s and 1950s mark the most vigorous era of her research on Afro-Cuban culture and religions. She remained in Cuba until 1960, when she departed to Miami and continued to publish within the field of Afro-Cuban studies. Cabrera's first book, *Cuentos Negros de Cuba*, was published in 1936. First published in French, a Spanish edition did not appear until 1940. Her most widely known work, *El Monte*, was published in 1954.[14] *El Monte* is considered a classic in Afro-Cuban studies, surpassing any study of Afro-Cuban religions prior to its publication. The book highlights, in particular, Roman Catholic elements within Afro-Cuban religious practices. Debunking the myth that all Afro-Cuban religions are the same, Cabrera's research focused on the three major religious groups on the island: Los Ñáñigos (a secret male religious society), Regla de Ocha (popularly and mistakenly known as Santería), and Congolese religions (which include, for example, Palomonte).

Cabrera's work must be contextualized in light of the 1920s surge in Afro-Cuban studies, most notably the *Afrocubanismo* movement. The roots of *Afrocubanismo* (Afro-Cubanism) are multiple, yet one of its starting points was a reaction to the work of white scholars such as ethnographer and criminologist Fernando Ortiz. (Cabrera was, interestingly, the sister-in-law to the father of Ortiz.) Rejecting a liberal, assimilationist approach to Afro-Cuban religion and culture, especially as found in the early work of Ortiz and more conservative efforts to erase African culture in Cuba, Afro-Cubanists offered a radical alternative. The *négrismo* movement, one that predated Afro-Cubanism, emphasized the exotic nature of blacks. This exotic depiction of blacks was rejected, and an alternative construction of Afro-Cuban and consequently Cuban identity was proposed. "Afro-Cubanism proposed for the island a creole identity, a composite multicultural, multiracial identity in which the African was central."[15] Afro-Cubanists called for a radical break in the manner in which Afro-Cuban culture was understood and appreciated on the island. Thus while figures such as Ortiz represent the birth of Afro-Cuban studies on the island, the movement that is knows as Afro-Cubanism was a reaction to white scholarship on the Afro-Cuban community.

An explosion of Afro-Cubanism occurred in the 1920s. Multiple factors contributed to this renaissance. As Carmen Gómez García notes, this movement must be situated in light of broader global movements. In Europe, a surge in ethnographic research on African cultures during the 1920s influenced various cultural sectors, including music, dance, literature, and painting.[16] This is significant in Cabrera's case, given that her first text was published in France. The Harlem Renaissance in the United States also influenced Afro-Cubanism, often very directly.[17] Afro-Cubanists were both black and non-black (Alejo Carpentier being an example of a prominent white figure). Ultimately, Afro-Cubanism was a movement fueled by a rediscovery of Cuba's African heritage. While interest in African culture predated this movement, the manner in which Afro-Cubanists depicted and celebrated Afro-Cuban culture marked prior efforts. The movement thrived between 1926 and 1938.

An overview of Cabrera's corpus is impossible in such limited space. Her writings are massive in scope. Publications range from books on the various Afro-Cuban religions to popular medicine to herbal studies to animals in folklore and magic to linguistics. My focus is her research on Afro-Cuban religions, in particular three dimensions of her methodology that are fundamental to understanding her long-term contribution: her transcription of Afro-Cuban narratives; her emphasis on the Roman Catholic elements of Afro-Cuban religious practices; and her consistent defense of African cultures. These three areas represent elements of her corpus that are not only central to understanding her work but also significant in light of the contemporary concerns of Latino/a and Latin American theologies.

In the area of Afro-Cuban religions, Cabrera's methodology is characterized by her efforts to transcribe as literally as possible the information her informants passed on to her, primarily in the areas of mythology and folktales. This aspect of her work is seen as the most innovative component of her corpus. Cabrera's goal was to gather information directly from the elderly members of the Afro-Cuban community and offer as literal a transmission as possible. As the prologue to *El Monte* highlights, she did not want to change their words or judgments, only offering clarification when it was deemed essential. Joseph Murphy has argued that through her transcription of oral tradition into printed text Cabrera has transformed the very nature of Afro-Cuban religions, transforming a purely oral tradition into a written one.[18] Underlying her methodology was a desire to represent the psychological world view underlying Afro-Cuban mythology. Magic, the spirits, and animism mark her work. Cabrera's desire to transmit this spirituality, argues Jorge Castellanos, makes her work a precursor to Latin American magical realism.[19] While not contesting its scientific value, Guillermo Cabera Infante describes her method as "anthro-poetic."[20] This desire to give voice to voiceless Afro-Cubans, an ignored and marginalized population among Cubans and Cuban Americans, is a central thrust of Cabrera's corpus and shares affinities with the methodologies of Latino/a and Latin American theologies.[21]

A second central methodological gesture in Cabrera's corpus is her emphasis on the Roman Catholic elements of Afro-Cuban religions. Cabrera argues that while Afro-Cubans practiced their own religion, this does not mean that they were not Catholic. Underlying her research is the question of whether Afro-Cuban religions conflict with Christianity. Cabrera argues that many practitioners of Regla de Ocha, for example, are also Catholic. Their public religiosity is white Catholicism, while their private religion is that of Africa. "For those in both religions (Catholicism and Santería), the only thing that varied was the names of the gods. When asked how she could worship Christian and African gods together and at the same time, an old lady asserted: 'God is the same but with a different necklace.'"[22] Cabrera contends that evangelization did not radically transform the world view of Afro-Cubans, primarily due to the lack of catechetical instruction. This is the case for rural slaves in particular. "Superficially Afro Cubans were Catholic, but they continued to be authentic Africans, and to Olodumare and to all the orichas they would talk, as they do today, in Anagó, in Yoruba, for they do not lose their language."[23] Cabrera argues that while slaves were definitely shaped by the Catholic context of Cuba, they never lost their African cosmological core. Her research reveals the heavy use of Roman Catholic symbolism, rituals (including Mass and baptism), and prayers within Afro-Cuban religions.

As noted above, Afro-Cubanism emerged as a response to and critique of scholarship that either exoticized or sought to erase Afro-Cuban culture from the island. Cabrera, though not traditionally situated within Afro-Cubanism, can be seen as a kindred spirit to the movement. Unlike her predecessors, such as Fernando Ortiz, whose early work sought to eradicate African culture from Cuba, Cabrera always defended the value and importance of the Afro-Cuban for Cubans. As she argues in her article "Las Religiones Africanas en Cuba," much to many Cubans' shock and remorse, African culture is just as valid a cultural category as (Spanish) Cuban culture. She compares the dismissal by Cubans of Afro-Cuban culture to the European dismissal of Latin American cultures.[24] The article "La Influencia Africana en el Pueblo de Cuba" directly combats prejudice against Afro-Cuban cultures by dismantling the myth of white (European) superiority over African and Indigenous cultures.[25] Cabrera outlines the various manners in which Afro-Cuban culture has come to saturate Cuban culture as a whole. Cabrera's research on Afro-Cuban culture thus has sociopolitical implications for Cuban and Cuban American peoples. In naming and seeking to unravel racism toward Afro-Cubans, Cabrera forced Cubans to face the very racism they often seek to ignore within historical and contemporary Cuba and in the Cuban American community.[26]

Cabrera's methodology is not without flaws. In her attempt to document the "purest" accounts of Afro-Cuban mythology, her scholarship pays little attention to the manner in which her social location and that of her informants shaped her research. Cabrera was not interested in the lives of her informants; she was interested in their stories. D. H. Brown notes that both she and her brother-in-law, Fernando Ortiz, "were far more interested in their 'informants' as transparent folkloric repositories than as agents whose biographies and social conditions were significant and would compel attention."[27] In addition, Cabrera's whiteness, as well as her outsider status within the world of Afro-Cuban religions, clearly affected her work. Nonetheless, in spite of certain limitations, one cannot deny her ground-breaking contribution. She is an innovative pioneer in Latin American religious studies, and she deserves a prominent place in Latino/a and Latin American theologies.

IMPLICATIONS

In light of this brief introduction to La Caridad and Cabrera, I would like to explore three implications that emerge from a serious consideration of Afro-Cuban religion within Latino/a and Latin American religious/theological studies. The first is the need for more intentional scholarship on the Cuban and Cuban American contexts. Given the overwhelming presence of Cuban American theologians within Latino/a theology, the silence surrounding Cuba is perplexing. Miguel De La Torre links this primacy to the economic and racial privilege of the Cuban American community as a whole in the United States:

> When exilic Cubans are lumped together with Mexicans, Puerto Ricans, and other Latin Americans under the term Hispanic and/or Latino/a, the power and privilege achieved by the Miami community, largely composed of those with light skins and of upper- and middle-class status, is masked by the religious discourse claiming a Latino/a religious commonality. . . . The desire of Latino/a religious scholars to evoke a pan-ethnic unity diminishes the reality of how sexism, racism, and classism are alive and well within the Exile Cubans' constructed religious and political space.[28]

De La Torre argues that due to the influence of Latin American liberation theology Cuban American theologians ignore their reality because they want to erase their political privileges and stand in solidarity with the oppressed. In other words, to reflect theologically from the Cuban American context would undermine the image of Latinos/as as poor, brown, and marginalized. While I agree with De La Torre's assessment of the ambiguous relationship shared between the Cuban American

political context and some of the principles of Latin American liberation theology—especially its early infatuation with Marxism—I find his
depiction of the Cuban American community limited and erroneous.
Nonetheless, there is a clear disparity when one looks at the fact that the
majority of the first two waves of Latino/a theologians are Cuban American while Latino/a theology remains relatively silent concerning Cuba.
This is especially perplexing when one considers Latino/a theology's
emphasis on social location and contextuality.

A second implication of this study is the need for a more porous understanding of Latino/a and Latin American theologies. This is a press-
ing question for Latino/a theologians in particular, especially those who
wish to articulate a contextual theology with a heavy historical foundation. Latino/a theologians have focused a great amount of attention on
distinguishing themselves from their Latin American colleagues. In its
early years Latino/a theology was considered a subset at best of Latin
American theology. Given the prominence of Latin American liberation
theology, the work of Latino/a theologians was often eclipsed, ignored,
or replaced by their Latin American colleagues. Thus Anglo scholars
believed that if they included a Gustavo Gutiérrez or a Jon Sobrino in
their curriculum, the Latin American and Latino/a question was simultaneously covered.

This is not the case. As A. Figueroa Deck points out, "We are not
Latin American theologians 'passing through.' We are North Americans
of Hispanic origin. We have one foot, as it were, in the Third World and
another in the First."[29] Latino/a theologians, as bridge people between
the First and Third Worlds, face the ambiguous position of being people
on the margin, living between two cultures. They are never fully accepted by the dominant U.S. culture, yet their countries of origin also
reject them. They are neither, yet they belong to both. This both/and
position is at times a place of crisis and confusion. Yet it is also a site of
creativity, a space where Latinos/as can draw from both cultures and
create something new, a Latino/a reality that contains elements of both
yet whose whole is much greater than its parts.

This bridge reality is echoed by Luis Pedraja when he writes:

Latinos and Latinas live at the juncture of cultures, in the hyphen
that joins their multiple heritages into one embodied reality. We
are both Americans and Hispanics. We often find distinct aspects
of both cultures existing together in our lives. . . . Yet, because we
embody different traits and cultures, we live on the boundary between contexts, existing in both as a living bridge between the cultures, races, and contexts that gave us birth.[30]

I could cite numerous examples from the works of Latino/a theologians that reiterate the same point: Latino/a culture is distinct from Latin American culture. The work of Latino/a theologians is connected to yet separate from Latin American theology. One should not confuse the two; although Latinos/as and Latin Americans have a shared history, they are not the same people.

I am fully aware of the reasons Latino/a theologians have spent substantial energy on distinguishing themselves from their Latin American colleagues. There was clearly, at first, a certain confusion concerning the role of, and at times a dismissal of, Latino/a theology. This is seen, for example, in the substantial dialogue one finds between black and Latin American liberation theologians, which pales in comparison to dialogue between blacks and Latinos/as, and for that matter, Latinos/as and Latin Americans. To put it bluntly, Latino/a theology has not been taken seriously by the theological academy. This has changed over the past few years, and today Latino/a theology is recognized as a vital and independent voice.

My concern, however, is whether, Latinos/as perhaps protested too much. In other words, in distinguishing ourselves so vehemently from our Latin American colleagues have we rhetorically cut ourselves off from the wealth of Latin American resources that constitute our history? And when we choose to write about that history, does our theology become Latin American or remain Latino/a? In my own work, I stumbled across this question when I wrote my first book on Latin American church mother Sor Juana Inés de la Cruz.[31] My book was marketed and categorized as Latina theology. Is it? I am not so sure. True, I am a Cuban American and my work is influenced by my hermeneutic as a Latina. However, the subject matter of my text was a Latin American figure. Thus which is it: Latin American or Latino/a theology? I would argue both, yet given the politics of identity within the theological academy my book cannot be both. A similar question arose for me when writing this essay, for much of my research focused on Cuba. However, in an effort to write a historically grounded theology, I must, as a Latina theologian, turn to Latin America in a substantial manner.

This concern has significant implications for the construction of Latino/a theology rhetorically and the politics of identity. In distinguishing ourselves so sharply from our Latin American colleagues have we ruined our ability to speak authentically about Latin American topics? How do we write a Latino/a theology that is historically informed by Latin America without negating our distinctiveness as Latinos/as? I find it noteworthy that there are very few Latino/a church historians and that most accounts of Latino/a history begin with U.S. involvement in Latin America's histories. It is my hope that in raising this question a more fluid understanding of Latino/a and Latin American theologies can be constructed, one that takes seriously the distinctiveness of their present conditions yet recognizes their shared history.

A third implication that emerges from this study is the need for more direct scholarship on Afro-Latin and Latin American religiosity by both Latino/a and Latin American theologians. Research on La Caridad and Cabrera raises distinctive issues regarding this theme. Within the disciplines of Latino/a and Latin American liberation theologies, Mariological reflection on La Caridad is scarce. For Miguel De La Torre, La Caridad is a liberationist figure that contests white privilege and represents the birth of the Cuban people:

> Her apparition accomplished two tasks. First, she symbolized the birth of Cuban identity, the birth of *cubanidad*. Cuba's patron saint ceased being a European white figure. Instead, the Divine appeared in the form of a bronze-colored woman, a color symbolizing death (the color of the mined copper responsible for the death of Amerindians and Africans) as well as life (the color of the Cuban new race). Second, to the oppressed she gave dignity. Rather than appearing to the white Spaniard religious leaders, she identified with the economic and racial outcasts, appearing in the color of oppressed Cubans. A biracial *virgin* severs the bond between inferiority and nonwhiteness, for the Divine is represented as colored.[32]

De La Torre raises some important points, particularly on the dynamic of race and power and its theological significance. The function of race in the apparition is a vital point to explore. The appearance of a bronze statue is extremely significant, for as De La Torre rightly highlights, the Divine takes the form of nonwhiteness. In a society in which whiteness equals power and authority, where the Spaniards had the ultimate access and control over the sacred, the appearance of a bronze Marian statue demonstrates God's solidarity with people of color. Through the apparition of La Caridad, the Divine takes the form of the oppressed communities of Cuba, the slaves and the Indigenous. Whiteness is no longer the sole color of the sacred.

The form of La Caridad's appearance is significant, but as De La Torre's citation implies, so are the individuals to whom she appears, who in a manner in which she challenge the dominant order. Spanish clergy and authorities are not the individuals that stumble upon her statue in the waters of the Bay of Nipe. Instead, she is discovered by a slave and two Indigenous brothers. The subversive nature of this is perhaps most clearly seen in the manner throughout Cuban history that the racial identity of these three men has been changed in order to suit the needs of those in power. La Caridad appears to three oppressed men within an oppressed community, demonstrating her solidarity with them. Her constant presence within the mining community demonstrates her solidarity with those who were forced to dedicate their lives to backbreaking labor at the hands of Spanish authority. Consequently, the how and the who of La Caridad's apparition are not the only dimensions of her narrative that are significant; the where is also revelatory of her solidarity with oppressed communities. She does not appear in the centers of power but in nature, away from the colonial order. She is discovered in the waters while three men are engaged in an everyday task, the gathering of salt. Mary thus reveals herself in the everyday life of an oppressed community. The sacred is present in the everyday, within those mundane moments that we take for granted. La Caridad also reveals God's presence and preferential option for the powerless.

Though La Caridad appears to two Indigenous men, Juan Moreno's participation in this event is significant. While the Indigenous play a significant role in New World Marian apparition stories, slaves and blacks are notably absent, even in areas where a significant portion of the population was black. Moreno's participation in the story of Cachita is significant in this regard, even though the narrative still contains the participation of two Indigenous men. It is notable that Moreno becomes the main witness and author of the apparition. As historian M. E. Díaz highlights, "It is as if in the case of the Virgin of El Cobre, slaves wrote themselves—and were allowed to write themselves—into a mainstream story, altering a genre from which they tended to be excluded regardless of their evangelization, creolization, and incorporation into the New World."[33] It is ironic that only after a white man is included in the story that La Caridad comes to be seen as paradigmatic of Cuban identity.[34] The slave presence in this narrative and the location of this devotion within an Afro-Cuban community are a radical break from conventional Marian apparition accounts, demonstrating, as the authors above highlight, the Marian preferential option for the oppressed.

Lydia Cabrera is an intellectual foremother to Latina and Latin American religious scholars. Her corpus, considered one of the most well-known and extensive bodies of writings on Afro-Cuban religions is a vital moment in the history of Afro-Latino/a and Latin American studies, religious studies, feminist scholarship, and Cuban and Cuban American intellectual history. It is ironic that a woman whose scholarship is so well known to Cubans and Cuban Americans has yet to appear in the writings of Latino/a and Latin American religious/theological studies in a substantial manner. Her work challenges the assumption that Cuban women and their descendants have no intellectual history. In addition, her work, as a white woman specializing in Afro-Cuban religions, challenges the dualistic categorization of black-white and Latino/a-black studies. Jorge Castellanos notes with amazement, for example, her work with the *ñáñigos*, a secret society of African men, considering Cabrera was a white woman who pertained to Cuban aristocracy.[35] As a white woman specializing in African religions, her corpus begs the question of how one defines Afro-Cuban studies: by the author? the subject? As a Cuban woman working within Afro-Cuban studies she also pushes one to re-evaluate the construction of black and Latino/a and Latin American studies. Does her work not fall into both camps?

These questions and others that emerge from this essay are a modest attempt to begin multiple conversations within the fields of religious and theological studies. While one could argue that theology is not an appropriate site for the study of Afro-Cuban religions, the Afro-Cuban nature of all Cuban and Cuban American culture and religiosity (including Roman Catholic) contests that claim. The Afro-Cuban devotion to La Caridad and Cabrera's assertion that *Afro-Cubanidad* saturates *Cubanidad* force the contemporary scholar to take Afro-Cuba seriously. In addition, an emphasis on Afro-Cuban culture and religion breaks open a significant conversation on the construction of race, culture, and national identity. Like its implications for the categories of Latin American and Latino/a studies, this field forces a more porous understanding of what have become rigid identity categories. The silence surrounding the faith life of the Afro-Cuban community is glaring and must be corrected. As Silvia Regina de Lima Silva notes, "We cannot omit the great question about the face of God that sometimes is hidden and manifested in the Afro-Latin American experience."[36] The experience of the Divine is indeed found in the religious faith and expression of Afro-Cubans, and they merit the full and rapt attention of the theological academy.

Notes

[1] Prominent Latino theologians Alejandro García-Rivera, Orlando O. Espín, and Roberto S. Goizueta are all Cuban Americans. Miguel De La Torre is the only Cuban American religious scholar who writes specifically about the Cuban American community in a substantial manner. See "Constructing Our Cuban

Ethnic Identity While in Babylon," in *A Dream Unfinished: Theological Reflections on America from the Margins*, ed. Eleazer S. Fernandez and Fernando F. Segovia (Maryknoll, NY: Orbis Books, 2001), 185–202; *La Lucha por Cuba: Religion and Politics on the Streets of Miami* (Berkeley and Los Angeles: University of California Press, 2003); "Ochún: (N)either the M(O)ther of all Cubans (n)or the Bleached Virgin," *Journal of the American Academy of Religion* 69, no. 4 (December 2001): 837–61; *The Quest for the Cuban Christ: A Historical Search* (Gainesville: University Press of Florida, 2002). Also see Miguel H. Díaz, "Dime con quién andas y te dire quién eres (Tell me with whom you walk, and I will tell you who you are): We Walk with Our Lady of Charity," in *From the Heart of Our People: Latino/a Explorations in Systematic Theology*, ed. Orlando O. Espín and Miguel H. Díaz (Maryknoll, NY: Orbis Books, 1999), 153–71; Alejandro García-Rivera, "Wisdom, Beauty, and the Cosmos," in *Cuerpo de Cristo: The Hispanic Presence in the U.S. Catholic Church*, ed. Peter Casarella and Raúl Gomez (New York: Crossroad, 1998), 106–33; Ada María Isasi-Díaz, "La Habana: The City That Inhabits Me: A Multi-Site Understanding of Location," in *La Lucha Continues: Mujerista Theology* (Maryknoll, NY: Orbis Books, 2004), 122–56.

[2] John M. Kirk, "(Still) Waiting for John Paul II: The Church in Cuba," in *The Latin American Church in a Changing Environment*, ed. Edward L. Cleary and Hannah Stewart-Gambino (Boulder, CO: Lynne Rienner Publishers, 1992), 147–65.

[3] Ibid., 152.

[4] Olga Portuondo Zúñiga dates the apparition at 1613. María Elena Díaz, in her excellent study of the slave community in El Cobre, dates the apparition at 1604. See Olga Portuondo Zúñiga, *La Virgen de la Caridad del Cobre: Simbolo de la Cubanía*, rev. ed. (Madrid: Agualarga Editores, 2002), 75; and María Elena Díaz, *The Virgin, the King, and the Royal Slaves of El Cobre: Negotiating Freedom in Colonial Cuba, 1670–1780* (Stanford, CA: Stanford University Press, 2000).

[5] Moreno's role in the slave community is not limited to this religious apparition. At the age of seventy-seven he was given the position of captain of the local militia, a role that entailed military and religious duties. Moreno represented the slaves of Cobre when the Crown attempted to transfer them to Havana. He was an advocate for the slaves and a mediator between them and Spanish authorities. Moreno played an active political role among the Cobre slaves and was, for some time, seen as their leader and representative to the Spanish. It is interesting to note that the recording of his testimony and his prominent position occur around the same time period. Juan Moreno is not the only Afro-Cuban to whom La Caridad appeared. Onofre de Fonseca, who was chaplain of the shrine of El Cobre from 1683 to 1710, introduces the narrative of the girl Apolonia to his written account of *La Virgen*'s presence among the Cobre community. Daughter of one of the miners, Apolonia was on her way to visit her mother when La Caridad appeared before her telling her where she wanted her temple built. This second apparition story is not as widely known

within Cuba, and its later date, coupled with a lack of firsthand testimony, makes its historical validity questionable.

[6] How this statue arrived in these waters is a topic open to much speculation. Did it fall off a Spanish ship? Was it brought to the island and somehow fell in the ocean? Many scholars argue that it is in fact an image of Spanish origins brought to Cuba. A Marian image named Our Lady of Charity was the object of devotion in Spain in the mid-sixteenth century. This image, found in the town of Illescas, resembles the Cuban version and is also named Nuestra Señora de la Caridad. North American historian Irene Wright argues that the images are identical. In her 1922 account of her visit to the shrine in Spain she describes discovering the mirror image to the Cuban devotion. She also highlights, importantly, that Illescas is near Toledo, the home of Captain Sánchez de Moya. Sánchez de Moya was in charge of the Cobre community at the time of La Caridad's apparition. See See Irene Wright, "Our Lady of Charity," *Hispanic American Historical Review* 5 (1922): 709–17. A different theory of the statue's origins has been proposed more recently by Cuban historian Olga Portuondo Zúñiga, who has written the most comprehensive history of La Caridad to date. Portuondo Zúñiga proposes the theory that the image itself may have been constructed in Cuba and not in Spain or other parts of Europe. Francisco Figueroa Marrero, the last specialist to restore the image, claimed that the head of the image was made of some sort of vegetable or corn paste. This sort of material for icons was very typical of the Indigenous. Figueroa also depicted several layers of paint on the image, which implies the possibility of heads being changed. One coat of paint was yellow, a ritual color for the Indigenous (Portuondo Zúñiga, *La Virgen de la Caridad del Cobre*, 58–60).

[7] Díaz, *The Virgin, the King, and the Royal Slaves*, 100.

[8] Thomas Tweed, *Our Lady of the Exile: Diasporic Religion at a Cuban Catholic Shrine in Miami* (New York: Oxford University Press, 1997), 23.

[9] Ibid., 23.

[10] Portuondo Zúñiga, *La Virgen de la Caridad del Cobre*, 71.

[11] Ibid., 163.

[12] Ibid., 209–10.

[13] Thomas Tweed, "Diasporic Nationalism and Urban Landscape," in *Gods of the City: Religion and the American Urban Landscape*, ed. Robert A. Orsi (Bloomington: Indianapolis University Press, 1999), 133.

[14] Lydia Cabrera's publications are extensive. Among her most significant works are *Los Animales en el Folklore y la Magia de Cuba* (Miami: Ediciones Universales, 1988); *Cuentos Negros de Cuba*, 2nd ed. (Madrid: Ediciones CR, 1972); *La Lengua Sagrada de los Ñáñigos* (Miami: Colección CR, 1988); *El Monte: Igbo, finda, ewe orisha, vitti nfinda* (Miami: Colección de Chicherekú, 1971); *La Sociedad Secreta Abakuá* (Miami: Ediciones CR, 1970); and *Yemayá y Ochún: Kariocha, Iyalorichas Y Olorichas* (Madrid: Forma Gráfica, 1974).

[15] George Brandon, *Santería from Africa to the New World: The Dead Sell Memories* (Bloomington: Indiana University Press, 1993), 92. For an excellent

overview of Afro-Cubanism, see Robin D. Moore, *Nationalizing Blackness: Afrocubanismo and Artistic Revolution in Havana, 1920–1940* (Pittsburgh: University of Pittsburgh Press, 1997).

[16] Carmen Gómez García, "Cuban Social Poetry and the Struggle against Two Racisms," in *Between Race and Empire: African-Americans and Cubans before the Cuban Revolution*, ed. Lisa Borck and Digna Castañeda Fuertes (Philadelphia: Temple University Press, 1988), 221.

[17] For a study of the relationship between Afro-Cubanist poet and essayist Nicolás Guillén and Langston Hughes, see Keith Ellis, "Nicolás Guillén and Langston Hughes: Convergences and Divergences," in Borck and Castañeda Fuertes, *Between Race and Empire*, 129–67.

[18] Joseph Murphy, "Lydia Cabrera and La Regla de Ocha in the United States," in *En Torno a Lydia Cabrera: Cincuentenario de "Cuentos Negros en Cuba" 1936–1986*, ed. Isabel Castellanos and Josefina Inclán (Miami: Ediciones Universal, 1987), 246.

[19] Jorge Castellanos, *Pioneros de la Etnografía Afrocubana: Fernando Ortiz, Rómulo Lachatañeré, Lydia Cabrera* (Miami: Ediciones Universal, 2003), 192.

[20] In ibid., 199.

[21] I am in no way implying that Cabrera is a proto–Latin American theologian. She is not. However, in Cabrera's corpus one finds a kindred spirit as a historical source for Latino/a and Latin American theologies. Some Latina theologians share her emphasis on oral tradition. See Ana María Pineda, "The Oral Tradition of a People," in *Hispanic/Latino Theology: Challenge and Promise*, ed. Ada María Isasi-Díaz and Fernando F. Segovia (Minneapolis: Fortress Press, 1996), 104–16; Jeanette Rodríguez, *Stories We Live/Cuentos Que Vivimos: Hispanic Women's Spirituality* (Mahwah, NJ: Paulist Press, 1996).

[22] Lydia Cabrera, "Religious Syncretism in Cuba," *Journal of Caribbean Studies* 10, no. 1–2 (Winter 1994–Spring 1995): 86.

[23] Ibid.

[24] Lydia Cabrera, "Las Religiones Africanas en Cuba," in *Páginas Sueltas*, ed. Isabel Castellanos (Miami: Ediciones Universal, 1994), 539.

[25] Lydia Cabrera, "La Influencia Africana en el Pueblo de Cuba," in Castellanos, *Páginas Sueltas*, 542.

[26] Scholars on the race question (or problem, depending on one's source) in twentieth-century Cuba differ wildly in their interpretations of this era. It is clear that racism existed in pre-Castro Cuba; nonetheless, blacks in Cuba were able to advance socially, particularly in the areas of politics and government. However, while the majority of Cuba's armed forces in the struggle for independence from Spain were black, very few blacks were admitted into positions of leadership in the new republic's government. The 1912 race war in Cuba also demonstrates that stories of a racist-free island are myths. Independence leaders such as José Martí, who argued for a de-racialized understanding of Cuban identity, offered an idealist position that differed radically from the everyday life of Cubans. What is clear in the history of the first sixty years of the twentieth century is that the birth of Cuba as a nation was a tumultuous process in

which questions of race and national identity featured prominently. Various excellent studies on this theme exist. See Alejandro de la Fuente, *A Nation for All: Race, Inequality, and Politics in Twentieth-Century Cuba* (Chapel Hill: University of North Carolina Press, 2001); Rafael Fermoselle, *Política y Color en Cuba: La Guerrita de 1912* (Madrid: Editorial Colibrí, 2002); Aline Helg, *Our Rightful Share: The Afro-Cuban Struggle for Equality, 1886–1912* (Chapel Hill: University of North Carolina Press, 1995).

[27] David H. Brown, *Santería Enthroned: Art, Ritual, and Innovation in an Afro-Cuban Religion* (Chicago: University of Chicago Press, 2003), 293.

[28] De La Torre, *La Lucha por Cuba*, 18.

[29] Allan Figueroa Deck, "Introduction," in *Frontiers of Hispanic Theology* (Maryknoll, NY: Orbis Books, 1992), ix.

[30] Luis Pedraja, *Teología: An Introduction to Hispanic Theology* (Nashville: Abingdon Press, 2003), 21.

[31] Michelle A. González, *Sor Juana: Beauty and Justice in the Americas* (Maryknoll, NY: Orbis Books, 2003).

[32] De La Torre, "Ochún," 849–50.

[33] Díaz, *The Virgin, the King, and the Royal Slaves*, 97.

[34] Miguel H. Díaz offers a slightly different interpretation of La Caridad, simultaneously attempting to focus on the narrative as it has been transformed throughout Cuban history while also analyzing the historical account of the apparition. He too emphasizes the significance of race in the narrative, though for him the "three Juans" are the center of his reflection. Centering on the oral tradition that there were three men named Juan—a slave, an Indigenous, and a *criollo*—to whom the statue appeared and consequently saved in the midst of a storm, for Díaz, La Caridad comes to represent the interconnection of European, African, and American Indian peoples. This distortion is seen positively, even to the point that the reduction of the men to the name of Juan is viewed as having theological weight. For Díaz, the transformation of the narrative, by way of oral tradition, to include a *criollo* can be interpreted as promoting the racial equality of the three men on the boat. He does not view the exclusion of one of the Indigenous brothers as a whitening of the story but instead gives it a positive spin as a model of racial equality. While I am not averse to Díaz's interpretation, I view the removal of one Indigenous brother and the insertion of the *criollo* as a way of undermining the subversive nature of the apparition. La Caridad was not discovered during a time of racial harmony, but instead during what was perhaps the bleakest moment in Cuban history, during the enslavement and genocide of nonwhite peoples. Her appearance to members of the forgotten sectors of the Cuban colony should not be diminished by including a white man. She did not appear to a white man, the discovery of her statue was outside of the realm of Spanish authority and involvement. While the image of Mary appearing to the three "races" of Cuba as they row together on the Bay of Nipe—something that never would have occurred at that time period, for can one really picture a white Spaniard rowing a boat for an African slave?—is a beautiful one, this picture of racial harmony is a falsehood that weakens her

solidarity with the Indigenous and slave communities. See Díaz, "Dime con quién andas y te dire quién eres."

[35] Castellanos, *Pioneros de la Etnografía Afrocubana,* 209.

[36] Silvia Regina de Lima Silva, "Black Latin American Theology: A New Way to Sense, to Feel, and to Speak of God," in *Black Faith and Public Talk: Critical Essays on James H. Cone's Black Theology and Black Power,* ed. Dwight N. Hopkins (Maryknoll, NY: Orbis Books, 1999), 190.

8

Because of an Ethiopian Woman

Reflections on Race, Gender, and Religion in the Biblical World

Maricel Mena-López

The biblical people found themselves in a crossroads of the world that linguists and some historians have usually called Afro-Asian. The African world and the Asian world were not separated, as biblical science supposes when it denies any African influence in the Syro-Palestine region.[1] Although the cultural legacy proceeding from western Asia has predominated in the study of the religion of Israel, questions must be asked about why the hieroglyphic materials from Canaan have prevailed in the historical reconstruction of Israelite religion and not the sacred sources of Egypt.

Despite this neglect, research in the last fifty years has shown that the Egyptian legacy was not an insignificant aspect of the religion of Israel,[2] and I argue that the same could be said with regard to the Ethiopian legacy. The silence of scholars concerning the African peoples that bordered on the Semitic world seems due above all to racism, both explicit and implicit, and such racism has prevented an adequate integration of this research into biblical studies. This essay seeks to contribute to remedying this situation by unmasking the racism and sexism present in the biblical narratives and in the history of research on the Israelite religion.

To accomplish my objective, I turn my attention to one of the many biblical mothers who have still not been well studied from a feminist perspective in biblical theology. Her name is Zipporah, the wife of the patriarch Moses. The silence around her is due in part to the fact that she appears only in short, isolated accounts that come from diverse sources or traditions. Little notice is taken of her because she is seen as simply an "extra" in the story of the Exodus, whereas Moses is the principal actor and his father-in-law, the father of Zipporah, is a secondary actor.

In the story of Exodus, Moses, the leader of the Hebrews enslaved in Egypt, had to flee to the desert of the Midianites after killing an Egyptian who had assaulted a Hebrew laborer. In the desert Moses married the daughter of a priest of that region, variously called Jethro, Hobab, or Reuel. During Moses' stay in the desert Yahweh appeared to him, as recounted in Exodus 3:13–15. This text reveals that before the time of Moses, the God of the Hebrews was not Yahweh; only after Moses did the Hebrews come to identify the gods they had previously adored with Yahweh.

Where did Moses learn the name Yahweh, and what was the religion of the patriarchs like? The biblical texts naturally affirm that the initiative came from Yahweh, but such theological explanation does not satisfy the student of religions. Even before Moses, references can be found to the use of this divine name by various desert tribes (Midianites, Kenites, and Cushites). The biblical account of the meeting between Moses, a fugitive from justice, and his father-in-law in the desert is traditionally taken to be an important key for understanding the book of Exodus (Ex 18:7–12). The father-in-law is portrayed as a priest of Midian who offers sacrifices to Yahweh on behalf of Moses. Furthermore, Cain, who is identified as father of the Kenites (Jgs 4:11) and the Cushites (Gn 10:6–8; 1 Chr 1:8–10), appears in Israelite mythology as a worshipper of Yahweh (Gn 4:3). The same can be said of Zipporah, who in Genesis 4:24–26 performs the circumcision of her son as part of the worship of Yahweh.

Most scholars agree that the pre-Israelite history of the God Yahweh begins among the Kenites, a clan belonging to a larger tribe known as Midian, but they make no reference to Cush or Ethiopia,[3] the region from which Moses' wife came, according to tradition (Nm 12:1). Precisely here is where I propose to deepen our understanding in the course of this essay.

Before entering into that, however, it is interesting to note that the few lines dedicated to Zipporah in the biblical texts characterize her as an enchantress, a sorceress, and a foreigner. Indeed, her contribution to the religion of ancient Israel, or proto-Israel, seems to have resulted in foreign magic's not being condemned. Although in some sources she appears to be of Cushite or Kenite origin, she is also reported to come from Midian. In some cases she is called by her own name, Zipporah, and in others she is simply the "wife of Moses" or the "daughter of the priest Jethro."

If the Exodus tradition preserved the memory of this woman in several narrative sources (Midianite, Kenite, Cushite), then why does the classical exegesis study her only on the basis of the Kenite (Midianite) source? Is there possibly some African legacy in the nascent worship of Yahweh? Is it possible to reconstruct the priesthood of women on the basis of these traditions? Such questions serve as a framework for my attempt to study the process of racialization and sexism to be found in the traditional Euro-centric exegesis and for proposing new epistemological paradigms in biblical studies.

RACE AND SEXISM IN BIBLICAL STUDIES

To begin the discussion, it seems important to define what is understood by race and by sexism in this essay. By race I understand the social constructions mediated by power relationships and their pretensions to evaluate individuals on the basis of congenital or phenotypical traits. Sexism is understood here as acceptance of the supposed inferiority of female biology and female social roles; it involves creating inequalities and seeing men's bodies as incarnations of the Divine.

Racism and its operative aspect, racial discrimination, are a violation of human rights.[4] Racism has been justified, codified into laws and institutions, and socialized by the most diverse types of political, economic, philosophical, biological, theological, and religious means. "Racism is not just a problem of skin color. Its deeper nature resides in the effort to disarticulate a group of humans by the negation of its collective identity."[5]

The lack of collective identity derives from a lack of historical references that allow African women and men to reconstruct a self-image that is worthy of respect and esteem. The construction of the identity of a person is something historical; it is a process carried out in history. But how can persons or groups with racial or ethnic identities that differ from the dominant identity be represented equitably in nations whose institutions do not recognize their particular identities, that is to say, their difference?[6]

According to Charles Taylor, the particular identity of human beings is modeled on the basis of knowledge or the lack thereof; that is to say, persons or groups may be affected by the way they are portrayed by other people, especially if it is through negative or devalued images; they may also be adversely affected by the lack of historical, social, anthropological, theological, or other reference points. For the present author, lack of recognition or inadequate recognition may be one of the principal sources of oppression, insofar as it reduces people to a false and distorted mode of being.[7] Such sources of oppression are manifest in society in general, and especially in those educational processes that pay inadequate attention to cultural contents and social values.

Furthermore, I find that biblical studies give evidence of a lack of recognition of the influence of African peoples in the religion of Israel. When the presence of these peoples does become evident, scholars have recourse to what we here call *racialization*. On the one hand, racialization refers to the injection of a racial element into a situation where it does not exist or is not important; on the other, it refers to the fact that biblical studies are almost always filtered through a white, androcentric process of interpretation and editing.[8] Such a process has ignored the historical role of the groups considered "unimportant" in the construction of Judaism and Christianity, such as women and the peoples and cultures of African origin, among others. Androcentrism and whiteness are the norm. They elevate the status of white men of the Western Semitic horizon, while women and blackness are considered a deviation from this norm.

It is important to emphasize that analyses done from a perspective of race and ethnicity do not always lead to greater sensitivity concerning the disparities of social power between men and women. It is precisely in this area that the analytic instruments of feminism have helped to create awareness of the need to question the explicit sexism in the sphere of religion by using a critical, transformative perspective. It is evident that women participate actively in the world of religious activity, such as Masses, rituals, and community meetings; indeed, they participate much more than men do. In the Abrahamic religions, however, dominion over the sacred is part of the masculine domain, for men are the ones who control rituals, dogmas, theologies and doctrines. Before the patriarchy existed, it is possible that it was women who realized these same activities that men do today in the religious world, and some biblical texts bear witness to this despite their androcentric language.

A major portion of biblical studies is influenced by the racialization and the sexism of the texts and the narratives. Such racialization and sexism derive from the racism and machismo of the world of the interpreter. A clear example of this can be seen in the common interpretation of Numbers 12:1, where Miriam and Aaron, sister and brother of Moses, have murmured against Moses because of the Ethiopian woman that he took as a wife. The commentary of Werner Schmidt on this verse is as follows: "Numbers 12:1 mentions a Cushite woman of Moses. Probably this passage refers not to an Ethiopian woman (according to the Greek and Latin tradition), but to a member of the tribe of Cusha (Cushan), which in Habakkuk 3:7 is mentioned in parallel with Midian; this isolated tradition refers to the same region of the Midianites."[9]

For Schmidt, the woman does not come from the country of Cush but from Midian; he thus denies any possibility that the woman is Ethiopian, while at the same time he doubts whether she is really the wife of Moses. For him, she is simply a woman that Moses found in the desert, not a legitimate wife, and this is the reason for the complaints of Miriam and Aaron. Such arguments show how the author perceives ethical and moral problems where they do not really exist.

A particularly racist assumption is that the cause of the murmuring of Miriam and Aaron was the color of the skin of Moses' wife. It seems to me that, quite to the contrary, the texts show no concern for race; the problem is a crisis of leadership among the two brothers and the sister who have been charged with leading the Israelite people to the promised land. The text itself proves effectively that there is no reference to the color of Zipporah's skin: "Miriam and Aaron too criticized Moses over the Cushite woman he had married. He had indeed married a Cushite woman. They said, 'Is Moses the only one through whom Yahweh has spoken? Has he not spoken through us too?' Yahweh heard this. Now Moses was extremely humble, the humblest man on earth" (Nm 12:1–3).[10]

The first verse makes plain that a dispute over power existed among the three siblings. Miriam and Aaron are not content with Moses' leadership. To express their discontent the redactor uses the root *dabar*, "word" or "murmur," an important rhetorical device that makes them heard by Yahweh (v. 2). What is interesting here is that to achieve their objective they make use of the woman of Moses: not the Midianite woman but the Cushite woman. The text takes care to stress this forcefully by mentioning the fact not once but twice. Is she the woman he married, or is it someone else? The Hebrew verb *laqah*, "take," has the meaning of "take as a spouse,"[11] and for this reason most translations render this text "because of the Cushite woman that he had taken as a spouse."

This woman is only a pretext used by Miriam and Aaron to state their real complaint: "Has the Lord indeed spoken only through Moses? Has he not spoken through us also?" But why are their complaints heard directly by Yahweh and not by Moses? Verse 3 gives us the answer:

Moses is a meek man and possibly for that reason does not react to them. Still other questions arise: Does Moses' wife have some special importance in the nascent worship of Yahweh? Is Yahweh listening only to defend Moses, or is it also because a prophetess of his religion is involved?

These verses portray a struggle for power, but I suspect that the power is in some way related to the leadership exercised by Zipporah. Can it be that Zipporah is a prophetess of Yahweh? Numbers 12:1–3 does not give us a clear answer to this question. Only by having recourse to inter-linear and intertextual interpretation can we draw conclusions in this regard. Perhaps examination of Exodus 4:25–26 will help us to continue our investigation.

Racist interpretations assume that Miriam's skin color is white, but in my judgment this needs to be proved. Why is Miriam justly punished with leprosy, a disease that leaves the skin white as snow? Why was she not punished with some other disease that would blacken her skin? (Nm 12:10). Such questions lead me to believe that the problem does not concern race, since Miriam herself is not white.

One problem for the biblical interpreter is the place of origin of Zipporah. The footnotes in the Jerusalem Bible assume the mention of Cush refers to the tradition of Moses' Midianite marriage. That is to say, they assume that all takes place within the geopolitical Semitic world.

For a long time the tendency of Old Testament scholars has been to negate the participation and the influence of the African nations in Isra-elite history. Especially as regards geography, a distinctive place is given to the Asian region that includes Syria, Palestine, Arabia, and Mesopotamia. Egypt is studied only briefly and as part of the Ancient East, instead of separately as a part of Africa. In the same way, when we look at a map of "the land of the Bible," we find a tendency to "de-Africanize" it. In other words, "most maps present only the areas of Syrio-Palestine and the region to its east, and if there is some representa-tion of Africa, it is restricted to Egypt."[12] Maps of the eighteenth and nineteenth centuries that supposedly describe all the places named in the Bible omit the African nations of Cush, Put, and Cyrene. What is the reason for this neglect? Normally, the maps that do include Cush within Africa consider it to be part of the Ancient Near East. Is it not time for us to revise our geography? To do so, we need to revise also our under-standing of paradise, since Genesis 2:10–14 shows Africa to be included in the Garden of Eden.

The sexism implicit in the whole of Numbers 12 is shown by the fact that only Miriam is punished with leprosy, even though Aaron was

assumed to be guilty as well (Nm 12:11). The interpreter of the Jerusalem Bible generously assumes that Aaron was perhaps punished as well;
he blames the priestly tradition for having spared Aaron's skin. Nonetheless, for the tradition that underlies this scripture, Miriam's leadership is also important, as is noted in the petition that Aaron makes to
Moses: "Oh, my Lord, please do not punish us for the sin we have been
foolish enough to commit. Do not let her be like some monster with its
flesh half eaten away when it leaves its mother's womb!" (Nm 12:11–
12). Moses reacts favorably to this request: "Moses pleaded with Yahweh.
'O God,' he said, 'I beg you, please heal her!'" (12:13). Miriam is excluded from the camp for seven days; only after she is allowed back into
the community can the people continue on their way.

   Although sexism and racism are evident in this chapter, as I have argued, I would still like to investigate, in the following section, the different traditions relating to Zipporah, paying special attention to the theories about her place of origin.

TRADITIONS CONCERNING ZIPPORAH

   In the Hebrew Bible various traditions exist about Zipporah. Some
are related to her father, who is known by three different names. Two of
these names are in the Pentateuch and are attributed to the Midianite
tradition: Jethro (Ex 3:1, 18:1—Elohist source) and Reuel (Ex 2:18; Num
10:29—Yahwist source). (I refer to the sources, although I am aware
that the theories concerning Pentateuch sources are not yet set in stone.)[13]
Literary criticism holds that the name Jethro corresponds to the Elohist
redaction (E) and is closely related to the Israelites' leaving Egypt. The
emphasis on the Exodus and the occupying of land is an important theme
for the literature of the mid-eighth century B.C.E. after the invasion of
Israel by Assyria. Reuel comes from the Yahwist redaction (J), which
originated in southern Palestine and assumes a friendly relationship between the tribes of Judah and the other clans of that area. We are here
dealing with pre-Yahwist narratives, in which religion and the name of
Yahweh have not yet been institutionalized.

   In the Deuteronomic scriptures, whose language comes from the seventh century B.C.E., the name we find for Zipporah's father is Hobab,
and he is specifically associated with the Kenite tribes (Jgs 1:16, 4:11).
Up to this point the sources appear to coincide, except for the reference
found in the Yahwist text of Numbers 10:29, where Hobab is also called
a Midianite. Scholars resolve this problem by concluding that the Kenites

belonged to this Midianite nation. However, if our criteria take into account the antiquity of the texts, how must we treat them?

Schmidt[14] believes that Moses' father-in-law was a Kenite, because the Midianites and the Kenites were related by blood;[15] in such a case there would be only one tradition. This affirmation by Schmidt is deduced from the fact that, according to Genesis 15:19, while the Kenites are Abraham's descendants, the Midianites were descendants of Keturah, the wife of Abraham (Gn 25:1, 1 Chr 1–2). For their part, according to the genealogies of Genesis 10:6–8 and 1 Chronicles 1:8–10, the Cushites appear to be descendants of Ham, the father of Canaan. If these genealogies bear some resemblance to reality, then why cannot Kush, who is a descendant from one of Noah's sons, from whom the nations emerge, also be considered a relative of the Midianites and Kenites?

An independent tradition exists, according to which Moses' wife is of Cushite origin and appears alone, without an allusion to her father's name (Nm 12:1). The identification of this territory with the tribes of Midian is due to the fact that the Cushites of Habakkuk 3:7 appear to be associated with the Arabs.

Traditional exegesis continues to find dubious the historicity of Moses' marriage with a Cushite, since uncertainty exists about whether the tradition comes from the Bronze Age or is a later anachronism, from the times of Persian or Ptolemaic Judaism. In this latter period Cush appears as a place of refuge to which an Egyptian pharaoh retreats in order to reestablish himself and return to drive the foreigners out of Egypt.[16] In this period Egyptians and Cushites would have enjoyed close relations.

Although the already cited literary criticism discerns three traditions with different dates, the criteria take note only of the antiquity of the accounts. Such a presentation makes clear the way Eurocentric logic operates: it unifies and fuses together different traditions that preserve their particular characteristics, even though they occupy the same geographic space. In this way the Kenites and Cushites are robbed of their specific identities and are combined into the Midianite culture. While such logic unifies some entities, it excludes others; for example, the authors find no problem in assuming the Kenite origin of Moses' father-in-law, but they deny the probability of Zipporah's being Cushite. The unity between Midianites and Kenites is based on the fact that the founder of Yahwism in Israel is an Egyptian, who is considered a Semite by most scholars.

Nonetheless, it is well known that the history of the liberation of the Hebrew people as described in the book of Exodus mixes Palestinian traditions with Afro-Asian traditions. The Exodus includes some traditions

that come from Palestine (Joseph) with others that come from Egypt
(Moses) and still others from the land of Midian (Sinai)—and I would
add also from Ethiopia (Zipporah). Such an observation may frighten
some people, but the time has come for us to understand that the history
of Israel has interfaces with the African peoples. For that reason I propose to study in the following sections the Kenites and the Cushites as
independent tribes that made an important contribution to the religion
of Israel.

WHO WERE THE KENITES?

The Kenites were considered to be the true worshipers of Yahweh. Of
course, since they came from the south, they joined with the Israelites
during the journey through the desert (Jgs 1:16). One clan of Kenites left
the tribe and settled in the north under the leadership of Heber, during
the time of Deborah and Barak (Jgs 4:11).

Some researchers even conclude, in the light of Exodus 13, that it was
from the Kenites that the Israelites received a good part of their mono-
theistic theology; this passage, however, treats directly only matters of
social organization. The Rechabites, a clan of the Kenites (1 Chr 2:55),
were of an ascetical bent and insisted on the need for maintaining the
nomadic habits of the followers of Yahweh (Jer 35:8–11).

The Kenites were always portrayed as being on friendly terms with
the Israelites. Their alliance with Moses and the sharing of a common
religion probably helped establish close bonds of friendship between them
during the years when Israel was in the desert (Nm 10:29–32). No indi-
cations exist of any enmity between the two nations (cf. 1 Kgs 27:20;
30:29). The Kenites apparently shared also in the Babylonian exile and
in the restoration, but they no longer appear as a distinct tribe; probably
they were assimilated by the Jews. Yahweh, before becoming the God of
Israel, was the ancient Kenite god of fire, whose dwelling place was the
summit of Sinai.[17]

The Kenites were also ironsmiths and worshipers of fire. Moses' father-in-law came from this people and perhaps introduced his son-in-
law to this form of worship. The association of the Hebrew God with a
local divinity is by no means absurd. It is possible that these people had
observed the mysterious volcanic phenomena on the summit of Sinai
and believed that the gods had their abode there. It is well known that
Yahweh revealed himself on that summit with fire and smoke. Indeed, in
Exodus he is called "the God of the mountain" (Ex 3:1).

Yahweh sometimes appears as the god of fire, as when he appears in the cloud of smoke that covers the peak of Horeb and in the flames of the burning bush (Ex 3:1–6). For that reason he is also called the "God of the bush," though this expression requires clarification. The Hebrew term would require a translation such as "he who dwells in the bush," or better still, "he who resides for a time as a guest of the bush." Although the relations between the Kenite religion and Yahwism are evident, I suspect that the African heritage plays no small part in Israelite religion. For this reason I propose to investigate further the African origin of the religion introduced by Moses, the Egyptian, and by his wife, Zipporah, by way of Ethiopia.

WHO WERE THE ETHIOPIANS?

The Hebrew scriptures refer to Cush in a number of ways: there is mention of the land of Cush or Cushan, there are individuals called Cushi, and there are people labeled Cushites. Such references occur in a variety of contexts: some in narrative passages, others in the prophetic books, and still others in proverbs. There are a total of seventeen such references in the Hebrew scriptures. However, some biblical scholars doubt that Cushan is the same as Cush, the kingdom located to the south of Egypt; they consider it possibly some other group, such as a tribe of Sinai. The argument is simplified in order to avoid controversy, and the balance is tilted in favor of the region of Sinai.

Recent research cites possible Egyptian references that come from the fourteenth and thirteenth centuries before Christ, the period when the name Yahweh would have originated, perhaps near a place called Reuel.[18] Such references confirm the existence of the cult of Yahweh before the development of the Israelite nation.

In order to support arguments concerning the Cushites to the south of Egypt, further questions need to be asked about certain Egyptian epigraphs that contain the name of the god Yahweh. Excavations in Timna, to the south of Eilat, reveal the existence of a temple dating to the twelfth century B.C.E. This temple was characterized by pottery that the archeologists later called Midianite. The temple contained an urn similar to the tabernacle of biblical tradition, with a serpent of bronze.[19] It is curious to note that, in all the sources prior to the priestly redaction, this is the only zoomorphic symbol associated with Moses (Nm 21:8–9).

The bronze serpent that Moses had made was destroyed during the reform of king Hezekiah, along with images of the goddesses Ishtar and Asherah, who were worshiped in the high places (cf. 2 Kgs 18:4).[20] In those days the serpent was called Nejustan, a proper name alluding to the material of the image *(nejoset)* and to the figure of the serpent *(najas)*. Serpents were common icons in the Afro-Asian regions. In Egypt the serpent was the emblem of life and had connections with the sun and the moon. In the "Book of Gates," in the tomb of Ramses VI, there appears the figure of the serpent called the Leader. Over the serpent's head appears the text: "She is the one who creates the Dawn before the god Re does. She is the one who guides the great god to the door of the eastern horizon."[21] In the Egyptian "Book of the Dead" the serpent is said to "vacillate between love and hate of the gods."[22] The serpent symbolized sacred power, both beneficent and hostile. The dual character of the serpent represents the joys and tragedies of human life.[23]

A series of poetic fragments in the Old Testament suggests that at some point in time Yahweh lived outside Palestine, although the geographic details are not precise (see Dt 33:2; Jgs 5:4–5; Ps 68:7–8; Hb 3:3). Such names as Sinai, Seir, and Paran refer to regions to the south of Palestine. There is documentation for "YHWH of Teman" in inscriptions found in Kuntillet Ajrud, in northwest Sinai and to the south of Kadesh; they date to around 800 B.C.E. According to Tryggen D. Mettzinger, "The biblical texts that describe the arrival of YHWH from Seir and other places point toward the region that exists between the Dead Sea and the Gulf of Aquaba."[24] Mettzinger, then, assumes that Midian is an Arab country situated between the southern point of the Dead Sea and the northern part of the Gulf of Aquaba. However, extra-biblical data coming from texts engraved on the walls of Nubia, formerly known as Ethiopia and presently as Sudan, contain inscriptions that, according to testimony, are the most ancient in which the name of the biblical God appears. The texts are found in temples dating back to the reign of the pharaoh Amenophis III (1400 B.C.E.) and in buildings of the epoch of Ramses II, around 1250 B.C.E. Both inscriptions mention the Shasu Bedouins.

Why is there no consensus about the presence of the Cushites in the region where the biblical religion first unfolded? And why is this relevant to a critical feminist reading of liberation? These two questions take on meaning in this context because of the arbitrariness with which biblical scholars divide biblical texts into those that are historical and those that are mythical. The African traditions are treated as myths without foundation, while the Semitic traditions are considered by academics to be *true* because they have a historical basis. Sometimes it is even made to appear that biblical studies are neutral and that interpretation is not affected by ethnocentric bias. It is wrong to reduce mythical narratives simply to the question of whether they have a historical basis or not, for they transcend the compass of Western, lineal history; they challenge biblical studies to examine the texts and their contexts with symbolic and anthropological keys.

These questions are important in another respect, since we suspect that the Yahwism introduced into the Palestine region by Zipporah considered women priests to be normal. In Zipporah's culture, women had direct access to the divinity and even dared to challenge its power—this, at least, is the conclusion that seems reasonable from our examination of the following text: "You are my blood-bridegroom!"

> On the journey, when he had halted for the night, Yahweh encountered him and tried to kill him. Then Zipporah, taking up a flint, cut off her son's foreskin and with it touched his feet and said, "You are my blood-bridegroom!" So he let him go. She said, "Blood-bridegroom" then, with reference to the circumcision. (Ex 4:24–26)

This text has generally been considered enigmatic, almost inexplicable, by most biblical commentators,[25] who argue that it is dealing with an ancient tradition. The context of these verses suggests that the attack occurred at some spot in the desert on the way to Egypt. In the prior verses, Moses took his wife and his son and returned to the land of Egypt after having received the order to return there from Yahweh (Ex 4:18–23). The unity of these verses with the previous ones is seen precisely in verse 23, where Yahweh threatens to kill the firstborn of the Pharaoh if he does not let the Israelites leave Egypt.

When we read these verses, though, the question arises: what is the motive for the attack? The Hebrew text is ambiguous, especially in its use of personal pronouns. Did God attack Moses or his son? Whose feet did Zipporah touch? According to Jorge Pixley, if the attack was against the child, then it was Yahweh's way of chastising Moses for not having circumcised him.[26] For Hans Kosmala, however, the story is intended to justify the Midianite practice of circumcision of infants.[27] If this is the case, then we are dealing with an etiological story, that is, a text that explains the origin of circumcision in Israel. Such an explanation runs counter to other passages on circumcision, such as Genesis 17 and Joshua 5, since here it is a woman who acts as priestess and performs the ceremony of circumcision. And she does so in a truly ancient fashion, using a sharp stone.

If, to the contrary, it was Moses' life that was being threatened, then how do we explain such an attack, since he was the man chosen to lead

Israel to liberation? For Brevard Childs, the reason Zipporah took the child and circumcised him was that Moses was under some type of attack and incapable of responding.[28] I am quite opposed to this argument because it minimizes the activity of the woman. The rapidity with which she went into action shows, it seems to me, that what she did was a common practice in her culture. We therefore see how the scriptures are sometimes read so as to deny women access to public space and to the official activities ordinarily attributed to men.

This delimitation of spaces has consequences for women's roles and their participation in social institutions, especially in matters of cult. For that reason, both in the religion of Israel and in religious history generally, the leadership of the official cult is rarely a function or a space occupied by women. It is, however, evident that before patriarchy was established women acted as priestesses. Only afterward did their space depend on the authority and the auspices of the patriarch, the father and the lord. Such asymmetry of power is written into the definition of values and the prescription of norms that prevail in society: "The masculine parameters will be the ones that prevail as the norm and that are understood as universal, whereas feminine values will be considered special or particular."[29] The generally accepted opinion in biblical studies is that Zipporah assumed the role of priestess because Moses was being attacked by God. It is interesting to note here that the sexist language is also defended by women. For example, Athalya Brener argues that Zipporah acts as a "recognized sorcerer [male] or as a consecrated man."[30] why does this author not recognize Zipporah as a priestess? We see here that, although official religion confines women to the domestic realm, there is active participation of women in religious life prior to the monarchy in Israel.

Zipporah the priestess is the one who performs the *Berit Mila. Berit* means "covenant," and *Milah* means "to cut" or "to take away." *Berit Mila* (holy pact) is precisely the covenant that consists in cutting and/or taking away the foreskin that covers the end of the penis, the male reproductive organ. The *Berit Mila* constitutes the greatest and most important holiness in all Judaism, since on it depends the eternal union of every male Jew with his Creator. This divine covenant is realized by a *mohel*,[31] a male Jew who must be an expert in the matter, have a close relation to the spiritual world, keep all the laws of the Torah, and respect God; in sum, he must be an extremely pious individual with irreproachable social conduct. Zipporah appears to have these qualities and so realizes this divine covenant. An essential part of the circumcision ceremony is the *Dam Berit* (covenant of blood)—a bit of blood must emerge at the moment of the *Berit Mila*. This operation is considered to be among the most ancient performed in the ancient world; it was practiced in Egypt, especially in the pharaonic family, and also among the Canaanites, the pre-Islamic Arab tribes, and the African tribes, as well as among other peoples such as Tartars, Malaysians, Polynesians, Australians, and Indians. Many of them continue the practice to the present day, with certain differences in age, forms, techniques, and so on.[32]

This woman Zipporah emerges from the shadow of her father (Reuel/Jethro) and her husband (Moses) and now appears as a savior in a mysterious, dangerous situation. Moses finds himself in mortal danger, and she performs the act of expiation by offering to God a part of the masculinity of Moses. Zipporah emerges as the savior of Moses; she responds to the divine attack by performing the ritual of circumcision, cutting off the foreskin of her son and touching Moses' feet (a euphemism for genital organs) with it, while pronouncing the words, "You are my blood-bridegroom!" (4:25). The expression "blood-bridegroom" is enigmatic. The fact that the narrator tries to explain the expression suggests that the received text was already ambiguous (4:26b). In the end, the biblical author does not explain how Zipporah knew that the way to get free of the menacing situation was by performing the ritual of circumcision. We can intuit, however, that she was familiar with this God, that she knew him very well. Her familiarity with Yahweh enabled her to confront him directly.

The controversy surrounding these verses has to do with attempts to explain the demonic aspect attributed to God in the story. The attack described in this account is similar to God's attack on Jacob in Penuel (Gn 32:23–32), in which a man touches Jacob's hip socket and dislocates his hip. In response, Jacob holds on to the attacker and asks for his blessing. From that moment Jacob knew Yahweh, for he saw him face to face (Gn 32:30). In a similar way Zipporah touched the "feet" of Moses, and Yahweh let him go. The story of Zipporah does not end with a blessing, as such, but with the final phrase, "Blood-bridegroom then, wiht reference to the circumcision." This statement implicitly gives the assurance that Yahweh will deliver his loved ones from death. The great similarity between the two narratives is interesting, though most interpreters claim that the parallel is inexact because it is improper to attribute a demonic side to the God of the Israelites. But are such attributes not comparable with those of the God who orders Abraham to sacrifice his son Isaac? This brief text serves to reinforce the fearful character of Yahweh, since it comes immediately after the threat against the pharaoh's firstborn. The religious principles assumed by Yahwism introduce into human history a profound dualism between man and woman, God and world, good and evil, reason and passion, heaven and earth, God and Satan, life and death. The overcoming of this dualism, which marks our philosophical traditions, becomes a basic challenge in the search for an ethics that liberates the bodies of women.

Although Zipporah in this text is portrayed as a priestess, she is relegated to a peripheral role by the authors of Exodus 2:16–22 and 18:1–9. In 2:16–22 she is given by her father as a wife for Moses, to whom she bears a son named Gershom. Zipporah appears again in Exodus 18:1–9, but this time she and her sons are taken by her father and grandfather back to her husband, Moses, although in the story it is not clear whether she had gone to her father of her own accord or was dismissed by her husband. The highlight of the story is the encounter of Moses and his father-in-law, Jethro, who meet on Mount Sinai, the place where Yahweh revealed himself in the bush to Moses. The significance of the meeting is the union of the two patriarchs, Moses and Jethro, with Yahweh, the liberating God.[33] Jethro is a priest who before had practiced the cult of Yahweh on this mountain; on learning of Yahweh's freeing Israel from Egypt, he worshiped him in this same place (18:6–12). The fact that this priest worships Yahweh allows us to conclude that Yahwism entered Israel through Zipporah and her father. It is clear, however, that most biblical commentaries pay little heed to the important role that Zipporah plays in this regard.

All these reflections lead us to propose the need for new epistemological paradigms in dealing with biblical texts. That is precisely what I intend to elaborate in the next section.

NEW EPISTEMOLOGICAL PARADIGMS IN BIBLICAL STUDIES

Black feminist biblical interpretation is challenging the traditional scriptural scholarship to view history from a different perspective, using a focus that is not necessarily that of Western Semitic culture. When we say *focus*, we refer to our viewpoint or localization, the position from which we observe, analyze, and understand the world. Our perspective should not be confused with the Eurocentrism, which imposed itself universally on all peoples by means of violent tactics and historical falsification. Eurocentrism abstracts the elements common to many peoples and structures them in a generalized vision on the basis of its classical Greek and Roman reference points. Of course, it prescinds from the fact that African peoples established the very bases of Western civilization itself. The Aryan ideologues of the last century strove not only to minimize the importance of the Egyptian contributions to the formation of

Greek culture but also to de-Africanize the Egyptians as much as possible.[34]

The spreading of the idea that the Ancient World was basically Caucasian derived from the process of racialization that had its roots in the concepts of European superiority that arose during the colonial epoch in the Americas. The classical world that we understand to be our cultural origin found its deepest roots in the world of East Africa (Egypt, Libya, Ethiopia). The understanding of the world on the basis of the Aryan model is quite recent, and for that reason I have proposed returning to the ancient model, the one witnessed to in the biblical tradition.

According to this model the people of the African continent influenced the peoples of the Mediterranean. As Martin Bernal affirms, "If I am correct in defending the collapse of the Aryan model and its substitution by the revised ancient model, it will be necessary not only to rethink the fundamental bases of 'western civilization,' but also to recognize the penetration of racism and 'continental chauvinism' in all our historiography, that is, our philosophy of writing history."

Bernal recognizes that there was no problem with the ancient model, but that it was rejected for external reasons by romantic racists of the eighteenth and nineteenth centuries, who did not consider it probable that Greece, the *cradle of humanity*, was the result of an admixture of native European, African, and Semitic colonizers.[35] Because of their bias, the ancient model had to be rejected and replaced by something more acceptable.

Both the violent and nonviolent methods of domination of the European model have resulted in ideological conjectures that are quite different from the construction of a theoretical perspective rooted in the African experience. They are different because the search for an African focus does not assume a universalist dominant posture; it does not assume that its elements are universal and therefore applicable to all other human experiences. Rather, it is a pluralist conception that attributes value to the world view proper to each people. E. L. Nascimento synthesizes this pluralist perspective well: "The main task of African-focused academics consists in studying, analyzing and affirming that which differentiates the African point of view, while at the same time identifying the supposedly universal postulates of Eurocentrism and demonstrating their specific nature."[36]

In questioning Eurocentric epistemologies, we recognize that they are constructions conceived in a given time and space and perpetuated over time. Such epistemologies are unaware of the ancient models of knowledge created by peoples and cultures that lived outside the Aryan world.

The option for African-centered biblical studies seeks precisely to undo this error. We therefore propose the following epistemological principles:

- Israelite history should be considered from an anthropological perspective, so as to take seriously the way in which it narrates history through religious myths and customs that form part of a larger world, with roots in Africa and Asia.
- Recognition should be accorded not only to a Mediterranean world, but also to an Atlantic world; this is a world that shifts the focus from the Eurocentric Western world to the four cardinal points, a world linked by the Atlantic Ocean, in which parallel cultures establish relationships on their own, at the margins of the Mediterranean world.
- Recognition should also be accorded to a world that precedes the Mediterranean world. More than ten thousand years ago there was contact between the peoples of Asia Minor and those of Africa, stretching down the Nile as far as Tanzania. These neighboring cultures were constantly moving back and forth and interacting. We find evidence in philology, in letters and poetry, and in iconographic and monumental art that these worlds were always in contact. Babylonians, Assyrians, Libyans, Sumerians, Ethiopians, Egyptians— all were in communication with one another as colleagues, adversaries, vassals, or sovereigns.
- A challenge must be made to the "argument from silence" put forward by archeological positivists, who argue that if something has not been found, then it could not have existed in significant quantities. Yet it is virtually impossible to prove the absence of something. We know that many ancient peoples were quite present in history but were made "absent" by a selective type of historiography and philosophy. Many buildings made of mud and wood in sub-Saharan Africa, for example, cannot be reconstructed archeologically, but that does not mean that those buildings and peoples did not exist.
- History should be read with respect for the cultural centers involved. A break needs to be made with the Eurocentric values and patterns, in order to attain a new logic of relations among cultures. For that reason I continue to raise the question, why does biblical scholarship ignore the African roots in the biblical traditions when they are plainly present there? Why is it so difficult to accept that the biblical world was also black? I am not proposing that we invent something new, only that we pay attention to something that is already in the text. We need to allow the texts to have odor, color, taste,

body; we need to let them transmit life as we penetrate them. In this way we break through paradigms and seek out other logics and methods of interpretation.

- Value must be accorded to the contributions that women have made in the field of feminist exegesis and to their reinterpretations of the great theological themes: ecclesiology, Christology, sacraments, theological anthropology, spirituality, morality, ethics. I consider this point extremely important, especially since working within a cultural perspective always runs the risk of hiding the asymmetries of power with regard to gender. Precisely for that reason I have studied the prophetess Zipporah, with the hope that this African woman's voice will help us reformulate the monolithic theories with regard to the configuration of Judaic monotheism.

FINAL CONSIDERATIONS

The tendency of the scriptures to restrict women to secondary roles reveals that the language used in the redaction and interpretation of the texts is androcentric and patriarchal. Even when there is evidence of the agency and the authority of women in certain biblical texts, this is no guarantee of inclusive language. For this reason the task of rescuing women's specific functions in the cultic life of the Bible is quite difficult and must be done on the basis of conjectures. Even so, an audacious new feminist consciousness makes available a wider array of methodological instruments for analyzing texts and their interpreters.

In Zipporah we behold a woman who defies the destructive power of the God of the Israelites (and hers as well) and who is also portrayed as the only person capable of defusing the divine wrath. With the expression "You are my blood-bridegroom!" Zipporah opens up to Yahweh the possibility of new relations that go beyond the imposed geographical and cultural limits. At the same time, she reveals to us an alternative model of relations of comradeship between men and women.

Even if my reading of the text does not allow us to affirm with certainty the Cushite origin of Zipporah, due to the limits of biblical scholarship, it does help to unveil a gruesome system that condemns peoples and cultures to oblivion. It is a system that has destroyed the collective consciousness of whole peoples and thus contributed to the loss of identity of African-descended peoples. I hope that this study will be of assistance in reaffirming the struggles of black women for the transformation of the present reality; may it strengthen their striving for a black and beautiful future for those who come after us.

If Yahwism became strong in Israel because of an Ethiopian woman, then religion in Israel was in principle a patrimony, or rather a "matrimony," of women! However, these priestesses were displaced by the power of men. Who knows, the destiny of our tradition might well have been different because of women's work!

Notes

[1] Peter Nash, "O papel dos africanos negros na história do povo de Deus," *Estudos Teológicos* no. 42 (March-April 2002): 5–27.

[2] Ronald J. Williams, "Egito e Israel," in *O legado do Egito*, ed. J. R. Harris (Río de Janeiro: Imago, 1993), 267–301.

[3] In the biblical tradition Ethiopia and Cush were considered synonyms. The Masoretic text used Cush and the Septuagint transcribed *Xous* in the ethnographic list of Genesis 10:6–8 and 1 Chronicles 1:8–10, where Cush is listed as the son of Ham. In classical antiquity this name was changed to Aetiopia by the Greeks. See A. M. Ali Haken, "A civilização de Napata e Méroe," in *A África Antiga,* vol. 2, ed. Gamal Mokhtar (São Paulo: Editora Ática y Organización de las Naciones Unidas para la Educación, la Ciencia y la Cultura UNESCO, 1980), 326.

[4] Racism and racial discrimination violate the Universal Declaration of Human Rights: "Everyone is entitled to all the rights and freedoms set forth in this Declaration, without distinction of any kind, such as race, color, sex, language, religion, political or other opinion, national or social origin, property, birth or other status" (UN, Universal Declaration of Human Rights, Article 2,).

[5] Abdias Nascimento et al., "Dia Internacional Contra a Discriminação Racial," in *Thoth Escriba dos Deuses: Pensamento dos Povos Africanos e Afrodescendentes,* ed. Abdias Nascimento (Brasília: Gabinete do senador Abdias Nascimento, 1997), 37.

[6] Joaquim B. Barbosa Gómes, *Ações afirmativas e princípio constitucional de igualdade: O direito como instrumento de transformação social: A experiência dos Estados Unidos* (São Paulo: Renovar, 2001), 74.

[7] Charles Taylor, *Multiculturalism: Examining the Politics of Recognition* (Princeton, NJ: Princeton University Press, 1994), 26; Walter Silveiro, "O Multiculturalismo e o reconhecimento: mito e metafora," *Revista Universidade de Sao Paulo* 42 (June-August 1999): 44–55.

[8] By androcentric I understand the linguistic constructions of history that tend to downplay the role of women as active participants in history. See Elisabeth Schüssler Fiorenza, *As Origens Cristãs a Partir da Mulher: Uma Nova Hermenêutica* (São Paulo: Edições Paulinas, 1992), 56.

[9] Werner Schmidt, *A fé do Antigo Testamento* (São Leopoldo: Sinodal, 2004), 107.

[10] Biblical quotations in this essay are from *The New Jerusalem Bible,* gen. ed. Henry Wansbrough (Garden City, NY: Doubleday, 1985).

[11] See BibleWorks, *Lexicon,* Hermeneutika Computer Bible Research Software (2001), available at http://bibleworks.com; Internet (accessed November 11, 2006).

[12] Randall C. Bailey, "Beyond Identification: The Use of Africans in Old Testament Poetry and Narrative," in *Stony the Road We Trod: African American Biblical Interpretation,* ed. Cain Hope Felder (Minneapolis: Fortress Press, 1991), 166.

[13] Milton Schwantes, "E Sara riu," in *Ecce Mulier: Homenagem a Irene Foulkes,* ed. Silvia Regina de Lima Silva (San José, Costa Rica: Universidad Biblica Latino-Americana, 2005), 43.

[14] Schmidt, *A fé do Antigo Testamento,* 107. See also Jorge Pixley, *Êxodo* (São Paulo: Edições Paulinas, 1987); Frank Crüsemann, *Preservación da liberdade. O decágolo numa perspectiva histórico-social* (São Leopoldo: Sinodal, 1995).

[15] See Dt 10:19; 24:14–15; Ex 23:9. The Kenites were considered almost siblings of the Israelites, while the Jebusites, the Rechabites, the Hittites, and other foreign races were looked on favorably (Jgs 1:16; 5:24; 2 Sm 11:6–11; 15:19–22; 18:2; 24:15–25; Jer 35:1–19).

[16] See Karen Joines, *The Serpent Symbolism in the Old Testament* (Haddonfield, UK: Haddonfield House, 1974), 8.

[17] Edwin Oliver James, *Historia de las Religiones* (Madrid: Alianza, 1975), 63.

[18] Moshe Weinfeld, "The Tribal League at Sinai," in *Ancient Israelite Religion: Essays in Honor of Frank Moore Cross,* ed. Patrick D. Miller, Jr., Paul D. Hanson, and S. Dean McBride (Philadelphia: Fortress Press, 1982), 305.

[19] Beno Rothenberg, *Timna: Valley of the Biblical Copper Mines* (London: Thames and Hundson, 1972), 163.

[20] Halpern Baruch, "Kenites," in *Anchor Bible Dictionary,* vol. 4, ed. David Noel Freedman (New York: Doubleday, 1992), 17–22.

[21] Joines, *The Serpent Symbolism in the Old Testament,* 48.

[22] Ibid., 97.

[23] Mary Coden, "Eva y la serpiente: el mito fundamental del patriarcado," in *Del Cielo a la Tierra: Una Antología de Teología Feminista,* ed. Mary Judith Ress, Ute Seibert-Cuadra, and Lene Sjorup (Santiago: Sello Azul, 1994), 215.

[24] Tryggen D. Mettzinger, *Buscando a Dios: Significado y Mensaje de los Nombres Divinos en la Biblia* (Córdoba: El Almendro de Córdoba, 1988), 40.

[25] Brevard Childs, *The Book of Exodus* (Philadelphia: Westminster, 1974).

[26] Pixley, *Êxodo,* 50.

[27] Hans Kosmala, "The Bloody Bridegroom," *Vetus Testamentum* 12 (1962): 25.

[28] Childs, *The Book of Exodus,* 103.

[29] Eleine G. Neunfeldt, "Práticas e Experiências Religiosas de Mulheres no Antigo Israel: Um Estudo a Partir de Ez 8, 14–15 e 13, 17–23" (doctoral thesis, Escola Superior de Teología, São Leopoldo, 2004), 27.

[30] Athalya Brener, *A Mulher Israelita: Papel Social e Modelo Literário na Narrativa Bíblica* (São Paulo: Paulinas, 2001), 102.

[31] *Mohel* is a term that comes from the biblical Hebrew *muwl*, which means "circumcise." The *mohel* is the one who performs the circumcision.

[32] See the Jewish movement Jabad Lubavitch Argentina, available at http://www.jabad.org.ar/Mohel.asp; Internet (accessed November 7, 2006).

[33] Rita J. Burns, "Zipporah," in *Anchor Bible Dictionary*, vol. 6, ed. David Noel Freedman (New York: Doubleday, 1992), 1105.

[34] Nascimento, "Dia Internacional Contra a Discriminação Racial," 38.

[35] Martin Bernal, "Introduction," in *Black Athena: The Afroasiatic Roots of Classical Civilization (The Fabrication of Ancient Greece 1785–1985)*, vol. 1 (Piscataway, NJ: Rutgers University Press, 1987).

[36] Elizabeth Larkin Nascimento, "Sankofa: Resgatando a Cultura Afro-brasileira," *Revista Thoth Escriba dos Deuses* [Brasília] 1 (1997): 221.

9

Dialogue of Memories

Ways toward a Black Feminist Christology from Latin America

Silvia Regina de Lima Silva

A group of women of African descent, on the road to discovering their black identity, had the surprise of encountering the religion of their ancestors. This encounter developed into a relation of faith and affection in which the traditional African religion, as experienced in the diaspora, came to give new meaning to Christian experience. My interest in working on the theme of a Latin American black feminist Christology emerges from such experiences. The text that I propose to develop here seeks to build bridges, establish dialogue, drink from different founts, and speak of faith lived on the religious frontiers. To that end I seek to recollect black women's preserved memory, as well as the black body, as spaces that give witness to new experiences of faith.

This essay seeks to be a contribution to a reflection on Christology that is open to dialogue with other theological positions and interpretations. Out of Christian experience and in dialogue with ancestral religious traditions, I set myself a twofold task: first, to rediscover the importance both of the historical and everyday experiences of women of African descent and of their myths and religious experiences; second, to explore paths that might lead toward a deconstruction of the dominant Christology and provide elements from the Jesus traditions that can contribute to dialogue among the different memories and traditions.

My aim is that this reflection contributes to the task of creating a Latin American feminist Christology that has an intercultural and ecumenical perspective. In order to achieve this, I draw on the analysis of a biblical text.

SOME HERMENEUTIC KEYS

A black feminist Christology shares with other feminist theologies the hermeneutic principle[1] of critical feminist consciousness.[2] Furthermore, it assumes as a critical principle the affirmation and promotion of the full human condition of women.[3] For black women, the principle of the full human condition of women implies not only a commitment to working against sexism and classism, but also a rejection of the racist structures of society. Consequently, the search for a critical feminist rereading of the Bible should aim also at overcoming racial discrimination, which continues to be present in everyday reality. Such racism is often founded on biblical texts and interpretations and even finds occasional expression in theological formulations.

Maricel Mena-López, a Colombian biblical scholar, affirms that the first step in a black reading of the Bible is approaching black history, with its myths and liberating memories. The second step is going to the biblical text and communing with the myths and memories rooted in the Jewish and Christian traditions. Thus the biblical text is read from a black perspective and with the tools of feminist analysis. Equally necessary, however, is a critical-historical approach that is conscious of the subjectivity of the scriptural exegete, as well as of the questions that the exegete raises and of the body that he or she has. Such close study of the text raises questions about what is said, but also about what is not said; it interrogates the silences, the voids, and the omissions.[4]

The critical feminist hermeneutic attempts to liberate the biblical text from the patriarchal reading that has predominated throughout its interpretative history. The feminist reading seeks to set loose the liberation forces within the text in order to widen and enhance the paths of life and freedom for groups and communities of women readers. Such a way of reading opens up new horizons, puts names on new realities, and creates a new symbolic universe. A feminist reading of the Bible is directed to women and men of faith, but also to those who purposely seek to challenge the influence of the patriarchal tradition in the life of women.[5] Recovering and dialoguing with those memories that rescue our identities as women, as part of a people, are liberating and reinforce our dignity; they encourage us to create alternative spaces and relationships.

MEMORIES REDISCOVERED

The first memory I would like to call up comes from the Yoruba tradition, in which ancestors hold a central place. The deities are conceived as personifications of the basic forces of nature and of ourselves, and narratives about them are understood symbolically.[6]

Recalling Ochún

Ochún is the divinity of the beauty of life, mistress of gold and of love.[7] Her name is the name of a river located in Nigeria. She is the goddess of fertility and of wealth. Cult is rendered to her under many names, and she manifests herself in different ways, especially as a warrior, resistant and powerful.

> When the Orixas came to earth, they organized meetings to which women were not admitted. Ochún became angry at not being taken into account and being unable to participate in the decision-making. To avenge herself, she made the women become sterile, she dried up the rivers and she prevented the activities of the Orixas from having favorable outcomes. In desperation the Orixas went to Olodumaré and explained that things were going badly on earth, even when decisions were taken in assembly. Olodumaré asked if Ochún was taking part in the meetings, and the Orixas answered that she was not. Olodumaré explained to them that without the presence of Ochún and her power, none of their labors would yield results. Upon returning to earth, the Orixas invited Ochún to take part in their assemblies. They spent much time pleading with her and insisting. Finally, she accepted. Immediately, the women became fertile again, the rivers began to flow, the projects of the Orixas turned out successfully and life returned to earth.[8]

Some traditions of African origin relate the notion of the feminine to vitality and see it expressed in social relations, where women appear as chiefs, elders, wives, and mothers; women especially manifest the energy that creates life and keeps it present in the universe. This myth should be read on the basis of the historical circumstances experienced by women, for only within this context can it be reinterpreted. In black history, the understanding of cultural heritage is linked to social circumstances in which women, for their own survival and that of their children, have made the role of defenders and protectors of real, concrete lives their very own. Theirs is a history of resistance, persistence, and insistence, of breaking with patterns and paradigms of the racist, patriarchal society. These nearly forgotten memories are recovered in an effort to prevent the death of the religion of the ancestors and so to recover the voices of the Divine, which becomes manifest in the history and the body of each one of us.

These are words that synthesize the experiences of many women; these are memories that strengthen women of African descent. Some stories are bearers of liberating memories, while others have the power of condensing many other stories. I would like to share one of these stories with you. I am thinking especially of the example and the words of one of our ancestresses: Sojourner Truth.[9] Born between 1797 and 1800, she was given the name Isabella and lived as a slave in New York. In the speech that follows, we find a woman who speaks from a consciousness of herself and who denounces the power relations of a patriarchal, sexist society.

> That man over there says that women need to be helped into carriages, and lifted over ditches, and to have the best place everywhere. Nobody ever helps me into carriages, or over mud-puddles, or gives me any best place! And ain't I a woman? Look at me! Look at my arm! I have ploughed and planted, and gathered into barns, and no man could head me! And ain't I a woman? I could work as much and eat as much as a man—when I could get it—and bear the lash as well! And ain't I a woman? I have borne thirteen children, and seen most all sold off to slavery, and when I cried out with my mother's grief, none but Jesus heard me! And ain't I a woman?[10]

The words of Sojourner Truth express what has been the social and historical experience of countless black women. Her words give evidence of a situation of submission, exploitation, and worse, since they come from the context of slavery. At the same time, Sojourner Truth views society with irony, pointing out the contradictions of a system that is patriarchal and racist as well. She turns the system upside down. She stands up on her own two feet, takes a good look around, and makes use of her words to talk about herself. She abandons the position of being observed and defined by others, and she becomes her own principle of self-definition and self-evaluation, characteristics that are found in black feminist thought.[11] She talks about herself, but also about those who wish to subjugate her. Hers is a thought that, due to the toughness of her life, challenges the established order.

Black feminist reflection arises from this ground, from standing firm on one's own feet, from having legs like roots sunk deep into the earth, so as to be able to take from history, from the past, and from the ancestors the strength and the critical vision needed to deal with the present.

Such strength and tenacity break out of the places assigned by the racist-patriarchal world, and they open up alternative spaces of dignity, life and liberty, which can be occupied by black bodies. Thus, equipped with this critical vision and standing on our own two feet, we examine the biblical text.

Hearing the Biblical Text as a Memory

The biblical text is a memory that I propose to recall. The biblical text that I analyze here treats a memory that tends to be forgotten, at least from women's perspective.

I refer to that woman of Bethany who found Jesus and anointed him before his death. Regarding this woman's gesture Jesus announced: "Wherever throughout all the world the gospel is proclaimed, what she has done will be told as well, in remembrance of her" (Mk 14:9).[12] Despite Jesus' words, the symbolic and prophetic action of the woman has not succeeded in becoming part of the evangelical knowledge of most Christians.[13] Rather, it is a memory relegated to oblivion. We take up this text as a symbol of the many forgotten memories of women.

The text is found in the Gospel of Mark (14:1–11), but it also appears in the other Synoptic Gospels (Mt 26:6–13; Lk 7:36–50) and in the Gospel of John (12:1–8).

Mark locates the incident in the context of the passion and death of Jesus. It is a time of persecution, murders, attempts to silence dissonant voices, and ideological control by religious and political powers. The deaths of some are meant to teach the rest. It is a time of searching for the guilty and the suspect (Mk 14:1–2).

> He was at Bethany in the house of Simon, a man who had suffered from a virulent skin-disease; he was at table when a woman came in with an alabaster jar of very costly ointment, pure nard. She broke the jar and poured the ointment on his head. Some who were there said to others indignantly, "Why this waste of ointment? Ointment like this could have been sold for over three hundred denarii and the money given to the poor"; and they were angry with her. But Jesus said, "Leave her alone. Why are you upsetting her? What she has done for me is a good work. You have the poor with you always, and you can be kind to them whenever you wish, but you will not always have me. She has done what she could: she has anointed my body beforehand for its burial. In truth I tell you, wherever throughout all the world *the gospel* is proclaimed, what she has done will be told as well, *in remembrance of her*" (Mk 14:3–9).[14]

Dialoguing with the Text

The initial question for dialogue is: what memories does the text help us to rescue? The encounter of the woman with Jesus took place in the context of a supper in a house in Bethany—indeed, the text speaks of the house of a leper. The passage is located between two other texts that offer the historical context in which the narrative develops. The prior unit, 14:1–2, informs the reader of the time of year of this supper, that is, just before the feast of Passover. After the anointing, which occupies the central unit, there follows the story of the betrayal by Judas. We will analyze this passage, so rich in gestures, expressions, and metaphors, as a text that represents, to a fair degree, the biblical-theological activity of black women.

Text and Contra-text: Gratuity and Creativity in the Midst of Threatened Life

The story is inserted amid stories of pain and suffering that are fruits of injustice. The text opens up a space of light that allows something different to appear amid words heavy with death and deceit; it tells of a gratuitous, prophetic, revolutionary gesture. It is life opening up space within pain, within the patriarchal world's scheme of death.

The contrasts in the text are vivid. We might even speak of admixtures of different vital dimensions: life and death, good and evil, joy and sadness. One dimension brings forth the other. Such words as *deceit, prison, death, burial,* and *money* are found in the text, but there are also references to other realities, revealed in words such as *perfume* and *good work.*

Money is present throughout the text. The word *money* appears explicitly in the third segment (14:11), but the same word is part of the semantic universe of the central section (14:3–9) as well. There is talk of very expensive perfume (14:3), waste (14:4), selling (14:5), three hundred denarii (14:7), the poor (14:11)—all terms related with the world of economics and money. Two distinct logics are expressed in the text. One is the logic of calculation and profit, which permits even the purchase of information and, behind the money, the betrayal of a friend; the other is the logic of friendship, gratuity and affection.

This passage about the encounter of the woman with Jesus in Bethany is a counter-text, a counter-current text that shines forth for its contradiction of the context in which it is found (Mk 14:1–2, 10–11). The text and the woman seem out of place. They are witnesses; they call forth memory of themselves. Woman and text are menaced by the looks, words, and gestures of the patriarchal world that considers them aliens and intruders. The "proper" guests bother the woman, they "upset her" (14:6). The text definitely appears out of place, for it is an uncomfortable memory, this memory of a woman and her perfume. The woman's act is of itself a theological and ideological act. We might well say that it is a theology that is expressed through the body and through gestures; it is a theology without words, a caress that breaks down barriers and crosses borders. It therefore makes possible a different experience of the sacred; it becomes an experience of the sacred within the woman that overflows in relating to the body of another, the body of Jesus.

The Body as a Hermeneutic Space

The woman's body holds a central place in the narrative. The guests discuss and debate about her body, her presence, and her gesture. It is a body that is out of place, or at least out of the place expected of it and assigned to it in the patriarchal world. Her body is what she does; she becomes herself through her gesture. Her body does not speak but acts, and the action also troubles people. Silence is kept about her identity. Her gesture of breaking the jar of perfume is a definite, concrete act that happens suddenly. It is an act that transgresses and causes murmurs.

There is also the body of Jesus. Mark describes these final days of Jesus' life in the form of a tragedy. The drama intensifies in the midst of conspiracy, imprisonment, torture, and death.[15] And here the two bodies meet, that of Jesus and that of the woman, bodies in relation. One body allows itself to be cared for by another. A body that is threatened and pursued is approached by a body that expresses affection, care, and recognition. Anointing his head might be seen as a confirmation of Jesus in his prophetic mission.[16] The woman's gesture and attitude constitute a prophetic and political act. In the midst of death threats, it is a risk-ridden affirmation of life. The gesture irrupts into a milieu heavy with violence and announces something different. The gesture also identifies this woman with Jesus' own prophetic mission; it is an expression of her ideological solidarity[17] with the path and the project of Jesus.

A New Theological Locus

Moving through the different spaces in the text and following the narrator's perspectives make it possible to find new theological loci. The first site offered is Bethany, in Hebrew "house of the poor one." The memory of the stories about Jesus makes it the meeting place for men and women friends, including the family of Martha and Mary. Bethany is the scene of the encounter in the house of Simon the leper, where Jesus is reclining at table, possibly a common meal, like supper. To be having supper in the house of a leper is a violation of the rules of the social order. The text presents this "dis-order" clearly in opposition to the dominant order; it is a counterculture opposed to the hegemonic culture.

A Memory of Two Suppers

The encounter of the woman with Jesus happens in a house, during a supper, the Supper of the Anointing. It is an encounter on the fringes of society, one that upsets the established order and features a clearly feminine initiative. This text of the Supper of the Anointing is followed by the text of the Last Supper, known as the Institution of the Lord's Supper. The text of the Last Supper, throughout its long interpretative history, has been understood by ecclesial tradition as a foundational text of Christianity, but it has also become an alienating text as far as women are concerned. It has been used to justify the exclusion of women from full participation in the ecclesial ministries.

The Supper of the Anointing is the supper of inclusion, full of affection, prophetic spirit, and ruptures. It is the supper that preserves another memory: "In memory of her." It preserves the memory of a woman who communicates Divine Wisdom. As the presence of Divine Wisdom, she anoints Jesus, the one sent by the same Divine Wisdom, who not only proclaimed the *basileía* of the God of the poor but also took part in table fellowship with the excluded ones of Israel.[18] It is he who is here anointed as prophet of this community of outcasts.

Of Perfume and of Grace

The house of the leper is filled with the fragrance, and everybody can smell it. The perfume enters through the nose, and soon it seems to reach all parts of the body. The perfume is of pure nard, an herb that originated in India and that is recalled in the love poems of the Song of Songs (1:12; 4:13–14). The woman's gesture provokes the indignation of the others in the house. An economic subtext runs throughout this passage,[19] but let us rather just enjoy a little more the perfume. Let us leave the disputes and return to the fragrance.

Perfume has an element of gratuity; anointing with it is a priceless gesture done out of folly. It is giving all that one has, a gracious gesture that opens space within the text and within reality and allows the experience of something new. It is the "already" of God's reign; it is feasting in the midst of pain and threats. It is beauty. Gratuity is precipitous, "loses its head," breaks the jar, pours it all out, keeps nothing for afterward. The "afterward" is that very moment, as the "before" also was then. Gratuity condenses time. It is self-giving, and self-giving through desire, and so it becomes a principle of liberation.

Christology as the Rescue of Liberating Memories

What memories do the texts preserve? Who are those that preserve these memories that get erased little by little? In Luke's Gospel an anonymous woman gets transformed into a sinner (Lk 7:36–40), and there is no longer talk of preserving her memory, of announcing her gesture wherever the gospel is proclaimed. This is the way that women's traces keep getting erased little by little, along with the traces of Divine Wisdom.

Christology is sometimes mentioned as a limitation on interreligious and intercultural dialogue. We may ask, however, what memory of Jesus can be recovered for theological reflection by women of African descent. For a black feminist Christology, I propose that we try to recover the traces of Divine Wisdom in the first traditions of the Jesus movement. These traces, as Elisabeth Schüssler Fiorenza states, are often hidden behind androcentric language and the kyriocentric setting of these texts.[20]

As the patriarchal, oppressive face of God becomes more and more evident, women seek out other allusions and other images that lead to the encounter with Divine Wisdom. This encounter makes possible a different experience of God, one that helps us recover other stories and memories of the way Divine Wisdom becomes manifest in the lives of women in the history of our peoples. I believe our objective must be to adopt an interpretative method that helps us recover those liberating memories and those revealing, inspiring words of God, and such a method must become a practice that extends to all the dimensions of life.

Such a method can be seen also in the practice of Jesus, who as an inspired person searched out in his nation's history those memories and traditions that strengthened people and communities and that helped them to recover faith and to experience the Divine in themselves and in their encounter with the "other." The biblical text is an inspiration for an exercise that begins in life and that ends in life itself. It fosters an attitude in the face of everyday existence that makes it possible for us to read the past and recover liberating memories, such as those of Ochún and Sojourner Truth, so that we may unite ourselves with them and with other foremothers, who were and continue to be presence and light along the way, word and companions on the journey, caretakers of Divine Wisdom. For women of African descent, recovering memory is part of our having faith in the living memories. The memories of the ancestors take on flesh, make themselves present, become incorporated into our lives, and take on new life in our bodies.

For black women, then, the good news of the gospel will always be accompanied by the announcement of "that woman," along with the announcement of our ancestresses and our liberating memories. They are memories rescued from history, from the ancestral religion, and brought to life in cults and celebrations. They are memories that break through the frontiers of time and space and communicate with one another by bringing life and happiness to their daughters.

The Scent of Perfume That Remained in the Air

Good news, broken flask, pieces thrown on the floor, marks and footsteps and oil stains . . . and a pleasant odor in the air. Someone passed through here and left her traces. Black feminist Christology from Latin America reflects on allowing yourself to be led by the scents that are in the air. There is so much to sniff and smell. There is desire to discover good things; there is commitment to deconstructing a Christology that for too long grounded a theology that justified the suffering of women and the various forms of oppressing and discriminating against women and others. The path of Christianity became too narrow and restrictive because of the dominance of a patriarchal, ethnocentric Christology. The search for a black feminist Christology implies a subversion of the established order and a rediscovery of very simple, immediate experiences of Jesus. Such experiences perhaps do not point toward a "lord," but they can resemble an encounter with a close friend, or with a man who has known pain and can therefore hear our cry, as Sojourner Truth put it. In this way we encounter a Jesus who can enter into dialogue with other liberating memories that we as black women carry within us, a Jesus who is not bothered when these memories reveal themselves through our bodies. Such a Christology is discovered and is strengthened in alternative spaces, in the houses of Bethany, in the houses of the poor and of the lepers, far from the great temples of the religious powers and perhaps also from the academic establishment that is bound to upholding a single, inflexible truth. It is a liberating reflection that inserts itself into a global praxis of liberation.

CONCLUSION

To bring my reflection to an end, I would like to share some possible visions or pathways that open up through or are opened up by a black feminist Christology.

The way forward for a black feminist Christology from Latin America is fundamentally through interculturality. For biblical study, this means beginning with consideration of the text and with a search for the interculturality that is present in the text, preserved in the memories that created the text and that are part of the biblical background. These recovered memories of the Bible stories and the life of Jesus enter into dialogue with our own memories and our ancestral wisdom, much of which is preserved in the lifestyles and the cultures of the women of the diverse peoples.

In the course of this essay I have used the word *Christianity,* but only for lack of another, more adequate term. I have insisted on speaking of the experiences of Jesus. I have not mentioned the historical Jesus, even though serious studies on this theme are multiplying on all sides. I share the opinion of those scholars of biblical theology who hold that such studies manifest persistent tendencies of the kyriarchal currents that "attempt to secure Christian identity in terms of the Western 'logic of identity.'"[21] I recognize that these studies contain valuable elements that can contribute to a feminist or black feminist Christology, but, still, more important than searching for the historical Jesus is recovering the many easily available stories of Jesus and dialoguing with them.

The stories of Jesus seek to go beyond the uniqueness of christological dogma; they aim to recover the plurality of biblical symbols and metaphors about Jesus. This wealth of symbolism and metaphors opens up the possibilities of dialogue. Dogma tends to close us down, while images open us to imagination, dialogue, and the construction of new meanings within our different contexts and cultures.

Such a Christology thus makes possible an encounter with the divinity that we have within us. It also draws closer to Jesus' own efforts to question and delegitimize the religious power of his time, which had taken control of God's name. This means discovering a religious experience that strengthens us as complete persons, full of dignity and created for happiness; it is a religious experience that strengthens the community as a place for experiencing the values of God's reign. Such a community is at the same time a prophetic one; it is light and grace in the midst of violence and death.

Notes

[1] On the principles of Latin American feminist theology, see María Pilar Aquino and Elsa Tamez, *Teología Feminista Latinoamericana* (Quito: Ediciones Abya-Yala, 1998), 59–69; for a treatment of feminist hermeneutics, see 78–105.

[2] This principle belongs to the legacy of feminist biblical studies. It seems to me important to recall the three accents or tendencies that until the decade of the 1980s characterized the study of texts by feminists identified with the Christian tradition. The first involved studying texts specifically about women, in order to refute the well-known interpretations used against women; the second used the Bible in a general way to arrive at a theological perspective that offered a critique of patriarchy; the third studied texts about women in order to learn from the history and the stories of ancient and modern women who have lived in patriarchal cultures. See Katharine Doob Sakenfeld, "Feminist Uses of Biblical Materials," in *Feminist Interpretation of the Bible*, ed. Letty M. Russell (Philadelphia: Westminster, 1985), 56.

[3] This principle is presented by Rosemary Radford Ruether. She states: "The critical principle of feminist theology is the promotion of the full humanity of women. Whatever denies, diminishes, or distorts the full humanity of women is, therefore, appraised as not redemptive" (*Sexism and God Talk: Toward a Feminist Theology*, 10th anniv. ed. [Boston: Beacon Press, 1993], 18–19).

[4] Maricel Mena-López, "Eu sou um trovão: Pensando ma metodologia bíblica negra e feminista," in *Abrindo Sulcos: Para Uma Teología Afroamericana y Caribenha*, ed. Maricel Mena-López and Peter Nash (São Leopoldo: Sinodal, 2003), 170–74.

[5] Letty M. Russell, "Introduction: Liberating the Word," in *Feminist Interpretation of the Bible*, ed. Letty M. Russell (Philadelphia: Westminster, 1985), 17.

[6] Clyde W. Ford, *O Heroi Con Rostro Africano: Mitos da Africa* (São Paulo: Selo Negro, 1999), 168–71.

[7] Oxum is called *Ialodë*, a title conferred on the woman who occupies the most important place among all the women of a city; she is the queen of the rivers and exercises her power over the water; she is the goddess of wealth, of copper; and she is a woman warrior.

[8] Pierre Verger, *Orixás, Deuses Yoruba na África e no Novo Mundo* (São Paulo: Corrupio Comércio, 1981), 174.

[9] For a biography of Sojourner Truth, see Olive Gilbert, "Narrative of Sojourner Truth: Based on Information Provided by Sojourner Truth 1850," available in "A Celebration of Women Writers," at http://www.digital.library.upenn.edu/women/truth/1850/1850.html; Internet (accessed December 12, 2004).

[10] Sojourner Truth, "Ain't I a Woman?" (speech delivered at the Women's Convention, Akron, Ohio, 1851). Available online.

[11] On this topic, see Patricia Hill Collins, *Black Feminist Thought: Knowledge, Consciousness, and the Politics of Empowerment*, 2nd ed. (New York: Routledge, 2000).

¹² Biblical quotations in this essay are from *The New Jerusalem Bible*, gen. ed. Henry Wansbrough (Garden City, NY: Doubleday, 1985).

¹³ Elisabeth Schüssler Fiorenza, *As Origens Cristãs a Partir da Mulher: Uma Nova Hermenêutica* (São Paulo: Edições Paulinas, 1992), 9.

¹⁴ The words and expressions that I have emphasized are important for the commentary I will make on the text.

¹⁵ Ched Myers, *O Evangelio de São Marcos: Grande Comentário Bíblico* (São Paulo: Edições Paulinas, 1992), 426ff.

¹⁶ Schüssler Fiorenza, *As Origens Cristãs a Partir da Mulher*, 10.

¹⁷ Myers, *O Evangelio de São Marcos*, 426.

¹⁸ Elisabeth Schüssler Fiorenza, *Jesus: Miriam's Child, Sophia's Prophet: Critical Issues in Feminist Christology* (New York: Continuum, 1995), 139–43. The author refers to Divine Wisdom as found in the Q source. The possibility of rereading Mark's gospel and seeking the traces of Wisdom there is a task for future research.

¹⁹ Myers, *O Evangelio de São Marcos*, 427.

²⁰ Schüssler Fiorenza, *Jesus: Miriam's Child*, 133.

²¹ Elisabeth Schüssler Fiorenza, *But She Said: Feminist Practices of Biblical Interpretation* (Boston: Beacon Press, 1992), 141. See also Schüssler Fiorenza, *Jesus: Miriam's Child*, 5–12.

10

Between Oppression and Resistance

From the Capture of the Imaginary to the Journey of the Intercultural

María Cristina Ventura Campusano

The vital experiences of black women have clearly marked one of the perhaps lesser known, but not for that reason less significant, currents of feminist theology. This essay seeks to be a helpful contribution to those feminist theological reflections that make a decided option for critical analysis. I believe it is possible, by means of such analysis, to find answers to the hermeneutic challenge that intercultural dialogue presents to feminist theological thought in Latin America.

The proposal of intercultural dialogue begins with openness to and practical implementation of respect for difference, mutual knowledge, cross-cultural learning, and mutual cooperation for the affirmation of human dignity. *Interculturality* is understood to be "an eminently polyphonic process in which the accord and harmony of the diverse voices is attained by continual contrast with the other and by continual learning from the other's opinions and experiences."[1] In this way, interculturality is considered to be an experience of constantly journeying toward the "in-between," a space where no stagnation or accommodation is permitted, but where continuous movement of our thoughts and actions, in relation with other peoples and cultures, is fomented.

Such a position is an intermediate one, giving primary importance to the interrelational, which highlights cultural differences. As Fredric Jameson affirms, the very act of expressing cultural differences "calls us into question fully as much as it acknowledges the Other, thereby also serving as a more adequate and chastening form of self-knowledge."[2] It is a question of looking toward oneself in the encounter with the other. In that look, we affirm ourselves in our identities and at the same time assume a commitment to defend human life and dignity.

Since I wish to stress the importance of frontier spaces, my present focus—between oppression and resistance—aims to contribute to reflection on the reality of the "inter-mediate" spaces that characterize postcolonial discourse. Such spaces, as I understand them, allow for the formation of social subjects on the basis of their differences of race, class, gender, generation, sexual orientation, and social position. Those "inter-mediate" spaces, understood as social realities where cultural differences find expression, are nourished by the social imaginary (*imaginarios sociales*), which in turn arises from specific cultures[3] and at the same time contributes to them, thus influencing social relations.

For the present reflection I consider it fundamental, first, to grant centrality to the experience of black women in their construction of everyday intermediate spaces. Second, in regard to strategies of interpretation, I consider biblical exegesis to be a means for dialogue that allows us to ask about cultural differences and intercultural perspectives and to explain how these differences are recorded. Finally, I propose to explore how the intercultural hermeneutic can be of help in discovering interpretative strategies for creating a world in which black women, men, and children can live in justice and in permanent interrelation with other human groups.

OUR TRAVELING THROUGH DIFFERENT WORLDS AND CULTURES

This type of analysis, which gives priority to intercultural themes and reflects principally on the interconnected character of oppression and resistance, allows us to think in terms of different worlds and cultures. At the same time, it motivates us to move toward abandoning those stable, ready-made images that limit imagination and impede the creative and re-creative force exerted by an imaginary that is capable of provoking encounters among different spaces and times.

From my perspective, it is necessary to propose above all an imaginary that allows for the growth of social subjects that desire to dream about living on the frontiers, in that space where one is not on either side, where no controls are needed and where life can be preserved. From within that space we are able to desacralize the evident assumptions of cultural supremacy.

Putting forth an intercultural proposal involves the obligation to counteract not only the prevailing cultures of the North, but also any other dominating forces. Accordingly, we should keep in mind the relations of domination that exist even among countries of the South, and in our own particular case, the relations between the Dominican Republic and Haiti. For years now there has been a tendency, encouraged by the dominant classes of both nations, to consider Haitian culture inferior to Dominican. As a result, a great variety of sociopolitical schemes has been implemented to attempt to demonstrate the superiority of one people over the other.

In the cultural context of the Dominican Republic, the images used to sustain this prejudicial way of thinking have become quite obnoxious: "Haitian people are dumb," "Haitian people are filthy," "Haitian people are . . . ." Such images become operative in diverse ways, fundamentally through relations of gender, class, and race. At the same time, however, notice must be taken of the labors that have been carried out by different individuals and groups, both Dominican and Haitian, in deconstructing these imaginaries that attempt to convert simple differences into tools for satanizing cultures. These image complexes have the effect of hampering mutual respect and of preventing recognition of the drumbeats that unite both people.

Language, whether spoken or written, is a tool of power. Literary works such as those of Edwidges Danticat[4] are quite suggestive in helping us critique the ways in which Dominican thought has been destructive with regard to the cultures of both peoples, and especially in relation to the ethno-political formation and the history of Dominicans. Danticat proposes new paradigms for envisioning the Haitian and the Dominican cultures in their different manifestations and relations. She views the cultures as different, but as having common roots and a common history, which allow for true experiences of interculturality.

In her work *Cosecha de Huesos* (harvest of bones), the author recounts in the form of a novel the experience of the massacre perpetrated in 1937 by the Dominican dictator Leónidas Trujillo, which had the aim of smothering the common flame that was identifying and uniting the two peoples. In this novel we find stories in which the two peoples appear to be a single people, their characters appear to be a single character and their shores appear to be a single shore. All of Danticat's writings are important for our present reflection, but here I have selected some dialogue concerning the experience of a midwife:

> " . . . If doctor Javier doesn't come, you'll have to do it!"
> "Madam, it's time. . . ."

As soon as he arrived, doctor Javier rushed . . . to the bed of Madam Valencia. . . . Madam Valencia handed him her son. "Why didn't you send for me?" . . .

"Amabelle, do you remember the exact time when they were born?"

"It was still morning. . . ."

"And how far apart were they born, Amabelle?

"I don't know," I said.

When it was time to bathe Rosalinda, doctor Javier lifted her up. . . . "She has some dark curls behind her ears," he dared to say to Madam Valencia.

"It must be the father's family," responded Papi, running the tips of his fingers over his white, sun-burnt face. "My daughter was born in the capital of this country. Her mother was of pure Spanish blood. As for me, I was born near the port of Valencia, in Spain."

Doctor Javier followed me to the pantry. "So you are a midwife, Amabelle, and you never said anything about it?" he asked. "How did you know what to do with those babies?"

"In Haiti my parents were healers. When it was necessary, they delivered babies."

"Valencia says that the little girl had problems," he said. "It seems as if the other baby had tried to strangle her. . . ."

"If you please, doctor, I would not condemn those little ones by saying such a thing."

"Many of us start out in the womb as one of a pair of twins, and we do away with the other," he insisted. "Sometimes two babies are born at the same time, but one is born dead and the other is healthy. . . . "

"I am thankful that ours have both survived. . . ."

"Let me tell you something else, Amabelle. You should leave here and become a midwife in Haiti."

"I am not a midwife. . . . And I have not crossed the border since I was eight years old."

This text is rich in images and details; its oppositions and correlations provoke a fascination that is more proper to poetry, but this is a poetry that makes the reality manifestly present, without hiding anything. Each character has a defined function and an appropriate form of speech. The themes of race, gender, class, and sexual reproduction appear quite naturally in the text. Amabelle was a midwife—"didn't she know it?" people asked, caught by surprise. She had a wisdom[5] that she inherited from her mother and father, who were healers. She knew how to save lives. The story of Amabelle's experience allows us to realize not only what life was like under the dictatorship, but also what kinds of positions men and women had within the system.

The doctor insists on his stories of death, but Amabelle continues to trust in life: "I am thankful that ours have both survived"—a boy and a girl. That is what matters to this midwife. And they hadn't sent for the doctor. The text subtly insinuates that the births of children make some profound social difference and have also certain political implications. This becomes visible through the names that are given the children. The mother chooses the name Rosalinda Teresa for the girl, in honor of her grandmother (22). The boy's name, Rafael, was chosen for his father, "in honor of the generalissimo" (45).

Amabelle is happy that she did not have to decide between life and death (38). For her, the most important thing is life. The difference between Amabelle and Valencia is represented in stereotypes of ethnicity, race, gender, and class. The ethnic-racial differences do not really appear to be so great: "Rosalinda has some dark curls behind her ears,"[6] the doctor warns. This detail is corrected immediately, however, by Papi's insisting on the mother's Spanish origin. For Amabelle, recognizing the difference does not prevent her from making this other woman's pain her own, even if she represents the dominant class. "She never thought that those people could do her damage!" She also resists the idea of crossing the border and leaving what she has and the people she knows. Only when she feels that her life is threatened will she make that decision (163).

In our communities we have many stories of midwives who intervene when the doctor doesn't arrive in time. They are Haitian midwives and Dominican midwives who exchange knowledge among themselves— didn't anybody know? They are midwives who become accomplices of the women who are giving birth. They know not the hour nor care about the time it will take, but they do know that time is significant and that the differences cannot be negated or simply summed up, because "in some way they occupy the same space."[7]

IN THE BIBLE: MEMORIES OF WOMEN, COMPLICITIES, *CONVIVENCIA* (LIVING TOGETHER)?

The story of Amabelle and Valencia brings to mind other stories, especially the memories of biblical women. According to Musimbi R. A. Kanyoro, the aim in reading biblical stories is not just to find the patterns of ancient customs, but to pay attention to the leads that the text can provide us for changing customs.[8] In this light, reading the Bible appeals to me because I approach it as a text that, while forming part of a culturally destructive colonial project associated with a patriarchal, androcentric system, offers the possibility of dialogue with the ancient memories of women of different cultures. These biblical women and their cultures, by interrelating, manage to keep themselves visible; moreover, they challenge the desire for historical homogeneity of which the colonial system was so proud and that the current neoliberal globalization seeks to reestablish.

The rhetoric of any text is important to take into account, for each text has an intention and seeks to justify to the reader the actions recounted. The intentions of the biblical text are not only religious, but also political. The process of formation, canonization, and transmission of the Bible has taken place under the aegis of authority and power. As feminist biblical criticism makes clear, the Bible can be and has been used as an instrument of domination, but it also can be and has been interpreted in ways that work for the liberation of women and of all oppressed, marginalized social groups.

Such is the context in which we should read texts such as Exodus 1:8–22. Like the passage I presented earlier, this scriptural text introduces the memories of women: it tells the story of midwives who team up with expectant mothers and help them give birth to their babies. The midwives are portrayed as disobeying laws and forgetting about the commands and the dangers. They seem to be interested only in saving lives. In contrast to the novel dialogue presented above, however, the biblical text does not allow the women to speak for themselves. Rather, the text speaks for them, so that the action of the midwives is known only through the author's ideological perspective.

In this sense, the Bible narrative preserves the memory of how women in general were socially constituted in the past, in terms of gender, race, and class relations. This story takes place in Egypt and reflects on the interactions between the Hebrew people and the Egyptians. Of course, many of the stories of Israel's origins and relations with Egypt have to do with the traditions found in Genesis and Exodus.

As part of the account of Israel's liberation from Egypt (Ex 1—15), the narrative of Exodus 1:8–22 is directly related to Exodus 2:1–10, which recalls the role women played in the Exodus.[9] The first chapter (1:1–7) gives an account of how the children of Israel settled in Egypt and became exceedingly numerous, long after Joseph and the first generation. When the new king arose, "who had never heard of Joseph" (1:8),[10] everything changed for the Israelites:

[The Egyptians] gave them no mercy in the demands they made, making their lives miserable with hard labor: with digging clay, making bricks, doing various kinds of field-work—all sorts of labor that they imposed on them without mercy.

The king of Egypt then spoke to the Hebrew midwives, one of whom was called Shiphrah, and the other Puah. "When you attend Hebrew women in childbirth," he said, "look at the two stones. If it is a boy, kill him; if a girl, let her live." (Ex 1:13–16)

Verse 15 mentions the midwives, but their nationality is not precisely specified in the ancient text. In the Septuagint version "Hebrew" can be read as describing not the midwives themselves but the women with child: "the midwives of the Hebrew women." Since the text leaves open the question of nationality, we may allow the possibility that some cultural interchange between Hebrews and Egyptians existed, whatever the ethnic origin of the midwives. The contact between the two peoples was indeed longstanding: "the time that the Israelites spent in Egypt was four hundred and thirty years" (Ex 12:40). This is more than sufficient time for mutual apprenticeships.[11]

Verse 16 uses the phrase "look at the two stones." The word *obnayim* (stones) appears to mean a type of two-stoned seat on which the birthing woman kneeled. Although some interpretations translate the term as "genitals," I here give preference to the former meaning because it represents a cultural practice that seems to have been widely known. According to Roland deVaux, the use of two stones to make a birthing stool has been documented in the rabbinic era and also in certain places of the modern Near East.[12] Some texts indicate that birthing sometimes took place on the knees of the mother or of someone else, whether midwife or family member (Gn 30:3; 50:23; Jb 3:12). In any case, what appears to be common practice is the participation of the midwives at the hour of giving birth (Gn 35:17; 38:18).

Quite significant is the appearance in the text of the names of these two midwives: Shiphrah and Puah. As is well known, documenting the names of women in the Bible is not common. This is so not only because the Bible is a text with androcentric bases, but also because, in general, the experiences and voices of women play a small part in it. Furthermore, not all the voices included in the Bible are the voices of all women. For that reason, in my opinion, the presence of these names makes clear the power of the memory of the midwives, even in this androcentric, patriarchal story. In such a context, being a mother was women's principal role, and the midwives are therefore honored for the role they played.

Although these women's experiences have been used for the benefit of a patriarchal ideology that makes heroes of men on the basis of women's actions,[13] we must recognize that there still exist memories of women who create histories that cannot be forgotten or evaded.

In this sense, Carolyn Osiek, reflecting on minority-group women in the United States, writes that "all women . . . do not necessarily stand in solidarity against the oppression of women, but that racism and classism have determined the relationships of rich and poor, slave and free women. . . . We are learning slowly and painfully that women's reading of the Bible and of their lives is affected by race and class as much as by sex."[14]

I propose to read this text, therefore, on the basis of the experiences of black women who are midwives. They are the experiences of Haitian and Dominican women and of women from other parts of Latin America and the world. The medical labors of such women who accompany other women are often rendered invisible today. We wish to emphasize the way in which these women, whether from different cultures or not, can become agents of life: "But the midwives were God-fearing women and did not obey the orders of the king of Egypt, but allowed the boys to live" (Ex 1:17).

This verse really says nothing new with regard to what is traditionally expected of biblical women. Thus, Elisabeth Schüssler Fiorenza states that it is important "to see the bible as a perspectival rhetorical discourse that constructs theological worlds and symbolic universes in particular historical-political situations."[15] As I have noted in earlier sections, the principal role of women in the Bible is having children or of caring for children.

Drorah O'Donnell Setel understands that these women, who are central in the dramatic image of giving birth, are portrayed throughout the narrative as heroes (Exodus 1:8—2:10).[16] The midwives exhibit admirable qualities; besides initiating the resistance against the Pharaoh's oppression, they were "God-fearing women." We can thus affirm that they were women who acted wisely;[17] they were wise women. "The midwives said to Pharaoh, 'Hebrew women are not like Egyptian women, they are hardy and give birth before the midwife can get to them'" (1:19). For Renita J. Weems, the theme of difference is inherent to the story: there are differences between Egyptians and Hebrews, between slaves and masters, between Hebrew women and Egyptian women, and between girls and boys. On the basis of these differences, the story portrays the social conflicts reflected in the memory of the struggle between those who have power for dominating and those who have power for resisting.[18] These differences, which provide the setting for the text, are manifested as relations of power.

The midwives' attitude of "fearing God" serves the ideological interest of the narrator, who does not portray the differences as matters of fact but seeks to exploit them and insists on binary inferior/superior relations. Weems states that "certainly, the narrator's claim is not for ethnic, but religious superiority: the god of Israel who stands in the shadow of the Hebrews is superior to the god of Egypt."[19]

Nonetheless, I believe that stressing the difference between the Hebrew women and the Egyptian women goes beyond purely religious motives. The affirmation that "Hebrew women are not like Egyptian women, they are hardy," highlights a difference in the women's bodies, which is also used to show the superiority of the Hebrews over the others. Such a procedure gives evidence of how gender, race, and ideology work together in this text about midwives.

When differences are emphasized in terms of superiority/inferiority, it is difficult to achieve true recognition of the midwives and the other women. However, when difference is valued as an element favorable for the forming of relations of mutual respect, then a transformation of images occurs, one that seeks to affirm that no person or culture is inferior to another.

For that reason I consider it important to pay heed to the warning of J. Cheryl Exum: "Even if there is a positive side to our recognition of the midwives' experience in resisting the Egyptian Pharaoh (1:19), we also run the risk of supporting the narrator's ideology, which spares no effort in showing how this Pharaoh is so dumb that even women are able to deceive him."[20] Ignoring Exum's warning would result in an attitude that continues to support those image complexes that affirm women's inferiority to men. However, hardly anyone would run the risk of arguing for the inferiority of one culture to another, instead of conceiving that cultures and identities are forged in their mutual dealings with one another. In this sense, I find valuable the contribution of Raúl Fornet-Betancourt, who states that "cultures are frontier processes. The frontier, as a basic experience of being in continual transition, is not only a frontier that marks off one's own territory and traces the limit between what is one's own and what is foreign. . . . The frontier is created and established in the very interior of what we call our own culture. The other is both within and outside of what is our own."[21]

A hermeneutical perspective that gives priority to dialogue between cultures does not allow for generalizations. Similarly, such a perspective avoids portraying the Egyptians as powerful monsters operating against the powerless Israelites; precisely such an image is present in the ideology created by the Exodus narrative. A hermeneutical perspective that gives priority to dialogue thinks in terms of powers that encounter one another in practices of domination and resistance. As Jean-Paul Sartre points out, the dialectic between the singularity of the universal and the universalization of the singular takes place in the structuring of situations.[22]

In this sense, a hermeneutic of intercultural dialogue strongly urges us to deconstruct the symbolisms that have often been used to describe or identify human groups or cultures, whether in the Bible or elsewhere. As is shown in the work of many patristic writers who treat the relations between the Egyptians and the Ethiopians, there exist interpretations that prescind from the interrelations recounted in the text or the interests of the text's editors.[23] Such neglect has strengthened ideologies that emphasize the differences of inferiority/superiority, thus impeding fluid dialogue among cultures. We should keep in mind, however, that, although the Exodus text makes an effort to satanize Egypt, within the Bible more generally Egypt appears as the original host of the Israelites and of other neighboring peoples, especially in moments of great famine.[24]

For that reason, I would like to observe that the construction of images on the basis of the daily experience of bordering peoples, when it is done in terms of a superior/inferior polarity, not only impedes dialogue between the peoples but also prevents the strengthening of both. Along this line, as the text of Edwidges Danticat also illustrates, I suggest the need to break with the imaginary of superior/inferior and to move rather toward true encounter. Amabelle is a Haitian midwife who uses her practical knowledge to save the lives of children of another culture, but that other culture is also in some way her own. This is a woman who later takes the risk of defending people of her own group and who, with a mix of confidence and distrust, decides to cross the border, although it would appear to be too late.

In the story of Amabelle, the border appears to be a decisive place, the place where the plans on one side and on the other get woven together. The border is thus a political place. However, she does not feel a need to cross it. Only when her life is threatened on one side or another does she cross to the other side, even though in political and economic terms the two sides are not very different from each other.

THE MIDWIVES: DIFFERENCES AND ENCOUNTERS
THAT RAISE CHALLENGES

Our reflection on these two texts, one fictional and one biblical, raises some concerns that need answering if we wish to advance in our proposal for an intercultural theological hermeneutic. The first concern has to do with the texts being embedded in contexts where the interrelational is a given. The relations of gender, race, class, and sex are evident in both texts. Both the midwife Amabelle and the midwives Shiphrah and Puah are conditioned not only by the sociopolitical contexts, but also by the cultural settings from which they come. In both cases, the image complexes seem to swirl around relations of power.

A second concern has to do with the significant differences between the two texts. In the case of Amabelle, it is noteworthy that her experiences are related in her own voice, so that a greater understanding of the interrelations between the two cultures is allowed. At the same time, the story shows how gender, race, class, and sex are intimately connected to the experiences of domination and resistance. In my view, this means that interculturality should be understood as an experience that takes place in daily life.

In the biblical text, however, the women's voices do not appear directly; rather, the text speaks only of what they did. What the women did or did not do, what they spoke or kept quiet, all is conditioned by the sympathies of the narrator. Nonetheless, these women were favored, since "God was good to the midwives" (Ex 1:20). That text I have used about Amabelle does not reveal the similarity of fates between her and the biblical midwives, but the complete work does, even if her end was less marvelous than theirs.

The third concern has to do with the reality of oppression or domination. Even though our proposal treats of interculturality, this concern is not thereby annulled. Rather, this reality is manifested in the way cultural differences are structured and in the way they are expressed through liberation or resistance. The intercultural viewed as process, therefore, does not mean that the interchange of values, meanings, and priorities is developed only in harmonious collaboration; it can also be a process that is deeply antagonistic, conflictive, and even incommensurable. Nonetheless, this process highlights the right that each culture has to its own voice. The other social subject involved in the process, even if it is a history of oppression, always contributes an original discursive perspective that shakes up one's own securities and certainties.[25]

Amabelle and Valencia are from different cultures, both in their daily activities and in their image complexes, and they are not considered to have the same social value. Madam Valencia is a Dominican mistress of Spanish descent, married to a soldier of the generalissimo's guard. Amabelle is a Haitian survivor of the 1937 massacre who reached the madam's house as a child. Although she grew up beside Valencia, Amabelle is a domestic servant.

Still, Amabelle's attitude always manifests the affection she feels for the family that received her. For me, it is significant that she never speaks of being inferior but rather is simply grateful. She relates to Valencia freely and spontaneously. Furthermore, she does not inquire even about her civil status, that is, about the actual state of her rights and responsibilities in the country. Her responsibilities appear to be limited to the daily concerns of caring for the family. Apparently, the real or imaginary barriers with regard to her citizenship do not cause her fears, traumas, sentiments of discrimination, or inferiority complexes.[26]

With regard to Shiphrah and Puah, there is not much information about them—they might be Egyptian, or perhaps Hebrew—who knows? They are the midwives who receive orders from the Egyptian Pharaoh. Despite the androcentric rhetoric of the text, we can well imagine the ingenious efforts of these midwives to devise and execute ways to save the Hebrew boys. Their efforts are consistent with their everyday actions of helping to care for the lives of all children. Ironically, due to the inferior social position of women, the orders given are to leave alive only the baby girls.

Amabelle assumes the job of helping to give birth to the little twins. She does not have to face the dilemma of deciding which one to leave alive. For that reason she is happy, though we do not know for "fear" of whom, since the text makes no mention of God. Amabelle's outlook, however, might well be interpreted as a manifestation of the celestial Wisdom, who has been present in her own life and in the life of her ancestors, from whom she learned to be a midwife. Wisdom is understood as that "cosmic figure delighting in the dance of creation, a 'master' craftswo/man and teacher of justice. She is the leader of Her people and accompanies them on their way through history."[27] However, this interpretation cannot hide the fact that Amabelle receives orders not only from men, but also from Valencia, her mistress.

Our fourth concern has to do with how the feminist theological community, in view of all this, is called upon to continue its critical dialogue with contemporary cultural studies, which appears to be at once complex and problematic, for all talk of culture makes us walk along avenues of ambiguities. Participation in the design of cultures often turns out to be an uncomfortable and disturbing activity of surviving and supplementing, but its glowing presence can also bring moments of pleasure, illumination, and liberation.

In this sense, feminists in both Africa and Latin America define culture as a double-edged weapon, since it provides women with resources for affirming their own integrity and lifestyle, while at the same time it reinforces patriarchal forms of domination that work against women.[28]

This same argument is made by Letty M. Russell in her reflection on the hybrid character of modernity and western Christian religion, which supposedly offer the world freedom and life, but at the same time impose global imperialism, oppression and the negation of African cultures.[29]

PREPARING FOR THE JOURNEY TOWARD INTERCULTURALITY

What does it really mean, then, to speak of interculturality in the face of the concrete reality of some cultures that dominate and others that are dominated?

This question, I suggest, obliges us to reflect on the importance of social image complexes in our discussion of cultural differences, and especially of interculturality. Human groupings construct their identities by affirming their distinctiveness on the basis of social image complexes, but those same image complexes also hinder us in our ability to identify the snares of power relationships imposed by the hegemonic cultures. As a result, the proposal of interculturality turns out to be something that we must still seek to make visible, and in many cases it is something that we must still design and build.

In my opinion, when we speak of culture(s) within the intercultural experience, we must assume the task of reflecting on the importance of interculturality not only in and of itself, but also in relation to its broader sphere, content, and context. This concern for the cultural environment means emphasizing the international spaces of historical realities, where cultural differences are inscribed in the "inter-mediate," or rather in the reality of the culturally hybrid.

On the basis of the texts analyzed in this essay and of experiences that I have shared with other people, I would like to suggest that the "inter-mediate" spaces are necessary for intercultural exchanges. According to Jung Young Lee, those spaces are more than a limit for making explicit the meaning of marginality, where no one's world is independent; rather they exist in relation to the other and in relation to the opposite.[30] According to Homi K. Bhabha, those spaces allow for the "beyond," in the sense of exceeding the barrier or the limit, because the "beyond" means spatial distance, marks an advance, and promises the future.[31]

In terms of the construction of discourse, our entering into the world of Amabelle and into that of the biblical midwives has helped us discover the unequal and disparate forces of cultural representations that give evidence of a world where social and political authority are being disputed within the world order to which these representations refer.

The discourse of the texts in question intervenes in the discourses that seek to grant hegemonic "normality" to the unequal development of nations, races, communities, and peoples, that is, to the unequal development of interpersonal relations, as in the case of Amabelle and Valencia. Similarly, our study of the unequal relation of Shiphrah and Puah has served to analyze the patriarchal and ethnocentric interests that are present in the narrators of the biblical texts. In this sense, Denys Cuche observes that "cultures are born of social relations that are always unequal relations. To think that there is no hierarchy among cultures would be to suppose that the cultures exist independently of one another. If we affirm that all cultures deserve the same attention, that does not mean that all are recognized socially as having the same value."[32] Nonetheless, in our concern to overcome inequality, we manage to express the urgency of our protest in the face of what is real and what is being threatened by the political and the historical in all their diversity.

At the same time, taking into account the present-day reality, nobody can deny that it is difficult to speak of interculturality without taking as a starting point the realities of current cultural displacements.[33] Only on the basis of these realities can considerations of interculturality or intermediate spaces make clear the need for rethinking ways to affirm human rights, nationality, the needs of citizenship, and relations of gender beyond the dynamics of economic, cultural, and political exploitation.

Faced with all these tasks, we see clearly the need to develop a new system of the imaginary that allows us to live beyond the borders of the present time and that highlights our temporal and social differences, but without hierarchies, whether supposed or imposed. It also seems clear that this proposal is not one that can be realized by a single person or a single group; it needs to be a collective task that involves and interrelates other persons and groups. At the same time, those who have always been in the centers of power can and must "re-learn"[34] the ability to see other social groups from an open posture that allows other centers to exist and corrects the asymmetries within the power structures.

Finally, reflecting on interculturality also involves reflecting on citizenship. Citizenship cannot be restricted. In intercultural terms, the decision to cross the border is not taken out of fear of what can happen on one side or the other, but out of the freedom that people have to take steps toward encountering other people and continuing to grow as human beings. It is a question of making explicit the concern and the practice that every person should have for the full development of all cultures. In this sense interculturality is a political act that promotes the valuing of difference as a way of living in liberty.

Notes

[1] Raúl Fornet-Betancourt, *Trasformación Intercultural de la Filosofía: Ejercicios Teóricos y Prácticos de la Filosofía Intercultural desde Latinoamérica en el Contexto de la Globalización* (Bilbao: Desclée de Brouwer, 2001), 29.

[2] Fredric Jameson, "Foreword," in *Caliban and Other Essays*, ed. Roberto Fernández Retamar (Minneapolis: University of Minnesota Press, 1989), xi–xii.

[3] Culture is understood neither as a datum nor as a heritage that is immutably transmitted from generation to generation, but as a construction that has its development in the history of the relations of social groups among themselves. See Denys Cuche, *A Noção de Cultura Nas Ciencias Sociais*, 2nd ed. (Bauru-São Paulo: EDUSC Editorial Universidad Santa Catarina, 2002), 143.

[4] Edwidges Danticat, *Cosecha de Huesos* (Bogotá: Editorial Norma, 1999), 18, 25, 28, 31, 32.

[5] "Wisdom is a state of the human mind and spirit characterized by deep understanding and profound insight. It is elaborated as a quality possessed by the sages but also treasured as folk wisdom and wit. Wisdom is the power of discernment, deeper understanding, and creativity; it is the ability to move and to dance, to make the connections, to savor life, and to learn from experience. . . . It is a radically democratic concept insofar as it does not require extensive schooling and formal education" (Elisabeth Schüssler Fiorenza, *Wisdom Ways: Introducing Feminist Biblical Interpretation* [Maryknoll, NY: Orbis Books, 2001], 23–24).

[6] This is an expression used in the Dominican Republic to indicate that a person has African blood. In this context, people are frequently desirous of hiding their black roots, which are common in the Haitian people.

[7] Charles Taylor, *Philosophy and the Human Sciences* (Cambridge: Cambridge University Press, 1985), 145.

[8] Musimbi R. A. Kanyoro, "Cultural Hermeneutics: An African Contribution," in *Other Ways of Reading: African Women and the Bible*, ed. Musa W. Dube (Atlanta: Society of Biblical Literature; Geneva: World Council of Churches Publications, 2001), 107–8.

[9] J. Cheryl Exum posits that, when the ideology of the text is revealed in biblical literary analysis, it is certainly possible to appreciate the importance that women have in these opening chapters of Exodus, but it is also clear that the object of attention is a masculine baby, Moses. While he becomes the central figure and eventually dominates the story, the women gradually disappear. See J. Cheryl Exum, "Outras considerações sobre personagens secundárias: Mulheres en Êxodo 1:8–2, 10," in *De Êxodo a Deuteronômio a Partir de Uma Leitura de Gênero*, ed. Athlya Brenner (São Paulo: Paulinas, 2000), 82–95.

[10] Biblical quotations in this essay are from *The New Jerusalem Bible*, gen. ed. Henry Wansbrough (Garden City, NY: Doubleday, 1985).

[11] In the symbolic image system of the Egyptians, the relation man/woman is seen and projected as essential for the existence of Egypt, on the basis of the

circularity of behavior. See Margaret Marchiori Bakos, *Fatos e Mitos do Antigo Egito*, 2nd ed. (Porto Alegre: EDIPURS Editora Pontífica da Universidade Católica do Rio Grande do Sul, 2001), 32.

[12] Roland de Vaux, *Instituições de Israel no Antigo Testamento*, trans. Daniel de Oliveira (São Paulo: Editora Teológica, 2003), 65–66.

[13] J. Cheryl Exum, citing Julia Kristeva, wonders what effects result from the fact that the biblical editors responsible for maintaining social and symbolic order seek to manipulate the women in Exodus 1:8–2:10 by portraying them in a positive way that is worthy of imitation by the women of Israel and other women who read the text. Furthermore, citing Esther Fuchs, Exum points out that "the feminine characters in the text often reveal more about the dreams, fears, aspirations and preconceptions of their masculine creators than they do about the real life of women" (Exum, "Outras considerações sobre personagens secundárias," 86–87).

[14] Carolyn Osiek, "Reading the Bible as Women," in *The New Interpreter's Bible: General and Old Testament Articles Genesis, Exodus, Leviticus*, vol. 1, ed. Leander E. Keck (Nashville, TN: Abingdon, 1994), 186.

[15] Schüssler Fiorenza, *Wisdom Ways*, 4.

[16] Drorah O'Donnell Setel, "Exodus," in *Women's Bible Commentary*, ed. Carol A. Newsom and Sharon H. Ringe (Louisville, KY: Westminster John Knox Press, 1988), 28–34.

[17] The fear of God is presented principally in the sapiential texts as the principle of wisdom. This fear not only prepares people for knowledge but also possesses an eminently critical function by maintaining an awareness that the cognitive faculty relates to a world ruled over by mystery and awakens the confidence needed to be open to teaching. The truly wise person is surrounded by the "unknown of God" and is at the same time a "singer of the divine secrets." See Hans Walter Wolff, *Antropología del Antiguo Testamento* (Salamanca: Ediciones Sígueme, 1997), 277–80; Brevard S. Childs, *El Libro del Éxodo: Pentateuco: Comentario Crítico y Teológico*, trans. Enrique Sanz Jiménez-Rico (Estella, Spain: Verbo Divino, 2003), 53.

[18] Renita J. Weems, "The Hebrew Women Are Not Like the Egyptian Women: The Ideology of Race, Gender, and Sexual Reproduction in Exodus 1," *Semeia* 59 (1992): 30.

[19] Ibid., 32–33.

[20] Exum, "Outras considerações sobre personagens secundárias," 87.

[21] Raúl Fornet-Betancourt, *Interculturalidad y Globalización: Ejercicios de Crítica Filosófica Intercultural en el Contexto de la Globalización Neoliberal* (Frankfurt: IKO; San José, Costa Rica: Departamento Ecuménico de Investigaciones, 2000), 68.

[22] Jean-Paul Sartre, "L'Universel Singulier," *Situations* 9 (1972): 190.

[23] See Gay L. Byron, *Symbolic Blackness and Ethnic Difference in Early Christian Literature* (New York: Routledge, 2002), 57.

[24] For more on this, see R. J. Williams, *A People Come Out of Egypt: An Egyptologist Looks at the Old Testament* (Leiden: Brill, 1975), 231–52.

[25] Fornet-Betancourt, *Transformación Intercultural*, 41.

[26] Virginia Vargas Valente, "Una reflexión feminista de la ciudadanía," in *Antología de Teoría y Análisis Feminista: Teología Feminista Intercultural* (reading material in preparation for the Inter-American Feminist Symposium, México City, July 2004).

[27] Schüssler Fiorenza, *Wisdom Ways*, 27.

[28] Musimbi R. A. Kanyoro, *Introducing Feminist Cultural Hermeneutics: An African Perspective* (Cleveland: Pilgrim Press, 2002), 9; Elsa Tamez, "Cultural Violence against Women in Latin America," in *Women Resisting Violence. Spirituality for Life*, ed. Mary John Mananzan et al. (Maryknoll, NY: Orbis Books, 1996), 11–19; Mercy Amba Oduyoye, *Daughters of Anowa: African Women and Patriarchy* (Maryknoll, NY: Orbis Books, 2000), 82.

[29] Letty M. Russell, "Cultural Hermeneutics: A Postcolonial Look at Mission," *Journal of Feminist Studies in Religion* 20, no. 1 (2004): 28.

[30] Jung Young Lee, *Marginality: The Key to Multicultural Theology* (Minneapolis: Fortress Press, 1995), 47.

[31] Homi K. Bhabha, *El Lugar de la Cultura* (Buenos Aires: Manantial, 1994/2000), 20.

[32] Cuche, *A Noção de Cultura Nas Ciencias Sociais*, 143–44.

[33] H. K. Bhabha states that "we learn our hardest lessons from the life and thought of those who have suffered the condemnation of history: subjugation, domination, diaspora, displacement" (Bhabha, *El Lugar de la Cultura*, 212).

[34] In his proposal for an intercultural philosophy, Fornet-Betancourt uses this term to indicate that "relearning" is learning to understand and present one's own word (and action) as always "respective" of the other. See Fornet-Betancourt, *Transformación Intercultural*, 91–100.

11

Indian Wisdom and Spirituality

Dialogue and Encounter with Indigenous Women

Christa P. Godínez Munguía

This chapter seeks to examine the wisdom and spirituality of the indigenous people of America (whom we call Abya Yala) on the basis of dialogue and encounter with some Latin American indigenous women.

BEGINNING AN INTERCULTURAL DIALOGUE

I conceive such dialogue and encounter as intercultural, since all of us have been molded by different cultures, even though we all share being born and living physically in Latin America. Our dialogue seeks to serve as a link and a bridge between the indigenous reality that, though being only a few hours distant from our view, remains marginalized, remote and invisible for many people who live in the large cities. The distance that separates us from indigenous reality is not just a matter of kilometers but is also, more seriously, something conceptual, tending at times to oblivion. Many people believe that indigenous peoples no longer exist.

Many, of course, even question whether such a dialogue can be intercultural, since for them the indigenous peoples generally have no culture—the remains of their culture are to be found only in museums. Those who see matters this way have a rather poor concept of what culture really is, or they reduce the term to the modern culture of the West or to written culture. They fail to understand the anthropological principle that holds that culture is a human constant, in all times and all places.

Certainly all peoples live by means of their culture, which defines their way of being and provides them with the tools they need to situate themselves in the world. The indigenous peoples possess millennial cultures that have been passed on from generation to generation, not necessarily by writing, but through oral traditions, rites, symbols, and stories. The Amerindian peoples have voice and word; the word is one of their essential values and the depositary of their wisdom; it is a word that must be listened to and that must be made heard in our society. Our goal here is to accept that word and to recognize its concrete, critical contribution to our humanity. We seek then to undertake an intercultural dialogue that aims at mutual fecundation and enrichment among diverse cultures.

I approach the indigenous peoples from a culture that is *mestizo,* urban, and Westernized. I live in Mexico City and work in an academy, but I have had the opportunity to share in various experiences of encounter and dialogue with the indigenous communities of Mexico. Moreover, I have long had a great interest in learning from the wisdom and the spirituality of the indigenous peoples of America, as well as of other continents, whether by immediate experience or through their writings and symbols. Much of this wisdom has been preserved and transmitted through the agency of grandparents and parents, who are still viewed in these cultures with great respect and veneration.

THE *EKKLESIA* OF WO/MEN AND THE INDIGENOUS VOICE

One of the conceptual tools that I have found useful for this work is the notion of the *ekklesia of wo/men,* introduced by Elisabeth Schüssler Fiorenza. She states: "When I speak of ekklesia of wo/men . . . I do not speak of a women's church that excludes men. Nor do I speak of one group of women as a unitary entity."[1] She explains further:

> Theologically, the expression ekklesia of wo/men asserts that "salvation" is not possible outside the world or without the world. G*d's vision of a renewed creation entails not only a "new" heaven but also a "renewed," qualitatively different earth freed from kyriarchal exploitation and dehumanization. To articulate ekklesia, i.e., the assembly of full citizens, means to name an alternative reality of justice and well-being for all, without exception.[2]

Kyriarchal exploitation and dehumanization refer to our present situation, where "elite Western educated propertied Euro-American men have articulated and benefited from women's and other 'non-persons' exploitation."[3] In our case, besides Euro-American men, there also exist Latin American *mestizo* males who have joined with the former in their kyriarchal exploitation and dehumanization of the women, men, and children of the indigenous peoples.

The *ekklesia* of wo/men is a notion that I believe exists already among the indigenous peoples. Listen to the voice of María Vicenta Chuma Quishpilema of Ecuador:

> From our experience we know that the situation of indigenous women is the same as that of their men, but it is aggravated by the division of roles socially imposed by the ideology of the oppressor culture. That other culture's way of seeing and acting has for more than five centuries made us forget that for us, as our old people say, it takes two hands to kneed the bread.[4]

She also criticizes the system:

> The western system tries in many ways to give a purely feminist content to the struggle of indigenous women. It bases learning projects and leadership training on models of self-esteem and on very coercive proposals with respect to domestic violence. It uses an ideology of "gender solidarity" that eliminates the difference between well-off women and poor women, between women citizens with full rights and country women with few rights, between white or *mestiza* women and indigenous women—all for the sake of "women's unity" and the unity of the struggle against the "domination of men." With this unilateral approach they bias the struggle through a system that works against the indigenous population as a whole and that provokes major distortions like "machismo" in the same indigenous communities.[5]

Chuma Quishpilema recognizes also that the wisdom of these peoples has helped them face these same difficulties, though not without problems. Many indigenous peoples are indeed convinced that machismo is an import from Western culture. It is like a virus that arrived in the sixteenth century with the colonizers, since for the indigenous peoples male/female complementarity has long been fundamental in all the labors and responsibilities that are part of community life. Moreover, for some indigenous peoples, such complementarity helps define their mission of reproducing in human life the twofold image by which they contemplate the divinity, as father/mother.

WHAT HAPPENS IN OTHER INDIGENOUS COMMUNITIES?

According to Marisela García Reyes, the disease of machismo afflicts also the homes of some of the Tseltal indigenous communities in Chiapas, Mexico, where the women are often beaten, maltreated, oppressed, and badgered.[6] Although the woman is said to be the owner, it is not always so, because the man also rules and oppresses there in the home. The women spend most of their time in the house, but it is not a place of liberty, rest and recreation for them, but rather one of oppression when the men maltreat them, beat them, fight with them, or get drunk.

Drunkenness, alcoholism, and the sale of alcohol have often been denounced and resisted by the women. In many ways, through strong speeches, symbols, drawings, socio-dramas, tears, resolutions, and so forth, the women have spoken their word, and I can give testimony of that. They treat this problematic as if it were a thornbush that is destroying the community and needs to be rooted out completely. The women who have posts of service in the community make a serious commitment to treat the problem, and in this sense they are concerned for the *ekklesia* of wo/men, since this is a problem that affects both women and men. Alcoholism among indigenous men has on many occasions been exploited by certain *mestizos* to destroy and rob communities of their assets. Alcoholism is indeed an ally of the kyriarchal oppression of indigenous women and men. Besides suffering these evils of machismo and alcoholism, many communities of Chiapas have also had to live in fear because of the presence of the army, the police, and armed highway bandits. "We women do not have the freedom to travel alone since we run the risk of being raped."[7]

THE DIFFICULTIES OF DIALOGUE WITH INDIGENOUS WOMEN

Earlier I made reference to the word of Vicenta Chuma Quishpilema. I say "word" here in the singular, and not "words" in the plural, because for the indigenous peoples the word is a reality that molds, gives life, gives meaning, sustains, and forms part of their essence. This vital function of the word can be better understood if we take into account that the indigenous peoples have kept alive their long oral tradition. They claim that authentic people are "persons of the word" and not of the dispersed, empty "words" that provoke death. On hearing the word of Vicenta, we ought to be aware that she had to learn Spanish or *castilla*, as Spanish is commonly called in many indigenous communities of

Mexico. Vicenta has translated her mother tongue into *castilla*. She is
speaking to us in a tongue that is not her own, and this is not easy, but
she wishes to be heard and therefore has made an effort to learn *castilla*.
For her part, Marisela García Reyes, whose mother tongue is Spanish,
has learned perfect Tseltal, and thanks to her I have been able to know
and get closer to the Tseltal peoples and the situation of their women,
for not all women speak *castilla*, and many of us who deal with them do
not speak their tongue well. In this zone, in fact, the majority of the
women speak only Tseltal, since they ordinarily stay at home and take
care of the land. In contrast, their husbands generally leave home to
look for work or to sell their products to the *mestizos*; they therefore
must know *castilla* in order to do business. What I have noticed especially in these indigenous communities, above all in the conversations
among women, is that communication is not reducible to spoken language but is broader and includes symbols and attitudes, along with
gestures of acceptance, rejection, affection, support, or indifference.

    Indigenous women, as well as the men and even the children, possess
a fine sensibility that quickly grasps what we wish to tell them, even
beyond our words. In fact, these peoples have had so many experiences
of *mestizos* and foreigners who did not keep their word that they prefer
to listen to the heart of people and so detect their diverse and sometimes
devious intentions. If the word goes hand in hand with the heart and the
attitudes, then it has a worthwhile content, and a fruitful dialogue can
be had.

    In my own experience I have had the help of translators, both indig-
enous and *mestizo*, but in fact much of the dialogue has taken place
through attitudes and gestures, through encounters of prayer and faith,
through joyful and festive celebrations, or through shedding tears for
the sickness and death that continually besiege them. The spirituality of
the Tseltal peoples is one of resistance, struggle, perseverance, generosity, service, hospitality, and openness, in a constant, patient communal
spirit.[8] The word is therefore communal; everybody is invited to say
their word, and whatever time is necessary is taken, in speaking and
listening, in word and silence, so that all may express themselves and
consensus be reached. We have much to learn from such practice.

INDIGENOUS SPIRITUALITY ACKNOWLEDGED
IN DEVOTION TO THE VIRGIN OF GUADALUPE

    Much has been said in Mexico, and in all of Americas, about the
importance of the Guadalupe event for the evangelization of the country

and the development of Mexican culture. The Virgin of Guadalupe has been viewed as either an indigenous or a *mestiza* woman, depending on the origin of those who approach her. Here we would especially like to recover what she means in the indigenous tradition, since our aim is to listen to and learn from the indigenous voice that is to be found also in our *mestizo* reality.

What have indigenous people seen in Maria of Guadalupe? They have found in her someone who loves their culture and their indigenous way of being. They know that Maria revealed herself as an indigenous woman speaking a native tongue, the Nahuatl language of Juan Diego.[9] Maria of Guadalupe did not need translators to speak with Juan Diego, nor did she need translators to speak other native tongues. Besides, her word and her heart were united, so that the content of her word brought forth life. Juan Diego heard in his own language that someone accepted him with great affection, just the way he was, speaking to him in his own cultural symbols. Such an experience caused a rebirth of his heart, which had been trodden down by the Spanish conquistadores—it was a recovery of his dignity, a saving sign. The experience of salvation that is narrated in the *Nican Mopuhua*[10] is one that is re-created and relived by every member of the indigenous peoples and by the community as such in the depths of their hearts.

It is worth noting that the notion of heart among the indigenous peoples is similar to the biblical notion of heart. The heart not only is the seat of feelings but signifies also the most intimate recesses of the person; it is the place of decisions and of encounter with divine wisdom. When the Virgin speaks to Juan Diego, therefore, she speaks to his heart; that is where her word reaches directly, the word that will console and strengthen him. For that reason she tells him: "Know, and be sure in your heart." Her words seek to restore the heart of the person who has been humbled and cast aside by the colonizers' oppression. Dialogue with the Virgin of Guadalupe is experienced as a saving and liberating dialogue. Thus is it presented in the story of Guadalupe, and thus is it lived by indigenous people today. Indigenous women say that they find in her consolation and a heartfelt desire to struggle for their community, in order to be able to strengthen and expand the heart of their communities constantly. They see themselves as continuing the labor begun by the Virgin of Guadalupe, that is, consoling, strengthening, and giving life to people's hearts.

The wisdom of indigenous spirituality encourages perseverance and constancy in the struggle to defend and generously care for the community. Such a spirituality thus promotes three fundamental elements found in the heart of their culture: hospitality, respect for agreements, and community spirit. The struggle and perseverance of the members are shown in their willingness to accompany the community faithfully "in good times and in bad."

Indigenous women and their communities are enriched in their relation with the Virgin of Guadalupe through two forms of approaching her. One is through the image of the Virgin, and the other is through the story of *Nican Mopohua*. When they see the image of the Virgin, they realize that she is not static but dynamic—she is in movement. If we observe her image, we observe that one of her legs is flexed in a walking position. She is a woman who walks with her people. Furthermore, they recognize a full coherence between her word and her heart, her face and her heart, her word and her attitudes. The Virgin has a word, she gives her word, and she keeps it; they know that she *respects agreements* and does not deceive. Her word is one that expresses *hospitality;* she takes in Juan Diego and everybody else. For that reason she wanted a little house, a chapel, to be built, so that everybody could find her there—not only those of indigenous origin, but also those of *mestizo*, Spanish, and other backgrounds. In that place she will be *generous*, though she already is, splurging her love and compassion. In her word she says:

> I greatly wish and earnestly desire that my chapel be built on this spot. In it I will show and give my love, my compassion, my aid and my defense to all the peoples. For I am the merciful Mother, of you and of all the nations that live on the earth. May they love me, speak to me, seek me and confide in me. There I will hear their laments and will cure all their miseries, disgraces and pains.[11]

She restores those who are wounded, forlorn, and humiliated in heart. This loving generosity is also symbolized in the variety of blossoms that Juan Diego found in the barren terrain, where only thornbushes were growing amid rocks and boulders. In the Nahuatl world view that flowering place that symbolizes life, health, well-being, the dignifying of creation and all living beings, is given the name Xochitlalpan (from *xochitl*, "flower," and *tlal*, "earth"), the place of the Flowering Earth. In this "little house" that she wishes to be open to everybody, the community spirit that is present is continually being built up in the *ekklesia* of wo/men and is turning the Virgin's prophetic word into reality. And the community spirit is animated precisely by the Holy Spirit, who inspires the *ekklesia* to continue realizing the Xochitlalpan, so that what ultimately inspires and enlivens the Xochitlalpan is the loving presence of divine Wisdom with us and among us.

We can thus state that the indigenous spirituality that existed even before Christianity takes form and becomes conscious in the Virgin of

Guadalupe and her story. Today we find that spirituality alive in the flowering hearts of the indigenous women and in the heart of their communities.

THE INDIGENOUS WOMEN'S COMMITTED WAY OF WALKING

What do we know of the indigenous women's struggles and their committed way of walking? What do they tell us and share with us?

From the church point of view, it has been difficult for them and for all indigenous peoples, given the intolerance with which Christianity confronted the native religious traditions and cultures. Not only were the missionaries distrustful of the indigenous traditions, but their Western culture injected a strong dose of machismo into the native culture. The pre-conciliar church offered no real alternative: the services were run by men, since only they were allowed access to the priesthood. That epoch is still remembered by Tseltal deacons who as boys had to learn Spanish and Latin in order to serve during Mass as acolytes. Some women also remember those days and claim that there were really two types of church service: those performed in the parish and exercised only by men, and those other services that were celebrated in the communities and performed by both women and men.

A dichotomy seemed to exist between what people could do in the church and what they could do in the communities. Thus, when Jerónima Hernández López gave an ecclesiology course in 1996 in Bachajón, Chiapas, she displayed a drawing in which the church was represented as a man: "This was the Church before." Then she showed another drawing, in which the church was represented as a male-and-female couple, and she commented: "Now the Church is complete, since before the companion was lacking," meaning, of course, the participation of women.[12] As a matter of fact, many of the jobs in the indigenous community are taken on by married couples, people who have already demonstrated their ability and responsibility toward the community. Similarly, in the church, ministries are now taken on by both men and women.[13] Furthermore, some Tseltal women whose security does not depend on having a husband or a house put all their heart into helping their community and other women who are suffering. There are women catechists and chapel leaders who have never married and who are at the service of the chapel and the community. The wives of deacons have a house and a husband and besides are extraordinary ministers of the Eucharist, but their heart does not dwell only on their own family or their own house; they go out into the midst of their communities in order to help them expand their heart. We also know of a group of *ach'ixetic*, the Tseltal term for young single women, which is also applied to Tseltal religious. They are women "who decide not to marry or have their own house, but to live in community and serve other women. They make a commitment with women and strive to relieve their suffering, open their eyes and help them find their liberation. Although they suffer hunger and exhaustion, and at times pain, their heart is not concerned with security, for they do not even receive a wage."[14]

Such commitment to evangelizing service performed by indigenous women has given rise, since the conciliar renewal, to a variety of ministries and positions, which found support also in the fourth Conference of Latin American Bishops, held October 12–18, 1992, in Santo Domingo: "It is important that we have female leadership and that the woman's presence in organizing and leading the new evangelization in Latin America and the Caribbean be promoted. We must encourage the development of a kind of pastoral work that may advance indigenous women socially, educationally, and politically" (no. 109). Mentioning explicitly *campesina* and indigenous women, the document also emphasizes that it is necessary to "condemn whatever affects women's dignity by attacking life" and to "foster the means for assuring a decent life for those women who are most vulnerable" (no. 110).[15]

The voice of the indigenous woman has also been heard within civil society, in the resistance of the indigenous peoples, and in their unity with other organizations. Some communities have discovered that without the participation of the women, the government officials pay them no mind. "So we see how women, whom we consider to be weak, have struggled and have overcome, as in San Miguel C'anxanil, when they drove the soldiers out of the community, or as the women of Guaquitepec, who spoke strongly against the remunicipalization."[16] Women of different communities have prevented the security forces from entering their towns. Women are most often the persons principally concerned about caring in different ways for the life and welfare of the community. "The weak ones of the community are strong and brave, and if we unite the weakness of the women and the weakness of the indigenous people, then we find much strength with the help of God."[17]

María Vicenta Chuma Quishpilema states that the force of indigenous protest throughout the Andes has found expression in recent years, especially in the 1992 celebration of "500 Years of Indigenous Resistance," as well as in the proclamation of the Decade of the Indigenous People and the creation of regional and continental spaces of indigenous action, such as the First Continental Summit of Indigenous Peoples. Such events and processes have opened up bright perspectives for the indigenous movement, and for indigenous women in particular, in their struggle to recover their cultural and social identity; in their demand for the recognition of plurinational, multicultural, and multilingual states; and in their search for different forms of autonomous government, territoriality, and sovereignty. Furthermore, women have participated actively in the defense of the land and indigenous territory, as well as in the development of the productive and distributive forces in the communities.[18]

Here we discover another element of the indigenous wisdom and spirituality, namely, respect for Mother Earth, for nature. The earth is the place where community life is carried out; it is the place where Wisdom is encountered. The indigenous peoples consider their relation with the earth to be one in which the earth itself is seen as a living subject. They care for her and venerate her for all that she gives them. They ask permission to sow in her or to build a house on her, lest such labors cause her harm. Women have an especially direct relation with the earth; it might be said that there is an intimate communication between women and "woman earth." Both are integrated into the cycles of nature, both collaborate in producing and sustaining life. Women have a keen sensibility for understanding earth's problematic, for they know how to dialogue with her. They care for her and defend her; they make an effort to learn different ways of cultivating her and fertilizing her, using only natural substances in order to protect and preserve her. Women challenge us and teach us to preserve and protect the harmony of the ecosystem and to struggle against those who would make use of the earth in an exploitative, hoarding, irrational way.

WHERE TO JOURNEY TO . . .

In the course of this study we become aware that we must open ourselves up ever more to dialogue and to listening to what we are being told by the indigenous peoples, and especially by the women, those who are so close by, yet so far from our own Westernized reality. If we do not listen, we run the risk of ceasing to grow in our own humanity, of refusing to recognize all the wealth contained in their wisdom and spirituality. Besides the valuable contribution they offer to other Latin American peoples and to all humanity, their voice helps the true indigenous blood in our own *mestizo* veins to flow more freely. If we reject them, we are denying or forgetting an essential part of our own history.

We also become aware that the indigenous wisdom and spirituality find an echo in the Christian message, which we can enrich for ourselves through intercultural and interecclesial dialogue.

Combating kyriarchal exploitation and dehumanization, therefore, means helping God's vision of a new creation to become reality, giving form and structure to the *ekklesia* of wo/men as an alternative reality of justice and well-being for all.[19] It means helping to realize the project of the kingdom that was proclaimed and inaugurated by and in Jesus. It means promoting fraternity and sorority on this earth and creating what for the indigenous peoples is the project of the Xochitlalpan, the Flowering Earth without evil, which would truly be a qualitatively different, thoroughly "renewed" earth.

Notes

[1] Elisabeth Schüssler Fiorenza, *Jesus: Miriam's Child, Sophia's Prophet: Critical Issues in Feminist Christology* (New York: Continuum, 1994), 27. On her use of the term "wo/men," Schüssler Fiorenza explains in this book that it "seeks to indicate that women are not a unitary social group but rather are fragmented and fractured by structures of race, class, religion, heterosexuality, colonialism, age, and health" (24).

[2] Ibid., 27.

[3] Ibid., 14. The analytical category kyriarchy means "the rule of the emperor/master/lord/father/husband over his subordinates" (14). See also 34–43.

[4] María Vicenta Chuma Quishpilema, "Las mujeres en la construcción del Estado plurinacional" (women in the construction of the plurinational state), presentation, Second Continental Summit of Indigenous Peoples and Nationalities of *Abya Yala*, Quito, Ecuador, July 21–23, 2004. Available at http://icci.nativeweb.org/cumbre2004/chuma.html; Internet (accessed July 12, 2007).

[5] Ibid.

[6] Marisela García Reyes, *Mujeres sabias y de corazón valiente: Catequesis sobre Judith, Ruth y Susana*, private ed. (Chiapas: CEFIPI, 2000), 92.

[7] Ibid., 14.

[8] I speak here of the Tseltal indigenous peoples of Mexico, who are those I know best because of an agreement between our Religious Science Department at the Universidad Iberoamericana and the Jesuit Mission in Bachajón, Chiapas, which serves the Tseltal communities. This agreement provides support for courses and training for indigenous community workers. Many indigenous peoples, in Mexico and throughout the Americas, share the same basic spirituality as the Tseltals.

[9] The Nahuatl language is still spoken in the states of central Mexico.

[10] The *Nican Mopohua* is the story of the Guadalupan event. *Nican Mopohua* in Nahuatl means "here it is narrated, here it is told in order." I use here the Spanish translation of Clodomiro Siller (*Guadalupe: Luz y Camio de Nuestra Realidad. Texto Náhuatl del Nican Mopohua* [Mexico: CENAMI Centro Nacional de Ayuda a las Misiones Indígenas, 1985]).

[11] Story from the *Nican Mopohua*.

[12] Jerónima Hernández López is an *ach'ixetic*, that is, a Tseltal religious woman. She gave conferences in the interregional ecclesiology course in the Jesuit Mission of Bachajón, Chiapas, in November 1996. Presented in this course also were several works and testimonies from various Tseltal indigenous communities, in which they describe the model of church that they are living: a participative model of communion, where a diversity of ministries, assumed by women, have flourished.

[13] See Christa P. Godínez Mungúian, on "Posibilidad de nuevos ministerios laicales" (Possibility of new lay ministries), in Memorias del VII Simposio Internacional de Teología, Universidad Iberoamericana, September 10–12, 2003.

[14] García Reyes, *Mujeres sabias y de corazón valiente*, 70.

[15] Latin American Bishops' Conference, "New Evangelization, Human Development, Christian Culture: Fourth General Conference of Latin American Bishops," in *Santo Domingo and Beyond, Documents and Commentaries from the Historic Meeting of the Latin American Bishops Conference*, ed. Alfred T. Hennelly, S.J. (Maryknoll, NY: Orbis Books, 1993), 104.

[16] García Reyes, *Mujeres sabias y de corazón valiente*, 66.

[17] Ibid., 24, 66.

[18] Chuma Quishpilema, "Las mujeres en la construcción del Estado plurinacional."

[19] Schüssler Fiorenza, *Jesus: Miriam's Child*, 27.

12

"I Am Very Happy Despite Everything, Thanks to God!"

On Women with HIV/AIDS

Yury Puello Orozco

Trying to relate together the dimension of celebration and the reality of women with HIV/AIDS might seem to border on the absurd. Since the idea of writing on the interconnection between these two topics first occurred to me, I have had to struggle with the sentiment of perhaps dealing with something inadmissible, especially since I am not a bearer of the virus myself. Such were my thoughts until I began to do my research on women, AIDS and religion. Quite soon I discovered, in the very experience of these women, the possibility of interrelating the two seemingly disparate realities. What once seemed inadmissible and paradoxical turned out to be quite real, in the very lives of women who are bearers of HIV/AIDS.

As I thought about this relationship between the women affected by HIV/AIDS and having the desire to celebrate, several questions occurred to me. How can we think about celebration, joy, feasting, in the shadow of an epidemic that causes such fragility and so many problems of health and well-being in the people infected? It would appear more logical to relate the experiences of such persons only with the suffering, sadness, and desperation that such a disease seems to unleash. Indeed, it would appear to be much more logical to speak only of sadness and suffering when writing of women with HIV/AIDS.

My point of departure for this essay has been my experience with several women whom I knew in the city of São Paulo, Brazil, when I was working on my dissertation for a master's degree in theology and with whom I have stayed in contact.[1] I have had the chance to talk with them about the impact that the disease has had on their lives, and I have come to know their fears, their sorrows, their joys, and their hopes.

All the ideas and images I had about bearers of HIV/AIDS were changed as a result of my getting to know these women through frequent contacts with some of them and very close relations with others, as well as through participation in activities and meetings where concerns of interest to them were discussed. Such experiences opened up horizons for me and revealed new possibilities for reflecting on the celebration of life by women with HIV/AIDS.

At the start I thought I was going to find women who were despondent, guilt-ridden, disillusioned with life, and withdrawn into suffering; they would be living quiet, immobilized lives, considering AIDS to be a punishment for their sins. What I found, though, was quite different from all that I had imagined. Their lives were hard due to their precarious economic situation, family conflicts, or opportunistic infections, but the women that I met talked much about themselves, their desires, their hopes, and their new loves. They see and feel life as something beautiful and hopeful, the kind of life that the music of Brazilian singer Gonzaguinha celebrates and commemorates in his song "What Is It? What Is It?":

> To live and not feel shame is to be happy
> —To sing and sing and sing
> the beauty of being an eternal apprentice
> —Oh! My God, I know, I know
> That life should be much better and will be
> but that doesn't keep me from repeating
> —that it is beautiful! it is beautiful and it is beautiful!

This discovery of mine, by no means free of ambiguities, is what leads me now to write about the possibility of celebrating even in the midst of suffering. Indeed, these women, though they continue to suffer, feel pain, have fears, and even at times despair, are still endowed with an interior energy that is far stronger than their pain, a force that lifts them up and inspires them to carry on.

They speak of God and their relation with God; they speak of the strength that they find for dealing with life. I simply do not find in their testimony the elements needed to develop a theology centered on suffering. To the contrary, the relationship these women feel with the divinity I find to be something dynamic and revitalizing.

ATTEMPTS TO TRANSCEND A THEOLOGY
CENTERED ON SUFFERING

Taking a topic like this, which in the conventional mindset is related to pain, suffering, and death, and treating it in terms of celebration, hope, and life might seem to require that we follow the path of traditional theology, which generally concentrates on an exaltation of suffering as a way of earning merit and as a necessary condition for salvation.

It might also be seen as necessary to have recourse to the theology of the naked God or the hidden God, a theology that sees God's manifestation in the silences of people who are abandoned, suffering, and excluded, so that such people, from their very nonbeing, might come to encounter God and be transformed.

Still another path might be through the theology of original sin, which treats fallen human nature and suffering as our justly deserved condition and considers expiation necessary in order to reach a state of encounter and reconciliation with God. It might even seem that the only available resources are the theologies based on the suffering God, those which have exalted suffering to the point of making it a value in itself.

Theology that exalts suffering may end up justifying the injustices committed against women and may even contribute to women's understanding and accepting such injustices as their inevitable destiny, or at least the result of their part of the history of original sin. This supposedly deserved destiny is precisely what has immobilized women and has made them feel impotent and resigned, clinging to the image of a God who out of love suffers passively.

A cross-centered theology also has fateful consequences for women. For this reason, from the moment women started to develop their own theological reflections, this symbol of the cross, among the most important in Christianity, was also one of the most questioned. Theological reflection about "crucifixion of the flesh" emphasizes especially the negation of pleasure and joy; it satanizes and silences this dimension that is so important for human fulfillment. Carrying the cross has meant silence, humiliation, abandonment, and even disparagement of women's own lives. "My life was not life, it was only suffering. For what?" (Débora).[2]

All such theologies have constituted an obstacle to developing other theological conceptions, based on the principle of rescuing the full humanity of women. As Elizabeth A. Johnson states, "The ideal of the helpless divine victim serves only to strengthen women's dependency and potential for victimization, and to subvert initiatives for freedom, when what is needed is growth in relational autonomy and self-affirmation."[3]

Our desire to break with the centrality of suffering in our theologies and in our cultures does not seek to negate this basic human condition. Rather, our aim is to show that the exaltation of suffering as a condition for finding God and one's own self has contributed to a negation of women's true fulfillment and has left them malformed vis-à-vis society and the churches. The realization that traditional theological reflections and formulations bear the marks of a kyriocentric style of thought has led feminist theological criticism to reinterpret certain symbols and to develop theological reflection on the basis of the transformative experiences of women.

The image of the crucified or tortured person who is sacrificed for the sake of humanity finds no echo or resonance in our present times, which, rather, reveal to us women who are being born anew, are reencountering themselves, are crying out, and are daring to propose new forms of life and new ways of encountering divinities.

In my view, the challenge before us is one of rescuing the experiences of women in their own contexts in order to understand and interpret the full complexity of life, with all its sufferings, joys, and other contingencies. The complexity of all life, but especially women's lives, challenges us as feminist theologians to create our own language and our own theological reflection, taking as our starting point the experiences of women's lives. This is one of the ways of deconstructing the theologies that have long been sustained by a conception of men's power over women.

WE STILL FIND STRENGTH TO LIVE

Our Lady of the tempests and the original mysteries,
when you arrive, the earth trembles from its left side.[4]

Why not say that these women, who now arise with fresh energies emanating from their renewed bodies, with great feasting and rejoicing, with all the new delights of encountering and rediscovering themselves, make tremble from their left side all those theologies that obtain their patriarchal power from exalting the suffering and the pain of women?

Now reborn from the deepest part of their being, these women challenge us starkly with their reflections. With all the irreverence of being women infected by such a stigmatized virus, they tell us: "Yes, I am going to die, but I do not know when—just as you, who do not have the virus, do not know when you will either!" The reflections of these women on their own situation confront us with ourselves and point out ways for us to rethink ourselves and our lives.

This essay does not seek to emphasize HIV/AIDS as a cause of suffering or as the principal reason for the transformation of these women. Rather, the central theme is that HIV/AIDS, as a profound event in their lives, is what has given them the opportunity to recognize themselves today as agents and subjects of change. This profound event is related precisely to the opportunities they discovered upon being treated as women who have the virus.

The growth of AIDS among women and the impact it has had on them have revealed their greater vulnerability in facing the epidemic. The rapid increase of this virus among women is not the result of irresponsible relations on their part. To the contrary, it has more to do with the way that gender relations have been established between men and women in society.

For that reason, both in public policies and in the institutions that work with women and AIDS patients, efforts are made to deal with this epidemic by taking into account such factors as gender and the concrete conditions of women, whether socioeconomic, political, religious, racial, sexual, or even biological. Many institutions have invested resources in supporting projects to help women to recover their dignity and to motivate them to partake in activities to defend their rights. Thus women who have the virus have discovered that their association with women's organizations has strengthened them, and they have found opportunities for taking part in networks and events where they exercise an active role.

Starting out from the treatment centers, they have linked themselves together in social and community activities and thus have been able to discover both their weaknesses and their potentialities and to boost their self-esteem. This new reality has provided them with both the challenge and the opportunity to transform their personal lives. In the words of Sara, "It's necessary to face reality. I am well, thank God. If it were not for the treatment and God's help, I would be dead. But no, now is when I am going to really live."

As these women reveal, coming down with AIDS, along with everything related to it, is giving them energies to live. They are stronger women, and most of them, I would even dare say, discover themselves to be true subjects, capable of acting in society and exercising leadership. They are women who communicate the meaning and importance of joy and solidarity, especially among other women.

As a result of such discoveries, they do not experience AIDS as a sickness that makes them depend on their families, the government, or anybody else, but rather as an event that divides their lives into a before and an after. In the after, they found the opportunity for a better life.

Contact with and knowledge of these women allows us to speak of celebration, because through their encounter with their deeper selves their lives find new meaning in celebrating. They celebrate life from the depths of life itself, from what each one most truly is and feels, from their own reality.

> Despite having the virus, I feel ever more valued, ever more strong. Other people say, "Ah, but you have AIDS. How do you live?" I live quite well. I don't get bogged down in sickness, but strive after health. I take care of myself, you know, and keep living my life. I have good company, look out for myself, treat myself well, and take my medicines right on time. From the moment they told me I had the virus, I have been taking the medicines at six in the morning, two in the afternoon, and ten at night—always at the precise hour. I always have lunch at the right time, so that I'll have time to take the medicine afterwards and not be careless. I weigh almost 93 kilos [205 pounds], so I think I need to lose weight. I already put on several shows with our project group; you know, we created a group to put on shows. I did it for three years. (Isabel)

The discovering of new possibilities in life has allowed these women to be happy and to celebrate. Affirming the hope for a better life is the energy that bursts into their lives and makes them discover that their condition as virus bearers is not a synonym of death; rather, it is a life-giving event that allows them to remove the cumbersome bandages that were covering up their bodies, their desires, and their womanly being.

Having HIV/AIDS makes these women aware of the meaning and depth of their lives, because they celebrate out of the very reality and the conflicts that their situation generates, and they draw strength and vigor from the same sources. The women celebrate because they experience their lives as surrounded with good things, positive expectations, and challenging discoveries. Their existential experience is what gives meaning to their lives as bearers of the virus.

"NOW I'M REALLY GOING TO LIVE. . . . I'M TAKING CARE OF MYSELF. . . . I'VE GOT A LOT OF CHALLENGES"

This is the way I think now: in order for women to be more womanly, to depend on themselves and not on others or on men, they have to take on the struggle. We are able to get into the struggle, looking out for our rights. Now I can do what I want. I don't want to depend any more on a man, no . . . (Noemí)

These women celebrate the recovery of their own dignity and have the courage to fight for their rights and to feel themselves subjects. I do not find any pessimism in their experiences, or any desire to take refuge in a theology centered on the cross or suffering.

Their courage and their way of dealing with the effects of AIDS on their existence are what led them to want to transform themselves and, through their own experience, help to transform the lives of other women. The reality of AIDS truly opens the way for them to discover themselves as subjects and agents of change.

Their ability to perceive themselves as subjects is greater when they become aware and make manifest that they were more exposed to AIDS as a result of their social, cultural and gender vulnerability, not because of the natural condition of being women. In this way, feeling themselves to be subjects makes them understand that their struggles and demands for integral health services are based on the rights they have won as full citizens, not on their being victims of a disease.

For these women, discovering themselves as subjects of change means taking on greater responsibilities, even as they have to confront new challenges. The epidemic produced by the accelerated growth of HIV/AIDS requires women to meet their own needs with qualified strength, and none are more qualified than the infected women themselves, with all their experiences, to become spokespersons and educators in these matters.

"GOD DID NOT TAKE AWAY MY DESIRE TO LIVE AND TO GROW"

Perhaps rescuing the image of a Divinity who joyously celebrates and accompanies women's lives will contribute to destroying the old androcentric, dichotomous, and marginalizing vision, according to which the figure of the woman sufferer is exalted and adored, while the figure of the woman who gives priority to the pleasures and joys of life should be punished. We find in Mary and Eve the symbolic representation of these two contradictory and prohibitive models.

The way women with the virus celebrate life challenges us to grasp the divine mystery that lies beyond suffering, pessimism, and the difficult situations of life. Grasping the mystery from this perspective offers us the possibility of comprehending that the sacred is experienced out of the integral fullness of life. The holy is experienced out of all the diverse situations with which we can arm ourselves from day to day, whether joyful, sad, challenging, conflictive, or whatever. By adopting this perspective, we will discover how to overcome the duality or polarization that exists between suffering and joy.

We progressively develop a profound relationship with God through the new being that comes to birth in the deep entrails of the events with which life presents us. As Ivone Gebara points out, "Celebrating is something fundamental in human life. We celebrate in different ways what is, what is loved, what is hoped for and what is lived."[5]

Ignoring what these women have experienced and are experiencing can make it difficult to perceive their intensity and their expectations with regards to life. As they themselves state, we have to celebrate and be thankful for all that "has gone right in our lives": the medicines, the health professionals, the support of people we have met, the institutions that have received us, and many other things besides.

> I am grateful to God, because, you know, when I first found out about it, there were no free medicines, but when I needed my own medicine, there was already AZT and there were other medicines. (Débora)

> I really believe that God's hand was there, you know? I trust a lot in God, because I became pregnant and I already had the virus, though I didn't know it. I found out afterwards, when the baby was born, you know? I know that the child has the virus, but there are no symptoms, and he is well. So I know that God exists, I trust much in God and I am grateful. (Noemí)

Such experiences lead us to encounter an image of the Divine that is concerned with the lives of people, that takes the side of justice, that participates passionately in the experiences of humankind, and so becomes indignant or saddened or joyful, and that challenges us, day by day, to undertake transformations.

What use is it for these women to celebrate? Or better said, what is there that is different about this celebration of women who are bearers of HIV/AIDS?

First of all, what I feel, in my meetings with these women, is that celebrating is for them an intense form of encountering the Divine; it goes beyond the limits and boundaries of theologies burdened with the image of a suffering, sad, passive God.

These women's encounter with the Divine is celebrated in a daring, challenging way. It is a divine experience of reciprocity, of company, of community, of God's experiencing with them the feeling of crossing frontiers of negation, in order to go on to their encounter with love, with their children, with suffering, with sicknesses, with music, with song, and even with death.

This celebratory experience is set in a hermeneutic key that contributes to the rescue of the women's dignity, since it allows them to conceive this experience as a way of rescuing their being, their existence, their self-esteem, and their true citizenship—and since what motivates them to celebrate is the fact of their feeling alive and having an important, recognized role in society. They therefore rejoice in what is good, and they are glad because something important is happening in their lives.

Confidence and gratitude to God are two sentiments that are constant in these women—confidence in life; confidence that all will turn out well; confidence in the medicines, in the doctors, in the people who work with them.

Thanks to their experience with AIDS, they are not daunted, and they see the positive aspect of the scientific advances and the benefits they are receiving. In all these things they feel the presence of divine forces, which help to make all this real in their lives. They discover the presence of divine grace that motivates them and encourages them in this new life.

It is as if AIDS arrived like a strong wind and unexpectedly ripped off the veil that was covering their eyes. Naked before AIDS, they find themselves face to face with one another, even though still part of a world that has made them into something they are not in reality: fragile and culpable women victims. Now they discover that they can manifest their suffering, but they can also manifest their desire to live and to struggle with wisdom and courage for a dignified life as full citizens.

In their struggle they find themselves confronted for the first time by their own alienation and ignorance about themselves, their bodies, their desires, and their sexuality: "By doing his will I ended up doing harm to myself. I didn't say anything. He always decided when and how. So, desire and pleasure—hah, it wasn't always that I felt them!" (Marta).

The virus finds in their unprotected feminine sexuality one of its principal means of entrance, and that sexuality is situated in a body that has been construed negatively by culture, belief, values, and subjectivities.

The experience of sexuality, now that these women are bearers of the virus, which is also transmitted sexually, has led them to reassess their lives and to discover their alienation and ignorance in this regard. Their prior reality consisted of silence and unawareness about their bodies and their sexuality, but now, in full possession of their sexuality, they have recovered and appropriated something of which they had before been despoiled: the right to feel pleasure, to enjoy knowledge of all their bodies' hidden nooks, and to be able to decide when and how. As Ana expresses it, "Today my life has changed. I am seeking work, and I have my children to raise. If any man comes along, it's going to be different, that's for sure."

They also celebrate the experience of feeling themselves to be bearers of good news for other women. "Our Lady of the tempests and of the liquid ways, when you come, the divinities dance. All is alchemy, all in you is miracle, Our Lady of energy" (music of Maria Betania).

Armed with the miracle of life and with new energies, the women are not content with meeting just among themselves. They go forth to encounter other women and to share their new life with them. The solidarity of the women who welcome and receive other women into groups and institutions contributes to the recovery of self-esteem and to the desire to live and struggle even as bearers of the virus. Solidarity among women is the reality we find in most of the institutions that work with women who have HIV/AIDS. It is a solidarity born of an understanding that the disease attacks women because of the conditions of vulnerability in which they find themselves. As in Ángeles Mastreta's story of the aunts, those women who whisper in people's ears and quietly transmit the wisdom inherited from other women, the women I have met are capable of creating new energies and of exciting fresh desires to live.[6]

Notes

[1] See Yury Puello Orozco, *Mujeres, Aids y Religión* 10, 2nd ed. (São Paulo: Católicas pelo Directo de Decidir, 2002).

[2] Débora, Sara, Isabel, Noemí, and Marta are women with HIV/AIDS whom I had the opportunity to interview.

[3] Elizabeth A. Johnson, *She Who Is: The Mystery of God in Feminist Theological Discourse* (New York: Crossroad, 1992), 254.

[4] Poem of Manuel Alegre, recited by Brazilian singer Maria Betania, on the recording *Diamante Verdadeiro*, Sony BMG, Ao vivo, 1999.

[5] Ivone Gebara, *Trinidade: Palavra sobre coisas velhas e novas: Uma perspectiva ecofeminista* (São Paulo: Paulinas, 1994), 50.

[6] Ángeles Mastreta, *Mujeres de Ojos Grandes* (Buenos Aires: Seix Barral, 1998).

13

Bodies, Discourse, Emotions, and Symbols in the Middle of the Empire

The Pedagogy of the Apocalypse

Violeta Rocha Areas

The book of the Apocalypse, otherwise known as the Revelation to John, is an impressive text. Reading it evokes quite varied sentiments and continually prompts the formulation of diverse messages. Revelation is an open invitation to enter into a world that is multi-hued, resonant, aromatic, violent, imaginative, cruel, and tremendously hopeful. This book has even been viewed as "the space of the interpretative battle."[1]

Apocalypse, Revelation—beginning or end? The Nicaraguan poet Michèle Najlis invites us to wonder: what if the Apocalypse is nothing more than the beginning of Genesis, and vice versa?[2] Space and time, men and women, heaven and earth, demons and angels, victors and vanquished, empire and resistance—so many possibilities are contained in one little book, and they crisscross one another in a vibrant fabric of puzzles, stereotypes, struggles, and rereadings of a new world, of a new order, of new relations.

As a theologian who claims to be feminist, I confess my interest in this final book of the Christian Bible, just as so many others do in Latin America. I believe there is a complete pedagogical dynamic expressed in the bodies, emotions, voices, silences, signs, and symbols of the women and men of the Apocalypse. They exist in the middle of an imperial system that imposes death, inequality, and oppression, but they affirm at the same time their resistance to the system for the sake of the utopia, that space where the challenge of creating something new and different is vitally present through the movement unleashed by Jesus of Nazareth.

The category of gender is valuable for understanding this dynamic and for analyzing the masculine and feminine roles present. These roles sometimes reinforce stereotypes, functions, and perspectives that reaffirm gender inequality and that evoke an uncritical reading of the biblical text, and even a certain evangelical "terrorism" that obscures the complex weave of the biblical narrative.

A FEMINIST PEDAGOGICAL PROPOSAL
FOR READING REVELATION

The apocalyptic genre introduces us to a world full of stories, visions, oracles, ecstasies, adoration, allegories, and suffering; it even includes revisions of history and hope. This world is presented through images in which language plays an important role. The power of both language and images produces different effects on readers. While various exegetical approaches to the text are useful, the following question, of a semiotic character, seems to me especially valid: how do we develop a reading of Revelation in which the pedagogy and the didactic of language and images can offer us new perspectives of feminist interpretation?

I propose some analytical criteria that might prove useful for answering this question:

The Language of Revelation as a Reflection on Context

The language of Revelation has been considered a kind of "anti-language," that is, a language corresponding to a context of crisis. Such language is characterized by replacing old words with new ones while keeping the same basic grammar; in this way a new vocabulary is created, one able to make new identifications.[3] Thus we find different words being used to express a single basic concept; for example, the terms *God* and *Jesus* can be used interchangeably, as can the terms *Satan* and *Roman Empire*.[4]

Furthermore, the language of Revelation allows us to discern and identify the social groups that exist within the text. Exegetical analysis of chapters 12, 17, and 21—22 allows us to identify collective symbols, which might also be called collective subjects. These symbols are organized in binary form, in such a way as to form a "social body" that makes evident the value systems that are present in the text. Some examples are:

God	Satan
Jesus	The beasts
The angels of God	The angels of the Dragon (Satan)
The woman dressed with the sun	The whore of Babylon
Jerusalem	Babylon
The saints and the martyrs	The idolaters and the murderers
The new creation	The old creation

The designation of characters with the definite article not only makes possible an identifying link but also constructs an anaphoric relation.[5] The text uses the definite article seventeen times to specify names or nouns. The author (or authors) of Revelation would thus seem to be using the literary figure of anaphora, since there are common and familiar reference points that establish the relation of the reader with the personages represented in images.

A Language Expressed in an Androcentric Key

The relations of power, the sexual terminology and the warlike elements contribute to reinforcing the androcentric aspect of the language. The powers that are present represent both symmetrical and asymmetrical relations. Sometimes the text presents equivalent powers: certain actors or subjects win the battle, others lose it, and their action progresses up to the final moment, when there is only one victor. There are also powers that are absolutized, whether as God or as Satan. If we consider the context and accept that there is a full deployment of powers, we should not be surprised to find strong expressions of warlike language or forceful use of the aforementioned images, which produce different effects on readers.

The warlike language is associated with the holy war, a well-known theme in ancient Jewish traditions, with the difference that here the central character is Jesus Christ. This war seems to have been unleashed because of the cry for justice or for vengeance that is expressed in Revelation 6:9–10. Sentiments of hate and violence are part of this warlike language. The images used in Revelation 1:16, 2:12b, 19:15, and 21 feature a sharp sword, a symbol of war and of death.[6]

The war takes place both in heaven and on earth, and different figures play diverse roles. The text thus describes a cosmic war in which no domain is spared. In the process, sexual language is used at two levels: (1) in concepts such as seduction, adultery, prostitution, giving birth, fornication, and purification; and (2) in the roles corresponding to these concepts: prostitute, virgin, mother, wife, husband.

The opposition between pure and impure or between worthy and unworthy is linked to the book's sexual terminology. The bodies of women and men, as well as their relations, become a hermeneutic key for understanding the social roles they represent.

The Power of Images and Symbols

Elisabeth Schüssler Fiorenza describes Revelation as rhetorical discourse that has persuasion as its final objective.[7] This power of persuasion consists in producing different effects of resonance with respect to the general context, the readers involved in the reality, and the ideologies that lie behind and help to interpret these images and symbols. Even so, we should raise a few questions: How are these images and symbols conceived in a patriarchal culture and an imperial context? How are the images interiorized in a culture in which images are a main didactic means for facilitating comprehension and learning? How do these images give shape to an ethics and a lifestyle? The social roles that appear in the text may throw some light on these questions. Such roles are divided into feminine and masculine:

Feminine Roles	Masculine Roles
Prostitute	Virgins
Prophetess	Servants
Wife	Husband
Mother	Holy warriors

The roles for women have been associated with the exercise of seduction, which can occur in various ways: at an intellectual level, as suggested by the teaching of Jezebel; through the exuberant appearance of the great prostitute, who leads to lust and fornicates with the kings of earth; or by means of the signs and wonders that the beast works upon the poor, the rich, the small, the freemen, and the slaves (Rv 13:6). As regards the role of mother and wife, women may also interiorize the suffering of the woman at childbirth (chapter 12) and the hope for a new creation based on the image of the mother-wife (chapter 21).

In contrast, the roles associated with men are not easily understood: warriors, saints, servants, prophets, and virgins. The image of the warrior represents the ideal of force, military strategy, weapons, and death. This image leads to another: war. The male virgins demonstrate their virginity as a basic requirement for following the Lamb. To that end they must avoid the contamination of women through sexual contact.[8]

The other roles that men play as servants and prophets, or as ancients who sing and adore the Lord, seem to represent a liturgical and prophetic setting of masculine character.

Symbolic Language as a Pedagogic Means

The author of Revelation develops the text as a great dialogue from beginning to end. The book's introduction tells of the revelation of Jesus Christ being given to his servant John through his angel, and John transmits it to those who hear the words of the prophecy. John not only speaks, however, but also writes, discerns, and leaves spaces open for others. The structure of the book seems to be organized according to these basic questions: For what? Of what? Of whom? The book thus presents a pedagogy of apocalyptic and of prophecy in epistolary form.

But how can we claim that the book is organized pedagogically in light of the allegedly poor quality of the Greek language used in the text? If the thesis of S. E. Porter is valid, we are dealing with the work of grassroots groups that are writing for other grassroots groups and using a didactic methodology of a symbolic and participative character.[9] Pablo Richard considers the Greek language of Revelation to be a type of protest against and resistance to Hellenization and Hellenism.[10] If we consider this position plausible, then the language of Revelation could be considered an eminently grassroots option for developing the discernment and the organization of groups of women and men in a situation of conflict.

The process presented by John the Visionary may be described in three stages: seeing, understanding, and writing, which would seem to constitute a pedagogy for discerning history and participating in it, a process that might be called a pedagogy of prophecy. Prophetic texts of the Old Testament demonstrate the pedagogical meaning of prophecy in terms of seeing/hearing, writing/proclaiming or announcing/denouncing, as well as in terms of persuading/dissuading with regard to certain behavior. The discernment process is carried out through the use complicated images, symbols, messages, and so on. The symbolic language invites us to develop a process of construction and deconstruction of symbols by using such pedagogical techniques as numeration, images, times, places, ascendant and descendent movements, actions, letters, liturgy, signs, and the scenes of heaven, earth, and sea. The strong oral quality present in the book, evident in the "mighty voice," the hymns, and the prophecies, helps us to decode and understand its content. Ugo Vanni speaks of the literary motif of Revelation, suggesting that the book is organized as a great opera.[11] All this is a pedagogy of dialogue, of liturgy, of images—in sum, it is a pedagogy of resistance that permits grassroots groups to read and interpret its contents in such a way as to engage in dialogue together and sustain the utopia.

BODIES, DISCOURSES, EMOTIONS, SIGNS, AND MYSTERY

The category of gender helps in making visible the respective gender roles, but we need also a more holistic comprehension of the biblical text, one that includes the categories of class, ethnicity, and other possible variables. The function of the genders in their day-to-day and political dimensions is fundamental for a critical feminist interpretation of liberation, but these other categories also help us view women's bodies and men's bodies as hermeneutical supports for grasping the significance of the body and of sexuality in the Bible.

The bodies in Revelation, in their diverse expressions, are signs, symbols, and also word. The discursive and rhetorical element is present in the intense oral quality of the book, and even in the silences. This rhetoric is conceived in images, emotions and symbols that may reinforce the ideology of the empire and the patriarchal culture, but which also are capable of disclosing, criticizing, and reorganizing that same ideology and culture in order to transform them.

The Apocalypse presents us with female bodies that are controlled/ protected/persecuted/destroyed but also open to life and hope. The book presents us also with male bodies that are controllers/controlled/persecuting/persecuted/destroyed and likewise open to life and hope. In the end, these images reveal bodies and sexualities in conflict, bodies politicized, brilliant minds and persuasive intellects, fecundity and virginity, life and death! The women stereotypes are divided into good and bad: Jezebel the prophetess, who teaches and seduces in Revelation 2:20–23; the woman dressed with the sun in chapter 12; the great prostitute in chapter 17; and the female spouse in chapters 21 and 22. Taken together, they represent both transgressive bodies and good news in history. The woman dressed with the sun and the great prostitute are both considered sign and mystery.

Chapter 12 tells us that "a great portent appeared in heaven: a woman clothed with the sun, with the moon under her feet, and on her head a crown of twelve stars" (v. 1). These figures form a celestial pattern "sun-moon-stars" that defines her state as cosmic. The woman has the leading role as agent in a program of giving birth. This woman-sign will fulfill her role between the apparent dynamic of power and her real fragility, in the face of threats from the other sign in the heaven, the dragon, who will pursue her until the very end.

The semantic contour of the woman may be represented as follows (see Figure 13–1):

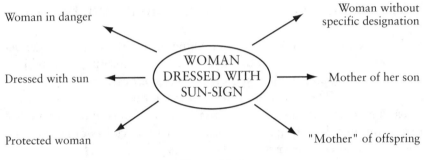

Figure 13–1

If the woman of chapter 12 is a collective subject, she may be conceived as a prophetic community that lives its faith in a context of constant danger, where the tension between life and death creates alternatives and strategies of struggle for gaining the definitive victory. The image of the woman is used positively in two senses: it comes from the heritage of the collective memory of a people who have messianic hope, and it is oriented toward assuming a prophetic role, one that is lived in the midst of pain and suffering, where the value system is determined by joy and fidelity despite the price that must be paid (v. 11). The woman assumes her role in the midst of ambiguities: on the one hand, her fragility and impotence; on the other, her desire to struggle and give hope to the world.

On the other side, chapter 17 introduces us to the great prostitute, who is referred to as a "mystery" that causes John to be "amazed" (v. 7). The woman sitting on the beast comes from the earth; she is not celestial.[12] She is dressed in purple and scarlet and adorned with gold, precious stones, and pearls; in a word, she embodies a wholly earthly figure of economic wealth. The mystery of her identity is revealed by an angel: she is Babylon (v. 5). Certain groups have names on their foreheads: some bear the mark of the beast (13:16; 14:9), while the 144,000 have the Father's name written there (14:1; 22:4).

In considering the woman's identity, the semantic contours shown in Figure 13–2 may be of help:

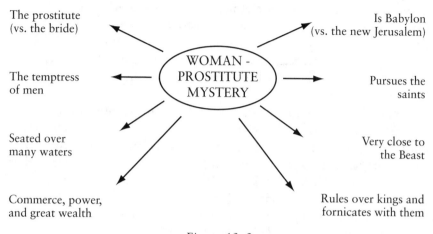

The prostitute
(vs. the bride)

Is Babylon
(vs. the new Jerusalem)

The temptress
of men

WOMAN -
PROSTITUTE
MYSTERY

Pursues the
saints

Seated over
many waters

Very close to
the Beast

Commerce, power,
and great wealth

Rules over kings and
fornicates with them

Figure 13–2

Nonetheless, all this appearance of power in the woman-mystery masks the fact that her control over everything is merely apparent and illusory. Her fragility is evident, and the beast itself will destroy her (v. 16). The beast will abhor the prostitute and will burn her with fire, the punishment prescribed in Leviticus 21:9 for prostitution. Her end is the fire, whose smoke will spiral up forever and ever (19:3).

The emotions of these two women are here expressed to the maximum in terms of fear, vulnerability, persecution, stupor, amazement, and the feeling of being protected and nourished.

A PROPOSAL FOR A FEMINIST LIFE ETHIC

If we accept the description of Revelation as rhetorical discourse of persuasion, then we need to raise further questions: What kind of persuasion are we speaking of? How are the images of women and men presented so as to gain the objective? I propose to establish several ethical criteria.

Groups Organized around Their Historical Memory and Their Faith

The author of Revelation integrates images and symbols of concrete realities in order to promote reflection about the world-to-come, where eschatological hope is present. From the perspective of this world of

hope we may speak of a life ethic, one that is based on recalling the
promises of a God who is present in history and also on the collective
desires that are maintained from generation to generation largely by the
oral, popular culture. Such collective desires are marked by stereotypes
and reinforce the traditional gender roles; it is therefore necessary to
interpret them critically.

Pablo Richard points out that apocalyptic provokes serious ethical
debate because of the violence and the hostility that appear to be transmitted in various texts.[13] Adela Yarbro Collins claims that Revelation is
a catharsis, that is, a way of expressing anxieties and sufferings, and that
such catharsis is basically healthful.[14] Our task, then, is to continue to
develop the work of deconstructing and reconstructing the texts in a
liberating feminine key. Carl G. Jung speaks of ordering chaos through
the symbolism of the *mandala*.[15] The book of the Apocalypse invites us
to be participants and beneficiaries of that symbolic world that sum-
mons us to understand symbols and myths on the basis of their historical contexts. For such understanding the study of the multiple meaning
of myths can be of great help. Knowing how to discern becomes part of
a pedagogical process that may lead to the mobilization and organization of groups and of peoples to live a new ethic of communitarian values. In this mobilization, the feminist hermeneutic can offer key elements for reinterpreting the texts and for generating a praxis of liberation.

Establishment of New Relations

While the adorers of the beast proclaim the power of the global empire by crying out, "Who is like the beast, and who can fight against it?"
(Rv 13:4), the followers of the Lamb proclaim,

> Now have come the salvation and the power
> and the kingdom of our God
> and the authority of his Messiah. (Rv 12:10).

This affirmation of God's kingdom is crystallized in the descent of the
holy city, the new Jerusalem, where other kinds of relations become possible. Affirmation of the kingdom and of God's authority is possible
only with the establishment of new relationships of gender and power.

Readers of Revelation will find in it both positive and negative images, which are made into symbols and anti-symbols, as we explained
earlier. The text also offers the image of the woman-spouse who is
figuratively transformed into the new city. In the expression "The Spirit
and the bride say, 'Come'" (22:17) the woman-spouse is presented as a

collective subject, the community of women and men who believe in this new creation and who actively await it.

I propose the following schema of discursive configuration for Revelation 21–22 (see Figure 13–3):

The celestial dimension is interpretable/visible/ tangible/terrestrial

A city built with the heritage of faith and the memory of others

A change of economic values

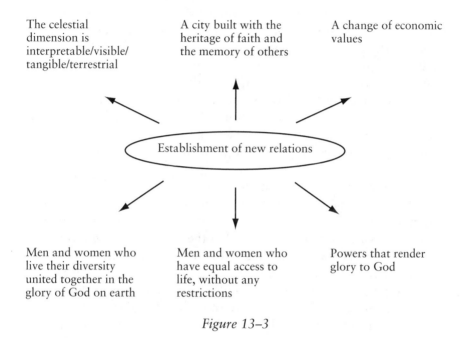

Men and women who live their diversity united together in the glory of God on earth

Men and women who have equal access to life, without any restrictions

Powers that render glory to God

Figure 13–3

CONCLUSION

In this essay I have used certain situations in order to reconstruct both the *Sitz im Leben* and the function of a language full of symbols and images that appears to constitute a pedagogical process for a group of women and men living in a specific context. I would draw the following conclusions.

Apocalyptic literature is frequently thought to be evoked by a situation of crisis, which is exacerbated by asymmetrical relations of power and by a violence that compounds the injustice and inequality. In the midst of this power struggle, utopian hope arises as a possible way to change relationships. A feminist critique of both the text itself and its symbols and images helps us to understand that the dualistic relation of genders that is present in the book responds in part to the community's political and socioeconomic situation of oppression.[16] The challenge for

a critical feminist hermeneutic is to reconstruct these images and to recover the liberating dimension of the women and men in the text.

According to Schüssler Fiorenza, rhetorical analysis cannot be conceived "as just one more mode of literary or structural analysis"; it is
also "a means for analyzing how Revelation and its interpretations participate in creating or sustaining oppressive or liberating theo-ethical
values and sociopolitical practices."[17] Thus, understanding the rhetorical structure of the Apocalypse, with all its images and symbolism, can
lead us to a practice of liberation in our present-day context of an empire that pretends to be permanent, eternal, and indispensable.

The profound subjectivity present in the narratives of Revelation is
made evident in the book's symbolism. Might not that subjectivity represent an alternative proposal or a need of the author to transcend that
socio-temporal reality by generating new meanings for those symbols
and images?

Revelation is set in a horizon of justice and hope. As Revelation 19:2
points out, the great whore that was corrupting the earth with her fornication has been judged. The horizon comes to full realization in chapters
21 and 22, which describe the arrival of the new order, where God will
live with God's people and all misfortune will be banished.

The collective subjects, such as the prophetic community (chapter 12),
the imperial power (chapter 17), and the new creation in the cosmic
sense (chapters 21 and 22) also have roles as political subjects that develop social relations that will bring about a new subjectivity, one that
will be realized on the basis of the attitudes of those same subjects toward life, power, crisis, and desire.

A phrase used during the protest movements in France in 1968 seems
to me to contain the whole of Revelation: Run, run, the old world is
chasing you. It is an old world that presents challenges, causes crises for
systems of values, and calls out for the arrival of the new world. This
new world is built up through relations, of equality, where the fear of
damnation has no reason to exist and where the tree in the middle of the
city has been given for the healing of the nations, of gender relations and
of earth's wounds. I believe that slogan is still valid.

Notes

[1] Tina Pippin, "The Revelation to John," in *Searching the Scriptures. A Feminist Commentary*, ed. Elisabeth Schüssler Fiorenza (New York: Crossroad, 1998),
109.

[2] Michèle Najlis, *Ars Combinatoria* (Managua: Editorial Nueva Nicaragua,
1988), 90.

[3] Revelation gives us an example of this in chapter 2, which makes evident the problematic of the seven churches: their adversaries, who are false teachers pretending to be Jews, do not belong to the true synagogue, but to the synagogue of Satan, where the faithful witness Antipas has been slain (2:13). See John E. Hurtgen, *Anti-language in the Apocalypse of John* (Lewiston, NY: Mellen Biblical Press, 1993), 13.

[4] Another example may be found in Revelation 1:5, "and from Jesus Christ the faithful witness, the firstborn of the dead, and the ruler of kings of the earth," and also in 12:9, "the great dragon was thrown down, that ancient serpent, who is called the Devil and Satan, the deceiver of the whole world." Biblical quotations in this essay are from *The New Revised Standard Version* (New York: Oxford University Press, 1991).

[5] A segment of discourse is said to be anaphoric when its interpretation (even if only literal) requires reference to another segment of the same discourse, which "interprets" the meaning of the anaphoric segment.

[6] J.-G. Heintz does an analysis of symbolic correspondences and writes, "The sword corresponds to the devouring fire, which, more than a natural element, is the greatest expression of divine power within the ancient Semitic traditions" (J.-G. Heinz, *Image et Signification*, Rencontres de l'Ecole du Louvre [Paris: Documentation Française, 1983], 65).

[7] "Rhetorical analysis seeks to explore the persuasive power of Revelation's symbolic language within the book's overall structure of meaning as well as within the rhetorical situation that is inscribed in the text and rooted in a particular socio-historical matrix" (Elisabeth Schüssler Fiorenza, *Revelation: Vision of a Just World*, ed. Gerhard Krodel [Minneapolis: Augsburg Fortress, 1991], 20).

[8] There are different interpretations in this regard: an allegorical sense, a literal sense, a call to asceticism, a requirement for a small group, and so on. Carlos Mesters proposes interpreting these militants as those who are not contaminated by false gods. See Carlos Mesters, *Esperanza de un Pueblo Oprimido. Apocalipsis: Una Clave de Lectura* (Mexico City: Dabar, 1992), 62.

[9] J. Pierre Prevost takes this argument from S. E. Porter, who proposes understanding Revelation as one example of the popular Greek used in the first century. See Jean Pierre Prevost, "L'Apocalypse (1980–1992), in *"De bien des manières": La recherche biblique aux abords du XXIe siècle*, ed. Michel Gourgues and Léo Laberge, Actes du Cinquantenaire de l'Association Catholique des Études Bibliques au Canada (Montréal-Paris: Fides-Cerf, 1995), 446.

[10] Pablo Richard, *Reconstrucción de la Esperanza* (San José, Costa Rica: Departamento Ecuménico de Investigaciones, 1994).

[11] Ugo Vanni, *L'Apocalypse: Ermeneutica, Esegesi, Teologia* (Bologne: Dehoniane, 1988).

[12] Jean Pierre Charlier presents a synopsis of both chapters, wherein he shows the points of coincidence and opposition between the descriptions of the two women. See Jean Pierre Charlier, *Comprender el Apocalipsis*, vol. 2 (Bilbao: Desclée de Brouwer, 1993), 69.

[13] Richard, *Reconstrucción de la Esperanza*, 201.

[14] Adela Yarbro Collins, *Crisis and Catarsis: The Power of the Apocalypse* (Philadelphia, Westminster Press, 1984).

[15] Quite interesting is the article of Ingrid Rosa Kitzberger, "'Wasser und Bäume des Lebens'–eine feministisch-intertextuelle Interpretation von Apk 21/22," in *Weltgericht und Weltvollendung: Zukunftsbilder im Neuen Testament*, Quaestiones Disputatae Band 150, ed. Hans-Josef Klauck (Freiburg: Herder, 1994), 206–24. In this article Kitzberger uses Carl Gustav Jung's proposal for a *mandala* as a structure that presents an image of the world as it passes from chaos to perfect order and as an attempt at a self-cleansing of nature itself.

[16] Schüssler Fiorenza, *Revelation*, 122.

[17] Elisabeth Schüssler Fiorenza, *The Book of Revelation: Justice and Judgment*, 2nd ed. (Minneapolis: Fortress Press, 1998), 210.

14

Mary of Guadalupe

Icon of Liberation
or Image of Oppression?

María del Carmen Servitje Montull

Devotion to Our Lady of Guadalupe is of great importance to the faithful of Latin America because of its enormous potential for creating national and regional identification on a religious level. Volumes have been written about the devotion's Spanish and pre-Hispanic origins, about its development in the course of the centuries, about the authenticity of the apparitions, and about the art inspired by the devotion. In the last few decades, there has been much discussion about the ability of the *guadalpano* symbol to effect emancipation within the context of the Latin American theologies of liberation.

In the Latino (or Hispanic) communities of the United States, the image of the Virgin of Guadalupe has been a unifying emblem. For several Latina feminist theologians, Guadalupe is not only a sign of their identity but also an icon of their liberation as women. However, in Mexico the *guadalpano* symbol is more ambiguous, and indeed it is often manipulated for the purpose of further subjecting a marginalized people, and women in particular.

In treating this topic, I describe my own encounter with Mary of Guadalupe, presenting some of the historical context that allows me to bring out the Mexican character of the *guadalpano* symbol. In opting to view Mary of Guadalupe as either an icon of liberation or an image of oppression, I introduce both the perspective of liberation theology and the special viewpoint of feminist theology.

A PERSONAL CONTEXTUALIZATION

I approach the topic of Mary of Guadalupe from my own psychosocial context: I am a sixty-year-old woman, teacher and student of theology, daughter, wife, mother, grandmother, and friend. All these roles are important to me, and their many demands often cause me conflicts.

I am Mexican, the granddaughter of Spanish small-farmer immigrants. At the start, life for my grandparents and my father was difficult. I grew up in a large family in which austerity was a value, but so was concern for justice and for people in economic need.

Because of our family's Spanish background, we had very little contact with popular Mexican devotions. In my house there was no image or statue of the Virgin of Guadalupe. It was through the influence of a woman of Indian origin who helped my mother to care for us that we began going to the Basilica of Guadalupe each time a brother or sister was born, to offer him or her to the Virgin.

My secondary education was with North American religious sisters who respected Mexican devotions and had in the school images of the Virgin of Guadalupe. The religious education they gave us, however, was based more on the Bible and was grounded in a type of theology that was more rational and solid than that usually given in Catholic girls' schools of the epoch, which was the decade of the Second Vatican Council. Shortly after marrying, in the full ferment of 1967–68, I lived a year and a half in the United States, attending a very open, liberal university. The Catholic parish was the center of much liturgical, doctrinal, and social change, and my husband and I participated in the activities.

When I returned to Mexico, Guadalupe was still absent from my extracurricular pursuit of the incipient liberation theology of the 1970s. My two principal concerns at that time were the possibility of giving my children a liberating religious education and the difficulty of living in a way congruent with the gospel values that I had learned in my theology classes.

My husband's family could be defined as totally *guadalpana*; indeed, his grandfather, who was a well-known art historian in his day, wrote a book on what he considered, from a pictorial point of view, to be the foundation of the apparitions. The *guadalpana* devotion of my in-laws caused me considerable inner conflict, but I began to go along at least once a year on the family pilgrimage to the Basilica of Guadalupe. I always went with an attitude of respect, but also with a certain reserve regarding those devotional practices that were not "my thing."

In March 1997, after I had been studying many years, several companions and I took charge of organizing some academic sessions for which we chose the theme "Guadalupe, symbol of freedom?" For me, the experience was very inspiring, for it opened my eyes to the complexities and the possibilities of the symbol of Mary of Guadalupe. In the course of the sessions we analyzed the devotion from various angles; we studied the apparitions, the historical aspects, the relation to liberation theology, and the Jungian feminist perspective, but we did not include a specifically feminist theology.

In the course of the academic sessions, with the help of students of art history, we organized an exposition of *guadalpano* art. One image of this exposition that especially affected me was a photocopy of a modern painting whose creator nobody could identify at that time. In this painting, which only later did I learn was the work of the Chicana artist Yolanda López, is a young woman with Indian features, dressed with the tunic and the cape of the Virgin of Guadalupe, surrounded by the light rays of the *guadalpano* image. The young woman is wearing modern running shoes and stepping on the wing of the angel that is at the bottom of the painting (the angel's wings are now red, white, and blue, instead of the red, white, and green of the original image). The woman is holding in one hand the edge of her cape and in the other grasping a snake tightly just below its head.

Could the Virgin of Guadalupe be a source of liberation for women? For me, that question remained without an answer for some years. After finishing my licentiate in theological studies, I was able to enter more deeply into the area that most fascinated me: feminist theology. Once again there appeared, in the context of my studies, the question about the Virgin of Guadalupe.

HISTORICAL CONTEXTUALIZATION

The historical complexity of the *guadalpano* devotion is at once overwhelming and captivating. The data appear quite simple. The conquest of what is now Mexico by the Spanish, under Hernán Cortés, took place in 1521. This cruel conquest had strongly imperialist and economic motives, which from the beginning were mixed with evangelizing motives and attempts to convert the inhabitants of the invaded lands. The sincerity of the religious motives is a topic of much debate, but what is clear is that religious conversion, in some cases forced on people by threats and in other cases obtained by convincing people that their old gods were defeated, was a powerful arm for subjugating the native peoples of the recently conquered continent. Clodomiro Siller states: "The ideological justification for destroying these peoples' material infrastructure, for subjecting and repressing them socially and for satanizing the ground springs of Amerindian culture was simply that they were Indian peoples and that the Europeans had a mission to evangelize them."[1]

This destruction of the pre-Hispanic religion and imposition of Christianity involved an enormous ideological, emotional and social change. According to Serge Gruzinski:

The most disconcerting aspect of the Spanish Conquest was probably the introduction of other ways of apprehending reality that were different from those of the Indians, just as in our days they are not exactly ours either. . . . The evangelizers wanted the Indians to commit themselves to the Christian supernatural, that strange pivot of an exotic reality, without any visible points of reference and without any local roots.[2]

Christian Duverger gives a succinct account of the *guadalpana* apparitions:

On the 9th and 10th of December, 1531, the Virgin appeared to an Indian convert, of whom we know only his Christian name, Juan Diego. According to the legend, the Virgin communicated to him her desire to have a sanctuary on the hill of Tepeyac, to the north of the capital. When the bishop of Mexico, Zumárraga, denied both the apparition and the request, the Virgin appeared again (to Juan Diego) on the 12th of December; she asked Juan Diego to go and gather flowers from the top of the hill, to put them in his cape *(ayatl)* and take them to the bishop. When the Indian unfolded the cape, Zumárraga discovered the image of the Virgin miraculously imprinted on the cloth. The bishop bowed down. Two years later, thanks to a collection organized by Cortés and the bishop's office, a sanctuary was built on Tepeyac, and the faithful could then venerate the image of that "dusky," dark-skinned Virgin, who was called upon as Our Lady of Guadalupe.[3]

The hill of Tepeyac had long been an important center of pilgrimage for almost all Mesoamerica. Veneration of the goddess Tonantzin (our beloved mother) took place there; this feminine divinity was associated also with others, such as Tlazolteotl and Cihuacoatl. Richard Nebel says that Tonantzin was "a name that in ancient Mexico was applied generally to the earth goddesses and their many variants, who were held to be the procreators of the gods and of humankind."[4] This fact is no doubt what made veneration of the Virgin of Guadalupe so acceptable to the Mexicans, but it is also what made such veneration so suspect of being idolatrous, as the Franciscans claimed, especially one Fray Bernardino de Sahagún. The secular clergy, headed by Archbishop Zumárraga, and later by Montúfar, saw in the veneration of the Virgin of Guadalupe a way of persuading the Indians to become Christians.

Regarding the choice of the name Guadalupe to designate the apparition of Mary, Jacques Lafaye says: "The origin and significance of this name are still debated; there is some agreement . . . in recognizing an Arab root, *guad*, which was quite common in [Iberian] peninsular place names . . . ; the suffix has been interpreted . . . as being of Latin origin, *lupus*, wolf, so that we would have 'river of wolves.'"[5] In Extremadura, Spain, there exists a sanctuary called Guadalupe, where a dark-skinned virgin is venerated. Nebel notes: "The national sancturary of Guadalupe became, from the 13th to the 15th centuries, the center of . . . Spanish nationalism and patriotism. [Afterward] it became the most prestigious convent and one of the wealthiest centers of art and culture in the country."[6]

The most ancient source of the Guadalupe story is a document in the Nahuatl language, the *Nican Mopohua* (here it is narrated). The work is known only through the version published in 1649 by Lasso de la Vega, a priest of the Guadalupe sanctuary, although older oral traditions and references to the apparitions were found in some earlier historical works, such as the *General History of the Events of New Spain* by Fray Bernardino de Sahagún. Some authors claim that the text published by Lasso de la Vega was actually written by Jose Valeriano, an Indian student of Sahagún. This claim is dismissed by more recent studies. As Nebel explains: "To begin with, it can be assumed that the text of the *Nican Mopohua* developed historically in the dialectic of a society and a culture that was both Spanish (Western) and Mexican (native), until the moment when one or several editors were able to give the work its present artistic and poetic form."[7] Nebel analyzes the text of the *Nican Mopohua* and defines it as "an intercultural narration whose content and form blend together aspects of both the Christian European world and the Toltec-Aztec world."[8]

Another opinion is expressed by Miguel León-Portilla, who claims that Valeriano was indeed the author of this text:

The *Nican Mopohua* displays qualities that make it resemble the forms of expression frequently found in the stories attributed to Indian authors. Among the more outstanding features of the vernacular style, proper to Nahuatl narrative and evident here, are the following: frequent use of parallel phrases that express a single idea in slightly different ways; multiple use of "di-phrases," that is, the combination of two words that metaphorically yields a third concept; the creation of dialogues instead of just relating events; the frequent recourse to concepts of pre-Hispanic thought about the supreme divinity, death, and the merits and destinies of human beings."[9]

Nebel maintains that attention should be concentrated not on the "historicity" of the apparitions (which cannot be proved or disproved), but on their theological and religious aspect, without denying the validity of continuing historical-critical research. As regards the possible historicity, Lafaye asserts: "Modern methods of historical research, when it is a matter of establishing facts, do not consider acceptable those proofs that come from oral tradition. . . . [Devout] consensus proves only the existence of the devotion, not the miraculous origin of its object."[10]

The preceding arguments refer to the origin of the image itself, since there are no data that give evidence of its being made by Indians using European models. Lafaye, however, cites a text in which Sahagún has a witness testify that "it was a painting made by Marcos, an Indian painter."[11]

"MEXICANNESS"
AND THE *GUADALPANO* SYMBOL

Several authors have stressed the importance of the Guadalupe image in the formation of a Mexican national consciousness characterized by *mestizo* culture. Nebel states:

The Guadalupe event described in the *Nican Mopohua* clears the way for a "Mexicanization" of Christianity: the ancient culture and religion is accepted without prejudice to Christian identity. . . . As a consequence of this new "Mexican" worldview, the native people demand respect for their identity, the right to live and to act in accord with that identity and the right to self-determination as a "Mexican nation," which will both draw on the rich cultural and religious heritage of the past and unite it to the values of the colonial society.[12]

According to Lafaye, the people's recourse to Mary of Guadalupe at times of great disasters such as the floods (1629) or plague epidemics (1525, 1575, 1576, 1579, 1725–28, and 1736) had the following effects:

> In that cataclysmic atmosphere, the image of Guadalupe of Tepeyac had such a therapeutic effect (well known since the origins of the devotion) that she ascended from being just the protector of her devotees to the rank of savior of the whole social body. The thirst for survival and the desire for salvation, not in the great beyond, but above all in this life, was the true oath of fidelity of all Mexicans to the protecting image of Guadalupe.[13]

Lafaye stresses also the importance of Guadalupe as a unifying emblem, which is obvious from the way it is constantly used in the plastic arts and literature, in place names, and in naming sons and daughters. It is obvious also in the massive pilgrimages that millions make to the sanctuary of Tepeyac and in so many other popular manifestations of the devotion. Lafaye claims that the meaning of the Guadalupe symbol goes beyond its theological interpretation:

> If Guadalupe was the mediatrix between God and men, between God and Mexicans, her mediation was not limited to that. She was also the mediatrix between the king [of Spain] and the "Americans." . . . This almost political role, though, was less important than the spiritual currents that flowed through a society as fragmented as was New Spain. An olive-colored Virgin who appeared to an Indian, Guadalupe succeeded in converting creoles, *mestizos* and Indians into a single people (at least virtually), a people united in one charismatic faith.[14]

The Virgin of Guadalupe was the banner of the insurgent Creoles, such as Hidalgo and Morelos, who rebelled against the Spanish authorities and waged the War of Independence. The young Mexican nation, despite the constant fighting between conservatives and liberals, adopted Guadalupe as the champion of the homeland. And at the beginning of the twentieth century, states León-Portilla, "Guadalupe accompanied Emiliano Zapata, the most emblematic figure of the Mexican Revolution."[15] Having given this historical background, we now turn to a theological appreciation of Mary of Guadalupe.

THEOLOGICAL APPROXIMATION

Clodomiro Siller, in his description of the *guadalpano* theological method in Indian theology, shows that the *Nican Mopohua* "is the Indians' understanding of their own religious tradition as experienced in the new circumstances of colonialism and evangelization."[16] More specifically, Siller highlights several characteristics of the *guadalpano* text that identify it as imbued with Indian theology: it is written in the native language of the Indians, Nahuatl; its subject is the Indian people; it has a collective author; it uses symbolic and dialogic language; it uses "flower and song" as a means of reaching one's own truth and that of others; it is formulated within the people's cultural matrix; it gives importance to ritual; it denounces the situation of social injustice; and it creates a bridge between the ancient traditions and Christianity, which it accepts as something new.

In situating the Guadalupe phenomenon within the perspective of the continent's liberation theology, Nebel states:

> The Guadalupe event—a native theological tradition of the New World— . . . provides people with a multi-faceted experience of liberation: . . . politico-economic liberation, through a new order of life that brings with it health and salvation; socio-psychological liberation, through reestablishment of the dignity and the human rights of poor, oppressed people who are obliged to be silent; sexual liberation of the maltreated feminine and masculine natures, through rehabilitation of the people's lost personal dignity by the Virgin Mother of Tepeyac; and religious liberation from a God conceived as exclusively masculine, insofar as the feminine aspects of God, incorporated in Mary of Tepeyac, are added to the masculine components of the God of the Christians, and at the same time the personal aspect of the God of the Indians is included.[17]

Another theological interpretation of Guadalupe is that of the Latina feminist theologian Jeanette Rodríguez. For her, the Guadalupe event can be considered theologically from three aspects: "(1) popular religiosity, (2) Guadalupe as symbol of God's unconditional love, and (3) the need for 'feminine' metaphors for a more comprehensive understanding of the divine."[18]

Popular religiosity is the people's way of experiencing the faith. It has evolved over the centuries in counterpoint to the "official" ritual and

devotional practices of the hierarchy. Church authorities have often deni-
grated popular religiosity as a product of ignorance and superstition
and as "primitive and backward, perhaps even childlike."[19] Popular religiosity, according to Rodríguez, "is active, dynamic, lived, and has as
its object to move its practitioners, the believers, to live their beliefs. . . .
Popular religiosity not only narrates a people's own history, but also acts
it out and represents it. . . . It is the humanization of God and the
divinization of humanity."[20] Popular religiosity is based on the profound
conviction of believers that God is the foundation of existence and that
everything is in God's hands; it is colored by a spirit of intercession,
perhaps motivated by the great needs and the powerlessness that ordinary people feel in their daily lives. Rodríguez writes, "Popular religiosity is rooted in marginality and oppression."[21] For people in a situation
of oppression, religiosity that is divorced from their concerns and their
anxieties about survival has no meaning at all.

María Pilar Aquino has noted that popular Catholicism, especailly as
practiced by Latinos/as in the United States, has been interpreted as a
religion, not just a religiosity.[22] This popular religion, she continues,
"displays a thought structure based on participation, incarnation, and
reciprocity. Because of this, it adopts a 'logic of vital synthesis' within
which knowledge is acquired through affective participation, in which
the criterion for determining 'what is true' is that which sustains dignified living."[23] Aquino analyzes the functions and meanings of this popular religion in epistemological, hermeneutical, methodological, theological, ethico-political, and soteriological terms. She indicates that *mestizo*
reality is a central category of this popular religion, one that is highly
relevant in a theological method that chooses interculturality as its main
theological focus.[24] Aquino explains that "precisely because mestizaje
has been portrayed by dominant cultures as carrying a social value only
worthy of exclusion, a *mestizo/a* theology will highlight the vital synthe-
ses which 'new peoples' have interculturally created in order to explain
their own vision and their own identities."[25] She emphasizes that "popular Catholicism goes on revealing a God who defends, protects, corrects,
and nourishes the very same social groups the world disdains."[26]

In relation to this "vital synthesis" of *mestizo* reality in popular Catholicism, José Luis González states that popular religiosity "operates
out of a principle of participation that integrates the world in such a way
that everything is perceived as interdependent or relational."[27] If God is
viewed as a distant being, then Mary and the saints are figures close at
hand who are able to gain the favors that the faithful seek. The supernatural is not separated from earthly life; the two are in constant interaction.

The most persistent and ubiquitous figure in popular religiosity in Latin America is that of Mary of Guadalupe. She is the intercessor par excellence; she is the *mestiza*, dark-skinned Virgin who is closer to the people than any other religious figure; she is a symbol of inspiration and refuge for women on the fringes. In the sanctuary of Tonatico I met one Indian woman, vested in traditional garb, who explained to me that she would never abandon her devotion to the Virgin, despite the petitions of her daughters to "become more modern." She asked, "Isn't she just a little Indian woman like us?"

As a sign of God's unconditional love, Mary of Guadalupe is easy to identify with and to feel close to. Jeanette Rodríguez explains: "Our Lady of Guadalupe becomes a symbol and manifestation of God's love, compassion, help, and defense of the poor. She restores her people's dignity and hope and gives a place in the world and in salvific history."[28] For Rodríguez, Mary of Guadalupe is a manifestation of God's grace and an emblem with universal meaning; even though she is not God, "she is a metaphor for God."[29]

This brings us to the third characteristic of the Guadalupe event mentioned by Rodríguez: the way she functions as the feminine face of God. In a people colonized and "converted" by force to Christianity, divinity was often identified with a God who was masculine, strong, and dominating; he was a warrior fighting on the side of the conquistadores. The compassionate, merciful God whom the missionaries wished to preach became present in the figure of Mary, the loving aspect of divinity. Rodríguez states: "It is easy to perceive Our Lady of Guadalupe as the maternal or female face of God, because she evokes an unconditional love, solidarity, and never-failing presence at the affective level. But in doing so, we inaccurately remove these attributes from where they rightly belong: to God."[30] Both the traditional and the renewed versions of Mariology tend to promote a serious dichotomy to the extent that they attribute God's supposedly feminine characteristics to Mary in order to justify the patriarchal image of an exclusively masculine God.

Rodríguez takes various aspects of God identified by Elizabeth Johnson and applies them to Mary of Guadalupe. More than anything, Our Lady of Guadalupe reveals herself as a mother: "a maternal presence, consoling, nurturing, offering unconditional love, comforting."[31] Mary of Guadalupe brings divine compassion alive, for women feel that "she will understand them better than the male face of God because she too is female and a mother."[32] Rodríguez affirms that Guadalupe is the representation of divine power, which is a "dynamism centered around mutuality, trust, participation and regard."[33] This force enables the people to continue struggling against injustices and in solidarity with all those who suffer. Rodríguez sees in Our Lady of Guadalupe the manifestation of God as presence and source of creative energy.

FEMINIST THEOLOGY
AND THE IMAGE OF MARY OF GUADALUPE

In light of all the aforementioned, we need to reflect on the Guadalupe event from the perspective of a critical feminist theology in the Latin American context.

The Guadalupe phenomenon can be considered from the perspective of Mariology and the veneration of Mary, but care should be taken to distinguish Mariology and "Mariolatry." The latter is characterized by adoration of Mary as if she were a divinity, while the church has always held that the form of veneration due to Mary is hyperdulia, which is different from the worship of God. According to Esperanza Bautista, "Mariolatry has produced many excesses and even aberrations, while Mariology, which is an important part of Christianity, can help toward a better comprehension of the feminine face of God and the role of women in the history of salvation."[34] She recommends that we draw closer to what she calls the "objective reality" of the gospel in order to recover a more reliable image of Mary and arrive at a "dogmatic understanding" of the Marian event. Bautista recognizes that "in the course of the tradition, the development of the Marian cult exalted a series of virtues considered properly feminine: quiet devotion and generosity, along with decency, modesty and sexual purity; humility, obedience and submission; all joined to resigned acceptance of one's situation as the will of God."[35] Bautista does not consider the option of some feminists for the cult of the Goddess" as a solution for rediscovering the feminine dimension of God:

> This "return" to the cult of the Goddess seems more like a regression than an advance. Once Christianity broke with the circular idea of time and opened up possibilities for change by conceiving life as movement toward a goal, men and women were freed from the oppression of the eternal return, in which everything is forever repeated, without possibilities of change or of anything different from the ancient tradition.[36]

Elisabeth Schüssler Fiorenza goes even more deeply into the question:

Malestream Mariology and cult of Mary, feminist theologians point out, devalue women in three ways: first, by emphasizing virginity to the detriment of sexuality; second, by unilaterally associating the ideal of "true womanhood" with motherhood; and third, by religiously valorizing obedience, humility, passivity, and submission as the cardinal virtues of women.[37]

In order to escape from this "malestream Mariology" and stop contributing to women's oppression, even if unconsciously, Schüssler Fiorenza asks feminist scholars to go beyond the analysis of doctrinal language or cultic imagery: "They must also confront their socio-historical context and its politically conservative dominant Mariology."[38]

Schüssler Fiorenza distinguishes four approaches of the "malestream Mariology" that feminist theologians are often tempted take:

> The *Reformation approach* seeks to cut back mariological excesses; the *ideal-typical approach* understands Mary as the representative of a new church and humanity; the *doctrinal-mythologizing approach* attempts to integrate Mary "the divine mother and goddess" into the dogmatic system of the church; the *cultic-spiritual approach* celebrates Mary as quasi-G*ddess.[39]

She thus divides Mariologies into those that view Mary "from below" and those that view her "from above."

The first two methods mentioned above fall within the "from below" perspective. The historicizing method of Reformation theology can serve as a patriarchal, chauvinist instrument since, in demythologizing the figure of Mary, it tends to fall into a totally masculine type of religion. Feminist theologians, especially those working in third-world contexts, have sought to discover in the Bible a Mary who is "the liberated and liberating woman . . . the exemplary disciple, the poor woman of the people, the prophetic proclaimer of justice, the motherly sister, or the sorrowful mother . . . as a historical paradigm."[40] According to Schüssler Fiorenza, this method runs various risks: a certain dualism, an idealizing of the feminine aspect of Mary, and an anti-Jewish prejudice (for considering Mary an exception to her culture). The ecclesiological ideal-type method, based on biblical exegesis and hermeneutics, recognizes that "an almost unbridgeable chasm exists between the historical figure Mary of Nazareth and the queen of heaven and mother of G*d celebrated in the cult of Mary."[41] The Second Vatican Council helped produce an understanding of Mary that is free of the immature and unrestrained imagination of some forms of Marian piety, but Schüssler Fiorenza still finds such understanding to be guilty of "universaliz[ing] her (Mary) as the ideal type of being woman and the paradigmatic model of submission in faith."[42] She thus rejects the viewpoint of some feminist theologians of liberation such as Rosemary Radford Ruether, Ivone Gebara, and Maria Clara Bingemer, who understand Mary as an "image of the people . . . new humankind . . . always represent[ing] the church of the poor,"[43] since such symbolizations, according to Schüssler Fiorenza, help to reproduce patterns of subordination and submission, both for women and for men who are in socially marginal situations.

The Mariology "from above," according to Schüssler Fiorenza, is exemplified by the mythologizing-dogmatic method and the cultic-spiritual method. Of the first she states that, although there have been feminist attempts to reinterpret Marian dogma, "insofar as the mariological dogmas tend to make Mary the great exception among women, they reinforce kyriocentric attitudes and structures."[44] Regarding the cultic-spiritual method, Schüssler Fiorenza states that the "Marian cult and imagery have a very important function in correcting the one-sidedly masculine theological discourses about G*d, since the cult of Mary offers images and symbols for the renewal of G*d's language."[45] Schüssler Fiorenza mentions specifically the cult of Our Lady of Guadalupe, citing a text of Virgil Elizondo that speaks of this cult in these terms: "*it is no longer the European expresión of God nor the Nahuatl expresión of God but a new mestizo expresión* which is mutually interpretive and enriching."[46] Schüssler Fiorenza, however, alluding to certain feminist theologians who advocate this Guadalupe cult as liberating, expresses doubts as to whether the figure of Guadalupe is positive for women. Of course, she speaks from her European and North American context.

As regards the symbolism of the "G*ddess" and the modern attempts to resurrect worship of the "G*ddess," Schüssler Fiorenza states that "the salvific power of the biblical G*d of justice and love is not endangered by G*ddess cults but by the (ab)use of G*d as an idol for inculcating kyriarcal interests."[47] In order to demythologize and liberate both discourse about God and Marian symbolism, Schüssler Fiorenza suggests the four traditional ways of knowing about God: "the *via negativa,* the *via affirmativa,* the *via eminentiae* and the *via practica.*" The first way affirms what God *is not.* The second presents, in analogous language, our positive conception of God, which for Schüssler Fiorenza should contain not only our personal desires for liberation and welfare but also an inclusive conception of the *basileia* of God for everybody; in this process certain denominations for God that Mariology has taken from the symbols and names of the "G*dess" may be critically accepted. The third way emphasizes the inadequacy of any discourse about God that pretends to be the *only* way to speak of God; it proposes a plethora of titles for God. Finally, the fourth way "attempts to derive G*d-language and Marian symbolism from the praxis and solidarity of antipatriarchal liberation movements in both church and society."[48]

CONCLUSION

For the apparitions of Guadalupe there do not exist any contemporary testimonies that are really historical and verifiable. As scholars and academics, we should accept this reality. God reveals the divine self in many ways to Christians. We firmly believe that God is present in our lives, but this premise does not require us to think that God violates the laws of nature, nor does it require us to act contrary to reason. In the case of Mary of Guadalupe, as in other types of popular religiosity, we should not limit ourselves only to the enlightened rationality of Western modernity in evaluating the validity of claims. The concept of interculturality perhaps can help us understand this phenomenon. Raúl Fornet-Betancourt explains that interculturality "means . . . that *posture* or *disposition* by which human beings become enabled . . . and habituated to living 'their' identifying references *in relation* to so-called 'others,' that is, by sharing such references in mutual dwelling with others."[49] From this perspective we recognize that there are other historical realities that impel us to take account of the Guadalupe event as an element that helps to rescue the identity of a conquered people and to forge the new *mestizo/a* identity of "Mexicanness," an identity that has never been clearly defined and is often manipulated by interests that are not the people's.

A variety of texts allow us to discover the wealth of the *guadalpano* symbolism, with its roots in the pre-Hispanic pantheon, in the veneration of the "black Virgins," and in the practices of Extremadura in Spain. Although ambiguities can be found in the original text of the *Nican Mopohua*, which was discovered more than a century after the events that it narrates, the literary richness of the document is notable, especially in its use of metaphors and symbols from pre-Hispanic Nahuatl literature. It is a fine example of the "flower and song" genre of poetic and ritual texts that were common among the Indians of Nahua origin in the Central Plateau.

Furthermore, from a biblical viewpoint, the text of the *Nican Mopohua* might be included within the literary type of "apparitions," which was used in other accounts of appearances of Mary dating from the colonial epoch, for example, the apparitions of Our Lady of Ocotlán in Tlaxcala.

When we interpret Mary of Guadalupe from the perspective of liberation theology, Juan Diego is seen as the collective figure of the oppressed
people, the one who recovers his dignity by being chosen by the Mother
of God to take a message to the religious authorities. Indeed, the messenger himself is the message: this oppressed people has been chosen, on
account of its smallness, to represent the God of Jesus, son of Mary. This
is a vital reminder of the essence of the gospel for those missionaries
who, in the fury of the Conquest, often forgot what should have been
their true motivation for going to the recently conquered lands and who
adopted instead the practices and values of the conquering soldiers.

Mary of Guadalupe rescues the ancient beliefs and divinities within a
new complex of images. As Gruzinski puts it, the native imagination
was colonized,[50] but there remained, in the image of Guadalupe, a solid
core of the rich symbolism of pre-Hispanic beliefs. The goddess Tonantzin
survived in the minds and the hearts of the Indians in her new configuration of Mary of Guadalupe, the woman who helped them recover their
lost dignity and in many cases encouraged them in their struggles for
freedom.

With what eyes can we Mexican women of the twenty-first century
view Mary of Guadalupe? Speaking of the Guadalupe phenomenon,
Mercedes Navarro Puerto states:

> The figure of Mary . . , through her sensitivity to their problems,
> can tell women today that no essences or biologies are so deter-
> mined that they cannot be changed or reinterpreted by the culture
> and by one's own life project, with its personal relations and free
> decisions. Thus Mary, mother of Jesus, can symbolize the possibil-
> ity of change that is present in every culture and every person. She
> may therefore symbolize the liberty and decision-making capacity
> of each person. At the same time she may symbolize the fragile,
> vulnerable and contextualized condition of human beings and the
> cultures generated by them.[51]

Mary of Nazareth, in her appearance as Our Lady of Guadalupe, is for
us Mexican and Latin American women a faithful companion in our
constant struggle against the machismo that still dominates all levels of
our cultures.

Personally, my recovering an understanding of Mary of Guadalupe
has helped me recognize my own *mestiza* culture as a Mexican woman
and my sisterhood with the women of my country. It has strengthened
my determination to keep on struggling for the full dignity of all wom-
en, especially for those most marginalized by the dominant culture.

Notes

[1] Clodomiro Siller, "La Iglesia en el medio indígena," in *Religión y política en México*, ed. Martin de la Rosa and Charles A. Reilly (México: Siglo veintiuno editores, 1985), 213.

[2] Serge Gruzinski, *La colonización de lo imaginario: Sociedades indígenas y occidentalización en el México español, Siglos XVI-XVIII* (México: Fondo de Cultura Económica, 1991), 186.

[3] Christian Duverger, *La conversión de los indios de la Nueva España, con el texto de los Coloquios de los Doce de Bernardino de Sahagún (1564)* (México: Fondo de Cultura Económica, 1993), 109.

[4] Richard Nebel, *Santa María Tonantzin Virgen de Guadalupe: Continuidad y transformación religiosa en México* (México: Fondo de Cultura Económica, 1995), 91.

[5] Jacques Lafaye, *Quetzalcóatl y Guadalupe* (México: Fondo de Cultura Económica, 1977), 311.

[6] Nebel, *Santa María Tonantzin Virgen de Guadalupe*, 53–54.

[7] Ibid., 216.

[8] Ibid., 204.

[9] Miguel León-Portilla, *Tonantzin Guadalupe, pensamiento náhuatl y mensaje cristiano en el "Nican Mopohua"* (México: El Colegio Nacional y Fondo de Cultura Económica, 2000), 22.

[10] Lafaye, *Quetzalcóatl y Guadalupe*, 406–7.

[11] Ibid., 340.

[12] Nebel, *Santa María Tonantzin Virgen de Guadalupe*, 261.

[13] Lafaye, *Quetzalcóatl y Guadalupe*, 358.

[14] Ibid., 403.

[15] León-Portilla, *Tonantzin Guadalupe*, 15.

[16] Clodomiro Siller, "El método teológico guadalupano," in *Teología India: Primer encuentro taller latinoamericano* (México: CENAMI, 1991), 133.

[17] Nebel, *Santa María Tonantzin Virgen de Guadalupe*, 288.

[18] Jeanette Rodríguez, *Our Lady of Guadalupe: Faith and Empowerment among Mexican-American Women* (Austin: University of Texas Press, 1994), 143.

[19] Ibid., 144.

[20] Ibid.

[21] Ibid., 148.

[22] See María Pilar Aquino, "Theological Method in U.S. Latino Theology," in *From the Heart of the People*, ed. Orlando O. Espín and Miguel H. Díaz (Maryknoll, NY: Orbis Books, 1999), 34.

[23] Ibid., 34.

[24] Ibid., 35.

[25] Ibid., 37.

[26] Ibid., 41.

[27] José Luis González, cited in Rodríguez, *Our Lady of Guadalupe*, 147.

[28] Rodríguez, *Our Lady of Guadalupe*, 150.

[29] Ibid., 151.

[30] Ibid., 153.

[31] Ibid., 155.

[32] Ibid., 156.

[33] Ibid.

[34] Esperanza Bautista, "El culto de María en la liturgia de la Iglesia y en la religiosidad popular," in *María, mujer mediterránea*, ed. Isabel Gómez-Acebo (Bilbao: Desclée de Brouwer, 1999), 80.

[35] Ibid., 82.

[36] Ibid., 109.

[37] Elisabeth Schüssler Fiorenza, *Jesus: Miriam's Child, Sophia's Prophet: Critical Issues in Feminist Christology* (New York: Continuum, 1994), 164–65.

[38] Ibid., 166.

[39] Ibid., 167. On her use of the term *G*d*, Schüssler Fiorenza explains that such a spelling "is theologically necessary to visibly destabilize our way of thinking and speaking about G*d" (ibid., 191).

[40] Ibid., 169.

[41] Ibid., 170.

[42] Ibid., 171.

[43] Ibid., 172.

[44] Ibid., 174.

[45] Ibid., 176,

[46] Virgil Elizondo, cited in ibid., 177.

[47] Schüssler Fiorenza, *Jesus: Miriam's Child*, 178.

[48] Ibid., 181.

[49] Raúl Fornet-Betancourt, ed., *Crítica intercultural de la filosofía latinoamericana actual* (Madrid: Editorial Trotta, 2004), 14.

[50] Gruzinski, *La colonización de lo imaginario*.

[51] Mercedes Navarro Puerto, "El símbolo de María en la perspectiva de la psicología de la religion," in *María, mujer mediterránea*, ed. Isabel Gómez-Acebo (Bilboa: Desclée de Brouwer, 1999), 193.

15

Toward a Feminist Intercultural Theology

Olga Consuelo Vélez Caro

The intercultural horizon has established itself today as a theological paradigm that underlies all the contextual theologies.[1] Thus, to speak of a feminist intercultural theology is to do no more than probe more deeply into the contributions that that horizon brings to the theological task. In this essay I propose first to explain how we understand interculturality and the challenges it presents and then to point out its major implications for feminist theology. I have divided this chapter into three parts. The first part examines the meaning of interculturality, its hermeneutical and epistemological presuppositions, and the basic requirements of the intercultural task. For this part I make use principally of the works of Raúl Fornet-Betancourt,[2] one of the pioneers in the subject. In the second part I indicate, in broad terms, the most outstanding aspects of the development of Latin American feminist theology, with the aim of stressing the need for and the urgency of reflecting seriously on culture in the present decade. Finally, I show some of the possibilities that the intercultural horizon offers to the Latin American feminist theological endeavor.

This exposition is above all a sharing of intuitions, with the hope that they will be discussed and validated by the theological community. In this way I hope to make a contribution to the development of a feminist intercultural theology in our Latin American continent.

THE INTERCULTURAL HORIZON

Culture and Inculturation

To speak of the intercultural horizon is to speak above all of a new conception of culture, one that is relatively recent. For over two millennia,

248

culture was understood and viewed mainly in opposition to the "barbarity" of the cultureless hordes. Culture was a matter of acquiring and assimilating the tastes, abilities, ideals, virtues, and ideas that were imposed by means of a good family environment and a liberal arts education. Values were insisted on more than just facts. In this sense, culture was conceived as universal and normative. Its classics were immortal works of art, its philosophy was of the perennial sort, its laws and its structures constituted the depositary of the wisdom and prudence of humankind. Education in the classics consisted in imitating models, emulating ideal qualities, and seeking eternal truths and universally valid laws. This notion of culture in some way sought to produce the "universal human being," capable of managing any situation and of doing so brilliantly. Thanks to empirical studies of human beings, however, this notion of culture has changed dramatically. "The contemporary notion of culture is empirical. A culture is a set of meanings and values informing a common way of life, and there are as many cultures as there are distinct sets of such meanings and values."[3]

This new notion of culture has influenced various disciplines, including theology. Indeed, it has produced a new way of doing theology. Latin America has in recent decades become especially conscious of various contextual concerns—such as poverty, marginalization, subordination, exclusion, racism, and so forth—that have given rise to new theological perspectives. Many of these can today be acknowledged as true Latin American theologies, such as liberation theology, feminist theology, Indian theology, Afro-american theology, ecumenical theology, and others.[4]

These new theological perspectives are the fruit of understanding the theological task as a mediation "between a cultural matrix and the significance and role of a religion in that matrix,"[5] and of understanding culture in its empirical sense. "When the classicist notion of culture prevails, theology is conceived as a permanent achievement, and then one discourses on its nature. When culture is conceived empirically, theology is known to be an evolving process, and then one writes on its own method."[6]

Despite our previous assertions, the empirical notion of culture is commonly found to have been poorly assimilated or accepted by many people, including scholars. As Tamayo-Acosta points out, the classical notion of culture remains dominant because, "despite all efforts at dialogue, (such a notion of culture) still holds sway in the collective imagery of Christian individuals and groups, especially westerners, in the minds of theologians, in many evangelizations projects, even those that are 'liberated' and inculturated, in the organization of the churches and in the way the

churches are run from the center."[7] For this reason, speaking of an intercultural horizon is even today a constant challenge and a topic relatively
unexplored.

Another matter that needs to be explained is the change that has been
going on concerning the notion of inculturation. On a theological and
pastoral level this term has traditionally been used to express the need
for theology and evangelization to insert themselves into the diverse cultures in order to draw on what is good in them and purify the aspects of
them that are marked by sin.[8] This notion, however, assumes that there
is a preexistent universal theology or a "pure" gospel that can simply be
adapted to the different cultures. Such an assumption ignores a reality
that is inherent to the incarnational process of revelation: there is no
such thing as a "neutral" revelation; rather, all revelation takes place
within a determined cultural context. Therefore, when the gospel message reaches a culture, it already comes dressed in another cultural context, and as a result what takes place is not so much inculturation as an
encounter of cultures.

Accepting the fact that there is an encounter of cultures means decry-
ing the way in which Western culture has for centuries set itself up as
universally valid for all peoples and has imposed itself on other cultures.
It means recognizing that evangelization and theology have been done
from that universalist horizon and have not taken seriously into account
the empirical cultures they have tried to reach. As a result, we are now
obliged to ask about the best way to realize this intercultural encounter,
which inevitably involves examining the hermeneutical and epistemological presuppositions of such an undertaking.

Hermeneutical and Epistemological Presuppositions
for Intercultural Dialogue

Intercultural dialogue is a tremendous hermeneutical challenge. It
means accepting that the interpretation of reality is plural, and that such
plurality is true. The first premise is clear. Plurality imposes itself, and
the attitudes of tolerating, respecting, and valuing what is different are
recognized as necessary in the world in which we live. The difficulty
comes with the second premise. How can we accept that such plurality is
true? The classical mentality simply cannot accept that; it requires that
there be only one truth that organizes, hierarchizes, and validates all
reality. Such a mentality accepts plurality only so long as it fits within its
own designated parameters. Only by moving to an empirical mentality
are we able to accept the plurality of truth in a way that can be articulated. In other words, it is necessary

to move away from a mental model that works with the category of totality, that fixes and encloses the truth within such a category, toward a model that is free of that category and prefers to work with the idea of dialectical totalization, with the aim of expressing, by such a change of categories, precisely its change of attitude with respect to truth: for this model, truth is not a condition or a situation, but a process.[9]

Intercultural dialogue is possible to the extent that people recognize that no culture *gives* us the truth, not even the classical culture that has reigned for more than two millennia, but that all cultures are ways of seeking truth and of gradually finding it.

Some might ask: is not such acceptance of the plurality of truth simply a form of relativism? To respond to this objection, Fornet-Betancourt appeals to the Zubirian idea of *respectivity*. All that is real must be understood as something that is "respective to"; in this sense, one's own culture is true "with respect to," but also can change "with respect to." There thus emerges a movement of the intellect that overcomes relativism insofar as it remains backed by respectivity, the possibility of a non-totalitarian ordering of the real. Respectivity affirms the "plural version" of reality without abandoning it to isolation, which is what relativism would do; rather, it opens up the formal space for understanding its substantial connectiveness.[10]

Acceptance of the interpretative plurality of reality invites us, then, to create a new dynamic of universalizing totalization with the "other," based on mutual recognition, respect, and solidarity. This does not mean simply being benevolent with the "other" and receiving the "other" within my universe. It assumes something more: an attitude of mutual openness allowing for the transfiguration of my own reality and the "other's" reality, in search of a common space.[11]

In providing epistemological presuppositions for intercultural dialogue, Fornet-Betancourt indicates the urgency of establishing some basic conditions for understanding all that is culturally foreign to us:

- First, eradicating the conceptual hegemony of any culture that seeks to oblige all that is strange to conform to its norms.
- Second, relativizing knowledge within the exclusive domain of rationality and entering into the existential dimension of the other. Mutual exchange cannot be limited to the conceptual level, but must open itself up to understanding the other in his/her life and his/her corporality.

- Third, attempting to practice a respective understanding that minimizes the habits of subsumption and reduction that ethnocentrism tends to create in the exercise of intelligence.
- And, finally, cultivating the terrain of the "inter," where every hasty definition is an error, just as every precipitous declaration of harmony may be an underhanded expression of domination.[12]

Intercultural dialogue requires, then, the creation of conditions and spaces wherein all cultures may speak with their own voice; it also requires accepting and studying the creations of those cultures in such a way as to be able to value and develop them.[13]

In the Latin American context it is important to emphasize the concrete reality of oppression and marginalization experienced by third-world peoples and to consider what that means for their concrete cultures. Thus, allowing all voices to speak means letting them express themselves from the depths of their real, daily experience of the world of the periphery.[14] This marginalized reality, so often invoked as the starting point for the new way of doing Latin American theology, still has to fight to defend its space in the face of the domineering rationality.

The intercultural horizon, therefore, is offered to us today as a new historical possibility for transforming the currently accepted ways of thinking,[15] because it recognizes that human beings involve food, clothing, care, reproduction, and social organization (vital and social values), but that they also constitute the meaning and the value of their reality, of their history, of their context, of themselves (cultural and personal values).[16] Respect for human dignity, then, comes to be measured by our effective commitment to working both for the transformation of the socioeconomic conditions that affect the concrete lives of human beings and also for the cultural transformations that lead to the construction of "another possible world,"[17] one that has room for everybody.

Toward Intercultural Dialogue

In what does intercultural dialogue consist? I will not attempt an answer to this question yet; we have a ways to travel before being able to do so. For the moment I point out some of the elements that may be intuited. I again draw on the work of Raúl Fornet-Betancourt and his proposal for an intercultural philosophy, but we attempt to adapt them to all efforts of intercultural dialogue that may be proposed within any discipline.[18]

I begin, then, from the premise that there does not exist a single universal culture that is valid for all times and places; rather, there exist as many cultures as there are human groupings. In other words, Western culture is not the ideal to be reached by all peoples; many other distinct possibilities exist for human realization and social organization.

Intercultural dialogue, therefore, is a new and unexplored path that involves great challenges. Such dialogue means:

- Entering into unexplored territory, that is, not simply making a theoretical readjustment, but rather creating something new out of the potentialities of each culture in the search for common convergence, without accepting the domination or the colonializing tendencies of any cultural tradition.
- Overcoming the schemas that judge other cultural traditions on the basis of one's own culture, in order to allow all the voices of humanity to be heard.
- Starting from the assumption of human finiteness, both individual and cultural, which means, first, renouncing the tendency, proper to every culture, to absolutize or sacralize what is one's own, and second, promoting the habit of experiencing change and contrast.
- Renouncing every reductionist hermeneutic posture, that is, any posture that operates with a single conceptual or theoretical model as its interpretative paradigm. Expressed positively, intercultural dialogue means entering into a process of creative searching that takes place when the "interpretation" of both one's own reality and the "other's" reality emerges as the result of a common, mutual interrogation, in which each voice is perceived at the same time as a possible model of interpretation.
- Removing all cultures from any possible dominating center position and situating ourselves, instead, in interconnection and intercommunication. This means opening up the way to the practice of inter-discursive reasoning, that is, starting out from one's own cultural tradition, but knowing it and experiencing it not as an absolute construction, but as a crossing and a conduit toward intercommunication. Our culture would thus be something like a bridge; we cannot jump off it, but we must cross over it if we wish to get to the other shore.

This proposal for intercultural dialogue does not deny the possibility of arriving at consensus, of finding shared meanings and values, or of recognizing valid aspects for the construction of any human reality. What it questions is our resting easy with the notion of classical culture, which is inevitably taken to be Western, rational, white, masculine culture. Our proposal is that we make a decisive option for the empirical notion of culture and use it to revise all the investigations and developments of our different disciplines. Intercultural dialogue is carried on between contextual universes that manifest their will for universality through their acceptance of the polyphony of voices that constitute the universal and the true.

FEMINIST THEOLOGY AS A CONTEXTUAL THEOLOGY

Feminist theology is a contextual theology. It starts out from the discrimination, subordination and exclusion that have been suffered by women of almost all times and places. Then, following the canons of liberation theology, it judges such reality in the light of God's word, in order to make decisions regarding the actions that must be taken in order to transform that reality. The history of feminist theology on Latin American soil goes back now some four decades. Each decade has been marked by specific contexts that have led to progressively new levels of feminist awareness, which is in a process of continually renovating, actualizing, re-creating and empowering itself.

During the 1970s, in the context of the rise of liberation theology, feminist consciousness adopted a view of women as being historical subjects of liberation, in virtue of their condition of being doubly oppressed: socioeconomically and sexually.[19] A biblical hermeneutic developed that sought to rescue the feminine figures of the Bible, all with the purpose of denouncing the oppression experienced by women and of announcing the possibility of their liberation on the basis of the biblical imperative. During this decade there was no dialogue with the feminist movements because of a mutual mistrust (the women theologians avoided speaking of any demands that were unrelated to socioeconomic oppression, while the feminists rejected religion and distrusted the women theologians).

In the decade of the 1980s, feminist theology began to make overtures to the feminist movements, and the option for the poor was questioned for what it had to say about gender.[20] Women sought to do theology not only "about women," but also "from women." There was talk of women's theology, theology from women's perspective. Biblical hermeneutics sought to study all of the scriptures from the general perspective of women, and not only on the basis of oppression, though it was recognized that concrete life experience must also be included. Efforts were made to rescue the feminine aspects and images of God: God as both father and mother, the Holy Spirit as feminine, and so forth. Theology and the triune God were feminized. Efforts were also made to conceive the characteristics traditionally attributed to women as being especially important and valuable both for the production of knowledge and for the transformation of reality. Inclusive language began to take on importance in the circles of feminist theological production.

In the decade of the 1990s, the task of rescuing the feminine in existing theology was considered to be inadequate.[21] Theology needed to be reconstructed. The urgent need now was to work on theories of gender in order to develop more thoroughly a true feminist theological discourse and biblical hermeneutics. Thus the instrument of social analysis was replaced by that of gender theories. The body and everyday reality were proposed as acceptable hermeneutic categories. The attitude of submissive surrender that was often considered proper to women was deemed repugnant, and a non-sacrificial reading of redemption was sought. Work was done on feasting, on joy, on delight in corporality and sexuality (as in the Song of Songs). The Pauline texts were studied with new epistemological parameters. Gender theories were used in analysis of biblical texts. Questions were asked about how to contextualize the contributions of first-world feminists in Latin America.

For the new millennium the challenges are immense. The aspects that have been mentioned as most relevant in each of the prior decades continue to exert force, depending on the context of each collective of women. The history we have recounted does not mean that the later stages supersede the prior ones. Rather, it depicts rising levels of consciousness that progressively open up the horizon of reflection and encompass ever more diverse aspects of human reality. The situation of women cuts across all theological horizons and becomes the starting point for profound renovations and new pathways. The present decade makes especially urgent the evangelical imperative of promoting egalitarian relations wherein "there is no longer Jew or Greek, there is no longer slave or free, there is no longer male or female; for all of you are one in Christ Jesus" (Gal 3:28, NRSV).

Our main interest with regard to these Latin American feminist developments is to ask about the reach of the intercultural horizon in theological work. If the intercultural horizon considers contextual theologies to be one of its privileged spaces,[22] then we should ask what that horizon has to say about the development of Latin American feminist theology.

The brief survey presented up to this point allows us to see how feminist consciousness has passed from denunciation of the situation of the socioeconomic oppression experienced by women to denunciation of the patriarchal, androcentric cultures that have long dominated societies and churches. The introduction of the category of gender into feminist studies is a sign of women's new consciousness of the need to work for cultural transformation in order to bring about authentic historical changes. What I propose to do in the next section, then, is to point out certain developments that can advance the work of Latin American feminist theology by making more explicit the intercultural horizon.

TOWARD A FEMINIST INTERCULTURAL THEOLOGY

The basic intuition in the development of this article is that the intercultural horizon can throw new light on the mission of Latin America feminist theology in three ways:

- By making it possible for all voices to speak: those of women of different backgrounds and with diverse characteristics, and also those of men, who have their own voice and feelings in regard to this reality.
- By favoring knowledge based not only on the elaboration of concepts, but also on the existential dimension of the subjects involved.
- By developing the intercultural horizon into a concrete opportunity for transforming mentalities, so as to make possible a world that does not exclude anybody for reasons of sex.

Making It Possible for All Voices to Speak

The title of this section might seem contradictory at first sight. Feminist theology has given voice to all those women who have been in silence for endless ages. One half of the human race had been rendered subordinate at both a grammatical and a real level, but thanks to all the efforts of feminists, today some women at least have found their voice and are persistently making it heard. Nonetheless, the sheer variety of voices on the feminist horizon is ever more evident and provokes a number of questions. Can all those voices find space? Is it possible to link them together in a movement that continues to favor women, instead of creating an arena of confrontations among women? How do we weave the masculine voices, also plural, into the horizon of plurality of feminine voices?

These questions arise from lived experiences. Although the reality of women's subordination traverses all social groups and all cultures, it does not cause the same effects in all of them. Many women define themselves as non-feminist, manifesting thereby their refusal to be included in a movement, either because it appears to them unnecessary—they personally feel good about the social role they already have—or because they feel offended by some of the positions that the movement proposes. Within feminist theology we can also recognize such a plurality of positions, though they are not always articulated. A simple example is the difference between feminism of equality and feminism of difference. The first places its emphasis more on demands and struggles to gain conditions of equality in all the spaces traditionally reserved to men. The second is more focused on making the "essential" characteristics of the feminine gender—motherhood, care, tenderness, service, and so on—manifest, recognized, and valued in the public realm.[23]

Behind these two positions, as well as others, lies a diversity of feminine universes. The diversity of the group "women" is as great as are the different cultural and religious traditions from which they come; women are as different as are their academic formation, their socioeconomic condition, their affective experiences, or their experience of marriage, the single state, and/or maternity. Such differences directly influence the postures they take with regard to the feminist movement. Men also display diverse stances with respect to feminism, which may include indifference, disapproval, or even a feeling of being attacked or oppressed by feminist proposals. It should be noted, as well, that some men are sincerely interested in the critique of patriarchal society and support the feminist movement by involving themselves decisively in changes that also affect them.

This depiction of people's relation to feminism recognizes that any subversion of the established order causes confusion, denial, and often radical opposition to new proposals. A great effort is needed to commit oneself to changes that affect one's personal interests. It is not to be expected, therefore, that the majority will support the feminist proposals. All the same, feminist theology seeks out paths that allow more and more women and men to become involved in this theology that is called upon to realize this arduous task. In effect, feminist theology must scrutinize all existing theology to help ensure that its inputs and contributions are infused with the evangelical imperative of creating a truly fraternal, sororal, and harmonious humanity.

For this reason, the intercultural horizon, with its proposal for a dialogue in which all voices are heard, can foster the inclusion of more women and more men in a truly shared space, where all feel included and are enabled to speak with their own voice. Thus intercultural dialogue fosters in us an attitude that is favorable for this task of summoning all women and men to dialogue, not in order to try to legitimize one posture and then use it to approve or reject other postures, but to enter with true detachment from one's own position, with generous acceptance of what is "alien" and with sincere commitment to seeking the truth that is found only on the terrain of the "inter" and of mutual respect. Of course, we mean truth in the sense already mentioned, that is, not truth as something static and already attained, something that can be located "out there," but rather truth with "this here" and "respective to" qualities, like all fully human truth. Incorporating such attitudes of the intercultural horizon into feminist work will make it easier for more women and men to feel truly represented and welcomed within this horizon.

Furthermore, the intercultural horizon seeks to open us up to the unexpected, which, in the terrain of the social relationships between men and women, is a very exacting task. How are we to imagine a society free of the currently traditional roles and capable of conceiving differently the question of collaboration and mutual responsibility between the sexes? How are we to imagine a society in which men and women, in recognition of their full equality and dignity and their joint historical possibilities, build together a world that is fully human, without any discrimination, especially for reasons of sex? Intercultural dialogue, as was already said, does not consist in accommodating, translating, or reproducing the established culture; it is rather a matter of creating something original, something new, something that allows us to transform decisively the established order of gender.

In this same sense, intercultural dialogue invites us not to pass judgment on other cultural traditions using our own culture as a yardstick. This is another immense challenge for the feminist agenda. How do we approach the ways of dressing, of participating in politics, of forming a family, of living a cultural and religious tradition, without judging them from "our shore," but rather receiving them from "the other shore" in order to allow ourselves to be questioned and mutually transformed by them? Such an endeavor is impossible unless we start out from an assumption of human finiteness, which leads us to realize that every culture is relative and is continually changing with the passage of time and with the progressive advances in consciousness that humankind attains.

In the field of feminist hermeneutics we can recognize the fruitful labor that has been done.[24] Breaking with the prevailing interpretive schemas and daring to propose a hermeneutic of suspicion or of creative imagination has opened up new ways of reconstructing historically the origins of Christianity and the presence of women in the first Christian communities, thus disclosing the androcentric bias in the interpretation of biblical texts. The horizon of intercultural dialogue reinforces this work by continually rupturing the narrow interpretative schemas and by accepting and validating instead a hermeneutic that welcomes a variety of different voices, convinced that all of them have something to

contribute. Such interpretation is fully conscious of being based on plurality, on a common questioning that takes place, once again, on the
terrain of the "inter."

Such complete openness to hearing and validating the different voices
will lead a feminist intercultural theology to refrain from absolutizing
certain aspects of the feminist struggle. It will propose positions that are
themselves understood to be contextual, partial, limited by the space-
time of each culture. It will accept that the advance in feminist consciousness does not depend exclusively on setting certain goals and then
pursuing them at all costs, but on being able to experience in the heart of
the feminist project the diversity of rhythms, urgencies, and the diverse
situations in which women find themselves. It will also see the importance of incorporating the sentiments and opinions of men, of appreciat-
ing their lights and their limitations in trying to walk to the drumbeat of
this evolving history, of allowing masculine voices to express themselves.
They too must tell the part they have played in the traditional partition
of humankind, and they also can express their feelings in response to
feminist denunciations and demands. But at the same time they can help
us all progress toward a humanity that most definitely needs to be different, so that discrimination, oppression, or subordination of either of the
sexes in any human situation cease to exist.

What feminist theologians most want to emphasize in this regard is
that the intercultural horizon requires both openness to all the voices
and establishment of intercommunication among them all. We seek to
awaken a greater sensibility, so that all the labors of feminist intercultural theology are imbued with these attitudes and this necessary openness to all the voices, in their polyphonic cultural intonations, so that in
the end the concert of the feminist theological venture makes manifest
the harmony of all humanity.

Favoring Knowledge That Assumes
the Existential Dimension of People

Our proposal for an intercultural horizon obliges us to consider the
epistemological presuppositions for such an undertaking. We need to
become conscious of how we know and to make a definitive break with
the theoretical, conceptual matrix that approaches reality only at the
level of ideas and concepts to be debated. As do all contextual theologies, the feminist perspective assumes from the very start the presence of
the theologian's existential dimension, which is established at the very
beginning, at the starting point of the theological work. Only life experience is capable of bringing forth the kind of questions that generate

truly efficacious theologies. The suffering of the poor, discrimination against women, racism, extermination of indigenous peoples, growing pollution of the planet, and such have led us to create a new way of doing theology, one that seeks to render faith meaningful and effective in the concrete contexts where Christianity is lived. This existential aspect must clearly continue to be encouraged and favored in order to guarantee the relevance of theology. Knowledge emerges from the existential experiences of human beings. We know on the basis of our experiences, and only to the extent that we draw close to and express solidarity with one another, only to the extent that we try to enter into the existential universe of the other, will we be able to observe the world from "their" perspective and make of that observation a binding imperative for our own lives. This way of knowing involves surprising elements: it broadens the field of vision, and at the same time it shows us the smallness and partiality of our own vision; it also helps us to understand the different existential stances and value judgments of other people.

In this regard it is important to stress the continuing importance and validity of that knowledge which takes into account "the periphery" or the "reverse side of history." The intercultural horizon, like all current concerns—care of the planet, technological advances, and so on—cannot allow us to forget that, situated as we are in Latin America, we must reaffirm the preferential option for the poor. Today the poor are understood to be not only those who are impoverished by unjust structures, but also all those who are excluded from the hegemonic neoliberal economic system that thrives on fierce competition and allows only the strongest to survive. The present situation of humankind recalls Luke's gospel: "There was a rich man who was dressed in purple and fine linen and who feasted sumptuously every day. And at his gate lay a poor man named Lazarus, covered with sores, who longed to satisfy his hunger with what fell from the rich man's table" (Lk 16:19–21, NRSV). Unlike Lazarus, however, poor people today are anonymous; they are disposable rejects in a history that escapes from their hands and excludes them from its workings. Exodus 22:26–27 throws light on this alarming situation in which poor people find themselves today and invites us to frame some vexing questions. Where will poor people sleep in this world that we are today bringing forth? What will become of those darlings of God in this time in which we live?[25]

Theology must be committed to the transformation of history. Engaged in constant discernment, it is called to denounce this unjust system, to seek out and promote all possible alternatives for including the most disadvantaged. As theologians we cannot maintain our distance from these social challenges; even less can we fall into the temptation of believing that there is no other way or of renouncing our dream that another world is possible. Theology that bases itself on the following of the Jesus of history can and should expose the historical cynicism and inhuman injustice of *homo economicus neoliberalis*, who does not consider poor people as *subjects* of history, but rather as *merchandise* that is useful only if it produces profits and is despised and excluded if it does not yield economic gain. In this sense, we cannot ignore the grievous socioeconomic exclusion suffered by women, even though it is necessary to pay heed also to all the other situations experienced by women today.

The dynamism of God's reign, already present in history, requires us to achieve integration between our desire for eschatological plenitude and our small historical successes, between our desire for abundance and the limits established by scarce economic resources, between our desire for a reconciled, equitable society and our concrete struggles for citizens' rights, and between our desire for a humanity that is respected in its diversity and our affirmation of all the negated identities. In this horizon, which weaves together the grand utopias and the tiny historical achievements and which mixes the positive, gratifying realities (wheat) together with the negative, frustrating realities (weeds), Jesus' words of hope continue to resound: God reigns wherever people hunger and thirst for justice and wherever they work for peace (Mt 5:6, 9).

Besides cultivating this knowledge that flows from placing ourselves on the world's periphery, we must also place much more value on the knowledge that is born of love, intuition, solidarity, daily experience, of all that is small. Through our present-day questioning of the technical-scientific matrix that presumes to guarantee an unlimited development of the world, we are being allowed to recover the wisdom that arises from other forms of knowing that are best expressed in stories, myths, and ancestral cultures. This broader horizon provides the basis for the recovery of a more integral humanity and the positive acceptance of plurality. In reality, human beings know by means of their reason, but they also know by means of their feelings. Better still, they know through the wholeness of all that they are, namely, beings capable of knowledge and moral action, persons capable of affirming facts and making judgment values about them. If we learn to recover memory, to value artistic expression, and to let loose our imagination and our stories and, if we learn to recover, to prize, and to empower popular religiosity, then we will find opening before us new paths that must be traversed with a theology that seeks to thrive in the heart of all that is human.

Transforming Mentalities

Raúl Fornet-Betancourt claims that intercultural dialogue offers itself as a historical alternative for achieving the transformation of the usual modes of thought.[26] Why such stress on changing the usual modes of thought? What purpose is served by seeking such a transformation of mentalities? One possible answer comes from considering the non-efficacy of many social changes; often, even when conditions have changed, the social situation has not improved. Why? As we have already pointed out, human beings are much more than social organization. They are above all creators of culture, that is, forgers of meanings and values that make up their lives and those of their communities. Any transformation that fails to include all these human dimensions can rapidly become a new source of oppression and can lend itself to even greater social corruption and deviation.

In the realm of feminist work, all the aforesaid is an undeniable reality. Today, great efforts are being made to include women in many sectors of society where before they were denied participation. Many countries have government policies that promote gender equality. Education is ever more permeated by the perspective of gender, and educational institutions are reviewed in order to avoid sexual discrimination. Even so, the work is arduous. Attempts must continually be made to achieve a real and effective change of the dominant patriarchal mentality. Although denunciation of that mentality is necessary, it is not enough; what is needed is an attitude that encourages new ways of feeling, thinking, judging, and valuing.

The alternative of intercultural dialogue may well be a highly efficacious means toward such a transformation. To the extent that all the voices are heard, especially the previously silenced ones, and to the extent that other ways of giving meaning and value to reality are recognized as valid and credible, it will become increasingly possible for us to adopt fresh mentalities that are impregnated with gender equality and that establish new relationships for accompanying all the structural changes that are necessary.

CONCLUSION

The ideas expressed here seek simply to provoke reflection about the implications of the intercultural horizon for the work of feminist theology. The work itself is still to be done. The contextual theologies of Latin America started off from social concerns and sought to respond to them, but today we realize that such work does not go far enough. Along with social transformation, a cultural transformation must also be achieved. Our Latin American feminist theology, as it has been developing over the past four decades, is called upon to frame its work within an intercultural horizon in order to allow all voices to speak, in order to develop new ways of knowing, and in order, above all, to bring about a decisive transformation of the prevailing patriarchal mentality. Only thus will the fomenting of dialogue, of the "inter," of cultural transformation, make possible a world where black, white, *mestiza,* and indigenous women of all social classes and all empirical cultures can thrive and fulfill themselves, in a society that has forever banished exclusion and marginalization because of one's sexual orientation.

Notes

[1] See Juan José Tamayo-Acosta, *Nuevo paradigma teológico* (Madrid: Editorial Trotta, 2003), 37.

[2] I use principally the contributions indicated in Raúl Fornet-Betancourt, *Transformación intercultural de la filosofía* (Bilbao: Desclée de Brouwer, 2001). It is worth noting the author's presence at and contributions to the First Interamerican Symposium on Feminist Intercultural Theology. For more information on this symposium, see Maricel Mena-López and María Pilar Aquino, "Symposium Abstract: Feminist intercultural theology: Religión, Culture, Feminism, and Power," in this volume, xiii–xxviii.

[3] See Bernard J. F. Lonergan, *Method in Theology*, 2nd ed. (New York: Herder and Herder, 1972), 301.

[4] See. J. B. Libanio and Afonso Murad, *Introdução à Teologia. Perfil, enfoques, tarefas* (São Paulo: Edições Loyola, 1996), 249ff.

[5] Lonergan, *Method in Theology,* xi.

[6] Ibid.

[7] Tamayo-Acosta, *Nuevo paradigma teológico,* 31.

[8] Latin American Bishops' Conference, *New Evangelization, Human Development, Christian Culture: Fourth General Conference of Latin American Bishops* (Santo Domingo, Dominican Republic, October 12–18, 1992), note 13, in *Santo Domingo and Beyond: Documents and Commentaries from the Historic Meeting of the Latin American Bishops Conference,* ed. Alfred T. Hennelly, S.J. (Maryknoll, NY: Orbis Books, 1993), 75–76.

[9] Fornet-Betancourt, *Transformación intercultural de la filosofía,* 48.

[10] Ibid., 49.

[11] Ibid., 47.

[12] Ibid., 50–51.

[13] Ibid., 44.

[14] Ibid., 40.

[15] Ibid., 43.

[16] Lonergan, *Method in Theology*, 31–32.

[17] "Another world is possible" is the slogan of the World Social Forum. As of this writing, seven forums have taken place; four in Porto Alegre, Brazil (January 2001, 2002, 2003, and 2005), one in Mumbai, India (January 2004), the sixth forum was decentralized and held in three different cities of the world (2006: Bamako, Mali; Caracas, Venezuela; Karachi, Pakistan). The seventh version of the forum was held in Nairobi, Kenya, in January 2007. Regarding this information, see the World Social Forum website, http://www .forumsocialmundial.org.br/index.php.

[18] Fornet-Betancourt, *Transformación intercultural de la filosofía*, 29–31.

[19] Ana María Tepedino and María Pilar Aquino, eds., *Entre la indignación y la esperanza: Teología feminista latinoamericana* (Bogotá: Indo-American Press Service, 1998), 44–47.

[20] Ibid., 47–52.

[21] Ibid., 52–57.

[22] See Tamayo-Acosta, *Nuevo paradigma teológico*, 37.

[23] See Marta Colorado, Liliana Arango, and Sofía Fernández, *Mujer y feminidad en el psicoanálisis y el feminismo* (Medellín: Imprenta Departamental, 1998), 101–13.

[24] Elisabeth Schüssler Fiorenza, *In Memory of Her: A Feminist Reconstruction of Christian Origins* (New York: Crossroad, 1985), 3–40.

[25] Exodus 22:26–27 refers to a concern about what those who have no clothing will use to cover themselves when they sleep.

[26] See Fornet-Betancourt, *Transformación intercultural de la filosofía*, 43.

Contributors

Clara Luz Ajo Lázaro, b. Banes/Holguín (Cuba), doctor of religious sciences, specialized in historical theology (Universidade Metodista, São Paulo, 1998). She is currently professor of systematic theology at the Seminario Evangélico de Teología (Matanzas, Cuba) and a member of the Commission of Theological Studies for Latin America and the Caribbean (Comisión de Estudios Teológicos para América Latina y el Caribe, CETALC) of the American Episcopal Church. Her publications include *Teología y Género: Selección de Textos* (2002); "La Regla de Ocha o Religión de Santería. Elementos Para un Diálogo con la Tradición Cristiana," in *Religión y Género*, ed. Sylvia Marcos (2004); "Ochún y la Virgen de la Caridad del Cobre: Mezcla de Diosas y Rostros de Mujer," in *Vírgenes y Diosas en América Latina: La Resignificación de lo Sagrado,* ed. Mary Judith Ress et al. (2004).

María Pilar Aquino, b. Ixtlán del Río, Nayarit (Mexico), doctor of theology (Pontifical Catholic University of Salamanca, Spain, 1990) and doctor of theology *Honoris Causae* (University of Helsinki, Finland, 2000), is currently professor of theology and religious studies and associate director of the Center for the Study of Latino/a Catholicism at the University of San Diego. Her publications include *In the Power of Wisdom: Feminist Spiritualities of Struggle*, edited with Elisabeth Schüssler Fiorenza (2000); *The Return of the Just War*, edited with Dietmar Mieth (2001); *A Reader in Latina Feminist Theology: Religion and Justice,* edited with Daisy Machado and Jeanette Rodríguez (2002); *Reconciliation in a World of Conflicts*, edited with Luiz Carlos Susin (2003), and numerous articles on the feminist theological activity from the context of the Americas.

Nancy Elizabeth Bedford, b. Comodoro Rivadavia (Argentina), doctor of theology (Tübingen, 1994), is currently Georgia Harkness Professor of Applied Theology at Garrett-Evangelical Theological Seminary (Evanston) and *Profesora Extraordinaria No Residente* at the Instituto

Superior Evangélico de Estudios Teológicos ISEDET (Buenos Aires). Her most recent book is *El Mundo Palpita: Economía, Género y Teología*, co-edited with Marisa Strizzi (2006), which explores the intersections between economy, feminist theory, and theology. She is a member of a Mennonite congregation.

Geraldina Céspedes, b. Fantino (Dominican Republic), a member of the Congregation of Dominican Missionaries, is currently a doctor of dogmatic theology candidate (Pontifical Catholic University Comillas Madrid), and teaches theology at the Escuela de Teología Feminista de Andalucía (EFETA). Since 1992 she has worked in El Limón, a marginalized neighborhood of Guatemala City (Guatemala). She is also a founding member of the Núcleo Mujeres y Teología de Guatemala, co-director of the Centro Audiovisual de Comunicación y Educación (CAUCE), and serves on the board of directors of the journal *Voces del Tiempo* (Guatemala). Her most recent publications include "Lo Éticamente Sorprendente" (*Voces del Tiempo*, 2000); "Con las Lámparas Encendidas y el Delantal Puesto: Mujer, Servicio y Autoridad en la Iglesia" (*Alternativas*, 2000); "La Dimensión Misionera de la Iglesia Desde la Eclesiología de los Pobres" (*Voces del Tiempo*, 2002); "Espiritualidade: Corporeidade e Resistencia" (*Encrucillada*, 2004); and "Hacia una espiritualidad de la inserción" (*Misiones Extranjeras*, 2006).

Christa P. Godínez Munguía, b. Mexico City (Mexico), holds a licenciate in philosophy (Mexico), licenciate in theological sciences (Mexico), and M.A. in theology, with specialization in theology of religions (Institut Catholique de Paris). Currently, she is professor of theology at the Universidad Iberoamericana (Mexico) and doctor of theology candidate (Institut Catholique de Paris). Since 1996, she has been a collaborator of the theological education program of the Tseltales indigenous communities in the Jesuit Mission of Bachajón (Chiapas, México).

Michelle A. González, b. Miami, Florida (USA), doctor of systematic and philosophical theology (Berkeley), is assistant professor of religious studies at the University of Miami. Prior to her position in Miami she spent two years working with a Mayan community in San Lucas Tolimán, Guatemala. Her research and teaching interests include Latino/a, Latin American, and feminist theologies, as well as interdisciplinary work in Afro-Cuban studies. She is the author of *Sor Juana: Beauty and Justice in the Americas* (2003), *Afro-Cuban Theology: Religion, Race, Culture, and Identity* (2006); and *Created in God's Image: An Introduction to Feminist Theological Anthropology* (2007).

Silvia Regina de Lima Silva, b. Barra do Piraí, Río de Janeiro (Brazil), licenciate in theology and M.A. in biblical sciences (Universidad Bíblica Latinoamericana, Costa Rica), doctoral candidate in studies of society and culture (Universidad de Costa Rica, Costa Rica), is professor of biblical sciences at the Universidad Bíblica Latinoamericana (San José, Costa Rica) and a member of the Grupo ATABAQUE: Teología y Cultura Negra (Brazil). Her publications include *En Territorio de Frontera* (2001); "Além das Fronteiras: Teología Negra Feminista Latinoamericana e Caribenha, Síntesis e Desafíos," in *Teología Afroamericana II. Avanços, Desafíos e Perspectivas. III Consulta Ecumênica de Teologia Afroamericana e Caribenha*, ed. Antônio Aparecido da Silva and Sônia Querino dos Santos (2004).

Daisy L. Machado, b. Camagüey (Cuba), Ph.D., M.Div., M.S.W., is currently professor of church history at Union Theological Seminary (NYC) and most recently academic dean of Lexington Theological Seminary, Lexington, Kentucky, where she was the first Latina dean of an accredited ATS institution in the United States. Dr. Machado is also an ordained minister of the Christian Church (Disciples of Christ). A historian of Christianity in North America, she has a special interest in borderlands issues as they refer to U.S. Latinos/as, Protestant missions history, nationhood, and Latino/a identity. Her publications include *Borders and Margins: Hispanic Disciples in the Southwest, 1888-1942* (2003); *A Reader in Latina Feminist Theology: Religion and Justice,* co-edited with María Pilar Aquino and Jeanette Rodríguez (2002); "Voces De Nepantla: Las Teologías Latinas/Hispanas En Los Estados Unidos," in *Religión y Género,* edited by Sylvia Marcos (2004); "Latina Adolescents: Sliding between Borders and the Yearning to Belong," in *The Sacred Selves of Adolescent Girls,* edited by Evelyn L. Parker (2006); "Women and Religions in the Borderlands," in *Encyclopedia of Women and Religion in North America,* edited by Rosemary Keller and Rosemary Radford Ruether (2006); "The Southern U.S. Border: Immigration, the Historical Imagination, and Globalization," in *Rethinking Economic Globalization,* edited by Pamela K. Brubaker, Rebecca Todd Peters, and Laura A. Stivers (2006).

Maricel Mena-López, b. Cali (Colombia), doctor of religious sciences, specialized in biblical literature (Universidade Metodista, São Paulo, 2002). She is currently professor of scripture at the Pontificia Universidad Javeriana (Bogotá, Colombia) and coordinator of the Ecumenical Association of Third World Theologians of Latin America (EATWOT). Her recent publications include two edited volumes, *Abrindo Sulcos Para*

Uma Teología Afro-Americana e Caribenha (2004) and *Es tiempo de Sanación* (Revista de Interpretación Bíblica Latinoamericana, 2004); "Sou Negra e Formosa: Raca, Gênero e Religiao," in *Corporeidade, Etnia e Masculinidade*, ed. Amdré S. Musskoff and Marga Stroer (2005); and "Lectura de Lucas 1-2 Desde una Perspectiva Afro-Feminista" (*Revista de Interpretación Bíblica Latinoamericana*, 2006).

Yury Puello Orozco, b. Cartagena (Colombia), doctor of religious sciences (Pontifical Catholic University of São Paulo, Brazil, 2006), is currently a member of the NGO Catholics for the Right to Decide (Brazil) and an adjunct professor of theology at the Dominican School of Theology for the Laity. Her publications on issues of religion and AIDS include *Mulheres, Aids e Religião* (2002).

Violeta Rocha Areas, b. Managua (Nicaragua), M.A. in theology (Paris, 1996), M.A. in Gender Studies (Managua, 1997), doctor of theology candidate (Free University of the Netherlands), is currently president of the Latin American Biblical University (UBL) in San José, Costa Rica, and a biblical scholar of New Testament studies and feminist hermeneutics. In various capacities she participates in numerous continental and international conferences and has published extensively on issues of gender, violence, and the Bible; feminist pedagogy; gender, culture, and communication; and theological education, among others. A number of these publications have been translated into Portuguese, English, French, and German.

Jeanette Rodríguez, b. Manhattan, New York (USA), is a U.S. Hispanic/Latina theologian, professor in and chair of the Department of Theology and Religious Studies at Seattle University. She received her Ph.D. at the Graduate Theological Union (Berkeley) and is the author of *Our Lady of Guadalupe: Faith and Empowerment among Mexican American Women* (1994); *Stories We Live Cuentos Que Vivimos: Hispanic Women's Spirituality* (1996); *A Reader in Latina Feminist Theology: Religion and Justice*, co-edited with María Pilar Aquino and Daisy L. Machado (2002). She has published numerous articles on U.S. Hispanic/Latina theology, spirituality, and cultural memory. Inspired by faith and the theologies of liberation, she directs her personal and professional commitments to the service of justice. This commitment takes the form of understanding, articulating, and offering the insights of the lived-faith experience of U.S. Latinos/as to the larger theological enterprise. In 2002 she was the recipient of the U.S. Catholic Award.

Maria José Rosado-Nunes, b. Caxambú, Minas Gerais (Brazil), doctor of social sciences (Paris), is professor of sociology of religion and feminist theory at the Pontifical Catholic University of São Paulo (Brazil) and a researcher of the National Council for Scientific and Technological Development (Conselho Nacional de Desenvolvimento Científico e Tecnológico, CNPq, Brazil). She is the founder and coordinator of Catholics for the Right to Decide in Brazil, and has been a visiting professor at Harvard University (2003). Her research interests include Catholicism and modernity, and women's rights in the Roman Catholic Church. Her publications include *Vida Religiosa nos Meios Populares* (1985); "Pensando Eticamente sobre Concepção, Anticoncepção e Aborto" (*Conciencia Latino Americana*, 2005); "Gênero e Religião" (*Revista Estudos Feministas*, 2005); "Teologia Feminista e a Crítica da Razão Religiosa Patriarcal: Entrevista com Ivone Gebara" (*Revista Estudos Feministas*, 2006), and numerous other articles on feminist issues in society and in the Catholic Church.

María del Carmen Servitje Montull, b. Mexico City (Mexico), studied English Literature (Instituto Anglo-Mexicano de Cultura, Mexico), French Literature (Instituto Francés de la América Latina, Mexico), Human Relations Training (Universidad Iberoamericana, Mexico City), Lactation Consultant Training (La Leche League International, Franklin Park, Illinois, U.S.), and Licenciate in Theological Sciences (Universidad Iberoamericana, Mexico City). Currently she teaches feminist theology in the Department of Theological Sciences of the Universidad Iberoamericana. She is also enrolled in the university's M.A. program in theology and the contemporary world. She has taught a diploma course on Life Direction for Women in Transitions (Universidad Iberoamericana, Mexico City) and was a lactation adviser for La Leche League International. She is also involved in numerous activities to support the integral development and human rights of marginalized women. Her greatest interest is to retrieve the lost voices of women in theology and in the diverse religious traditions, and to unveil the explicit and implicit oppressions of women, especially in today's cultures and in Christianity.

Virginia Vargas Valente, b. Perú, is a feminist sociologist and researcher from Peru, founder and member of the board of directors of the "Flora Tristán" Peruvian Woman's Center. She is also a co-founder and active member of Latin American and Caribbean Feminist Encounters, founder of Women for Democracy (MUDE), co-organizer and participant in the Feminist Articulation of the MERCOSUR, and member of the International Council of the World Social Forum. Vargas Valente is a professor at several universities of Latin America and Europe. She served as coordinator of Nongovernmental Organizations (NGOs) of Latin America and the Caribbean at the Fourth World Conference on Women in Beijing in 1995, where she received the UNIFEM prize. In recognition of her consistent and intense activity on behalf of the rights of the peoples and of women, the Latin American Association for Human Rights (ALOHU) conferred on her the Bishop Proaño Prize (1993), and the municipality of Miraflores (Lima, Peru) awarded her the Prize for the Defense of Women's Rights (1998). Among her many publications are *The Contribution of Women's Rebelliousness* (1989); *How to Change the World without Getting Lost: The Women's Movement in Peru and Latin America* (1992); and *Globalization and the World Social Forum: Challenges of Feminism in the New Millennium* (2003). She is also editor or co-editor of more than ten books on feminism, politics, democracy, citizenship, and globalization, and she has published numerous analytic articles on Peruvian, Latin American, and global feminism.

Olga Consuelo Vélez Caro, b. Bogotá (Colombia), doctor of theology (Pontifical Catholic University of Río de Janeiro, Brazil), currently is the director of both the S.T.B. and S.T.L. degree programs of the Department of Theology at the Pontifical Javeriana University, Bogotá, Colombia. Her most recent publications include *El Método Teológico: Bernard Lonergan y la Teología de la Liberación* (2000); *Reflexiones en Torno al Feminismo y al Género* (2004); *Decálogo do Educador e da Educadora: Comentários*, in collaboration (2006); and numerous articles on theological method, feminist theology, church, neoliberalism, and other current challenging realities.

María Cristina Ventura Campusano, b. Santo Domingo (Dominican Republic), doctor of religious sciences, specialized in biblical literature (Universidade Metodista, São Paulo, 2003). She is currently professor of biblical sciences at the Universidad Bíblica Latinoamericana (San José, Costa Rica) and also collaborates in the graduate programs of the Institute of Women Studies at the National University of Costa Rica (Heredia, Costa Rica).